# Enjoying Opera

## A BOOK FOR THE NEW OPERA GOER

*by Olga Maynard, author of*

THE BALLET COMPANION, a primer on the Romantic ballet.

THE AMERICAN BALLET, a study of the art from Colonial to contemporary times.

BIRD OF FIRE: STORY OF MARIA TALLCHIEF, study of a 20th century American ballerina in her setting.

AMERICAN MODERN DANCERS: THE PIONEERS, the history of the beginning of modern dance told through the lives of the men and women who created it.

# Enjoying Opera

## OLGA MAYNARD

Charles Scribner's Sons
New York

## ACKNOWLEDGMENTS

I acknowledge with gratitude the help of the American composer Conrad Susa, who read my manuscript in draft and made valuable recommendations.

Augusta Baker, Coordinator of Children's Services for the New York Public Library, and Mary Strang of the Library-Museum for the Performing Arts at Lincoln Center are two of the many librarians and educators whose encouragement and advice considerably aided me in writing ENJOYING OPERA.

I have also to thank Anne Gordon, Jeanne Thomas and Dale Heapps of the Press Department, Metropolitan Opera Association, for assistance in selecting photographs.

Photos 1–30, courtesy of The Metropolitan Opera Company; all except #15, #23, #30 by Louis Mélançon; #31 and #32 courtesy of The Metropolitan Opera National Company.

Musical quotations from *Hansel and Gretel, The Barber of Seville, Rigoletto, Otello, I Pagliacci* and *Samson and Delilah* are reprinted by courtesy of G. Schirmer, Inc., New York; from *The Marriage of Figaro* and *Salome* by courtesy of the publisher, G. Ricordi & C., S.p.a. of Milan. The excerpt from *Dido and Aeneas*, music by Henry Purcell, verse by Nahum Tate after Virgil, circa 1689, is from a libretto printed by Broude Brothers, New York, by special arrangement with Novello & Co. Ltd., London.

To Susan and Patrick Maynard
for pleasure;
and to Sara Kreger,
but not for pleasure alone.

"In art—music, painting, above all, sculpture—as in letters, what makes success is talent, and not ideas. The public (and I speak of intelligent people, the rest don't count . . .)—the public understands the idea *later*. To achieve this *later,* the artist's talent must manifest itself in an agreeable form and so ease the road for the public, not repel it from the outset. Thus Auber, who had so much talent and few ideas, was almost always understood, while Berlioz, who had genius but no talent at all, was almost never understood. There are two kinds of genius: natural genius and rational genius. Although I admire the latter immensely, I will not hide the fact that the former has all my sympathies. Yes, I have the courage to prefer Raphael to Michelangelo, Mozart to Beethoven, and Rossini to Meyerbeer. . . . I do not place the one group in second rank in order to put the other in first; that would be absurd. It is just a matter of taste. One sort of idea exerts a stronger attraction on me than the other."

GEORGES BIZET:
*Lettres à un ami,* 1865–1872

# Author's Note

*Enjoying Opera* is the title chosen by my editors at Charles Scribner's Sons for a book whose purpose is to put the new opera goer at ease in the opera house, the better to appreciate opera art. "Appreciation" often seems a hard, tedious task for the theatre goer but appreciation is really the accumulation of sufficient knowledge on which to acquire taste—the better to enjoy. This book is an Overture or introduction to what opera is, and what it is about.

It is not an orthodox "opera book" and I owe my reader an explanation of what it is not, so that he may use it for what it is. You will not learn how to sing, compose music or produce an opera by reading this book. It is not a text on opera, nor an analysis of the art, and it does not contain "stories of the operas." You are familiarly addressed because this material is drawn from my lectures on "Arts Appreciation" and is largely written to explain and reply to questions that have been asked me about opera—what it is, and why, how it got that way, when and where, and who made it so? This is, therefore, a very intimate sort of book, for the new opera goer who is a student, or someone on a job, or the lucky person who has "retired," and reached that glorious phase when one is free to enjoy at leisure everything in our world, including opera.

*Enjoying Opera* is for the theatre goer to whom opera is still a strange experience, an unresolved artistic adventure.

As a writer and lecturer I must always state that my approach to theatre is in the Greek definition of "a place to view." Opera is one of the theatre arts whose function is to entertain, not to educate and elevate. But theatre's ancient verities are magical: willing to be entertained, we are made to feel. And sometimes we are compelled to think. Opera has the facility of entertaining and of much more.

Opera was made known to me when I was young and ignorant, and I accepted it as one of the phenomena of civilization, like electricity and tram-cars. I lived with my parents in the Amazon forest and as soon as we left that sort of life we went to cathedrals and opera houses. I assumed that everyone in cities heard High Mass on Sundays and saw operas and ballets every night after dark.

In this innocence, I recall my first opera as *Pélleas et Mélisande,* which I swallowed at one gulp. No one had taught me to "appreciate" opera and I was not educated enough to know that Debussy had created an impressionistic opera which many audiences considered "difficult." The essential element I experienced from *Pélleas et Mélisande* was that people fall in love in ringing silence, the moment after the lightning strikes and the thunderbolt is loosed. Opera to me has remained an "experience" and it is this aspect of opera that I propose to introduce to you.

As an opera goer you will encounter *Pélleas et Mélisande* and determine your own intellectual and emotional response, because it will be your experience. The fact is: going to the opera is an exceedingly personal affair, like falling in love. No one can do it for you and you must actively do it yourself. You cannot sit in a chair and read a book and know all about opera. You have to go into the opera house and experience opera in performance and even then you will know only the one performance of the single opera. Opera is ceaselessly new because it is made and performed by human beings whose constancy is a divine inconstancy.

I think that of all theatre arts opera is best suited to American audiences and that, now that we have entered the age of the American opera tradition, we shall become a nation of opera buffs. I remember that when I first came to the United States ballet seemed strange as a "foreign" art to the audiences; in less than twenty years ballet has become the ubiquitous American dance, as common to "popular" media like movies and television as it is to the "legitimate" lyric theatre. Until recently, opera in America was within a few metropolitan opera houses —now opera is produced throughout the country, either by large touring troupes like the Metropolitan Opera National Company, or by local "regional" opera companies, many of them more avant-garde than the larger companies. We are in the process of creating a national opera tradition on the scope of the one which began in Europe during the High Renaissance and has lasted without lapsing into our times.

But in order to found a great national theatre we must cultivate a national audience and the American audience is a particular one, which I have observed as keenly as I have watched the American stage.

The English are reputed to take their pleasures seriously; we take ours with a lively curiosity, wanting to know the science as well as the art, the crafts as much as the aesthetics. When ballet was a novelty in this country the audience used to go backstage to examine the ballerina's shoes (and her toes, when permitted) to find out how a woman could leap about in the air like a rocket and twirl like a top on the tips of her toes.*

Many a new opera goer longs to look down the gullet of an opera singer to try to find out why opera singing sounds different to all other kinds of song, and why opera singers talk and even walk in manners different from the normal, or of the street. And the American theatre audience is of two kinds: one using the theatre in leisure for pleasure; the other using theatre not for pleasure alone, but for the purpose of extending study into it or out of it from other subjects in life and art.

You should accept the theatre as a foreign country, with its own language and customs, and use this book as a sort of guide and dictionary to put yourself at ease in the opera house. You cannot learn all about the world by visiting one small country so do not expect to know all about opera from one modest book.

Our educational system matter of factly includes "arts appreciation" in the curriculum and teachers are required to give students basics of theatre arts. In every city where there is a local opera troupe there is a policy for "student programs" for which teacher or parent must make preparation, or the student elects to prepare on his own.

* An anecdote illustrating this occurs in *The American Ballet,* a study of ballet in the United States, by Olga Maynard, publ. 1959, Macrae Smith Co.

I worked with teachers and librarians in compiling this book and I have included chapters which are specific but not exclusive to teacher-student use. The individual reader will adapt them to his own requirements.

A degree of repetition occurs in the text, not from carelessness but as recapitulation for the reader who uses this book before and after attending opera house performances. Remember that it is merely an Overture, not a whole *opus* in itself. And remember, too, that opera is a theatre art, presented for the entertainment of an audience. It is that and more to me and so I offer you my book in spirit *amabile, con brio ed piacevole*—in opera lingo: "amiably, with warmth, and in a pleasant manner."

*Olga Maynard*
*Autumn, 1965*

# Contents

# List of Illustrations

Characters and Scenes from:

# ✿ O N E ✿

# How to Use This Book

If you are reading for pleasure in leisure:

*The Beginning* and *Opera After Gluck* will tell you something of the romance of opera; how it began and where, who created it, and the influences of the street on the stage, the audience on the art.

*What Opera Is About* is the bare résumé of some well-known, well-loved operas.

*Opera: What It Is* . . . describes some of the science of opera making, how it is made into a form (shaped as sound) and through its instruments or players as orchestra and singers.

If you want to extend the main text into further information about opera, read *Notes* for *The Beginning* and *Opera After Gluck*, and especially the *Notes for Opera: What It Is* . . . ; the same chapter will describe the parts and sum of opera, how the orchestra evolved and changed in various eras, and how the singers are trained—why they look and sound like opera singers and like no other people because their art requires them to be a special breed.

*Overture* is an introduction or preparation for the new opera goer, to rid the reader of some prejudices and false notions about opera and to, I hope, engender the necessary enthusiasm and response required of an appreciative audience in theatre.

Teacher use of this book is directed to extensions of the above in: *An Approach to Opera Appreciation* and *Contemporary Ideas about La Bohème and Aida*, and *Highlights from Aida* is a brief guide to listening to opera recordings. *Aida for Example* is a general survey of the opera, useful for basic "Arts Appreciation" and *Aida's Composer* is illuminating for the creative process—how Verdi shaped the sound of *Aida*, who he was as a person and where and when he lived, et cetera. This is especially useful for teacher and parent use in establishing a human element in art. *Opera Lingo* explains terminology and the economy and purpose of its uses, and gives basic library reference for the reader who is a new opera goer. *Author's Note* and the quotation from Bizet's *Lettres* state the principles and intents of this book.

# ❧ T W O ❧

# Opera Lingo

Every profession has a vocabulary. In medicine, especially for pharmaceutical exactness, the terminology is Latin. English is the language of sports, whereby "baseball" is the same in every part of the world. Creating jazz, Americans contributed an idiom to musical language. Opera has its own lingo.

Because opera began in Italy and developed conspicuously there and in France and Germany, there are Italian, French and German words and phrases for some operatic statements or references. There is comparatively little difference between the first two, as in the Italian *buffa* and the French *bouffe*, descriptive of a kind of opera.

Opera is not foreign or "national" of itself but is a universal language, a man-made art form of great complexity and various styles: a world art which exists within its own traditions. The means by which it is produced, the systems by which its artistes are trained, and the styles and epochs of its evolution, are products and effects of opera artists, but not solely of one country or one national theatre.

Opera in America has a terminology largely based on the European, to which is added American vocabulary as translations of foreign language phrases. But a great deal of the "foreign" language phrasing in opera is pure opera vernacular which it would be absurd to alter. You do not refer to the literary plan of an opera as its "scenario," which is common to movies, but as *libretto*, the plural of which is *libretti* and, by American usage, librettos.

Some opera terminology is technical, primarily for the international uses of opera artistes, who commonly use three or four languages when speaking with each other, especially when discussing their work. An international opera language allows free communication between opera artistes of different nationalities, different tongues, and establishes a vocabulary through which basics of their work may be stated and recognized. As the audience, you are not obliged to master opera terminology but you will find that an elementary knowledge of opera vocabulary sharpens your perception about opera. Do not shun "foreign" phrases as an insuperable barrier between the stage and the audience. Even quite technical phraseology has a remarkable common sense and economy, as calling a certain style of song *da capo aria*.

*Da capo* is Italian for "from the beginning," and "aria" (*ahr*-iah) is Italian for "air," or melody. *Da capo aria* is sung in three parts and the third section is a return to, or repeat of, the first section. What could be used as a better phrase to describe this particular kind of song? You will find that exactness and economy are the principal virtues of professional terminology like "opera lingo."

I have offered English translations and some pronunciations for opera terminology and within the text, so that you will encounter them within their meanings, as examples. These will become natural and common to your approach to opera simply because they are of and belong to opera as a specific and useful language.

A reader wishing more amplification of operatic terms is referred to two superlative books: *The Concise Oxford Dictionary of Music* by Percy A. Scholes, and *The Concise Oxford Dictionary of the Opera* by Harold Rosenthal and John Warrack.

Opera jargon, of a non-technical nature, like the slang appellation of "opera buff" to an opera enthusiast or fan, has grown out of the romance of opera, through the involvement of the audience and the artists alike. The romance or story of opera is full of delicious scandals and extraordinary anecdotes, a vital, exuberant history in itself because opera was made for people by people and is a living, lively art. Opera is not natural and spontaneous but artificial and cultivated. This is the first thing and perhaps the only thing that you need to know about opera.

"Knowing opera" means "experiencing" opera in the opera house. But knowing about opera, finding out where and when a certain form developed, a style was inaugurated, a "school" came into being, are things you can learn from reading opera books. Opera was born and grew and for these reasons it has a story or history; a legend or life. For some of us in the audience, opera history has an immense fascination. It is a maze of persons and places, facts and figures, forms and formulas. Opera language may be stretched to encompass everything written about opera and all the memorabilia, besides, that is the accumulation of the art. A pictorial survey of opera houses, and opera productions through décor (scenery and costuming) is one exciting way of discovering the past and comparing it with the present of opera as a world-wide entertainment.

The American reader, almost invariably, is within reach of a library, an art gallery and a museum, and these are three main repositories of opera history. Consult the librarians in the Music department of your college, city or county library when you plan a reading course on opera. The finest such department is the unique Library-Museum for the Performing Arts at Lincoln Center, established by the New York Public Library in 1965.

My personal preferences for preliminary and elementary reading about opera are *Kobbé's Complete Opera Book*, edited and revised by the Earl of Harewood; *Knaurs Opernführer* by Gerhart von Westerman in the English translation by Anne Ross as *Westerman's Opera Guide*; and *A Short History of Opera* (2 volumes) by Donald Jay Grout. These books, with the music dictionary and opera encyclopedia previously mentioned (Scholes, Rosenthal and Warrack) are an excellent primary library for the teacher and a basic reading introduction for the serious opera goer. Individual taste, quite naturally, will dictate choice of reading. The funniest book I know on opera is the risible but exceedingly informative *Prima Donnas and Other Wild Beasts* by Alan Wagner. And some of the more articulate opera artists and impresarios have written biographies through which the opera goer may gain insight to personal predilections for opera art and the opera makers. *Composers on Music*, anthology edited by Sam Morgenstern, offers excerpts from literary materials on composers from Palestrina to Copland, and a fine reading guide in its *List of Sources*. The opera goer's appreciation of music will be immensely stimulated through *The Concert Guide* by Gerhart von Westerman, translated and edited by Cornelius Cardew. *A Dictionary of Vocal Themes*, compiled by Harold Barlow and Sam Morgenstern, will help you learn to identify famous airs.

# ✤ THREE ✤

# The Beginning

Opera may be approached from three main themes: technically, aesthetically and socially, all of which require research, analysis and evaluation. The romance of opera is in persons and places.

People were singing, dancing, acting and making music long before opera was conceived. In the age-old story of Drama and Music Opera is an infant. It is a modern, not an antique art, and although there are styles of opera consciously intended to be "natural," opera is sheer artifice. Its chief instruments of communication with the audience, the singers, do not sing or speak in natural ways but in a mode that is operatic.

This is an art that represents worldly sophistication and is the product of an ostentatious, material society. Opera was not born in a garret, the romantic habitat of a poor poet, but in the palaces of rich, indulgent patrons, for the purposes of expressing artistic ideas and communicating them to an appreciative audience. From this eminently cultured beginning, opera went out into the world and made a brilliant success, becoming as beloved by peasants as by poets and princes.

As soon as opera was formed it acquired a home: the opera house. This is a genuine architectural requirement of opera and for this reason opera is an art which has flourished within nations which established theatres as well as churches, courts, markets, schools and other public institutions. A European post-war manifestation was the rebuilding of opera houses as soon as war ended. In opera's history you will find that opera was cherished while nations were at war with each other or riven by civil revolt and riot. Opera is about three hundred and fifty years old but it is still vigorous and growing, taking root in every society which builds a home for it and nurtures its traditions.

Its universal attraction for the world-wide audience may be because *opera* means *works*, many arts as one art, and therefore opera has something to charm and interest every individual; an aspect to delight every single taste. Opera has magnificent pomp and pageantry and is the grandest of the performing arts. It is the world's most expensive entertainment and art form.

Towards the close of the 16th century a group of scholars and artists used to meet at the house of a Florentine nobleman, Giovanni Bardi, to discuss their ideas of art and theatre. They are known as "the Bardists" or the Camerata, the latter appellation derived from *in camera*, in private or in a chamber. Europeans of this period, the High Renaissance, were enamored of the ancient Greeks and the Camerata desired to achieve for their times the glory that had been Greece's in an older era. Factually, they wished to reform the theatre arts of their day.

In so doing they rebelled against formulas for musical composition and style of performance. From their rebellion came the new art of music, which we know as Opera.

Music in the time of the Camerata, as in our times, was of two general kinds: serious or "art" music, and the "popular" music, cruder in form, common to the people. The music of Medieval Europe was polyphonic and its acme was music for the church as masses and motets. Madrigal was the finest form of secular music, and beginning in Italy in the 13th century it was, by the 16th, in full flower. The madrigal had achieved, by the time of the Camerata, rich contrapuntal composition and was known throughout Europe. Introduced in England by Nicholas Yonge, a choir singer at St. Paul's Cathedral, it entered the mainstream of the music of English-speaking peoples.

The madrigal was the bridge between serious and popular music, between art and idiom. Madrigal composers often made use of street songs, the "pop" singing of the time, by adapting them to the madrigal form. Such adaptation altered the composition and delivery of the songs, but the root or source of many a stately madrigal lay in the music of the common people, the "music of the street."

Masses and madrigals were sung by several voices, as choirs, and the chorale, with or without instrumental accompaniment, was the serious or artistic style for Medieval song. Only common folk sang in solo form, and such singing was "pop" romantic music, idiom music that was not considered sacred or artistic.

The madrigal which had its root in a popular ditty would have decorated the original theme with polyphonic counterpoint, and, in performance, would be rendered by several voices, in a chorus. The Gregorian chant, the *cantus firmus* of church music, remained the absolute rule of aesthetic music but the madrigal, especially as an improvisation on its own terms on music of the common folk, expressed a more joyous, and individual concept of music.

The Medieval composers were in many ways very like "modern" composers today, who introduce electronic or "natural" and "non-music" sounds into the music of the 20th century. Avant-garde Medieval composers sometimes assumed "naturalness" to such a degree that they imitated bird-calls, shouts and street-cries, and interjected the sounds of whistles and hunting-horns in their music.

The madrigal was a song with several parts for several voices, sung without accompaniment, and in composing in this form Medieval musicians experimented with the human voice, playing it as a veritable instrument, and in orchestrations.

Music, not lyrics, was the main preoccupation of the madrigal composer—or, at least, for the *singing* aspect of the madrigal. Polyphonic music compelled a verbal distortion of language and the madrigal, in effect, was composed to be heard more as music than as sung music, in the way that we think of a "song."

The poets and musicians of the Camerata resolved to reform this style to what they believed the ideal of antique Greek theatre, where there had been no separations between dance and drama or music and poetry. The Camerata's new music would (they thought) restore Drama to its pristine position by requiring the text of a song to hold equal place with the music of a song. In short: every word, every syllable in a word, should be uttered by the singer and understood by the listener, when a song was sung. Above all, music must serve the spirit of drama; music should interpret the song as a whole, not embroider a theme without relation to the song, simply for music's "art" sake alone.

And these avant-garde Medieval artists declared that songs must be sung with naturalness, more within the ordinary ways of speech than the stylized utterances of the serious "art" music of the times.

The primary and perhaps crucial development of the Camerata was the *stile rappresentativo*, the representative style, in which the innovation was a recited narrative, called *recitativo*. Recitative (the English for *recitativo*) was not related to liturgical chant or to any of the then contemporary forms of singing. One of the Camerata, the composer Jacopo Peri, explained the principles of recitative by relating how he had studied people's ways of speaking and had adapted this mode to the new style of dramatic music. Music was incorporated into speech and vice versa. At the beginning of a piece of dialogue, in a dramatic musical presentation, the speaker would leave the musical harmony and return to it after variations in tempo. Emotion was an element of the new dramatic music. Tempo would quicken for some emotions, such as anger; tempo would slow for other emotions, as for sorrow.

This form of music-speech or dramatic music was performed by chorus and by single voice, in solo form.

The first experiment with the new form, the *stile rappresentativo*, was in a work called *Dafne*, for which the Camerata composers of music were Peri and Giulio Caccini, and the composer of the poetry or first libretto was the poet Ottavio Rinuccini.

*Dafne* in 1597 is the first chronicled opera performance, presented in the palace of the Camerata's second patron, Jacopo Corsi—who, with Bardi, was the first benign, suave influence on opera art. The *opus* or work (which was in actuality *opera*, plural for *opus*, because both music and poetry were involved as two commingled works) was described as *dramma per musica*, drama through music. *Dafne* was followed in 1600 by *Euridice*, by the same composers and librettist and, because its text was preserved, *Euridice* is the first known opera—hence, opera is said to have been born in the year 1600.

The Camerata is popularly said to have "invented" opera but, more correctly, this group crystallized the controversial, bold experiments of their times into the *stile rappresentativo*, which in *Dafne* and *Euridice* were used for the first time in whole works.

The genesis of opera was *intermezzo* or interlude, diversions as *entr'actes* (between the acts) of large scale entertainments. Some chronicles refer to these as *balletti*, and they generally contained dance, drama, pastorale (a form older than opera which continued, in its form, after opera was developed), and symphony, i.e. instruments playing together.

*Balletti* was an Italian entertainment, so popular that it was taken up enthusiastically in other nations, the French turning it into *cour de ballet* and the English into *masques*. Catherine de'Medici, wife of Henri II of France, had such a passion for *balletti* that she took it with her to court, where it diverted the French nobility to the extent that Catherine's children and children's children were dancers and balleto-manes. These elegant spectacles combined dancing, singing, instrumental music, and recitations. The subject matter was largely allegorical, the astute composers turning myth to good account to flatter the sovereign and the sovereign's favorites. Thus, in time, Louis XIV, the proudest man in Europe, would be willing to take his title of "Sun King" from a role in a ballet (*Le Roi Soleil* in *Ballet de la Nuit* by Lully).

Under Elizabeth I and James I the English revelled in sumptuous *masques*, variations of the grand entertainments as masquerades which the Italian princes had inaugurated a century or more before. The English poet-dramatist Ben Jonson and the architect Inigo Jones collaborated on *Twelfth Night Masque* in 1605, to produce a peerless scenic and dramatic work in the style of *masque*, entertainment by songs, speeches, dancing and finales of recitations and vocal chorus.

The form of singing, reciting and instrumental music, which is opera, might have emerged from the *masque per se*, in time, just as ballet itself came out of the large-scale *balletti*. But opera is considered to have come from the small diversion, the *intermezzo*, which the Italians fitted between the acts of *balletti*, probably to allow time for scenery and costume changes in the elaborate spectacles—which were of such length and production magnitude that our pageants and musical revues today would appear drab and skimpy in comparison.

These grand entertainments were put on not in theatre (which did not yet exist in the form of the opera house) but in the chambers and courtyards of palaces, whose princes subsidized an army of creative and performing artists as retainers. *Balletti* was more a social than a theatrical production, chiefly to advertise the pomp and position of the prince under whose auspices it was presented, usually for guest dignitaries, or to celebrate a gala event like the birth of an heir or a wedding between important houses. It was not gentle culture or aesthetic sensibilities which cultivated Renaissance arts but pure vanity and the passion to outdo one's princely neighbor in material show.

Italian nobles (some of appalling cruelty, like Galeazzo Sforza, duke of Milan) tenderly nurtured the arts in their savage, selfish bosoms—actively supporting the artists who lived on their bounties and so were able to create, experiment and improvise free of care and the need to earn a living by more pedestrian means. The Sforzas in Milan, d'Estes in Ferrara, and especially the Medicis in Florence had in their employ musicians and singers, ballet masters and dancers, painters and cooks all toiling towards one end: to make their master's social image such as would awe his envious friends and enemies. It is notable that opera was not born in a garret, the romantic habitation of the poor poet, but in the palaces of Bardi and Corsi.

Among the Camerata, Caccini was *musico* to the Medicis 1545-1618, during which period opera emerged gradually from its antecedent forms, became evident as *stile rappresentativo*, and underwent some evolutionary forms. In 1579 Caccini with musicians Pietro Stroggi, Alessandro Striggio and Claudio Merulo composed for the ubiquitous Rinuccini's text a work titled *Maschere d'Amazzoni* to be performed in honor of the marriage of Grand Duke Francesco de'Medici and Bianca Capella. For all we know now, this might have been of such "operatic" style and structure as to be, in fact, the initial opera. The title alone, incorporating the Amazons of myth, prove that Caccini and his collaborators were already speculating on the lost music and drama of ancient Greece. This was the thesis of the Camerata's revolt and reform in Medieval music, and the actual reason and beginning for opera.

Until then, dramatic presentations with music (in which the madrigal was the primary musical form) required choral accompaniment. Very infrequently, a voice sang one part of the music while the other parts were played by musical instruments. But when actors were on stage miming their roles the music was off-stage (singers and orchestra out of sight of the audience) and the musical accompaniment was in chorus, not solo voice, even when one actor held the center of the stage. Thus, a hero expressing his sensations of woe would, as it were, bewail in full chorus, not in an individual voice.

The new form of *dramma per musica* required that all the dramatic parts be sung (which entailed the services of singers on stage), some parts in solo and some in chorus. The recitative was a part of the new form, and the continuity of the entire production relied on the unity of the dramatic and musical entities. The music underscored or accompanied the singing and the early operas obviously treated music as the handmaiden of Drama.

In this assumption, the Camerata must have adopted as credo the definition given to music by Aristotle, who named it as the fifth constituent of drama. Rinuccini, the first librettist, went to mythology for his sources and his choice for *Dafne* (whose mother turned her into the laurel, to save her from being seduced by the amorous god, Apollo) is indicative of the histrionic sense which suffused early opera.

The first opera known to us which has been preserved for scrutiny (the music of *Dafne* has never been found), is *Euridice*, where the text followed the Greek legend of Orpheus's passionate quest of his wife after death. We do not know how the instrumental music assisted the drama but musicologists surmise that individual instrumentation was composed for each role, harmony prevailing. We do know that *Euridice* had expressive recitative and fine structural composition. The opera is occasionally produced from Peri's text and is a quaint experience for the modern listener, on whose ear the music falls more monotonously than excitingly. There is at least one delightful and immortal passage in *Euridice*, a chorus suggesting "Let us sing and dance"—as mellifluous as the flutes in its orchestration when it is heard in Italian: *Al canto al ballo all' ombr'al prato adorno*.

Peri as Orpheus sang to the Euridice of a noted singer and lutanist, Vittoria Archilei, and the opera *Euridice* inaugurated a vogue which began in Florence in a form which is described as the "Florentine opera" or opera period. Because its form differs from its immediate successor and usurper, the Venetian opera, it is interesting to note the differences in the audiences or patrons of these two opera modes.

Florentine opera was the entertainment of aristocrats, an artistic revolution encouraged by the rich and cultured like Bardi and Corsi. It was performed for the amusement of princes and cardinals of the church and in exalted themes which derived from antiquity. Daring as they were in their concepts for a new music, the Camerata failed to break entirely with precedent, by which choral music was the accepted form of artistic or "high-brow" music. The chorus was used more extensively than the solo voice in early operas and to distinguish it from later, more radical changes in Medieval music the Florentine epoch is classed as "choral opera."

It was an intimate sort of singing, contained within a room or chamber, and volume in singing was not then the requirement that it later became for projection from the stage into the auditorium.

There was a stage, raised as a platform and framed by a decorative proscenium arch, with wide steps leading down into the auditorium. Such a stage is shown in contemporary engravings as for the performance of *Euridice*. But all the drama was front-stage, scenic depth and décor were still lacking, and changes in scene apparently took place without pause, and with the minimum mechanics. Opera was far less opulent and technical in stage-craft than the *balletti* or *interludi* out of which it had been lifted.

Opera in the ideal of *Euridice* was still experimental and subject to influences, and many of these came from the audience, to stir the inventiveness of the opera makers. This influence made the opera aria paramount.

Solo vocalization with chorus and orchestra is a style first credited to a Roman Catholic priest, Philip Neri (canonized after death as St. Philip Neri), who is recorded as early as 1556 as staging performances of religious libretti for solo, chorus and orchestra in the church oratory (chapel or prayer-room). Thence came the word *oratorio*, a musical composition for solo and choir with orchestra, generally but not always on a sacred theme.

Neri died before 1600, the date of the affirmed birth of opera, but his inventions for the aria and opera are exceedingly important to note, predating the developments by the Camerata and their successive traditions in the Venetian and Neapolitan opera traditions.

Musicologists argue about the categories of the first oratorios and first operas and two schools of thought divide an early example by a Roman composer, Emilio de Cavalieri (*La Rappresentazione di Anima e di Corpo*) between these forms.

Probably the first innovation of the solo form within the Camerata was by the composer Vincenzo Galilei, father of the astronomer Galileo, who set an episode from Dante's *Inferno* and the *Lamentations of Jeremiah* from the Bible for solo voice accompanied by viols. Galilei's musical setting of dramatic sacred poem or prose is the basic form of oratorio and it appears to have inspired a fellow of the Camerata, Giulio Caccini, to develop the solo within poetic and dramatic texts.

Caccini (a collaborator of Peri in the operas *Dafne* and *Euridice*) was a singer of excellence, chronicled as *canto famoso*, famed singer. He was harpist and director of music for the de'Medici family in Florence and the favorite of Bardi, who wrote some short libretti for Caccini's compositions.

Caccini performed songs and recitatives to the accompaniment of the *chitarrone* (lute) and set a series of sonnets to music for solo voice and accompaniment by *theorbo* (lute) and is reputed to have had great success with the Camerata's distinguished audience, which on occasion included the leading political and social personages of the city of Florence, Giovanni de'Medici among them.

Firmly laying claim to his inventiveness, Caccini published a treatise on his compositions under the title *Nuovo Musiche* (New Music) and also printed his own music with Rinuccini's text for *Euridice* in January, 1601, three months after its première (as a libretto by Rinuccini with music by Peri and Caccini) on October 6, 1600. This establishes Caccini's *Euridice* as the first published opera and allows comparison between it and Peri's *Euridice*.

Peri was obviously the superior composer. He was also the favorite of Corsi, who succeeded Bardi as leader of the Camerata's audience, the cognoscente who were the first opera patrons. Although Caccini succeeded in publishing his opera before Peri published his, Caccini had to wait until nearly two years after *Euridice's* première to get his own version performed ( December 5, 1602, at the Palazzo Pitti) and such incidents as this plagued the poor man's life and exacerbated his jealousy. But Caccini appreciably developed the early form of aria through his own excellence as a singer and from his good fortune in having two daughters who were noted singers and instrumentalists.

One, Francesca (married to Giovanni Batista Signorini and there-fore found in some opera books under her husband's name), was the first female opera composer and the first opera composer to diverge from themes of antiquity into romance, as she did in her opera *The Liberation of Ruggiero* whose libretto was an epic romance by Ariosto. She sang the role of *Euridice* for Peri when she was aged thirteen.

Francesca, affectionately known by the diminutive *La Cecchina*, was a favorite of Maria de'Medici (for whose wedding to Henry IV of France the first *Euridice* was performed in celebration), and had two daughters who sang at court. Francesca had a voice of marvelous power and flexibility, and was probably the first authentic *coloratura soprano*, a term not in vogue in her time. Her father must, indubitably, have put her extraordinary voice to good use in his theme for solo voice, and La Cecchina sang herself into history as opera's first *prima donna*.

The great opera of the era was *Orfeo* by opera's first genius of music, Claudio Monteverdi, whose librettist Alessandro Striggio capitalized on Orpheus instead of his wife, Euridice, using the legend in its entirety while Rinuccini's text used only episodes, and patently arranged it to compliment the mortal bride and groom, Maria de'Medici and her husband Henry IV of France. The great difference lies in Monteverdi's actual work, so superior to that of other composers that it is Monteverdi's operas which actually commence the opera tradition. *Orfeo* is constructed to such excellent effect in its dramatic and melodic parts that it is performed without apology by contemporary opera troupes, able to stand on its own as a work, rather than (as with *Euridice*) as a curio.

Monteverdi and Striggio called the opera *La Favola D'Orfeo*, bringing into the terminology the *opera favola*, opera based on fable or myth, as a positive designation.

*Orfeo* was first produced in 1607, at Mantua; meanwhile another kind of opera, the allegorical style, was becoming known and admired. The first such was Emilio de Cavalieri's *La Rappresentazione di Anima e di Corpo*, presented in Rome (1600), and translatable as "The Representation of the Soul and the Body." The characters were personifications of abstract and idealized concepts of the Spirit, Intellect, Pleasure, and the story was a quasi-romantic moralization somewhat in the mode of the "Miracle Plays" of the period.

There were soon three kinds of opera: pastoral, as was *Dafne*; allegorical, in the trend of Cavalieri's opera (or oratorio?); and, probably drawing on the popular *balletti*, the "magical" opera where décor and stage mechanics embellished the plot. The introduction of stage mechanics and grand décor into opera removed it from its modest staging "in camera" and placed it in a new phase as theatre, from where it continued to develop until it commanded the greatest technical skills, becoming the grandest of performing arts. These developments were rather rapid because opera caught the general public's fancy and spread from city to city, as from Florence to Venice and Naples.

The first opera house was built in Venice in 1637 by a playwright-composer, Benedetto Ferrari, who believed that the new art would attract the audience en masse, as well as please the nobility. He was correct and Teatro San Cassiano was patronized by opera's first general audience: intellectuals, society folk, artists and hoi polloi. By the end of the century there were fourteen theatres in Venice, and more than half, and the most splendid, were devoted exclusively to opera.

At first, opera was scheduled during the carnival season, from Christmas to the beginning of Lent. It proved so popular that a season was added for the weeks during which the church celebrated the Feast of the Ascension. Eventually, there were three-month seasons three times annually, during which the Italians in every one of their major cities patronized opera performances. Within an amazingly short time Italians had become avid opera fans. Forty years after *Euridice* the new art was established as the national pastime of Italians, and little boys and girls in Italy dreamed of being discovered for opera with the same feverish excitement that their American counterparts later dreamed of being discovered for the movies.

Monteverdi, who was born in Cremona and was court musician to the dukes of Gonzaga from 1604 to 1613, went to Venice and there raised the standard of opera to its highest. He was director of music at St. Mark's Cathedral until his death in 1643, during the epoch when the aria came into vogue.

Florentine opera extolled the dramatic significance and considered the recitative the chief innovation of the new art. Venetian opera developed the purely musical element in melodic forms that glorified the singer.

Monteverdi (whose librettist Giovanni Busenello was the most conservative among the Venetians) remained faithful to the mode of dramatic recitative but his operas did not neglect the musical element for the dramatic. His individual style was characterized by a richness of harmony and the use of a large orchestra for his day: twelve violins of which two were solo instruments; five violas de gamba and two basses; a piccolo, three muted trumpets, a clarinet, trombones, two small organs (of the style of that time), two harpsichords, harps and other instruments. We do not know just how Monteverdi arranged his orchestra, only that he used them in solos and in groups, and it is assumed that not all the instruments were played at once, in fullest orchestration. Basically, Monteverdi's opera was within the form of Peri's and Caccini's; actually, Monteverdi's work was transfigured by his own genius.

In Monteverdi opera, we find the beginning of *cantilena*: smooth, melodic passages for the voice, and he was the first opera composer to use pizzicato as coloring for the orchestra, first to develop tremolo, trembling, as in the rapid bowing of stringed instruments.

Now opera began to embroider its music, as in *fioritura*, literally decoration of melody, often in an extemporaneous burst by an instrumentalist or a singer. Perhaps singers had done this sort of thing in madrigal, during the *entr'actes* or intermezzo diversions of the grand entertainments. Wherever it began it soon became the vogue in the new art which had so enchanted Venice, and presently every opera was decorated with *cantilena* and *fioritura*.

Venice, which led the civilized world in painting in the 16th century, elected to lead it again, in music, in the 17th, as it led the mode in dress and in every social fashion besides.

Opera, an Italian invention, was well suited to the Italian language (which as speech is lyrical in itself) and temperament and its new theatricality was typical of the Italian mode: extravagant materialism and lust for pleasure.

Opera's audience changed and thus changed opera styles. The gay, pleasure-mad Venetians, of all walks of life, flocked to theatres to be entertained, and required brilliant, even gaudy productions for their amusement. Décor became a part of opera and Italian "grand opera" developed magnificent productions in which the arts of sculpture, painting and design combined with poetry and music to form the single "opera" (as it came to be called) as several works of art.

The allegorical and "magical" operas, with their supernatural crea-tures and faërie themes, acquired a mysterious and fascinating aspect for opera, and required extraordinary visual effects. Sometimes these vis-ual effects altogether eclipsed the dramatic and musical aspects. When Cardinal Mazarin introduced Italian grand opera into France in 1645 the balletomane French seized on the elaborate machinery, some of it truly marvelous (Leonardo da Vinci designed some of the engineering feats) to embellish their ballets.

Less than half a century after its invention opera had rebelled against the Camerata's ideals, the first battle of music versus drama was fought, and the aria emerged, growing out of the *canzone*, a short, lyrical passage in opera.

The *recitativo secco*, or dry recitative innovated by the Camerata, bored the frivolous Venetians, and to relieve the tedium the opera makers developed *recitativo accompagnato,* recitative accompanied by instrumentation, eventually establishing a less stylized treatment of the vocal parts in opera. The *canzone* was melodious, and, as the full-blown aria, was accompanied by full orchestration.

Two Venetian composers frankly catered to the audience's taste and became the most successful and influential of the Venetian school: Francesco Cavalli introduced popular songs of the time into opera; Marc Antonio Cesti so liberally sprinkled *canzoni* through his works that the dramatic action would be interrupted for the sake of a song, even if at an unsuitable point of the story.

The subject matter of opera libretti changed, drastically, from lofty themes and epic characterizations to historical (based on recent, actual events, dressed up as classical romances) or comic, beginning to lean towards the commedia dell'arte. The moralizing ideals of the early operas yielded entirely to the melodramatic, fraught with human emotions, chiefly passionate love—which gave good reason for singing what Westerman calls "desperate duets."

Farce, undoubtedly, was a welcome relief from torrid passion and its anguishes. Opera began to assimilate some elements of commedia dell'arte for commedia per musica.

*Commedia per musica,* "comedy through music," was opera termi-nology in 18th century Italy, especially in the Neapolitan school. Comic opera was the opposite of *opera seria,* the appellation given to

17th and early 18th century Italian operas which were serious or tragic in theme.

*Commedia per musica* eventually became *opera buffa* for the Italians, and as such exists into our times. (It became *opéra bouffe* for the French, but the French opera genre that is *opéra comique* does *not* mean "comic" opera—about which more, in good time!)

Indubitably, comic opera derived from *commedia dell'arte*, slapstick, knock-about comedy that was purest burlesque. It was the entertainment of the people, and had developed in 16th century Italy in protest against the conventionality and pedantry of *commedia erudita.* All clowns are descended from Zanni, the stock figure of fun in commedia dell'arte. *Opera buffa,* when it was fully developed as such, won universal and instantaneous acceptance from the audience en masse, which had been prepared (for a century or two before) by the broad humor and sharp wit of commedia dell'arte to enjoy such themes. Molière and Shakespeare were two of many playwrights who borrowed characterizations and, on occasion, situations from commedia dell'arte.

The true *commedia* had no script or libretto and relied on the *soggetto,* an episode or incident on which to base the play. The story or plot was developed extemporaneously, the dialogue being created impromptu, and the complete presentation, whether it was staged in the market place and village green or in a palace courtyard, was superb as theatre. Portable stages were fitted with ingenious paraphernalia to achieve devilish tricks because malice and droll comment on topical events and personalities were prime characteristics of the *commedia,* as was its clever and often inspired buffoonery. At its peak, the *commedia* richly and elaborately costumed its stock characters (Harlequin, the soul of mischief; Pantalone, an utter oaf; and many others) and embellished the *soggetto* with incidental songs, dances, music and rhymes. It was an entertainment of long standing in Italy, France, Spain and England before *opera buffa* formed. The *Punch and Judy* street show, Stravinsky's *Petrouchka,* Shakespeare's Bottom in *A Midsummer Night's Dream,* the players in *Hamlet,* and the whole idea on which *Pagliacci* is formed came out of commedia dell'arte.

Characterization of human persons superseded symbolism in opera —not yet to the extent achieved in Mozart's works, of course. Mozart's dramatic and musical genius developed the human and personal elements of opera characterization, establishing the romantic foundations of 19th and 20th century opera. But from the raucous, bawdy creatures of the commedia dell'arte the Camerata's austere, artistic child drew associations and influences which turned that child, materially, into a more "human" course. Opera became vital and viable for the audience en masse.

I would say in summation: the first operas were in substance aesthetic experiments in which the Camerata and their emulators expounded and propounded theories for a "new music." These early operas were "art works" of exalted ideals, materialized as the creators' ideas. As such, an early opera was an end in itself. It appeared complete and entire, destined to convey nothing more and nothing greater than itself.

Seen in this light, the later opera differs in that it was productive of feeling beyond pure aesthetics. Opera began to appeal, and was consciously constructed by the opera makers to appeal to the senses. A tragic work or *opus* was no longer an end in itself; it extended far beyond the jurisdiction of its creator into the collective heart and mind of the audience. God alone knew, certainly not Leoncavallo, what would pass through the mind and twist the heart of a cuckold who attended a performance of *Pagliacci*.

Common experiences, experiences ordinary to the street, and "human" or everyday types, were the fortes of commedia dell'arte, which also had its romance (a roguish Pierrette, a love-sick Pierrot, et cetera) and invested heavily and to good account with the audience in what our "pop" media as "soap opera" on movies, radio and television consider "personal conflicts." A Duenna in commedia dell'arte or a zealous papa frequently thwarted True Love's Course, requiring the fabrication of hilarious episodes to distract attention from the lovers. Opera dramatists had only to adapt this "conflict" to a comic or tragic theme (turn it upside-down or inside-out) to find formulas in which "persons" assumed characters as well as action. The "I" or personal motif in opera was expressed through individual or solo song, hence the development of the *arietta*, the larger form as *aria*, the *arioso* (vocalization between true aria and recitative passages), the *canzone* and all forms of solo and duet.

On the premise that if a thing attracts the public, the public cannot have enough of it, opera composers strove to supply *canzoni* in a continuous stream of musical compositions. The Florentine choral opera style was supplanted by the Venetian solo opera style and on occasion the chorus was so shabbily treated that it became more an impediment than an asset in an opera. Opera now moved from the exalted "camera" or sheltered circle of the cognoscente into the wider world of popular entertainment and there the stage became subjected to influences from the street.

Soon cliques or coteries in the audience began to attach themselves passionately to certain singers, and the rise of the "star" performer in opera became one of opera's peculiar phenomena. Instead of coolly assessing opera as "Art" the audience en masse found empathy in opera through the singers, whom they conceived of as living and experiencing the incidents and events in the plot (the libretto) instead of being personifications of song; i.e. singers. The elaborate charades from myth and allegory, exalted themes which suited the tastes of the cognoscente, turned to plots closer to the styles of commedia dell'arte, which were basically human situation and characterization and, moreover, caricatures of ordinary events and common types.

Some musicologists believe that the fall of the chorus and the rise of the soloist in Venetian opera was for economic reasons. The theatre was commercial and the employment of a chorus, naturally, was more costly than the hiring of individual singers. Whatever the reason, the chorus grew smaller and was used less and less in opera, while the role of the soloist was glorified and glamorized. The singer sang more, sang more frequently, and sang louder in opera.

The female singer of supreme rank was called *prima donna,* first lady; and the chief male singer was *primo uomo,* usually a castrato. Soprano voices were the most admired and drew the highest pay. There were insufficient fine female soprano voices to satisfy the demand for arias because not enough trained women singers could be found, immediately following the first popularity of the aria.

Secular choir singers, male altos, were recruited into opera and soon composers made this type of voice the acme of vocalization, causing poor families (and some families of substance) to ensure their sons' careers by preparing them for the castrati. The first requirement was to make a boy a eunuch before puberty, by performing surgery on his testicles, so as to preserve the sweet, clear treble tone of the pre-adolescent voice.

The castrato became the singer of highest caste in Venetian opera, and it was usual for a male alto to receive a thousand ducats for a season, while the composer was only paid one hundred ducats, although he not only wrote the music but also, as a rule, rehearsed it, and worked in the orchestra. If he was lucky to hold the post of first harpsichordist, he was due to receive a small fee extra to his hundred ducats as composer.

The miserable librettist received no money at all and was supposed to rejoice that his verse was being sung. He did not usually have his libretto published in the Venetian opera, from whose early traditions few works have survived—it had been usual to record texts in Florence. Westerman estimates that at least six hundred operas were produced (and more may have been composed) in the Venetian style during the sixty years of its vogue in Italy, France and Germany; few examples were published and preserved.[1] Yet the libretto remained a fundamental and essential principle for opera.

The first opera seasons were ephemeral repertories, an opera house producing a work for one season and thereafter abandoning it, even when it was successful. Our method of preserving works in active permanent repertory and reviving old works seasonally was not the mode in early opera tradition. One libretto served a number of opera composers—we note that Rinuccini's *Euridice* was used by Peri and Caccini, and then again by Caccini when he was writing an opera on his own. The subject of *Euridice* served opera composers as far away as Germany, although the Germans had romantic myths and enchanting nymphs in their own folklore. Quite regularly, an opera's title and libretto would be lifted intact from one theatre and produced in another theatre, allegedly as the same opera, but with totally different music. The audience of an opera titled *So-and-So* in Vienna apparently neither knew nor cared that the opera of this title, composed in Venice, was to altogether different music. It only mattered to the later 17th century audiences that the opera be a grand spectacle, full of thrilling *canzoni* solo and duet.

Singers had now become the primary artists and opera houses promoted their popularity with the audiences. Maestros composed and arranged the music to suit the voices of their casts, cutting their coats to fit the popular fancy—and the abilities and fortes of their singers. Musically, there must have been a serious decline from Monteverdi's standards because then as now the composer's genius was exceptional, not commonplace. The poor hacks of musical directors or conductors who were ordered to "compose" *canzoni* for singers must have made makeshift music at best; execrable music at worst.

But this period, which might have brought opera so low as to extinguish it, increased the art in stature as well as popularity, by developing a style which is fairly close to that of contemporary opera. Cavalli and Cesti were not simple hacks. The first excelled in composing lilting melodies for songs, and introduced the barcarolle (a ⅔ measure) which later became integral to Venetian opera, and he had better grasp of structure than Cesti, balancing the merits of *recitativo* and *canzoni* to good effect. Cesti, one of the most prolific of opera composers, had less restraint and dignity and so sacrificed dramatic empathy for songs galore, but his works were very entertaining and, in form, were a series of popular songs, short recitatives and passages of virtuoso music, perhaps the original of the modern "musical" which is a theatre medium in itself!

And it was Cesti who originated the *da capo aria* in the next century. This was a solo in three parts, the third being a reprise, and it set a style which further enhanced the role of the singer.

## To Recapitulate:

The rise of the aria was the first public influence on opera; it was made popular and consequently important in opera simply because the audience en masse liked it and liked it so much that it clamored for operas with arias.

Opera had left the shelter and sanctuary of the private house, it was no longer being presented "in camera," but had gone abroad, into the world, where it became subjected to worldly influences. The audience's taste dictated the audience's favor and, to great extent, determined the standards and styles of opera performances.

The Camerata was made up of serious men who took themselves seriously. They had, as they believed, reformed the ancient Greek ideal in drama. In doing so, the Camerata devised a form, which naturally assumed a formula or *modus operandi*. It was *opera seria* or serious opera (a term which qualified Italian grand opera) in that theme, and treatment of theme, were serious. We may assume that every opera produced in the Florentine period provided debates of a scholarly and aesthetic nature.

The Venetian period was the advent of hoi polloi into the opera audience, an audience with cruder tastes, ruder humor, less time and inclination than the Camerata for subjective and objective dissertations on art. A different kind of audience attended opera and the physical theatre facility changed to accommodate the new art; the opera house was designed.

The court theatres (chambers set aside in palaces and mansions for staging theatrical performances) were of amphitheatre type, seating the dignitaries of the audience dead front and center, before the proscenium. The Venetian opera house was built in two or three tiers of boxes rising up to the roof from the floor, which we call the stalls or seats in the orchestra section. The gentry occupied the boxes, which were the most expensive seats; hoi polloi gathered in the stalls. The nobility maintained their opera boxes in style, because attending the opera had become fashionable as well as aesthetic. Rich families bought or leased an opera house box and kept it for generations, like maintaining family pews in the cathedral. One family, the Grimani, built an opera house and for several decades subsidized it, supporting it by buying out all the performances, to which they invited their friends to occupy the boxes and distributed the cheap seats in the stalls to the poor.

As the aria became popular with rich and poor, cultured and uncouth, the singer became the most important single artist. The audience did not see the composer on stage, it seldom knew the name of the librettist, and the orchestra was, in the course of opera evolution, hidden behind curtains, tucked out of sight under the stage, and, at most, a sound rising out of the orchestra pit. It was the singer and his song which touched the heart and imagination of the audience and many singers and not a few composers would capitalize on this rapport for centuries to come.

The Age of Scarlatti is the next epoch, which is that of Neapolitan opera. As the Venetian opera, at its worst, deteriorated into a tuneful potpourri with comic relief the libretti were blamed for falling far below the dramatic standards for opera and three poets in the imperial court at Vienna determined to refine and reform opera libretti. They were named Stampiglia, Zeno and Metastasio.

High morality and noble principles were again fashionable, the sentimental in poetic raptures ruled the rococo style, and the aria provided a delightful form in which to express emotion. Operatic verse or lyrics became the prime concept, the aria was dominant and dialogue and recitative latent in the new opera, which, in itself, was more aesthetically conceived than it had been in its Venetian period. All came about under the poetic influence.

Singing schools in the cities of Naples, Venice and Bologna had a ten or twelve year course of study for the student, whose education included dramatic training and dancing as well as sight-reading of music, virtuoso singing and at least an elementary knowledge of some instrument. Singers were developed to a large vocal range, with absolute evenness through the register, and fluency and suppleness to grant the virtuoso techniques in demand for opera. It is hardly to be wondered at that the prima donnas and castrati were temperamental, and ruled the opera houses they tenanted; they literally dedicated their lives to singing; the castrati yielded their manhood. Singers were the pets and tyrants of opera.

Pietro Metastasio was the most celebrated librettist of the era, and the "Metastasio aria" was a solo in three parts (the original of which lies in Cesti's aria): *da capo aria*. Metastasio was poet laureate and his undisputed authority (plus the charm of the aria form for the public) established his solo composition in three parts as the supreme aria form.

The virtuoso *da capo aria* introduced every scene, for which the star singer made a correspondingly grand entrée on stage. Operas as grand collections of arias, not too far removed from the mode Cesti set with his collections of songs, ushered in the mode of the Neapolitan opera. This was the mode that would sweep opera clear across fashionable Europe and Britain and, eventually, America. (We still use the aria as our chief link with an opera and its singer.)

Alessandro Scarlatti is considered the father of Neapolitan opera and it must at once be noted that, although he made good use of the aria (and in his later works glorified *da capo aria*) he was not unaware of the dramatic values of the recitative. Scarlatti was a prodigy, whose first opera was composed and produced in Rome when he was nineteen, so charming Queen Christina of Sweden that she became his patron. He composed one hundred and fifteen operas of which Westerman reports seventy to be extant. His techniques appreciably developed the traditions of "Italian opera," and in the thirty-six years he lived and worked in Naples (he was born in 1660 in Palermo, Sicily, and went to Naples in 1682) he single-handedly, it may be said, transferred the throne of opera from Venice to his adopted city.

Scarlatti and his emulators, who together form the "Neapolitan school" of opera, invented the "Italian overture," developed *da capo aria,* and injected new life into the *recitativo accompagnato.* Scarlatti's techniques were so widely imitated and borrowed that it is difficult to measure where each of his innovations began or how far their influences were diffused, as in opera ensemble, chorus and orchestration.

Opera, true child of *alma mater Italia* (from whom the Western civilizations derived theatre arts) was so expressly and expressively an Italian invention that "Italian opera" would remain, into our times, a qualification of compositional form and style; a whole "school" or technique and aesthetic to itself.

Thus Mozart, who created an era in opera within his works, composed Italianate opera even while he was establishing the German opera. His *Abduction from the Seraglio* and *The Magic Flute* were the first important operas written in German texts, and were the source and inspiration of later German opera, into the works of Richard Strauss. But Mozart's other operas, to Italian libretti, in general conformed to the style of "Italian opera."

The first "golden age" of Italian opera was the first opera epoch, in three styles: Florentine, Venetian and Neapolitan. In this epoch *opera seria,* or serious opera, was joined by *opera buffa,* or opera of a farcical type. The earliest *opera buffa* works of importance were composed by Giovanni Battista Pergolesi. His *La Serva Padrona,* which was premièred in Naples in 1733, was in fact *intermezzo,* a short (two-act) composition but involved the elements that were later to qualify *opera buffa.* Containing the elements of commedia dell'arte (the impudent servant whose effrontery wins the sympathy of the audience), it is the forerunner of Rossini's *Barber of Seville* and Mozart's *The Marriage of Figaro* and many such, besides.

Italians invented, innovated or conceived the origins of opera *per se*; serious opera, *opera buffa*, the aria and (from Monteverdi) novel orchestration. In the 18th century, Italian opera was literally an industry, and was commonly produced on a scale of magnificence. Opera houses were flourishing concerns, and another "golden age" arose from the composers Rossini, Donizetti and Bellini. Verdi, two hundred years after opera was formed, lifted the art to a stage of artistic and technical development that created yet another "golden age." The close of the 19th century brought *verismo*, realistic opera, into fashion—again, through an Italian composer, Mascagni (in his *Cavalleria Rusticana*, 1890). Italian opera has never yielded its domination of the opera stage and, today, while contemporary repertory is largely based on only three German composers, Mozart, Wagner and Richard Strauss, many Italian composers are represented: Rossini, Verdi and Puccini especially, also Donizetti, Bellini and others.

As a new opera goer you are more likely to see Italian opera than any other kind because Italian opera is the mainstay of contemporary repertory, especially for large, stable companies.[2] With some German opera, the Italian opera is universally loved and known—more so than French and Slavonic opera; or opera of the English-speaking peoples. This generalization, "Italian opera," covers not only operas originally composed on Italian texts but also operas that fall into the category of "Italian" in form and style.

Yet I must impress on you that opera is not purely an Italian form of music, which appears on world theatre stages intact as "Italian opera." Far from that, opera has positive national styles, predominantly that of "French" and "German" opera (which we shall gradually distinguish in the course of this introduction). Moreover, opera actually "went national" or became fiercely chauvinistic in ways which distinguish a trend as "nationalism" in opera art, for instance in Wagner's theories and principles, in the French composer Claude Debussy (in reaction to Wagner), and in the famous renegade Russians known as "The Five" (Balakirev, Borodin, Mussorgsky, Cui and Rimsky-Korsakov), whose operas show national musical and folklore idioms.

(The interested reader, wishing to understand what distinguishes these kinds of opera must research the works of the composers named above.)

Suffice to state here that "national" opera is a kind which so positively expresses and affirms a national ideology in art that it cannot possibly be mistaken as the music of another nation, but is singular and vividly representative of its own. For example: *Prince Igor* (Borodin) and *Boris Godunov* (Mussorgsky) are wholly Russian operas, as *Hugh the Drover* (Vaughan Williams) is English opera, while American opera, by the reason of our polyglot cultural heritage, is eclectic.

Thus, American opera is drawn from the Indian or indigenous, such as *Natoma* (Victor Herbert) and *Shanewis* (Charles Wakefield Cadman) but, more often, from émigré cultures, like the Negro: *The Emperor Jones* (Louis Gruenberg), *Porgy and Bess* (George Gershwin) and (a direct influence from Negro music) *The Cradle Will Rock* (Marc Blitzstein), which incorporates jazz. The first American opera must have been *Ponteach, or The Savages of America* in the 18th century but American opera is so generally thought of as a 20th century accomplishment that I have omitted it from the restricted limits of this book.

Opera among the English-speaking peoples began in England with *Dido and Aeneas* by a Londoner, Henry Purcell. He was a son of a Gentleman of the Chapel Royal who, at about the age of eight or ten (his birth date is not positively known) became a Chapel chorister, tutored by John Blow. Eight years later, Purcell was appointed composer for the King's band, and was thereafter organist of Westminster Abbey and one of three organists of the Chapel Royal. His *Dido and Aeneas,* a three-act opera with libretto (based on the third book of Virgil's *Aeneid*) by Nahum Tate, was first performed about 1689, when Purcell was presumably aged thirty. Six years later, Purcell died, and with him the wonderful flowering of "English opera."

Would that he had lived, because his *Dido and Aeneas* is a jewel that many musicologists hold as the single 17th century opera which comes closest to the contemporary opera ideal. Ewen movingly remarks that surely nowhere else in opera before Gluck is there to be found such integrity of music and text, song and dance, within a single artistic entity.

Moreover, *Dido and Aeneas* is a consummate example of artistic economy wherein not an iota of merit is sacrificed, but, rather, the spare principle enhances the substance of the work. Three principal characters: Dido, Aeneas and a wicked sorceress; Dido's handmaiden, Belinda, and few "extra" characters (attendants on Dido as courtiers, on the sorceress as witches, and on the hero as sailors) permit direct action in the plot, with sharply defined conflicts and climaxes. The most famous excerpt from Purcell's opera is Dido's *Lament*:

In Westerman's estimation, this is a composition of Monteverdian genius. Purcell composed what amounts to adaptation of the sailor's jig in his choruses for song and dance by Aeneas' men, interlacing the opera with contemporary or popular English melodies.

*Dido and Aeneas* is Purcell's only true opera, although he wrote about fifty stage works besides, two of which had libretti of literary worth. *King Arthur* in 1691 was written by John Dryden; and *The Fairy Queen,* the year following, was taken from Shakespeare's *A Mid-*

*summer Night's Dream*. These and others were musical plays with spoken dialogue and, had Purcell lived, might have evolved a wholly distinguishable form as "English opera." But Purcell founded no school, had no protégé who as emulator could succeed him and preserve or improve his work, and early "English opera" may be said to have been born and to have died within the creative span of one man's life (c. 1659–1695).

The next inspiration for opera in England came from the German Handel, who went to London in 1710 and, except for brief absences in Europe, remained there until his death in 1759. For half a century, Handel virtually ruled the English musical theatre.

It is interesting to note this composer's antecedents and the influences he brought with him into 18th century opera. To do so, we must go to German opera and *its* antecedents. These can be traced to pre-Renaissance and within much the same kind of social entertainments that were popular in Italy: processions, masquerades, courtly galas involving song, instrumental music, dance and speeches or recitations; and, of course, performances by traveling players, the "mummers" who dwelt in the mountebank sphere of the Western world. Westerman says that although chorale was dominant in early German music the solo was also known, especially for popular songs. But the Germans did not evolve opera; the Italians did, and the first opera in Germany is set as *Der Pastoral-Tragikomodie von der Dafne* in April 1627. What but the Florentine opus, *Dafne,* by the Camerata!

*Pastorale* was common in Europe from the 15th into the 18th century, and was the common designation for a drama of myth or allegory in a pastoral scene. This form of entertainment must have been especially well suited to *al fresco* presentation, and readily adapted to the chamber-sized theatre of the early Renaissance into Lully's era at the French court, the late 17th century. Lully, in fact, composed authentic *pastorale* long after opera was a fully established form, and as he was the Italian-born father of French opera, his penchants are worth observing.

The 1627 German *Dafne* (with a libretto written in German by Martin Opitz, a Silesian poet) had music composed by Heinrich Schütz, whom Westerman calls the great forerunner of Johann Sebastian Bach. It must have been considered a work of worth; it was a gala for the marriage of Princess Sophia Eleonora of Saxony to George of Hesse, which historians inform us was celebrated with particular splendor in the castle at Torgau.

*Dafne* was more Italian than German, despite the language of the libretto, and the first really "German" opera may be that composed by Siegmund Staden, first performed in Nuremberg in 1644: *Das Geistliche Walgedicht Seelewig*, a pastoral opera about a nymph, Seelewig, in a sacred grove.

The libretto was a poem by Harsdorffer of Nuremberg, who had traveled and studied in Italy and probably brought back the idea of the *dramma per musica*. Interestingly, overtones in this early German opera portend the "Good and Evil" and redemption themes of Wagner's later, esoteric operas; Seelewig is the embodiment of the eternal Soul, menaced by a woodland deity, Trugewalt, with more than a hint of satyriasis. Good shepherds save Seelewig from Trugewalt's pursuit; a host of jubilant angels sing the finale. Seelewig was a soprano, Trugewalt a bass, in the spirit and mode of a tradition that is further stated in this book, within *Opera: What It Is . . .*

As early as 1631 opera was an institution at the imperial court in Vienna, and Cesti composed a work (*Pomo d'Oro*) for première by the Imperial Theatre. This popular composer of the Venetian period lived in Vienna for a time, where he flattered Leopold I by obligingly using some of the emperor's compositions in his (Cesti's) operas. The insertion of such "German" songs into Cesti's Italian operas did not, by any means, constitute the birth or even the conception of a "German opera" form.

The small courts of the German principalities (Brunswick, Hamburg, Nuremberg and others) were less fashionable than the Viennese and could afford to be less modish in opera styles. Instead of slavishly copying the Italian, some of these, and with good sense, advocated a more national opera form. Brunswick boasts opera performances sung in German as early as 1639, and in 1690 opened a public opera house, built in the Venetian architectural styles, with five tiers of boxes. A most democratic spirit prevailed, and a nicely commercial one: anyone could buy a ticket to see the opera. An anecdote relates that the Duke of Brunswick, wishing to attend an opera performance, presented himself and was requested to pay for his seat; and did.

In such a vein, German opera was off on a stable economy but "German opera" did not progress very far, again, because of audience favor—this time, a preference for the Italian imported style rather than the native German one.

Italian composers capitalized on the German love of opera and Italian operas dominated the repertory of the German opera houses, causing the dissolving of the stubbornly chauvinistic Brunswick opera in 1755. German history, German folklore abounded in material suitable for romantic drama and German poets and musicians were certainly not lacking. It would seem, in retrospect, that the British and the German (between whom there was ethnic relationship) had everything at hand with which to make totally and triumphantly "British opera" and "German opera." They did not, and it may have been a matter of semantics as much as anything else.

The prevalent style for opera, during the early Italian periods in Venice and Naples, was melodic and, musically, the Italian tongue was expeditious for singing, especially in the thrilling tremolo and the agile, florid form of *fioritura*. Italian speech is (as has been mentioned) particularly well suited to styles of Italian opera singing. When the *da capo aria* was developed the Italian opera became an exquisitely sensuous pleasure. *Bel canto,* Italian for "beautiful song," is expressive of beauty of tone, purity of texture, facility of voice production, agility in ornamental passages, and the lyrical quality of the song. As an acquired taste by opera goers, *bel canto* exceeds any other single pleasure offered by opera. A man might stand as stiff as a stick, a woman lie as inert as a stone, and it would be enough to have beautiful singing from them without any attempt to inject drama in the work.[3]

The recitative was, on the whole, more dramatic than the aria and was still used for emotional and dramatic expression, but the declamatory style in opera (which might have been better suited to the English and German languages) never quite regained the pristine place it had held under the Camerata.

In general, opera in Germany was in the Venetian style (a formula in which *da capo aria* was the strongest element, and siciliano and barcarolle, purely Italian music, were evident) and the realistic approach to a German opera was not in the classical mode but through *Singspiel* (roughly: sung-speech). This was an earthy, popular concept rather on the style of *commedia per musica,* and later became the German equivalent of *opera buffa.*

Hamburg persisted in its attempts to found German opera and maintained, successfully (meaning, it paid its way or subsisted on its own economy), an opera house for more than fifty years.

The Hamburg opera attracted such outstanding native artists and the theatre was situated in such a prosperous community, that there was every indication, in its half century of existence, of its becoming the true German opera center. The style of Hamburg opera was realistic. Early plots were derived from Biblical history and the German opera makers introduced ordinary persons among Biblical characters, and popular songs among operatic compositions. The common folk in the Hamburg operas sang and spoke Low German, whether they appeared in mythical and allegorical plots or in contemporary dramas. After a while, realism got uncomfortably out of hand, with consequent lack of good taste. The poets, as librettists, appear to have been of the coarsest breed.

The opera *Stortebecker und Joedge Michaels,* about the lives and loves of the first-named (a bandit), required the singers to wear pig-bladders filled with blood and concealed under their costumes, so that when attacked in the course of the story the players would appear to bleed copiously. As Stortebecker was killed in the end the gruesome finale may be imagined.

The composer of the music for the horrific *Stortebecker,* Reinhard Keiser, and another composer for the Hamburg Opera, Georg Philipp Telemann, were musicians of excellence, fated to live and work in an era when they were offered paltry libretti and were required to please the fickle taste of the public at all costs.[4] One man who worked in Hamburg under Keiser succeeded in breaking away from the tawdriness of the worst Italian style, and without rebelling against the form. He was George Frederick Handel, a genius who was equally the master of *opera seria* and oratorio, turning to the second in earnest after he was deemed a failure in the first.

Handel was invited to London while serving as kapellmeister at Hanover, and in 1711 had an overnight success with his first opera in England, *Rinaldo.* The next year he returned and except for short absences thereafter lived and worked in England until his death in

1759. He was the undisputed leader of English music, occupying prestigious positions like that of first artistic director to the Royal Academy of Music, and the stream of operas that flowed from his invention had phenomenal successes.

At his acme, Handel employed the services of the greatest singers in Europe, among them two famed castrati Senesino and Farinelli, and was a despotic maestro—composer, conductor and impresario all in one. He was the popular musical idol of England, looked upon as an institution, adored and revered, until his sudden fall from favor, which brought him financial ruin, artistic ignominy and serious ill health. The fiasco was wrought by a turn in popular favor from *opera seria,* which was Handel's forte, to comic opera, of which the first and most flagrant example was *The Beggar's Opera* in 1728. Handel and *opera seria* never recovered from the attack, which this satire was, against baroque opera. The poor man turned to oratorio, producing his great *Messiah* in 1742. He went blind and died in 1759, while conducting the *Messiah* at Covent Garden. He is buried in Westminster Abbey, England's tribute to his great work in music.

Handel and opera and Handel and the English are phenomenal episodes in opera history. Socially, he was as unprepossessing as two fellow-countrymen, Beethoven and Wagner, and although he was honored by two English sovereigns (Queen Anne and her successor, who, conveniently for Handel, was the Elector of Hanover, his former employer) there were many among the English who detested him for himself and some who derided him for his opera styles. When the personal and artistic enemies of the composer coalesced as one claque (under the Duke of Marlborough) they worked hard to bring the lion down.

At one period, this claque hired an Italian composer, Giovanni Buononcini, to compose operas in competition with Handel's, these being produced at the Academy. Buononcini was very popular in Italy (about the peer there of Handel in England) and his advent into London opera was thought to be the death-knell of the German. It spurred Handel to compose one of his most successful operas, *Ottone,* and Handel hired Buononcini as his principal assistant. Handel was by then close to achieving for English opera the degree of splendor already enjoyed by the Vienna court opera. As an illustration of how close

Handel's works were to the Italian model, a satirical verse by a contemporary poet, John Byrom described the rival opera makers thus:

> Some say, compar'd to Buononcini
> That Mynheer Handel's but a ninny;
> Others aver that he to Handel
> Is scarcely fit to hold a candle.
> Strange all this difference should be
> 'Twixt Tweedledum and Tweedledee.

Not Buononcini but a poet as quick with wit as Mr. Byrom eventually caused Handel to be dishonored. The poet was John Gay, a friend and crony of Swift, who ironically remarked that "A Newgate Pastoral might make an odd, pretty sort of thing" as an opera, one with a prison-scene "which the Ladies always reckon charmingly pathetic," as Gay visualized it. First to last, Gay's libretto for *The Beggar's Opera* was intended to pierce society to its vulnerable quick. It was political and social satire as well as operatic parody, sardonically insinuating that all in power were corrupted and could be bribed.

*The Beggar's Opera* was an attack on vested authority, aimed chiefly at the British Prime Minister, Sir Robert Walpole. The glancing blow it hit Handel, the high panjandrum of music, was hard enough to knock him from his exalted place in the realm of music. A marvelously clever and audacious work for its time, Gay's opera remains a ceaselessly entertaining diversion.

As an "opera" it mocked the *opera seria* of Handel's style by pretending to be a gala composed to celebrate the wedding of two street singers. Since *Euridice* in 1600, it had been the custom to produce opera for the event of a princely marriage or betrothal. In such monarchical divertissements princes and princesses and their favorites (as during Louis XIV's era) were cast as symbolical and classical characters; Gay substituted for these "types" beggars, thieves and prostitutes. The hero was the complete anti-hero, being the leader of a band of highwaymen and a police informer on the side. This anti-hero was named Macheath, who was revitalized by the modern German composer Kurt Weill and his sardonic librettist Brecht two hundred years after being created by Gay, and recently became the subject of a "hit" song, *Mac the Knife*.

The music, as well as the plot of *The Beggar's Opera*, was deliberate parody, in which the "pop" songs of Gay's time, dance tunes and street cries took the place of the arias, ballet music and other formulas of the stylized opera. It omitted recitative and Gay impudently wrote, "I hope I may be forgiven, that I have not made my opera throughout unnatural, like those in vogue; for I have no recitative."

Handel, the despot, used to have horrendous rows with his singers; he lost the services of the castrato Senesino in 1733 after a quarrel, although Senesino had created numerous leading roles in Handel operas and was the singing idol of London for fifteen years.[5] The singers were not above having rows of their own and two of Handel's prima donnas, Faustina Bordoni and Francesca Cuzzoni, nurtured a bitter vendetta in the true Italian style. Making gay capital of the well-known feud, Gay wrote: "As to the parts [roles], I have observed such nice impartiality to our two Ladies, that it is impossible for either of them to take offence . . ."[6]

Such direct assault, such personal malice might have put *The Beggar's Opera* out of style once its arrows had hit the targets, which would have sent it into obscurity. It has been saved by its music as much as its wit, and in 1920 was the great hit of the London stage, where it ran for two and a half years. The score is the arrangement of a German composer, Johann Christian Pepusch.

Initially, it had an enormous success and audiences flocked to see Gay's beggars in such droves that Handel's operas played to empty houses, ruining the box office, forcing the Academy into bankruptcy and pauperizing Handel.

Handel went into partnership with a man named Heidegger and organized another company, which failed—because all his best singers were lured away to a troupe formed (and financed by the Prince of Wales) for the express purpose of ruining Handel's new company. But even if Handel had succeeded in holding his second company and had been capable of another fecund period of opera composition, Handel *opera seria* would not have regained its omnipotence. Macheath, the anti-hero, had killed the demi-god of music. Handel and *opera seria* were laughed out of business by comic satire of the *buffa* style.

Handel's sorrows did not end here, in English opera, for it was none other than *The Beggar's Opera* in adaptation that sparked the "new" German opera of the 18th century. In 1743 a burlesque, *The Devil Is Among Us or The Exchanged Wives,* was staged in Berlin with huge applause. Westerman says it was a translation from the English, "a coarse musical farce" like the Gay-Pepusch *Beggar's Opera.* Inspired by the latter, a Leipzig poet, Christoph Felix Weisse and the German composer Johann Georg Standfuss produced *Der Teufel ist Los* (The Devil Is Loose). Satire in the style of later modernists (Brecht in opera; Günter Grass in the novel) might have run rampant in German theatre except that Standfuss died and Weisse took as his librettist Johann Adam Hiller, who modelled his work more on French opera than on the English opera after Gay. Hence, the German *Singspiel* (begun in *The Devil Is Loose* and its precurser *The Devil Is Among Us*) became sentimental, instead of sardonic and satiric, under the romanticism of *opéra comique.*

And "pure German" they became, on order of Emperor Josef II, who commanded that the *Singspiel* (although in the French pattern of *opéra comique*) be sung in German. Joseph Haydn composed operas for the Esterhazy castle theatre, the Vienna imperial court theatre, and for the contemporary puppet theatre which was extremely popular in Austria, a few with German libretti, all in the Neapolitan style of *opera seria* or *opera buffa.* Goethe, says Westerman, was so captivated by *Singspiel* that he wrote a number of libretti, all refined and estimable but none so popular as the rustic and faërie texts of Weisse's operas. The Viennese *Singspiel* commanded two rival theatres, one managed by the impresario Emanuel Schikaneder, who was a popular actor. He was later to become the librettist of Mozart's *The Magic Flute.*

We come now to the era of Christoph Willibald Gluck, in the natural passage between the Neapolitans and Handel and Handel and his downfall (the English opera which was itself inspiration for the birth of the new German *Singspiel,* or comic romantic opera). We have, in this skimming of the opera history, skipped over the French opera, a development from the original Italian—the first "national" opera after the Italian origin and development.

Gluck is the artistic inheritor of influences from Handel and the German Hasse, so proficient in the Neapolitan style that the Italians called him *caro Sassone,* "dear Saxon," and of Rameau, contemporary of Handel and of Bach. Gluck is called by some musicologists "the father of modern opera," and he was a true reformer, in a way that Handel never sought to be, so that he marks the end of one era, the start of another—and he (with the Italian Luigi Cherubini) predated Mozart, Beethoven and Wagner.

As we know something of Gluck's German and Austrian antecedents, let us briefly note his artistic heritage from Rameau and the French opera.

We must regress a bit, to where we took leave of Scarlatti . . .

Opera waxed and waned in England and Germany but had an altogether different course in France, emergent but divergent from its Italian origins. It was not the only Italian invention which the French adopted and adapted to make a distinctively French thing. When Charles VIII of France crossed the Alps to seize the throne of Naples he and his army were amazed to find a nation given up (as were the Italians) to the pleasures of theatrical spectacle—song, music, dance, recitations and every imaginable feat of lyrical acrobatics. Thereafter, quip the Italians, the French stole Italian sauces to garnish French meats, Italian mistresses to decorate French salons, and Italian music and dance to make French opera and ballet.

Jean-Baptiste Lulli, son of a miller, was born in Arno and migrated from Florence to Paris at the age of twelve, where he Gallicized his name to "Lully." He had no formal musical instruction but he must have been a prodigy as well as an opportunist, and when he was fourteen his patron, the Chevalier de Guise, obtained for him the position of page to the household of Mlle. de Montpensier, the king's cousin. "La Grande Mademoiselle" was the richest heiress in France, a rashly impulsive old maid who appears to have been kind in a careless way. It was the vogue to patronize the arts—Louis XIV and his courtiers supported an army of musicians, and favored painters, sculptors and writers. In this era, a man made his fortune as easily with a violin in hand as he might have done with a sword.

Lully was an awkward lout with an unengaging disposition; he was assigned to the kitchen as potboy instead of as page to La Grande Mademoiselle. Somehow, he managed to make himself known to the music director and presently secured a place in the palace orchestra. He rose to leader of the violin section and fiddled away until chance allowed him to captivate the monarch by his talent for dancing.

Lully must have been like the general run of his countrymen: able to dance as easily as run or sing as naturally as breathing. And he was an adept comic, what we would today class as a *danseur caractère*. He danced so comically that the king laughed until he cried and when the tears stopped rolling down the royal cheeks, Lully was whisked away from the household of La Grande Mademoiselle into that of the king. Before Lully was twenty he was installed as Composer of Instrumental Music at court.

It was a musically rich court with a large orchestra, this like everything else to the king's taste. Louis liked strings and there was an orchestra of twenty-four violins known as "The King's Violins." Louis worked hard and played hard, and his court cultivated entertainments known as "pleasures," not only as audiences to ballets, operas and plays but also as participants in them, the king joining mostly in the dancing. In his mother's regency, while the French were in fact ruled by Mazarin, Italian grand opera was introduced into France but Louis obviously preferred ballet. To please his monarch, Lully invented a certain opera form.

The French affection for ballet was as characteristic as the Italian for opera. From the inception of *cour de ballet* under Catherine de'Medici ballet became part of the courtly fabric of French life. Henry IV fell in love with Charlotte de Montmorency while she was dancing in a ballet, and his queen, Marie de'Medici, declared she could not bear to give up ballet even when she was in mourning. When a stalwart warrior, Marshal de Bassonpière, was about to besiege a fortress, he turned to his aides and cried: "The décor and dancers are ready—let the ballet begin!"

French ballet already had operatic form before Lully, needing only a defining hand to be turned into what it became: opera-ballet, while retaining an identity separate to this form as ballet, thus creating two forms out of one artistic idea. The Duke de Luynes, under Louis XIII, a king who also loved to dance, had made ballet dramatic during his regime as supervisor of "Court Pleasures," with music taking on new importance and sung recitative replacing the declamatory speeches of an older style.

It was under Lully's supervision that "French opera" emerged in a distinct form, and it was art out of expediency, initiative over circumstances, because his king loved dancing as he also loved gardens, fountains, hunting and women. And Louis, who could not bear to be crossed, could be lavishly indulgent when pleased. Lully knew how to please; we do not hear Louis singing opera through history but see him dance often, and in public, from the age of seven, until his increasing portliness and exaggerated sense of dignity forced him to retire from the ballet as performer.

Since Louis was keen enough, why was not French music drama better established before the advent of the Italian, Lully? It *had* begun, and in the most admirable circumstances. By edict of the young king in 1661, a room in the Louvre was set aside as the Académie de Danse (a royal academy for training dancers), and was followed by issue of royal letters patent in 1669 for the establishment of a theatre (*L'Académie de Musique et de Danse*) to present opera and drama and dance with music.

This theatre is the same one we know now as the Paris Opéra and in the decade of the 1960's it reached its third century of uninterrupted history in teaching and performance.

That history of performance began with *Pomone,* an opera with music by Robert Cambert, the first French opera composer. He was given permission by Louis to build a theatre for the public performance of opera, for paid admission by the public, and Cambert opened his opera house in 1671 with *Pomone,* his librettist being the director of the Académie, Abbé Pierre Perrin. The choreographer was the king's own ballet master, Pierre Beauchamp.

Thus, French opera was in fact born out of Frenchmen, in *Pomone* by Cambert, Perrin and Beauchamp. This was its sole offspring in Cambert's generation because Lully usurped the Parisian composer and undertook, in his own name, to found the French national opera.

He did it on the Italian form, stretched to conform to French tastes, and he made use of every good grace already possessed by French arts. Lully maneuvered Cambert out of the theatre and won from Louis the exclusive right to produce operas in Paris. Cambert was driven out of his native city, went to England (where his second opera, *Les Peines et les Plaisirs de l'Amour* was produced) and eked out a living as a military bandmaster until his death there, in 1677, aged forty-nine. The French appeared not to rue his loss; they were ruled by Lully's forceful Italian hand, which even shaped Molière's playwriting.

Molière's concept for *comédie-ballet* was a stroke of genius for the playwright, and a stroke of luck for the Italian composer. Molière (yet another artist seeking to please the royal master) was engaged by Louis' minister, Fouquet, to devise a grand entertainment: a ballet and a comedy. Having few trained dancers in his troupe, Molière arranged the dances between the dramatic scenes, which gave the actors and dancers time to change costumes. With a playwright's sensitive imagination, he wove the dance and drama into one unified form and *Les Fâcheux* appeared (1661) as the genus of the new form: *comédie-ballet*.[7] It delighted Louis so much that Molière became a royal favorite —the work, however, did not endear Fouquet to his king enough to save the minister from his pending disgrace and fall.

Lully must have seen the efficacy of amusing the king with comedy and pleasing him with dancing, and the king was a fair representative of his subjects' preferences here. In order to divert the French (more afraid of being bored than of going to Hell) a composer or playwright had to produce diversions which in themselves contained diversions. Lully's genius existed in being able to weld the diversions together and make all organic and unified as "French opera."

Lully and Molière collaborated to good effect in *Le Mariage Forcé*, *L'Amour Médicin* and in a superb comédie-ballet *Le Bourgeois Gentilhomme*, in which Lully himself created the role of the Mufti. Lully composed a pastorale, *Les Fêtes de l'Amour* in 1672, which pleased the king, and the next year produced the cornerstone of French opera: *Cadmus et Hermione*.

He took as his librettist a French poet, Philippe Quinault, of the Corneille school; Quinault is considered the creator of French lyric tragedy. Lully also worked with Louis' favorite poet, Isaac de Benserade, but it was with Quinault that Lully produced his most important works—the best of which remained extant for more than a century. After Lully, the composers Gluck and Piccinni made use of Quinault's *tragédie lyrique*, for opera libretti. Corneille's work was adapted for opera by Donizetti, Gounod, Handel and Massenet. French libretti revived the classical spirit of the Camerata while Venetian opera had romantic libretti of such triviality as to be trumpery.

Lully's operas are distinguished by the "French overture," an innovation which was different from the "Italian overture" of Scarlatti (both are described in *Opera: What It Is . . .*) and the *reprise*, or repetition of melody which was later developed as *leitmotiv* (leading motive) for opera. He had a splendid orchestra and magnificent décors, and libretti of literary significance—perhaps a bit too stylized to sing easily, in the Italian manner. He leapt this hurdle by using recitative very sparingly and by having an aria sung at every possible opportunity, pleasing the French who were inclined to grow restive during long recitatives.

French ballet had previously used opera stagecraft to embellish its scenes; Lully commanded fine artisans for his scenic opera, in an age when one factory, Gobelins', was designing and weaving beautiful tapestries, and another factory was producing medals, portraits and statues, mostly of the king. The dancers were charmingly dressed, in tight bodices with tiny waists and billowing skirts. The "effects" must have been novel and clever; Louis himself took a hand in constructing Mme. de Montespan's marvelous bronze tree which perpetually rained perfumed water from its white metal leaves, and it may be imagined that no effort, no expense, was spared to adorn the operas for the king's pleasure.

Lully had an agreeable existence, sole arbiter of French music as his royal patron was sole arbiter of all things and persons French. In Lully's era (when Louis stopped dancing) the court ballets ceased and the professional dancers who had been the support of the noble amateurs turned to the theatre for their living. Lully was therefore able to mold professional ballet while molding the professional opera, and he established these in the Palais Royal, turning out the troupe of actors founded by Molière and installing his own company instead. Until his death, every work produced in the theatre was by Lully, who enlisted Beauchamp as choreographer, but himself directed every detail of a production and composed the music. At first, in the professional theatre, boys appropriately costumed danced feminine roles but Lully inaugurated the custom of women dancers and in 1681 his *Le Triomphe de l'Amour* featured four *danseuses* of whom the leader, La Fontaine, became the first *première* in the history of l'Opéra.

Lully was succeeded by a very popular French composer, André Campra, whose *Fêtes Venitiennes* was one of the Opéra's greatest triumphs. The Italians were responsible for the French mode of stringing several short works into one continuous work (opus and opus and opus to make *opera*) and Campra laid his scene in Venice, where the carnival, the picturesqueness of the city, and the barcarolle were immediately symbolical of *Fêtes Venitiennes*.

Orchestral development and "tone painting" in music were general trends after Lully and a great fetish for the "natural" began to affect opera art. But the form established by Lully remained untampered with—so much so that Campra remarked he could think of nothing to do to make the opera more popular, except to lengthen the ballets and shorten the skirts of the ballerinas. When this was done, under Rameau, it provided one reason for the fierce quarrel between the *bouffonistes* and *anti-bouffonistes*, in a row that shook French opera to its foundations and split it into two: *tragédie lyrique* and *opéra comique*.

Jean-Philippe Rameau was the antithesis of Lully in that he was an erudite artist, a trained musician who as a child (his father was a church organist) in Dijon studied harpischord, organ and violin. He was first of all a music theorist, founder of the modern theory of harmony, whose historic significance in this field, says Westerman, will always remain unchallenged. His published works: *Traité de l'Harmonie* (1772) and *Nouveau Système de Musique Théorique* (1776) are still valid.

Rameau began writing theatre music in 1723, producing *Hippolyte et Aricie* at the Opéra, and although he was immediately controversial he in fact saved the Opéra from a threat of bankruptcy, by drawing sufficient audiences to defray its production costs when the competition of Italian opera had seriously affected attendance on French opera.

In 1708 an Italian troupe came to Paris and had enormous success and thereafter capitalized on it by parodying French opera, which so amused the Parisians that they made it a vogue to enjoy having the national opera mocked and derided. Rameau's opera-ballets revived audience interest in the Académie (as the Opéra was still called). The finest of these was *Les Indes Galantes* (1735), a spectacular success then and in its revival at the Paris Opéra in 1952.

Rameau's characteristic was refinement and he extended this to music in the enrichment of harmony, the development of polyphony,

the reinvigoration of rhythm and the intensification of melody, all
with such discipline that he changed the baroque into a new, elegant
musical expression. He is extremely important in French music (he
was a harpsichordist of excellence) and in opera he developed orchestration and reaffirmed the nature of recitative, all with musical beauty
and dramatic truth.

He was an active participant as well as a target in the famous
*Guerre des Bouffons* (War of the Comedians) which broke out in Paris
in 1752 over an opera by André Destouches, contemporary of Campra,
who had been director of the Opéra under Louis XV. (Destouches
was also Superintendent of the King's Music and wrote ballets, operas
and church music, and, officially, held the same prestigious position
as Lully had owned.)

Pergolesi's famous *The Maid as Mistress (La Serva Padrona)*
was such a hit in Paris that it split the French worlds of letters and
theatre into warring factions, one enthusiastic over the Italian *buffa,*
the other not only against it but also against all Italianate opera and
violently pro-Gaul. The frenzy of the *Guerre des Bouffons* was such
that it persisted after the death of Rameau (1764) when all that was
Art could be denigrated as opposed to Nature—and that which was
"natural" had become a vogue, a philosophy and a cult. (Interestingly,
the war over Pergolesi versus Destouches opera in 1752 was waged
after the deaths of the composers, the Italian in 1736 and the Frenchman in 1749—they therefore were fought over in principle and not in
their personalities.)

Rameau was not a savant in his day, his most inimical opposers
being the members of the Paris Opéra's orchestra. They detested having to play his complex orchestrations. About 1737, Rameau's works
began gradually to replace those of Lully (who had established a one-
man repertory) and the Lullian monopoly was broken in truth (and
as an extension of the *Guerre des Bouffons,* as far as dance is concerned) when Rameau began to inaugurate the *danse haute* about
1730. If Rameau lacked the respect of the Opéra's orchestra, the ballet
more than made up for it and no wonder: Rameau instigated the grand
ballet renaissance, precipitating successive "golden ages" for the dance
which directly affected the popularity of opera. Within Rameau's era
ballet's great schism began, the rift in aesthetics which still divides

ballet and the balletomanes pro and con: is the acme of the art in the Soul, as expression, or in the Flesh, as technique?

The chief interpreter of the "soulful" ballet was Marie Sallé (b. 1707) who endowed her dancing with dramatic gesture and emotional fervor and drew a clique of admirers around her person and her style. The other Marie, surnamed Camargo (a French dancer of Spanish descent), advocated pyrotechnical feats which visibly affected some audiences in the same manner as opera audiences were aurally affected by the coloratura and castrati sopranos in their pyrotechnical feats of song. The battle was begun, never to end, between what the Franco-Russe choreographers have defined as "sowl" for *soul* and "juice" for stupendous vigor.

It was the difference in ballet even more than in opera that occasioned the war, which was waged parallel to and within the *Guerre des Bouffons,* between claques as "Ramists" and "Lullists."

Lully's dance had been *terre à terre* (dance of the earth; on the floor) in the geometric patterns invented by the first choreographer, Beaujoyeulx, another Italian immigrant to France, from the advent of Catherine de'Medici. Rameau had the imagination to recognize that the change in theatrical staging required an alteration in the dance. He, in fact, lent perspective or sight lines for the audience's view by advocating a greater turn-out of the ballet dancer's feet, itself a characteristic, with that of *aplomb,* of the ballet. In Lully's opera-ballets (where the choreography had been by Beauchamp) this turn-out, which was copied from the fencing stance, was about 45°. In Rameau's era, notably by Camargo, the dancer achieved something closer to the 90° turn-out (French: *le en-dehors*) later codified by Blasis, Italian ballet pedagogue (1803-1878). The exaggerated turn-out was anatomically necessary to give the dancer freedom of movement in every direction (it enables the thigh bone to rotate fully in the hip-socket) and it was an aesthetic necessity in theatre because it subtly enhanced the dancer's "line," the architectural and poetic entity of ballet.

*Cour de ballet* had been presented on the floor of the ballroom or salon, with the courtly audience seated around the dance area, sometimes on raised platforms (like bleachers), precisely in the conditions observed in contemporary "theatre-in-the-round," and, very often, for audiences grouped on actual terraces or galleries (as for the *al fresco* ballets staged in the gardens and courtyards for the nobility of Louis XIV's era). Professional ballet occupied the opera house stage (ballet had literally gone up in the world) and was now viewed as danced on a raised platform, with its audience on the floor below, or in boxes situated right, left and center of the stage. Quite obviously, the sight lines changed for ballet and in the older mode, the geometric patterns and the small turn-out, the dancers appeared foreshortened. Rameau altered the concept of ballet by encouraging inventive, physically adept dancers like Camargo to jump and leap, thus creating *danse en l'air,* which became a characteristic of ballet, and advocated the larger turn-out.

Camargo, quite carried away with herself, learned to dance with such brio and strength that the feats she performed in her day (1710-1770) are nowadays generally performed by the *danseur* rather than the *danseuse.* She became famed for being the first great ballet technician, for shortening the long skirt then worn to show off her feet and legs on stage, and for being the first professional dancer to wear drawers—a modesty which became the rule if not the regulation until the *chahut* (the cancan) broke the rule in 1830, after *bouffes Parisiens* had changed French musical and social mores.

Jean-Philippe Rameau was a theatrical and musical genius, who by the very richness of his gifts has been denied full recognition. He is claimed by opera and by ballet and as these two arts have existed in armed truce rather than in harmony, Rameau's greatness has been obscured instead of fully appreciated. It was only when the Paris Opéra staged his *Les Indes Galantes* in the 1950's that I, personally, understood the strikingly avant-garde ideas of the composer, who so far reached into our century that he experimented with "psychological stimuli" (as has been done in contemporary theatre), spraying perfume over the audience to emphasize sensation through the sense of smell as well as sight and hearing.

The revival of *Les Indes Galantes* has also given contemporary theatre understanding of the splendor of theatrical productions in Rameau's time. In the era of Louis XIV, magnificence was a hallmark of French opera. Jean Berain designed for Lullian opera and Rameau worked with Jean Servandoni, one of the greatest scenic artists of the time—it was this artist who designed the flower *divertissement* in *Galantes,* and the volcanic eruption in another of the opera-ballet's scenes. One good reason for Rameau's encouragement of the dancers at the Palais Royal (where the opera house was contained) was that the ballet's technique had become refined and accentuated; it was an art in itself (no longer merely a stylish adaptation of country and ballroom dances) and therefore worthy of the theatre. Accordingly, Rameau's opera-ballets employed dancers of consequence, including the first great *premier,* Louis, *le grand* Dupré.

It is necessary to interpolate these facts about French opera-ballet for the reader to recognize that it was a distinctive form, differing in idea and concept from the Italian opera. Unless these differences are known it is impossible to understand the violent altercation that raged in the *Guerre des Bouffons* and between "Ramists" and "Lullists"—and these battles have never been wholly resolved, because the ethics and theories for opera and for ballet continued to cause fiercely partisan ideals or "appreciation" in the audience, with, consequently, rabid opera buffs in claques. The ballet, of course, had its balletomanes.

*Castor and Pollux* (1737) is considered Rameau's masterpiece and he might have written another if he had not spent so much time penning pamphlets, either on pro-Destouches opera style (which was anti-Pergolesi) or his musical theories (he defined some chords as "inversions" of other chords, et cetera). Late in his career Rameau received public recognition, was knighted by the king and made composer of music at the court. He was exempted from paying municipal tax (besides receiving a pension) and when he died in 1764, was granted the honors of a civic hero's funeral.

The true *verismo* opera, or opera of a naturalistic style, came about in the Italian opera after Leoncavallo and Mascagni, and in French opera after Bruneau and Charpentier, but Rameau's "cerebral" music came under attack by Rousseau, whose revolutionary ideas decreed that only the "natural" was good. To an artist like Rameau, Rousseau's aesthetic ideal should have been anathema. They stood at opposite poles of French thought and fashion. Rameau represented Art and its order and elegance, and the arts were humanity's passionate defiance of Nature. The *danse haute* physically defied the law of gravity and the turn-out in ballet was altogether contrary to the natural way of movement. Rousseau, the literary beatnik of his day, believed in Nature which at its most ruthless was chaos or unruled instinct. And the French, at this moment in history, were of three "estates" of which the two high classes (clergy and nobility) numbered 300,000 and the third (the People), 20,000,000. Every Frenchman did not go to the opera but all the French were existing in the period of "enlightenment"—an abstract virtue that would shake the world.

In the great opera war of which Rameau and Pergolesi were the aesthetic protagonists we are presented with a philosophic quarrel in theatre and letters, the preface to the French Revolution.

Rameau alone withstood the tidal popularity of Italian opera which tended (as noted in German opera) to sweep away all other national opera and institute itself as the sole opera art. Rameau was particularly French in a classically elegant style and his refinements in French theatre seemed to negate the coarse and frivolous character of the Italian style. In a word, Rameau was an *urbane* composer.

In 1752, when Rameau was sixty-nine and only twelve years before his death, the raging literary row was resolved by the invention of another kind of opera: the *opéra comique*. Brandishing their quills, men of letters fought over Rameau. Friedrich Grimm found Rameau's ballets superfluous and excessive (who had dared complain about Lully's under the Sun-King?) and Voltaire wrote that Rameau had made music "a new art." The ironic Campra, who had advised shortening the ballerinas' skirts to increase the box office receipts at l'Opéra, prophetically commented: "Rameau will eclipse us all." But it would take Gluck to reaffirm Rameau's ideals and vindicate his principles and even so Gluck required royal patronage to persuade the French to admire opera in a lofty form. Under Rousseau, opera was to become for the people, of the people.

Rousseau condemned Rameau opera not only for aesthetic reasons but also for traducing the spirit of the French: "the French airs are not French enough." To show what *he* advocated, the philosopher dashed off the lyrics and music for an opera, frankly copied from Pergolesi's style (Rousseau had just attended several performances of *La Serva Padrona* in Paris). *Le Devin du Village* (The Village Soothsayer) was naturally, set in rural rather than regal scenes and was a primitive rather than a polished work. There were three characters and their *ariettas* and duets were patterned after naïve French folk songs. The work was designed to appear artless rather than artful and was sweetly pretty for the audiences who acclaimed the amateur composer. The *Soothsayer* had its première at Fontainebleau for Louis XV and was later (March 1753) presented for a season at the Paris Opéra—an unprecedented event, as only *tragédie lyrique* (the French *opera seria*) was housed at the Académie in the Palais Royal.

Louis XV, the last absolute monarch in Europe, fawned on Rousseau (the court applauded the *Soothsayer* with wild enthusiasm) despite the fact that Rousseau's notion to make French opera purely Italian was strongly opposed. At the première of his opera, the philosopher consented to occupy a box at Fontainebleau in the king's private theatre and took care to appear unshaven, unshorn and in picaresque deshabille, possibly to prove his "natural" condition as compared to the courtly one. He refused to grant the king an audience when Louis wished to compliment him on the *Soothsayer* and his effrontery so amused the court that it clapped the harder at l'Opéra. Campra alone might have heard, under the volley of applause, the sounds of tumbril wheels on the cobblestones, but in 1752 the Bastille was not due to fall for another thirty-seven years, by which time the composer of the *Soothsayer* should have been revolutionizing the heavenly harps for a decade.

Rousseau's *Village Soothsayer* may not be, in fact, the start of the French revolution, but it was the commencement of a theatrical form as *opéra comique*. This form, unrecognized as theatre art, was already a vogue at fairs, the kind that were so popular with the French that Marie Antoinette and her clique used to dress in the clothes of their maids and valets and steal off to enjoy them as "the people's pleasures." From about 1715 the term *opéra comique* was known at the Foire St. Germain for musical plays which parodied l'Opéra's *tragédie lyrique*. They began, we may say, in the spirit and much the mode of Italian *commedia dell'arte*, in rebellion and ribaldry and as satire on *commedia erudita*.

Rousseau was intent more on proving himself right and Rameau wrong than on composing opera, and he did not parody Rameau opera in the way Gay parodied Handel. Rousseau lacked Gay's wit and humor (but unlike Gay's collaborator, Pepusch, he composed his music, did not simply "arrange" it on others' compositions) and *The Village Soothsayer* was more pro-Pergolesi than anti-Rameau in form. In principle, of course, the *Soothsayer* was the antithesis of *tragédie lyrique*; the people of the Third Estate against the First and Second Estates. As such, the *Soothsayer* was rabidly revolutionary, an impudent challenge to the Bourbons as well as to l'Opéra.[8]

Rousseau was probably incapable of composing a whole original score so he simply linked his *ariettas* and duets together with spoken dialogue, thus setting the characteristic of *opéra comique* as a form or operatic structure. And he did prove, what may have been argued before, that the French language could be sung operatically. Unwittingly, the man who meant to laud the Italian style is credited with having invented a uniquely French style of opera because *opéra comique* is not "comic opera" (which for reasons of clarity I refer to as *opera buffa*) but *an actual form in itself, capable of being both tragic and comic.*

Under an agreement with l'Opéra, a theatre was established in 1715 as L'Opéra-Comique to produce musical plays with spoken dialogue, "comic opera" that did not positively compete with *tragédie lyrique*. But the *opéra comique*, after Rousseau, was defined as *opera with spoken dialogue* as well as the formal opera passages to music. In this form, operas like Beethoven's *Fidelio* and Bizet's *Carmen* are *opéra comique*.

Pergolesi influenced a number of French composers besides the amateur opera maker Rousseau, and one composer of serious opera, Pierre-Alexandre Monsigny, gave himself over so enthusiastically to *La Serva Padrona* that he ceased composing in any other style. A Belgian composer who is of French musical tradition, named André Grétry, developed *opéra comique* to its absolute and after him composers working in this form included François Boïeldieu, Adolphe Adam and Daniel Auber.

An Italian, Egidio Romoaldo Duni, elaborated on Rousseau's form, and *opéra comique* assumed other characteristics besides its pertinent one of spoken dialogue, such as a prevailing "naturalism" in theme and characterization, and "tone painting," a thesis that an idea, event or image could be "described" in orchestral music. It was very obvious that *opéra comique* enlarged the Rousseauian theme for the "natural."

The pastoral or rustic scene pre-empted the regal and Olympic abodes of opera-ballet and instead of princes and their fair Amazons, or gods and goddesses, common folk, hoi polloi, inhabited theatre arts.

Rousseau's caprice to make an opera succeeded in putting all *"les caprices des Danses de la Roi"* out of style, and the French were never less than *à la mode.* At the beginning of French opera, Lully and Benserade had worked hard to please Louis XIV, who danced as the shepherd in Lully's *Ballet of the Arts,* with his sister-in-law, Henriette d'Angleterre, as his shepherdess. Her *corps de ballet* comprised the king's two mistresses, Louise de la Vallière and Athénaïs de Tonnay-Charente, later de Montespan, and two young ladies of literary families, members of which could never resist courtly anecdote: the Mlles. de Saint-Simon and de Sévigné. The latter's mother wrote: "Ah, what shepherdesses and what Amazons . . . whom the centuries will never replace!" But by mid-18th century the French taste had changed for kings, philosophies and opera.

In all, French opera was eventually to acquire four forms, three of which are contemporary—the one which is obsolete is "French grand opera" of the early 19th century, with its apogee in Giacomo Meyerbeer; French "grand opera" being of grandiose spectacle and heroic-historical theme, and to such extent a "form" that it was never otherwise than within its style. It has become common to speak of "opera" as that kind which is not *opera buffa,* nor *opéra comique,* and these are the three French opera forms: *opéra, opéra comique* and the light opera, frequently of farcical or satiric mood, called *opéra bouffe.* Thus, any opera that fits into the *opéra comique* form derives from the French opera form of that term.

Characteristically, the French retained the old while adopting the new; *tragédie lyrique* survived and was magnificently reinstated and reformed under Gluck, while *opéra comique* developed as a form so distinctive in French opera that it would be recognized in world-wide opera *per se.* The French were reasonable as well as fashionable and however captivated they became by a mode they managed to extricate good sense from nonsense. But it had taken Italians to form opera and opera-ballet, and now it was the turn of a German to reform French opera. So doing, this German genius reformed opera as a whole.

*Che puro ciel* ("What pure light") sings Orpheus in Gluck's

*Orfeo ed Euridice* and the same rapt monologue might be addressed in opera to Gluck himself. He is the great reformer, so logical and sure that his genius has the quality of an angelic simplicity. Vindicating Rameau, he began with his *Orfeo* to establish the thesis of modern opera.

The art had progressed considerably already from the child born of the Camerata. It had several forms, it was of certain styles, and while these would continue to be developed or modified in successive eras, opera emerged after Gluck as the opera art we know today. Thus, Gluck is called the father or creator of modern opera and is the pre-curser of Mozart, a younger man and later composer, who was of the imperial court in Vienna, as was Gluck.

Christoph Willibald Gluck is one of the most famed and most romantic personages in opera, and the aid that Marie Antoinette of France gave his music is her good deed in the silly, naughty world whose ruin she helped precipitate.

Gluck was a Bavarian who, as a child, was trained in the violin, organ and harpsichord. At the age of twelve (1736) he went to Vienna and was employed in a princely household. Another prince, Melzi, took the boy to Italy where Gluck studied and wrote an early opera (*Artaserse*) and six more, none distinguished, before going to London. He got two of his works staged there, but received no encouragement from Handel and traveled back to Vienna by way of Paris, Hamburg and Dresden. After marrying a rich woman, Gluck obtained the post of kapellmeister at the imperial theatre and there met two men who helped to change his musical ideals. They were Count Giacomo Durazzo, who had charge of the Imperial theatres, and so could provide a house for Gluck's works, and Ranieri da Calzabigi, a poet who lived in Paris and absorbed the ideas of Voltaire, Rousseau and Diderot.

Gluck's uninspired early work was in the Italian mode and on Metastasio poetry, the two having combined to produce a stylized opera form which was so embellished with the rococo that the ornamental frills and ribbands had succeeded in binding and constricting opera. Gluck's genius was to unshackle these bonds and leave the art free, and also to unify and make gracious the component parts of opera as a whole. Much of his success was owed to his great librettist, Calzabigi. But chiefly Gluck's reform was in compelling the singer to be part of, not to rule, opera. And he did this without sacrificing the importance and beauty of song. All that Gluck wrought served opera well in his day and thereafter, but while he was innovating his reforms he excited such controversy as makes pallid the later one over Wagner's music drama. The French fought duels to settle arguments over Gluck, and the losers died when they could not support their arguments. The wordy debate in the celebrated *Guerre des Bouffons* was nothing compared to the bloody rows over Gluck and his rival, the Italian Piccinni.

By good fortune he was a childhood friend of Marie Antoinette, whom he taught to play the harpsichord and the child called Antonia, daughter of the redoubtable empress Maria Theresa, moved heaven and earth to promote her "dear musician" when she married into the Bourbon family.

Gluck did not at once win honor in Vienna, where his opera in the style of Rameau (a style in which simplicity and dramatic verity contrasted with the florid Italian opera, all artificiality and mannerisms) seemed sterile and cold. His first "new" opera, in the French ideal, was *Don Juan* (1761) to Calzabigi's libretto after a play by Molière, and in 1762 with *Orfeo ed Euridice* (the same theme and subject of the first opera in 1600) Gluck boldly asserted his reformative precepts. The opera failed to arouse any enthusiasm in the Viennese and two others: *Alceste* (1767) and *Paride ed Elena* (Paris and Helen) (1770) were equal failures.

Gluck's Orfeo was a character the opera audience of the day could not understand (some opera goers today cannot understand him either) because the conventional histrionics did not apply. In *Act III* when Orfeo sings *Che farò senz' Euridice*—"What is life to me without thee, Euridice"—people expected a loud and anguished outcry instead of a quiet lament.

*Alceste's* failure to move its première audience so saddened Gluck that he told a friend that Alceste had fallen [flat] at the theatre, to which the friend replied: "Fallen, yes—from Heaven!" But the utter disaster of *Paris and Helen* so enraged Gluck (he was not a man content to grieve in quiet like his Orpheus) that he decided to throw himself and his work on the hospitality of the French. He was doubly incensed by *Paris'* failure, having taken the pains to explain himself in a preface to *Alceste*, saying: "My intention is to purify music from all

the abuses which have crept into Italian opera through the vanity of
the singers and the compliance of the composers and have made the
most splendid and beautiful of all arts the most ridiculous and boring.
I tried therefore to bring musicians back to their real task of serving
the poetry, by intensifying the expression of emotion and the appeal
of every situation, without interrupting the plot or weakening it by
unnecessary ornamentation."

He carried this precept to such length that his *Paris and Helen*
was almost without theatrical action, and may be the first "psychological" opera because of its musical development of inner conflicts rather
than the enactment by conventional dramatic modes. It is an opera that
would seem singularly devoid of "happenings" to a contemporary audience—and not for one hundred and thirty-two years would Debussy's
impressionistic *Pelléas and Mélisande* cause such a scandal, so that the
French government would censure it and the première audience would
respond with hisses, boos and guffaws. Westerman considers that *Paris
and Helen* is Gluck's most valuable gift to posterity.

Calzabigi adapted Racine's *Iphigénie*, after Euripides, into a libretto and Gluck began composing a fourth opera in the "new" mode,
*Iphigénie en Aulide.* He was encouraged by a French diplomat at the
Viennese court to send it to l'Opéra, which Gluck did, confident that
it would be accepted. To his chagrin, the director of the Opéra rejected
the work, saying that if it were produced it "would kill all the old
French operas." And Gluck was advised not to go to Paris as he would
not be welcomed.

Marie Antoinette, the Dauphine, immediately insisted that her
favorite must be invited to Paris and her minister, Mercy, persuaded
the Opéra to accept *Iphigénie en Aulide.* Gluck arrived and was greeted
affectionately by his royal patron, who caused a minor court scandal
by receiving him in her private rooms behind the state bed-chamber.
(Court protocol decreed that the royal ladies should always be served
by others of their sex, but the wilful Austrian princess broke the taboo
and had a male hairdresser, Léonard the "Physiogonomist," and saw no
reason why she should not treat an old friend, her music teacher, with
easy familiarity.) But getting *Iphigénie* produced at the Opéra was
another matter altogether.

Mercy had connections at the Opéra[9] and he was at the moment bent on giving the little Dauphine her own way in all things which did not go counter to getting her to act and say what he wanted her to. Mercy ruled Marie Antoinette on instructions from Maria Theresa. The miserable young Dauphine turned to theatre as another woman (say: Louis' XIV's queen) might have turned to the church. Married to an amiable clod, Marie Antoinette found amusement and actually provided her husband with pleasure through theatre entertainments. She had (as Pierre de Nolhac commented) "an excessive love of pleasure" and at eighteen, not yet the Queen of France, her popularity was very great with her husband's people. Because she wished it, a production of Gluck's *Iphigénie* was scheduled.

How much Marie Antoinette loved opera and how much she loved getting her own way, were the scales on which Gluck's Parisian success was balanced. Marie Antoinette grew up in a musical city, member of a family friendly to music if not exactly musically gifted. She sang Mozart and Gluck in a small, pleasant voice—just true, but passable. Gluck was a countryman and therefore bound to be superior, in her estimation, to a French composer (Rameau) or an Italian (Lully) and she disliked French operas on principle—they committed the cardinal folly of boring her. The queen could endure calumny and death with a certain grace; she could not bear ennui.

Rameau had died (in 1764) and the worst elements of the Italian opera were being preserved (erroneously described by some writers as a Lullian renaissance) in what the French called *potpourri* opera, and the Italians dubbed *pasticcio* (pie).

*Pasticcio* was a common phrase to describe a popular opera form throughout Europe in the latter 18th century. It was usually a makeshift opera from an assortment of compositions, generally by one composer, sometimes by several. The audience en masse loved *pasticcio*, which required no intellectual appreciation whatever, since it was casually strung on well-known (and well-worn) melodies. At its most ambitious, a *pasticcio* might be held together with a plot for which new lyrics were written to suit a situation of characterization. Often, even this drama was lacking.

Gluck was not wholly above indulging in a little judicious pasticcio. When his *Orfeo ed Euridice* was performed in London in 1770 it had the "benefit" of additional choruses, recitatives and arias composed by Johann Christian Bach, lyrics by Pietro Guglielmi. Ingenuously, the program described these as "enrichment" of Gluck's work. By 1773 Gluck obviously eschewed these policies and declared to Marie Antoinette that his work stood alone and on its own "with no other adornment than its own beauty."

The Opéra singers were outraged when Gluck informed them (and the world at large) that he "had taken great care not to interrupt an actor in the heat of a dialogue in order to make him listen to a tedious *ritornello* nor to stop him in the middle of his speech at a favorable vowel." *That* might be nice for the actor but for the singers and instrumentalists it seemed a dangerous innovation. The singers were not only content but quite intent on seizing on a "favorable vowel" to stretch it as far and as high as possible (especially in coloratura) for some vocal high-jinks which excited the audience (just as a dancer, performing a series of aerial spins or "beats" would visually excite the audience). And the instrumentalists in the orchestra considered *ritornello* a right and a rite. It had grown from its original (*ritornello* is Italian for "little repetition") as a brief instrumental passage between scenes to instrumental passages everywhere possible, including between the vocal parts, sometimes within *da capo aria*. Its chief merit was drawing attention to the skill of the orchestra, as *coloratura* drew attention to the agility of the singer.

Gluck would never have been able to control the Opéra, a world to itself with its political machinations, except for Marie Antoinette's alliance. When rehearsals went in such ways as to oppose his commands, he threatened the artistes by the warning: "I shall go to Mme. la Dauphine [Louis XV had not yet died] and say to her: 'I find it impossible to get my opera performed.' Then I shall get in my carriage and take the road to Vienna."

Sorely as it must have wished he would, the Opéra bowed to edict and Gluck's opera was performed "without trills," this being the most startling diversion from the norm.

Poor Gluck almost lost his mind reforming the French and would leave rehearsals in such a pitiable state of excitement that once a crowd followed him through the streets, taking him for a madman because of his talking and gesticulating to himself. The Swiss Guard arrested the composer when he reached the Tuileries and one supposes he had afterwards to be calmed down by Marie Antoinette, who was also busily calming down the Opéra singers, probably using the same words with which her father, the Emperor Francis, had calmed the Viennese: "You know what he [Gluck] is like . . . But at heart he is a good man."

Gluck gave the French court a reason for one of its incessant vicious vendettas, by causing a faction to gather as "Gluckists" and another to form, in opposition, as "Piccinnists" around the body and body of works of Niccolo Piccinni, an Italian composer who enjoyed popularity with the French, especially with Mme. du Barry, arch-enemy of Marie Antoinette and, naturally, a detester of Gluck. Possibly, the mistress of Louis XV was less than enchanted by Gluck's favorite theme: conjugal love, in *Alceste* and in *Orfeo ed Euridice*.

The French audience did not quite know what to make of an opera without trills and the long recitatives were not to everyone's taste, but the opera had a great success. And no wonder, since the Dauphine never ceased applauding, compelling the audience to do the same. "The Princess seems to have joined a plot," remarked a contemporary writer of the Princesse de Lamballe "in order to please Madame la Dauphine."

The "plot" was to affirm Gluck's *Iphigénie* a success and Marie Antoinette's claque comprised herself and her husband, the amiable Dauphin, the Comte and Comtesse de Provence, the Duchesse de Bourbon, the Duchesse de Chartres, and the aforementioned Princesse de Lamballe. It was enough to subdue the formidable opposition of Mme. du Barry, especially as Rousseau approved of *Iphigénie*. "Since one can have such great pleasure for two hours," he exclaimed, "I feel that life has some advantages."

The Dauphine's triumph was complete the night after the première, when (criticisms silenced) people mobbed the theatre and guards had to be called out to restrain the crowd clamoring to see *Iphigénie*, an opera described as full of "many new beauties, grand, strong and simple" bursting forth "in passionate, moving and dramatic music."

Thunderous applause inside the theatre interrupted the opera, and there were emotional demonstrations during the première. When Achilles sang his warrior's song all the officers in the audience leapt spontaneously to their feet and drew their swords. When Iphigenia and Clytemnestra were saluted by the chorus singing *Que d'attraits, que de majesté*—What charm! What majesty!—the audience arose and bowed to the royal box, and Gluck's royal patron, Marie Antoinette. The little princess rushed home and wrote to her mother: "You can scarcely imagine what excitement reigns in all minds in regard to this event. We can find nothing else to talk about . . ."

*Orfeo* and *Alceste* were presented in French and gave more fuel to the fire, one blazing in enthusiasm for Gluck, the other in fervor for Piccinni, whom Mme. du Barry was determined to use to humiliate the Dauphine. Mme. du Barry had a reluctant ally in Piccinni, who admired Gluck enormously—so much so that his opera *Roland*, a huge success in 1778, was patterned on Gluck's principles in that the music was not divided into "numbers" in the Italian *pasticcio* style but within scenes (which followed the ideas of the text), and all recitative and *arioso* compositions existed *within* the musical structure, not independently or as superfluous ornamentation.

Piccinni had been an enormously popular composer in his native Italy. His *La Cecchina* (1760) is possibly the finest comic opera before Rossini's, and in 1762 he composed six operas, which were produced simultaneously in the six leading opera houses in Rome. The next year he was eclipsed by his own pupil, Pasquale Anfossi, which caused Piccinni to suffer a breakdown. When he recovered he declared he would never again write a note of music for a Roman audience and returned to Naples, where he stayed only long enough to reaffirm his former eminence. He next went to Paris, where *La Cecchina*, also known as *Buona Figliuola* (The Good-Natured Girl) had a great popular ovation.

Recognizing the publicity value of the vendetta between the opposing claques of "Gluckists" and "Piccinnists," the enterprising director of the Opéra engaged Piccinni to write music for a libretto for which Gluck was already composing. This was *Iphigénie en Tauride* (the same character who appeared in Gluck's opera in 1774, here removed in time and place from Aulis to Tauris). The text was by a French writer, François Guillard, who translated Calzabigi's libretto.

Undoubtedly, Gluck intended *Iphigénie No. 2* to outdo *Iphigénie No. 1*, and we may be certain that Marie Antoinette, now Queen, wished him, once and for all, to extinguish the fervor for Piccinni. She cannot have been pleased that *Roland* by the Italian was a thundering success while Gluck's own *Armide* (put on to compete with *Roland*) had failed to excite Paris. It was odd, but true, that an Italian composing *à la Gluck* would please the very audience that a work by Gluck displeased. Marie Antoinette did what she could to support Gluck and Rose Bertin and the "Physiogonomist" Léonard (who were called "artists" in charge of the Queen) invented coiffures *à l'Iphigénie* and *à l'Euridice* as compliments to Gluck. This was possibly a heroic concession by the Queen (Louis XV had died eight days after the première of the first *Iphigénie*, and Marie Antoinette's husband had become king, Louis XVI) for one assumes that the Grecian ladies occasioned more simplicity than usual in coiffure for the Austrian queen who wore such high plumes that she was sometimes unable to get into her carriage. But she spared no effort to promote her "dear musician," perhaps thinking affectionately of the year when she was eleven and Gluck had set Metastasio's poem *Parnasso Confuso* to music, for Antonia and her brothers to dance at the castle at Schoenbrunn for the marriage of Joseph II. Mme. du Barry no longer bothered Marie Antoinette. Louis XV had no sooner breathed his last than his mistress had been entrusted to the police, a prisoner of the State, and taken off to the Abbey de Pont-aux-Dames. But Marie Antoinette still promoted Gluck.

The composer was then aged sixty-five and *Iphigénie No.* 2 was to be his last triumph. For many of his admirers, then and now, it is his greatest opera although comparison between the two *Iphigénies* is inevitable. The first is distinguished by magnificent characterizations, especially of Agamemnon and Achilles. Kobbé sees Gluck's Achilles as the ancestor of Radames in *Aida* and "a whole line of heroic tenors," and Gluck's *Iphigénie en Aulide* alike to Mozart's Ilia in *Idomeneo* (it is this authority who calls Gluck the great-great-grandfather of modern opera). Westerman considers the overture the most brilliant part of the score.

*Iphigénie en Tauride* is better constructed with greater unity in all its parts, and such dramatic fusion that an extraordinary incident occurred while the work was in rehearsal for the première. In *Act II* Orestes sings *Le calme rentre dans mon coeur* (Calm returns to my heart) but the orchestral accompaniment simultaneously expresses his agitation. Confused, the players stopped. Gluck cried: "Go on! He lies! He has killed his mother!"

The opera received its première on May 18, 1779. Piccinni had delivered his *Iphigénie en Tauride* and now tried to withdraw it, but it was produced at the Opéra in January 1781 and ran for seventeen performances. Piccinni's prima donna was drunk at the première and caused a furor when the audience jeered that it had come to see Iphigénie in Tauris, not Iphigénie in Champagne.

Gluck's enemies were confounded when Piccinni and the German became the best of friends, taking their meals together and the Italian diligently trying to write operas exactly like Gluck's. A historian commented that while the claques as "Gluckists" and "Piccinnists" devoured each other the two men shared their dinners with each other.

Gluck's position was assured when he died (in Vienna, in 1787) rich and honored, leaving innumerable emulators and some pupils to expound and preserve his theories for opera. These composers took the Gluckian principles to Italy and Germany and supported them in France, and these three mainstreams of opera adopted the opera of Gluck as the form for opera—opera of a serious or exalted form—while developing other opera forms such as *Singspiel* in Germany. *Opera buffa* continued in Italy and was recognized as an opera form, world wide, just as was the French form of *opéra comique*.

Gluck had some final disappointments—his last opera, *Echo et Narcisse*, was not well received at the Opéra and Marie Antoinette never succeeded in getting the French to admire *Alceste*, even in French. Early in 1787, the same year Gluck died, she was hissed at the Opéra.[10] She had lost her old charisma for the French, who would put her to death for her follies and friendships only seven years later, when she was thirty-eight. Little Antonia had been fourteen when Gluck's *Paris and Helen* was produced in Vienna; that very year she had been married off to the son of the king of France. With the deaths of Marie Antoinette and of Gluck an epoch ended.

But opera from beginning to end was reformed. Gluck started his reform with the overture, of which he said "[it] should appraise the spectators of the nature of the action that is to be represented and to form, so to speak, its argument." Formerly, the overture, or instrumental prelude of an opera, bore no positive relationship to the opera itself. Composers made a sanguine practice of using an overture as best suited their needs, transferring an overture they liked from its original opera to as many other operas as they chose, using an overture to give audiences time to select seats, gossip with neighbors and settle down before the opera began.

Gluck was a stern disciplinarian and expected his audience to be seated and attentive from the first note of his music. He was equally strict with singers, who were not allowed to climb up and down the musical ladder in coloratura flights in Gluck's works. He strove to return to the ideals of the Camerata and of Monteverdi and he achieved in his century a simplicity and grandeur for opera. His own self-discipline was remarkable, for he wrote (to Duke Leopold of Tuscany in 1769, in the dedication of *Alceste*) "my most strenuous efforts must be directed at the achievement of a noble simplicity, thus avoiding any show of difficulty at the expense of clarity. I did not consider a mere display of novelty valuable unless naturally suggested by the situation and the expression, and on this point no rule in composition exists that I would not gladly sacrifice in favor of the effect produced. Such are my principles."

Gluck felt he had to win strong support of those principles, which were against those of Italian *fioritura*, in order to sustain them, and he anxiously entreated the Duke to permit him to "arm myself with the mighty protection of your Royal Highness' name, and therefore I entreat the favor of being permitted to prefix it to my opera," since if it appeared there as dedication the public would know that it had received the Duke's benign approval.

Before Gluck's, reforms or rebellions in opera had been ironic and satirical after the Camerata's initial organization of *dramma per musica*, as in Gay's *The Beggar's Opera* in England, its fascimile in Germany, and, of course, the *opera buffa* in Italy, while in France Rousseau's theme for *opéra comique* was in the style of Pergolesi's comic opera. Gluck seriously and determinedly brought about his own reform in the singular way of explaining it at great length, to powerful patrons, which no composer until then had sought to do.

He subdued the *da capo aria* (his librettist Calzabigi changed the style which had flourished on Metastasio's verse) and the aria was less rococo after Gluck, whose style was to write short musical passages and solos, closely woven into the drama. He entirely eliminated *recitativo secco*.

As result of Gluck's reform of the singer's role in opera the bar-

barous practice of castration was abolished, giving rise to a perpetual argument as to whether the castrati, indeed, sang more divinely than singers of conventional genders. The eunuch is still alleged to have reached the highest acme of song, in the style of singing advocated as most fashionable to opera, before Gluck.

Orfeo was created for a celebrated castrato, Gaetano (it is a role now sung by a contralto) but in *Alceste* Gluck broke with the castrato mode and the music he wrote for this character (a soprano) is so noble that he must have meant to emphasize the role to its nth degree. Westerman considers the most important music in this opera to be Alceste's aria in *Act I* ("Hear me, ye Stygian gods").

Gluck's music sounded very strange to the audiences of his time. It was pellucid, music so unworldly when compared to the Italian (whose characteristics were sweetness of melody and conscious charm) that Gluck's music seemed holy for being pure. The Abbé Arnaud said of an air in *Iphigénie en Aulide*: "With that one might found a new religion."

And, also, the means of making music had changed since the Camerata's time, when *nuovo musiche* was being invented on whatever instruments were available to the composers. A study, in literal description and by pictorial record, of orchestral instruments will give you keen understanding of the changes, physically, through which opera makers were able to change music. Such a study would also give insight into the temperaments of the opera composers—Wagner, for instance, who wanted a certain sound and a certain quality and quantity, invented his own instrument, the Wagner tuba.

Thus, Gluck inherited an art: Opera, which was already changed and enriched from what the Camerata had invented, and Gluck himself changed and enriched it further.

Opera had its legend or tradition, and a life form of its own. Like a human being, every opera had a beginning and an end, the beginning being its overture. Its end was the finale and that had been acquired too, in the course of time, as the last musical movement of a work, consisting of groups of various movements, sometimes containing formal arias and ensembles. Opera was not born full-fledged in all its parts—it did not have overture and finale, for instance. The finale was added to provide a close with a large ensemble in which opera achieved a grand climax.

The aria in all forms remained in opera and the ensemble and chorus (which had almost vanished from opera at one time) returned and took their places within the form. Ensembles became very much the vogue, artistically constructed songs for several voices, as trios, quartets, quintets, sextets.

The introduction of dance-songs into opera, like the Barcarolle in ⅔ measure and the Siciliano in 6/8 time, added their characteristics to opera music. Rameau, who had been chastised for being "cerebral" and not French enough, introduced the Quadrille, taking it from a French provincial dance, *quadrille de contredanse*, its earliest operatic use being 1745 in his *Les Fêtes de Polymnie*.

The quadrille had an enormous popularity in France and later a mode developed whereby opera melodies were fitted to the five parts of a typical quadrille, making a musical work of itself.

Recitative survived and the Italian opera developed *parlando*, a light, fluent, rapid recitative copied from the southern Italian dialects.

Opera's love scenes, grand occasions for music and drama, were in the arias and the duets. *Opera buffa* (from Mozart and Rossini) was to exercise greater freedom and achieve more virtuoso productions, richer forms even than the serious opera. *Coloratura* survived, becoming the prized attribute of the feminine vocalist of a certain voice range, and whereas it had been (and in serious opera remained) the aesthetic high point it also assumed uses as parody in *opera buffa*.

The opera audience was a theatre audience but it assumed a special character: people who were simply mad about opera, opera enthusiasts, became "opera buffs." They were like no other people, and a bit like bull-fight *aficionados*. The word "fan" came from "fanatic" and this was what opera audiences were, in spirit—willing to die on occasion for their ideals, as they did in the duels between the claques of "Gluckists" and "Piccinnists."

The Italians, as Westerman observes, made opera such a cult that they savored every performance of every opera, and went to experience a work over and over again, sometimes with changes in cast, seemingly indefatigable in their desire to know an opera inside out, and in every nuance.

The French, who love argument and relish debate, made opera a grand conversation piece as well as an art. In affairs such as the *Guerre des Bouffons* not only opera artists and opera buffs joined the fray but also people in cafés and journalists on newspapers and cheap periodicals. The French used to draw sword canes in the foyer of l'Opéra; later, becoming no less tractable but under sterner laws, they regularly beat each other over the head with furled umbrellas. Opera buffs took their pleasures so seriously or so passionately that they contributed to opera lingo, and became part of opera tradition. The very name "opera buff" which you will acquire if you become an opera enthusiast comes from the war among the *bouffonistes* and *anti-bouffonistes*.

Even the phlegmatic English were stirred, by the great claque pro and con Handel, over Gay's opera-ballad form, over various styles of opera that appeared in England (and London was a city particularly appreciative of opera), with a great schism in the Victorian era when the prima donna Jenny Lind toppled all the marvelous ballerinas who had enraptured Europe. In mid-19th century an habitué of the Royal Italian Opera House (the Covent Garden theatre that is now called the Royal Opera House) complained that "young persons by cunning contrivance of Shoe or Boot" (the ballet dancers) were stealing attention from the singers. Gentlemen went to see the ballet in such numbers that Wagner, a terrible-tempered composer, refused to include music for ballet in his operas. "You will be disturbed to know," ominously wrote the English opera buff, "that a great part of the Audience attends the Opera House only for the Pleasure of looking at The Ballet."

It is easy to understand why opera became so universally popular— what cannot be said may be sung, and what cannot be expressed in song may be danced. Opera had singing and dancing and music and speech and all the seductive arts to please the eye in shape and color and some magical illusions besides. And the ways in which people made national operas were very expressive of ideologies and economics. It is not only in public monuments that nations leave records. We are known by the way we sing and dance and make music, by the cuisine and our manner of making love and punishing crimes. Opera was a glass held up to all these, even to the kitchen, for out of it and the bedchamber came the characters of *opera buffa* to take their places with the princes and demigods of *opera seria*.

Gluck left the world to his successors, and opera as a fully formed art. If opera had been static it should have perished or remained a rare curio, but opera lived and in living changed and reflected change.

Only one month before Gluck died Mozart's *Don Giovanni* received its première; Mozart had already created *The Marriage of Figaro*. He had only four more years to live, time enough to produce *The Magic Flute*, in which there would be an air of which a 20th-century writer (George Bernard Shaw) would say: "It is the only music which might be put into the mouth of God without blasphemy."

After Gluck came Mozart, and Mozart was not the end; he was only another beginning.

# Notes

1. When a libretto was published, the librettist received royalties or proceeds from its sale. Few libretti were published in Venice. In France, however, Louis XIV ordered that all works performed at the Académie de Musique et de Danse must be printed and this was done by the State; all the important French operas, from the earliest eras, were thus preserved and it is to this decree of Louis that Westerman ascribes the rapid, brilliant blossoming of French opera. The role of the librettist must never be underrated; it is he who creates the skeleton and the full figure of the opera and he does it first, before the music is composed, so that the composer relies greatly on his librettist. The librettist usually determines the number of characters, and who's who in the opera and it is his job to make each of these speak and behave "in character" for the plot. It is the librettist who must convince the audience that the plot is of absorbing interest; the composer does not have to convince with his music, he can go about being as abstract and mysterious as he pleases, or on the contrary, he can musically amplify the literal aspect of the work. It is the librettist who furnishes the composer with a set frame, in scenes and acts, in characters and plot, and all the dramatic points for which the composer creates the parts of the opera as aria, duet, ensemble, chorus, marches, ballets, et cetera. It is the librettist who decides entrances and exits and just who and how many come on and go off in every scene and act. He must do all these things, as the playwright does for a play, within the limitations of a physical stage and the human state—for instance, he has to plan time enough for singers to change costumes and stage crews to change scenery. Then he must write the actual verse of the libretto, the words to be sung in various ways as recitatives, patter-songs or dialogue of the *opéra comique* type. He puts all these words into the various mouths of soloists, duetists, ensembles and choruses, and he does all this within a "style" as well as within the characterizations and plot. If he is writing *opera buffa* libretto he is required to be witty, to use jokes, *double entendre* and other humorous ideas and statements. This is perhaps the most difficult kind of libretto to write for opera because being funny in the theatre is a great deal more difficult than being serious or sad. Audiences respond more readily to tragedy than to comedy, especially subtle comedy. Adapting a novel or a play into opera is not easy because the librettist translates the subject from its medium into the medium of opera. This is a medium with its own rules and conventions, as described in *Opera: What It Is . . .*

Verdi's *Macbeth, Otello* and *Falstaff* are not simply Shakespearean plays set to music. His librettists Piave (*Macbeth*) and Boito wrote libretti based on the dramas and Verdi created operas out of them. Shakespeare's plays, we may say, were first destroyed and then created, block by block, as operas. It is a generality to say that an opera has been adapted from a novel or a play but the actual creation and craftsmanship of an opera is a major accomplishment, a work entire to itself. The finest poem which scans beautifully on the page may prove un-singable in an opera score, to the chagrin of authors who resist having their words altered. Puccini, Leoncavallo and Massenet were refused permission to make *Cyrano de Bergerac* into opera; Rostand felt that his words had music enough and did not require warbling over in song. Composers are hard to please and make enormous demands of librettists. Puccini took eight months to write the score for *La Bohème* but his librettists toiled over the text for two years, rewriting the final act five times. This libretto derived from a novel based on real-life persons, the romantic riff-raff of the Latin Quarter. Making it into a novel was far easier than remaking it into an opera, because *La Bohème* is in two dimensions: drama and music. A libretto is recorded in its vocal score, where the orchestral music is reduced to piano, the instrument of reference. The full opera score is very complex, with parts for all the singers and players, stage directions and other notations. Multiple copies are made, from which the singers and players learn their parts. The libretto which you are most likely to see in print is the vocal score, verse and melody. You do not need to be a musician to recognize the enormity of the task which faces creative artists who begin to make an opera. The preliminaries may take several years, during which time a singer has not sung one word or the orchestra played a note. The librettist, alone, has a herculean task, the composer another, and when they are finished their work the opera engages innumerable individuals from première through its exist-ence in repertories. A great deal of writing and recording goes on for an opera, first through copyists of the score, then by librarians for repertory, also by printers, who toil to bring the opera to that first stage of completion where it may, next, become the opera in rehearsal and production on stage.

 2. This is not to say that opera cannot be sung in English, the language of great poets and playwrights. Indeed, the Italian-American Menotti prefers to write his libretti in English (he has also written Italian-libretto operas). The English tongue is dramatic and flexible, capable of imaginative and realistic expression, and it is not inferior to Italian, French and German, the languages in which the great bulk of opera repertory is sung. What matters is how English is written to be sung in opera, and how the composer suits his music to English verse. The English language has its own particular syntax and semantic con-ventions; it does not, for instance, have the masculine and feminine genders of Romance languages and when foreign language libretti are literally translated into operatic verse they suffer inversion of word order because certain languages place the verb after the noun. These language conventions are important in opera because of the musical values required of libretto, which must have rhythmic shape and rhythmic variety. As a result, the majority of English translations from foreign language libretti must be adapted, rather than stolidly translated, and since the music was originally composed for the libretto's original language the music has to be considered in the translation. Unfortunately, these adaptations are not always fine enough to stand up to the original because opera producers

and opera house managers appear to employ language translators for the job of transferring libretti from the original foreign tongues into English. What is needed is a *musician* who is able to translate foreign languages into English; he alone can qualify the "English" adaptation with sufficient sense in verse to suit the opera's music. For my part, I would rather find out ahead of curtain time what the opera is about and make a study of the libretto sufficient to allow me to follow the musical and dramatic action, when the opera is being sung in a language I do not know, than suffer hearing a clumsy and stilted language translation which is ridiculous as speech and not especially fine as music, simply to know what is being said while it is being sung. To popularize foreign opera in English, opera composers must provide far better English libretti than is now the norm. There are, of course, many operas composed on English language libretti. English opera did not develop as such while the Italians were the flourishing opera arbiters because an "Italian" musical style prevailed which was, naturally, better suited to the Italian language than to any other. When English musicians composed operas on English libretti then and only then did "English opera" come about. The same is true of "French opera," as you will understand by reading *The Beginning* in entirety.

3. This giving rise to some aesthetic quarrels in theatre, as is current over Joan Sutherland, the Australian prima donna who is possessed of a beautiful voice but who falls short as an actress. She is the idol, in the 1960's, of opera buffs who enjoy revivals of *Norma* and *Lucia di Lammermoor* and other roles especially well suited to Sutherland's great voice.

4. Keiser had brilliant melodic gifts, which were squandered in superficiality; his private and professional life was wasted in frivolities and he is totally eclipsed in German music, but Hasse, himself a successful composer, counted Keiser among the world's great musicians. Handel worked under Keiser's direction for three years (1703–1706) at the Hamburg Opera, where three of Handel's operas were produced. Telemann, who succeeded Keiser, is one of the great German baroque composers, better known today for his cantatas, suites and sonatas than his operas, which are classed with the early German operas, the best known being *Don Quichote*, all in the French style.

5. To call an opera singer the "idol" of an audience is not excessive, when we know how the opera claques worshipped; to degrees of hysteria which led otherwise sane and sensible persons to commit follies and sins, one to laud the idol and the other to denigrate the idol's rivals. The castrati were particularly idolized, on stage and off, and while in a later age it became the fashion for gentlemen to have love affairs with ballet dancers it was formerly the vogue for great ladies to give their favors to the castrati—a singularly convenient person to have a love affair with since no "fruits of the illicit love" or illegitimate offspring could come about from the liaison to embarrass the ladies. For the castrati remained sexually potent but were incapable of breeding children. Their loves and lives are romantic anecdotes in opera history and their princely stations in the theatre brought them fame and fortune, which not unnaturally gave them very high opinions of themselves. Farinelli (1705–1782) was picked by Handel's enemies as an instrument for Handel's downfall and it was the castrato's alliance with this faction that helped break the composer. From 1737 Farinelli

lived in Spain, was paid a huge salary and given great political power as a court singer employed by the queen (Elizabeth Farnese of Parma) and no longer sang in public but directed the opera productions for which Madrid was famed in his period as favorite. When Elizabeth's son Charles succeeded his half-brother Ferdinand VI, whose reign Farinelli survived, in 1759, Farinelli was forced to leave Spain but continued to collect his salary, on which he retired in luxury to Bologna, where he died. Caffarelli, a third famed castrato, also sang for Handel. He was noted for his quarrelsome nature as well as his beautiful voice, but was hired for the latter, to sing privately for the Dauphine of France (1753) to cheer her during the months of her pregnancy. He survived duels which he fought to maintain the merits of Italian music over French, the Lisbon earthquake in 1755 and other disasters, and bought two palaces and a duchy in Italy with his earnings. In *The Barber of Seville* Bartolo refers to him in Rosina's singing lesson.

6. Gay had previously written several libretti for Gluck before producing his *Beggar's Opera*, so was adept as a librettist, and Pepusch was a very clever musical arranger. Pepusch did not compose an original score but brilliantly improvised a parody on popular songs and dance tunes, compiled as sixty-nine numbers of which twenty-eight were English, fifteen Irish, five Scottish and three French airs. Many other parts of the music used as the opera score had been composed as songs and dance tunes by anonymous persons and to these Pepusch added street cries, producing a musical mélange which was perfect for Gay's savagely ironic verse. *The Beggar's Opera* was produced at a London theatre managed by a man named Rich and the wags of the time pronounced it a work which made Gay rich, and Rich gay. Its re-creation by Brecht and Weill is known as *Die Dreigroschenoper* (The Threepenny Opera).

7. Molière got the idea of inserting danced passages into drama from the Jesuits, from whom he gained his education. The Jesuits were notable for their ballets, which were operatic in form. It is also notable that Molière's work provides opera with a reservoir of libretti; *Le Bourgeois Gentilhomme* is also Richard Strauss' *Ariadne auf Naxos*, and besides these composers others to make use of Molière's dramas include Bizet, Charpentier, Gounod, Grétry, Haug, Lattuada, Shaprin, Wolf-Ferrari, Zich.

8. Eventually, the French became thoroughly exasperated with Rousseau's pro-Italian musical tastes and rebutted them so entirely that they turned against Italian opera. The troupe which had brought *La Serva Padrona* to Paris in 1752 and stayed on to enjoy two years of fantastic success, was forced to pack up and leave the city to protect their persons from the wrath of the opera buffs of the Ile de la Cité. Taking to its heels, Italian *opera buffa* left a clear field to French *opéra comique*, which thrived through the Revolution. Compare this with a far different debacle in German opera where the Brunswick theatre was ruined in 1755 by the audience's preference for Italian opera. The opera house built in Hamburg on the Gansmarkt in 1678, expected to flourish on its "home" or local audience's natural preference for German opera, collapsed into bankruptcy in 1738, put out of business by the arrival of Mingotti's touring Italian opera troupe. The Hamburg opera house was torn down, just two years before Berlin got its first one, in 1740—a gift of Frederick the Great, as an edifice in

the Unter den Linden, where the opera was in the Italian fashion and language!

9. Mercy's connections at l'Opéra were chiefly through his mistress, Rosa Levasseur, member of a French family of opera singers. (One, Nicolas Prosper Levasseur, was the great French dramatic bass of the Meyerbeer era, and was later in his career professor of lyric declamation at the Paris Conservatory.) Rosa, as her reward, was given the role of Iphigénie as priestess of Diana in *Iphigénie en Tauride* or *Iphée deux* in l'Opéra lingo.

10. This insult is notable since Marie Antoinette had been, from her time as the Dauphine, a pet of l'Opéra. The Austrian princess allied herself with theatrical folk as the British Princess Margaret, sister of Elizabeth II, was to ally herself in the 20th century. "The best thing I have to tell you about the little Dauphine," a dancer wrote home from Paris in 1773 "is that she is loved by we of the theatre." On June 16 that year she was cheered so long at l'Opéra that the curtain was held past its lifting time and June 23, when she was greeted with "transports of joy and affection," she gave permission for the audience to applaud the performers in her presence, altering the French royal etiquette at the Comédie Française (which was presenting *Les Legs* and *Le Siège de Calais*). On June 30 at Théâtre des Italiens the play was *Le Déserteur* and called for the actor Clairval to cry "Long live the King!"—to which he added, (intending this, he said "to *fête* the Dauphine and Dauphin") "And long live his dear children!" "All this," wrote Mercy, "is addressed to Madame la Dauphine. One could fill whole volumes with the moving remarks that were made, the comments on [her] appearance, charm, and gracious, kindly air. . . ." "Had she been sensible," comments a historian of the Opéra ballet, "Marie Antoinette should have heeded the sign that from the Opéra season in 1775 she was less frantically applauded than before."

# ✻ F O U R ✻

# Opera: What It Is...

It might be easier to tell you what opera is not, than try to explain what opera is . . . Many new opera goers are puzzled about the differences in opera and, for instance, "musical comedy," two theatrical arts that have singing and music as distinguishing features. Is opera serious and tragic, and as such the opposite of "musical comedy?" No, because many operas are light-hearted and comic, while some "musical comedies" are somber. *West Side Story*, a landmark in the American musical comedy theatre, is based on Shakespeare's theme for *Romeo and Juliet* and, in its medium, is a true work of art.

"Musical comedy" derived from opera and is distinctive in its form. Between the genesis of *Oklahoma!* and its extension into *West Side Story* the "musical" has traveled approximately the same proportionate course as opera from Mozart to Menotti. Particular to its kind, "musical comedy" is a great achievement in the American musical-dramatic theatre, and sometimes its choreography and dramatic substance is more important than its tunes. No opera is ever greater than its music and opera music can and often does sustain a mediocre plot.

You are correct to assume, as most new opera goers do, that opera is "something sung," and that the singers are opera's primary performers. But there are different sorts of singing beyond even the kind of "popular" vocalizing that is ordinary and well known.

*A Cappella* (ah cah-*pell*-lah), Italian for "in the church style," is song by a chorus without instrumental accompaniment. It is a 16th century musical form.

*Cantata*, Italian for "sung," is a work for several solo voices, chorus and instrumentalists, although it is occasionally performed without instrumental music. Originally, in the 17th century, cantata was an extended vocal solo with recitatives and arias. Now, it is something like a short oratorio, without staging or conventional theatrical presentation.

*Oratorio*, which is as old as opera, has libretto, orchestral accompaniment, solo and chorus; it is rather like an opera divested of scenery and dramatic action. Oratorio, like opera, has arias and recitatives.

*Opera*, as we know it today, is a distinct art form, the sum of several arts and contributing works of art. Each work is an "opus" and the plural works form the "opera." To understand what opera is, you need to know how it began and why, when and where, and from whom and how it was born and grew. These things are briefly related in the chapter: *The Beginning*.

In the opera house you experience Art in a state of being; genius and order as a medium or form.

Note that I say "experience" and not that you "see and hear" opera. I need to impress on you here that opera is not simply heard in its music, or seen in its dramatic action, but, more precisely, opera is experienced as an audio-visual art. Opera is a happening which occurs as reality for the performers and the audience. It happens in a certain way, which is the medium or art form. The performers, who are called "artistes," are also technicians or craftsmen trained within the opera medium or form of expression. Therefore, opera has a mode and manner, and its language or vocabulary is particular (and we may say peculiar) to itself. Know what opera is, and accept it for itself—exactly as you know and accept a play is a play; a ballet is a ballet. But opera is far more complex and complicated than a play or ballet.

It is elementary knowledge that a play is acted, and a ballet is danced, as the substances of these art forms or mediums in theatrical expression. Opera also contains drama and sometimes dance, but it is erroneous to assume that an opera is a play set to music, or a ballet in which dancers sing.

I have read books and heard lectures which describe opera as "a play with music." This over-simplification, I find, confuses and disappoints the new opera goer, who assumes that an opera is, literally, a drama with musical accompaniment.

*Do not expect the opera to be communicative in the same way as a play*. And do not think of an opera as "a play with music" or as a drama in which the actors sing. The single intellectual approach to opera is an understanding of what it is—opera is a drama *in* music.

I feel that you must be free to approach opera in the way you prefer, as pure entertainment or studiously, as art, but I require you to understand and accept what opera is—a drama in music—in order to communicate to you something of what opera is about. Opera has a distinct form, in which other art forms appear, some of these being drama, dance and symphony—the last in its Greek meaning: "sounding together" or playing together of several instruments as orchestra. Opera's form distinguishes it, and that form has the attributes of several styles, for which see *The Beginning*.

Get used here to thinking of opera as artificial, not natural. Opera and ballet have to do with singing and dancing but this kind of song and dance is never spontaneous and impromptu; it is man-made, or cultivated, as art. Art is not natural because it is artificial. We hear people speaking of leaves "dancing" in the wind and of water "making music" but these are poetic fancies, not facts. Opera and ballet are physical as well as artistic facts. Ballet is a popular, well-known American theatrical art and it is useful to compare it with opera to clarify some statements about opera. Both opera and ballet make normal human accomplishments (singing and dancing) supernormal or idealized and their forms assume certain conventions which the theatre audience accepts as the artistic means of expression for opera and ballet.[1]

The size, theme, characterization and production of an opera may vary but an opera remains an opera within its form. Gluck's *Orfeo ed Euridice* has three characters; Verdi's *Aida* has a large cast of principals and two armies. Britten's *Billy Budd* has no female characters and is set with sailors on a ship at sea. Operas can and have been made about everything real or fantastic, including the moon (Haydn's *Il Mondo della Luna* and Orff's *Der Mond*) and all it shines on, like a sleep-walker (in Bellini's *La Sonnambula*). There are operas about saints and sinners, as Menotti has proved with his *Saint of Bleecker Street* and *The Medium*.

Two general classifications in which the opera's form as drama in music is contained are "classical" and "romantic." In principle, "classical" determines music as the servant of drama. If you have already read *The Beginning* you will know this to be the ideal of the Camerata, pursued by the first opera makers in the Aristotelian idea (in *Poetics*) that music is one of the six essentials of tragedy. "Romantic" opera is the triumph of music over drama.

Ideally, the two components as drama and music should be equal and unite to form a perfect work of art. Sometimes this occurs in opera but often one part presumes importance greater than the other, giving opera two generic classifications as "classical" and "romantic." The schism in opera has caused spontaneous creativity in opera, from which works emerged to set styles. If the composer was imitated and emulated, the style became an international mode. If there was violent reaction to the style, it developed a new creative ideal—for instance, Wagner developed music drama and Debussy reacted against the Wagnerian ideal with "impressionistic" opera.

We readily grasp the idea of a play because life is naturally a drama and we are actors, in ordinary life—forced to dissemble our feelings and protect our thoughts by "acting" parts which are assumed as the outer, visible self in order to preserve the inward, private person. The majority of us are not musicians and music is more difficult for us to understand than drama, but to know what opera is you must recognize it as an art existing in two dimensions: drama and music.

A play occupies one dimension and spoken drama generally follows one strand of action. When a play contends with more than one level of action it resorts to extraordinary effects, as in Christopher Fry's *A Sleep of Prisoners* (in which the actors communicate conventionally in dialogue and also in dreams) and in Eugene O'Neill's *Strange Interlude* (where the actors speak dialogue and, also, "unvoiced" thoughts). But regardless of the skill of the playwright and his actors, these devices are clumsy and the double-dimension of dramatic action has to take place through stage-craft, as tricks, in the attempt to convey the outer and inner world of the characters in the play. Opera has the virtuoso faculty of expressing several separate statements, simultaneously, because its drama is only one level of action, and its music can follow several separate and often different strands—the music augments the dramatic action as well as the sung or declaimed parts.

Opera can and does weave several separate strands of action, simultaneously. Drama alone, even with movement and gesture, cannot achieve this magic.

*It is the nature of opera to occupy plural dimensions of drama and music, with simultaneity.* Once you have grasped this, the nature of opera is no longer an enigma. And if you know your English poets, assume for opera what William Blake assumed for the being: an equilibrium of mind and soul with the body, which Blake called one.

Music passes in time and is composed on silence and sound qualified by pitch, tempo, rhythm, texture and intent. Opera moves in music as well as in time and space. The composer uses singers and players as parts to make musical statements and he will mingle themes, orchestrate, and employ a number of devices to express himself. An aria, for example, can be sung slow or fast, in a low or a loud tone. The composer uses singers and players in solo, duet, ensemble and chorus and commands an enormous dimension (that of music) in which he can do several separate and often different or divergent things, with simultaneity, so that drama and music occur as one.

In opera, drama and music happen together, at the same time. Opera is a physical as well as a musical fact, just as a quintet—a group of five singers or players or both performing together, at once; and/or a piece of music composed for five singers and/or players—is a physical as well as a musical fact.

Gluck makes Orestes sing lies while the music simultaneously reveals the truth about him, a bit of operatic legerdemain recounted in *The Beginning*. And Verdi, in *Aida*, makes Amneris as beautiful and venomous as a serpent; she addresses Aida: "Come, dearest one . . ." singing endearments and breathing lies.

Opera does not have "lyrics" as ordinary songs do—it is said to have "verse." Actors speak lines in a play; opera singers communicate in lyrical passages. Opera is sung and declaimed but it is never sung and spoken in the styles of the cabaret or the street. An opera is not a play in which actors sing, but a musical art form in which singers also act. Opera singers begin life with stronger voices than is "average," or with a musical gift that is not "ordinary" but then have to be trained or made into opera singers—a special and comparatively rare kind of singer.

Running and walking are natural or ordinary ways of moving, and jumping and leaping or turning in the air are normal, animal forms of movement. When these are performed according to codified techniques, to apply to a form of art, they become balletic. The human voice has tone and volume but opera requires the voice to achieve operatic styles.

Music has a larger, richer, more complex expression than speech and in singing words are repeated and phrases expanded to suit the music; for example in Dido's *Lament* in *Dido and Aeneas*. It takes longer to sing than to say something. Opera is wholly artificial in its mode of singing. People in ordinary life never behave as they do in operas. Even operas based on very ordinary persons, like the people in *La Bohème*, do not express themselves in commonplace manner. Mimi is a poor, shabby little consumptive of weak morals but Puccini chooses to make her sing like a diva, the goddess of opera. So doing, Puccini's Mimi is immortalized, a unique creation among her real-life counterparts, the archetypal Parisian midinette "Mimi Pinson," of whom the French tune-smith, Béranger, sang, in the "pop" *chanson* of the day.[2]

In opera, people think as well as talk in song, and they do it as their regular vocabulary—as we speak in ordinary life. But at the dinner table we do not sing to pass the butter and pepper and salt, nor apologize in an aria if the soufflé falls, nor would a guest (even a tenor) compliment you in song if you concocted a tasty casserole. In opera, singers sing without stint regardless of the circumstances and situations. A man sings when he falls in love, if he wants a barber to shave his cheeks, a king to spare his life, or a city to raise a siege. In opera a fellow will sing while his house is burning, his wife running off with his best friend, and his only child is being stolen away by gypsies.[3] In opera, they sing for joy and sing in sorrow; sing if life is bitter, and if life is sweet. Singing itself is the *reason* for opera.

An ancient proverb says that what cannot be said may be sung and what cannot be sung may be danced. Opera does all these and does them with more fervor and subtlety than they could have if done separately, because opera does them simultaneously and within productions or staging which amplify and emphasize all operatic effects. Opera is the supreme artifice, the most eloquent of theatrical arts.

### Its Parts and Sum

When you go into the opera house you are usually given a program, a kind of bill of fare which tells you (in a synopsis) the story of the opera and who's who in the cast, dividing the opera up into acts and scenes. As soon as the opera commences you will be aware of the singers on stage and the orchestra, probably in the pit.[4] The singers and instrumentalists are the performers, and hidden from the audience are the opera director, producer, librettist and composer and all the technicians and collaborating artists who have created the work for the performance.

You will now know opera in some of its several parts—all those that are placed on view and in the hearing of the audience. The singers will be appropriately costumed, and their dress alone will convey a great deal of the atmosphere of the opera. But, chiefly, the opera itself, the drama in music, will communicate its theme and create its characterizations.

Before curtain rise you are likely to hear the opera's overture, a word derived from the French *ouverture*: an opening. Listen to it attentively because the composer has employed it to set the mood for the work. Wagner called his introductory musical compositions "preludes," to emphasize them as creating the emotional and dramatic atmosphere for his operas.

The opera overture was inaugurated by the Italians, who called this part of an orchestration *sinfonia* and *toccata*, meaning that the part was played, not sung. Originally, an opera had no introductory instrumental phrases but began with singing, in a vocal prologue. Scarlatti innovated the "Italian overture" in three sections: the first fast, in fugal style; the second, slow; the third, again, in quickened tempo. Musicologists suggest that this was a musical ruse by composers to hurry laggard audiences into the opera house and give them respite to settle themselves in their places after a little gossip with friends in the theatre—and that the accelerated third part was to rush the audience to attention.

Lully innovated the "French overture" for an audience at Louis XIV's court, which would not have dreamed of offending that monarch by turning up late to a theatre performance, a hunt or a levee. Lully could afford to take his time, and did, commencing his overtures with slow, majestic music; inserting a fast middle section in fugal style; concluding with dance music like the minuet. The last part was to please Louis, a balletomane who liked ballets in operas and inspired Molière to put dance in plays. The French overture was such a distinguishing aspect of the architecture of French opera that Marie

Antoinette (trying to get Gluck's works admitted to l'Opéra) complained about Lully's overture pattern: "A slow start, called serious, which was generally played twice, and a quick return to the subject, called gay, which was usually in the form of a fugue."

Gluck was the first composer to integrate overture and opera and his *Alceste* and *Iphigénie en Aulide* have overtures which unify mood and style, the overtures establishing the emotional natures of the works. The closing phrases of these Gluckian overtures flow directly into the opening scenes of the operas.

Mozart integrated themes and phrases from his operas into their overtures and Beethoven, Weber and Wagner developed the idea until this became the formal statement of the opera overture. Wagner, as has been said, used preludes to establish mood, an example being the mysticism of *Lohengrin*. He, with Mozart, experimented with the overture form. Verdi, Wagner's contemporary, as a rule preferred prelude and of a short rather than long form, but many composers preferred to keep the overture independent of the opera so that it could be (and still is) played as a concert piece as well as an operatic overture. Rossini was one of these sanguine composers, some of whom used one favorite overture several times, for different operas.

While the overture bore no positive relationship to an opera, composers often borrowed or stole each other's works, so that one man's favorite overture (which seemed appropriate to another man's opera) might not only serve several of his operas but of other composers' operas as well. With the mass circulation of music by radio, television and phonograph this amiable thieving would be impossible to hide. In earlier times it was easy to do, and when it was noted it does not seem to have excited a great critical brouhaha.

Many operas and all operettas have overtures in which themes from the operas proper are mingled in a pleasant potpourri. Avant-garde opera buffs are inclined to sneer at this sort of overture (*Carmen* has one such) because modern opera ignores overture. Since the era of Richard Strauss opera tends to begin its dramatic action with the first note, as the curtain rises. *Billy Budd's* curtain rises while the stage is still dark, before the music even begins. But for many opera buffs the overture is the lovely ritual beginning of an opera.

After the overture, what next? This is according to the composer's choice, because there is no set formula for arranging opera's parts in order. There is seldom an aria in the early part of the first scene and when there is singers loathe late-comers who destroy the theatrical atmosphere. Jean de Reszke, the celebrated Polish tenor, used to omit singing *Celeste Aida* when he took Radames' role because this aria occurs very soon after curtain-rise in *Aida.*

In *Mastersingers of Nuremberg,* which has a magnificent overture, the first singing is within a church service, and in *La Bohème* half the first act passes before there is an aria.

Aria (*ahr*-iah), is Italian for "air" or melody. The formal aria has three sections, the first more or less complete in itself, the second a new section introduced for contrast, and the third a repetition or reprise of the first in whole or part. A short, simple aria, without the second section, is an *arietta.*

Some arias are composed, in the Italian mode, as *aria cantabile*: slow and level; *aria di portamento*: noble, and with long, smooth notes; and *aria di bravura,* which is for the purpose of showing off a virtuoso voice.

A *duet* is a vocal or instrumental composition for two and it may have separate parts, so that the performers sing or play "against" instead of "with" each other; and, vocally, it may be one instrumental part with two sets of vocal parts sung at once. The duet is often used in operatic love-scenes but on occasion a duet may be a quarrel or a statement and a soliloquy, or two soliloquies, and so on. It is customary for singers to muse aloud as well as sing aloud and they assume the theatrical license that even in a duet one singer may muse in secret while singing aloud.[5]

*Ensemble,* from a French word meaning "together," or all at the same time, is a musical passage for three singers, or singers and chorus, and *chorus,* group singing, is well enough known not to require explanation.[6]

The declamatory style of opera is *recitative,* monologue and dialogue in a terse, chanting style, which is *recitativo* in Italian, *récitatif* in French, and *recitativ* in German, all meaning: to recite.

Kinds of opera which employ recitative are *opéra comique,* which is not comic opera at all (as you will understand by reading *The Beginning*), *opera buffa* and *Singspiel.* These are operas in which dialogue has a part, as well as song.

The opera passes in acts and scenes, and an opera is generally in three to five acts, acts sub-divided into scenes as for a play or ballet, many of these necessitating changes of scenery. The opera makers attempt to have each act or scene hold a dramatic climax, so that curtain-rise and curtain-fall (and a pregnant space between) are punctuations of the opera—not interruptions. The opera is therefore planned very skillfully as a theatre piece, to allow the singers to change costumes, the stage crew to change scenery, the musicians to rest, the audience to refresh itself and for the opera, as a whole, to compel the attention of performers and technicians and audience, all alike, from beginning to end.

The content of an opera is seldom elusive for the audience, even if the opera is sung in a foreign language. Opera plots are among the most naïve forms of literary composition, seldom as subtle as a good play, generally turbulent with characterizations hinged on a quite straightforward plot—some of these being rather like the plots of "soap operas" on radio and television. Many opera plots are derived from classical literature or folklore of the most universal familiarity. The corpus of opera libretti is of great variety and comprises a whole romantic library in itself. 18th and 19th century operas have by now achieved sufficient fame to rank among the best known works in international theatre, especially for an opera goer. The regulation program almost invariably gives the audience the plot in story form for an opera, old or new.

If you take an opera apart to examine its several components you find that it is composed on libretto and score. These are usually by two different persons as collaborators. Sometimes the librettist adapts a work already existent (many operas have been made from myths and from old plays and ballads); sometimes he creates an original story and characters. When a libretto is expressly written for the composer it is called an original libretto; this is usually the case because the composer has, generally, a very good idea of what he wants to write music on, about and for. But few opera composers create their own libretti.[7]

Opera in its several parts is usually in overture or prelude, continuing through to the finale. Some parts of opera are arias, duets, ensembles and choruses, for singers and instrumentalists, and for the orchestra the music for entrances and exits, ballets, entr'actes, marches, et cetera. Kinds of operas have been identified, as classical and romantic, and as *opera buffa,* et cetera, but no one has ever needed to describe an opera as a "musical" opera. This is because music is the intrinsic nature of opera and "opera" is a qualification for the musical work of this name. The composer therefore assumes paramount importance in the work and the librettist, at his best, serves the composer or inspires him to create the most eloquent musical statements for the work. And while the librettist can, conceivably, sketch his libretto as he would the script for a play, the composer must provide music at length for the opera from start to finish; a monumental task!

The composer determines how he shall compose the opera—shall the music be continuous, or shall he divide the work into a series of movements, et cetera? He constructs the music in a style that remains constant and is recognizable, and he chooses to give the orchestra the leading role in the opera, or, on the contrary, to feature the singers. In the former choice, the composer creates instrumental music as his primary composition, and may do so to the extent achieved by Richard Strauss, in some of whose works instruments might be substituted for vocal parts without noticeable loss of the opera's substance. In the latter choice, which was Puccini's, for instance, the vocal parts are primary and the instruments are used for atmosphere and color. The operatic orchestra is elastic and its size varies according to the composer's choice—and also according to some opera fashions. Monteverdi composed for a comparatively large orchestra, in his era, but later composers hugely expanded the operatic orchestra to suit their requirements. Wagner even invented an instrument, a tuba, in order to obtain the sound he wanted. Hector Berlioz (1803-1869), a composer of the French school, dreamed of an orchestra capable of the greatest possible tonal combinations and musical effects—it would have required four hundred and sixty-seven instrumentalists and a choir of three hundred. Wagner composed *The Ring of the Nibelung* for one hundred and four instruments, the apogee of the giant orchestra of the 19th century.

20th century composers reverted to small orchestras, about the size used by Mozart. This became the vogue partly from choice, in the 20th century philosophy of music, and also because of a more stringent theatrical economy (especially in English-speaking countries) after two world wars. Richard Strauss' *Salome* (1905) and *Elektra* (1909) were composed for large instrumental groups; his *Ariadne auf Naxos* (1912) for an orchestra no larger than that used by Mozart.

Benjamin Britten in England and Gian-Carlo Menotti in America are two modern opera makers who have composed for a few solo singers and orchestras of thirteen to sixteen instruments—examples: Britten's *Rape of Lucrezia* and Menotti's *The Medium,* both in 1946 premières.

Large opera houses (the Metropolitan in New York and the Royal Opera, Covent Garden, London) maintain large repertories and must have a permanent orchestra of varied instruments, for playing the widest range of operas.

## The Orchestra

This requires a whole study to itself, how it evolved and developed, when and where it altered in size or character. Monteverdi was the first composer to use ensembles and the first to compose instrumental passages, without vocal parts, in opera. Under Scarlatti, ensemble and overture (as well as *da capo aria*) assumed greater importance. Until the middle of the 18th century keyboard instruments were the harmonic backbone of the orchestra, the bass parts being played by cello, double bass, bassoon and harpsichord. The strings became the dominant factor (Louis XIV's 24 violins) and were grouped to play a part in unison. Then they were divided and became the quartet of first violin, second violin, violas, and cellos and double basses. Beethoven separated the cellos from the basses to form the string quintet.

An 18th century opera may need an orchestra like this one:

| Brass and Woodwinds | Strings | Percussion |
|---|---|---|
| 2 trumpets | 9 first violins | 1 pair kettle-drums |
| 2 French horns | 8 second violins | 1 pair cymbals |
| 2 flutes | 6 violas | 1 triangle |
| 2 clarinets | 7 cellos | |
| 2 oboes | 6 double basses | |
| 2 bassoons | | |

The strings here predominate about two to one and for contrast the orchestra groups brass and woodwinds to play against the strings.

More normally, there is a division in the orchestra between brass and woodwinds. Note, also, the minimum percussion.

Wagner and Richard Strauss works in repertory would require an opera company to command an orchestra something like this:

| *Woodwinds* | *Brass* | *Percussion* |
|---|---|---|
| 2 piccolos | 4 trumpets | 2 pairs kettle-drums |
| 3 flutes | 8 French horns | 1 bass drum |
| 4 oboes | 4 trombones | 1 snare drum |
| 1 English horn | 3 tubas | 1 pair cymbals |
| 3 clarinets | | 1 triangle |
| 2 bass clarinets | *Strings* | miscellaneous bells, |
| 3 bassoons | 16 first violins | chimes, tambourines, |
| | 16 second violins | et cetera. |
| | 12 violas | |
| | 12 cellos | |
| | 8 double basses | |

Luckily for opera costs, instrumentalists often play more than one instrument, but even so an opera house like the New York Metropolitan is compelled to employ and maintain a large, accomplished orchestra as a significant entity in its army of artistes and technicians.

Conducting the orchestra is itself an art and one in which the conductor is trained. The act of directing instrumental groups dates to the 15th century, on the evidence of illustrative paintings of the century. At that time, music was not divided into bars, and the director's (the conductor's) gesture with hand or baton served to co-ordinate the instrumentalists as they played. Into the 18th century, conductors used a stick which they struck on the floor to mark time. Lully used this method of conducting, to his great rue. While conducting in 1687 he hit his big toe instead of the floor and an infection set in from which Lully died of blood-poisoning, having outlived Molière, his arch rival for Louis XIV's favor, by fourteen years.

The baton came into use about 1817, and was made fashionable first by Weber, next by Mendelssohn. The audience undoubtedly preferred the baton to the thumped-stick method of conducting; there are anecdotes of bitter complaints from the audience about the racket set up by the conductor's stick, over which noise one followed the music with difficulty.

The baton was made of bone or ivory, usually with an ebony

handle; nowadays it is likely to be made of plastic. And, as you will notice, some conductors prefer to use the hands, without the baton.

In the orchestra's early days the conductor sat in the middle and marked tempo on the organ or harpsichord, playing with one hand and beating time with the other. Beethoven conducted in this way but also used a baton—one of the first composers to do so. In the late 18th century the concert master or first violin took over the job of leading the orchestra, but as he usually stood in front, with his back to the musicians, he could not easily communicate with his fellow-instrumentalists. The conductor now generally stands facing his players, with his back to the audience—the first time this was done (turning his back to the audience) was for the première of Wagner's Festival Theatre at Bayreuth, 1876.

Is a conductor necessary for an orchestra? Disgruntled singers, smarting under the tyranny of a conductor, would like to say no but the conductor is more than necessary to opera, he is essential. The role of the conductor becomes even more pontifical when he is by temperament a magnetic person; then he becomes one of opera's star performers.[8]

Regardless of whether the composer allocates a larger or smaller importance to the orchestra in an opera (as if the singing is more featured than the orchestra) the conductor has to conduct singers and players, twice the job that it takes to conduct in the concert hall. The opera conductor concentrates more, for longer periods, and on a wider variety of problems and responsibilities than the symphony conductor. Each singer performs his role but the conductor (besides ruling the orchestra) has to keep track of the entire cast, on a crowded stage, and be ready to indicate the beat clearly and without fault or hesitation for an individual performer.

The orchestra is a great part of an opera's sum, because it accompanies all the singing and action and preserves continuity, even when singers fall silent—this is seldom, and singers are usually in full cry from curtain rise to curtain fall. The orchestra colors and defines characters and plot and does far more, because music can express a great deal in a shorter time than can be expressed by song or speech. In *Otello*, Verdi uses a very brief musical composition to send the poor, bedevilled, duped Moor into his wife's bedroom to smother her, and tells us everything we can bear to know about the anguish and passion of the deed. Shakespeare requires twenty-two lines to say the same thing.

A genius will use the orchestra in extraordinary ways. When Pelléas and Mélisande confess their love for each other they do not sing—Debussy created speechless rapture: the orchestra is still for two bars.

### The Singers

Singers come in two genders, male and female (and have been known in the neuter, as the *castrati*), in several physical shapes and sizes, and in about six kinds of voices. The first thing you need to know about an opera singer is that he or she is an *extra*ordinary, not an ordinary person.

However gifted you might be musically you are very unlikely to become an opera singer without extensive and specialized training. It would be impossible for you to put on an opera singer's costume and stroll on stage, to sing a role—first, your physical as well as artistic development must occur to qualify you for opera singing.

The opera singer is taught to sing and also to breathe and control his voice. The making of an opera singer takes place in lungs, larynx and sinuses: cavities of throat, mouth, nose and head. For men, breath development and control is primarily in the diaphragm; for women, in the diaphragm and through the muscles around the ribs.

Song is produced in the human body by the same means as speech but with considerably more development and control, especially of the larynx, the portion of the throat commonly called "Adam's apple." It is a cavity with nine cartilaginous walls, containing the vocal cords. In human beings (and in most of the higher evolution of animals) this cavity forms the upper part of the wind-pipe (the trachea). The opening at the upper part of the trachea and between the vocal cords is the glottis. Two pieces of cartilage (like two pieces of string or cord) are stretched across the glottis, which extends from the lungs up into the mouth. These pieces of cartilage are vocal cords, about half an inch long in the male and somewhat shorter in the female. (Vocal cords share in gradual physical growth and a child's are as small, sometimes smaller, than a female's.) Very efficiently, these cords open and close and the opera singer learns to manipulate and control them to produce the effects and sounds of the operatic voice.

Our vocal cords open and close naturally, as we breathe; the singer learns to breathe in certain ways so as to control his vocal cords. When they are wide open and held loosely, he can produce low notes, and sing in slow tempo, as for *andante* (an-*dan*-tay) passages. This is performed on an *inhaled* breath.

When the singer wishes to perform high notes he must force his vocal cords apart, stretching them across the glottis; this he does on an *exhaled* breath.

Vocal cords vibrate when stretched and in turn cause the air above them to vibrate at a corresponding speed. Singers speak of using "a column of air" to vibrate the cavities or sinuses which are resonating chambers for the larynx. Sounds as speech and song are made with the entire face and head; the vocal cords alone would be inaudible. Facial and cranial cavities (which are, in medical terminology, sinuses) serve as sounding boards and amplify the sounds from the larynx. If you have ever heard someone without teeth try to talk (or to sing!) you will understand the structural importance of head and face which work as sounding boards for the vocal cords.

Pressures of air which the singer controls affect volumes of sound and tonal qualities of singing. A loud tone, with rising pitch, is accomplished by vibrating very fast; but a loud tone, without rising pitch, is achieved by stronger pressure of air, increasing the amplifications of the vibration.

"Schools" or systems of training opera singers propound the theory that it is possible to direct a column of air into certain cavities, and not into others, to attain desired results in singing. Medical men consider this a physical impossibility but singers and their teachers insist that it is a valid method. The layman can change the "sound" of his own voice at will and, it seems to me, he does so by shutting off some passages or cavities to achieve a twang or a brogue or an inflection he deliberately seeks. I am not a singer but I do know that for certain languages one blocks off certain passages, the better to utilize others, as when one deliberately "talks through the nose."

To speak Russian, you must learn to enunciate in the hollow of your mouth (not from the throat) and the tongue is always pushed forward instead of held back in the mouth. For French, you must hold the organs of speech (lips, tongue, et cetera) taut; the upper lip must not be held tightly against the teeth, and the tongue must not be drawn too far backwards. The nasal French vowels (ã, ẽ, õ, œ̃) are produced by the vibrations of the air coming partly through the mouth, partly through the nose, not through the mouth only as for simple sounds.

Even when two languages are closely related, as with Portuguese and Brazilian, enunciations effect distinct changes in sounds. A clearer, slower and more harmonious enunciation (due in large part to the conservation of the timbre of unstressed vowels which Brazilian slurs or drops altogether) characterizes Portuguese. "American" is a new, versatile, exceedingly graphic derivation of "English," and, as any Englishman will tell you, it sounds altogether different from the mother-tongue.

Virtuoso singers have amazing agility and control because a virtuoso voice is one whose vocal cords will respond flexibly and speedily to the singer's commands or signals. How singers manage this is a veritable mystery, even to themselves; when asked, they resort to aesthetic abstraction and say they "feel" how to do it. Indeed, you *feel* how to make a sound when you speak, by making it in the front of your mouth, or the back, or in your nose, or deep in the glottis (which produces that horrid vocal sound called "glottid"). You know you are able to emit sounds from various parts of your face and head because your ear tells you the difference in these sounds. Just as, when listening to a vaudeville "imitator" we can hear him assume voices of well-known personalities, so perfectly that he is said to "sound" like the persons he is imitating.

If we accept (as I do) the opera singer's statement that he is able to move his voice about inside his face and head, then it is easy to understand what the various "schools" or systems of training voices propound as their methods of singing.

The Italian style, the oldest style of opera singing, does not force the sound out of the mouth but into the cavities of the face, the frontal sounding board of the larynx. The French term: *chanter dans le masque* (to sing in the face) expertly describes the method. Singers who adopt this method say that they literally feel the song vibrating inside their heads; they are singers who favor a bright tone.

The German school (which is favored by American opera singers, in the main) concentrates more on the throat and head cavities with a resulting sound called, variously, "hooded" and "hollow." A singer has explained to me that he hears the differences between the Italian and German singing as being *a*) in the "mask" or front of the face, very strong, clear and bright; and *b*) in the "hood" of the head and the "hollow" of the throat as being "from inside a tube," and of a "darker tone."

These effects are partially from individual control and partially from the singer's native aptitude. They may even have some relationship to national temperament; the Italian soprano Renata Tebaldi has a bright tone, while musicologists class the Polish soprano Elisabeth Schwarzkopf among the singers with the "hooded" tonal quality. Both singers are popular in American opera and present an excellent example of comparison between these two qualities of tone: that from the "mask" or facial resonance, and from the head and throat, or "hooded, hollow" resonance.

Could it be that the size and shape of a singer's head and face are dominant elements of the tone of his voice? And do the development and control of the vocal cords, for opera singing, have a physical effect on the larynx? Persons with very small sinuses are said to have little vocal resonance but when Francisco Tamagno (1850-1905) died and an autopsy was performed for the purpose of investigating his larynx, medical scientists could find no difference between the "voice box" of Verdi's great Otello and that of the ordinary man.

Equally unfathomable to the layman is the aspect of "control" by which singers throw or switch their voices when singing, moving the sound into the head, the throat or the "mask" of the face. Maria Callas in her best years was marvelous at this and made good use of it for spectacular dramatic effects.

The tensions which a singer exerts on his vocal cords are by other mysterious means, at least for the audience. Some singers can conserve the breath supply and close their vocal cords between notes; others, not so able, find that the breath has eased through the glottis before they have controlled their vocal cords. A violinist tunes his instrument by turning the pegs and trying the strings, again and again, until he has the instrument in tune—only then does he begin to play, and sometimes his instrument goes out of tune while he is playing, especially if damp temperature affects the strings. But the singer can find and fix tension on his vocal cords faster than it takes you to read this line. It is a matter of course to him when he is singing; it is, indeed, mind and matter working at the speed of thought.

To be truthful, very little is known about the human voice and most singers do not attempt to analyze, even to themselves, why they sing in certain ways, nor how they do so. A singer has expressed his greatest amazement to me as being not about the operatic voice but about the human voice; he finds it incomprehensible that persons without any vocal cords can still whisper!

Another source of wonder is pitch, when it is *perfect pitch*. Musicologists say it is a feat of memory; musicians, including singers, say it is a gift with which few are endowed. It is an unerring ability to recognize and produce (by singing, or on the instrument played) any given note, a sound established on the number of vibrations within a certain time, i.e. one second.

Every singer has a voice which is his alone. Unless you are remarkably knowledgeable about pianos, you will hardly be able to tell one famous maker's grand piano from another but when you listen to opera for only a short period you come to know the voices of the singers as well as you know the faces of your friends, and the handwriting of intimate correspondents. A voice's identity is first of all a matter of human personality and then a matter of "schooling" or training under a recognized system. But I adhere to the principle that the opera singer, like the ballet dancer, is first born, then made or trained. Bad teaching will destroy a potential singer or dancer but the best teacher in the world cannot succeed in creating a singer or a dancer from a being devoid of the talent of singing and dancing.

The audience must always be aware that in opera and ballet the artistes are not free and the performance is not impromptu; the artistes are technicians working within media which exact from them total or almost total acceptance of the presiding genius. For opera, the genius is the composer; for ballet, the choreographer. A "pop" singer need not have a voice at all if he has a winning personality and creates a style which makes audiences respond to him; the opera singer must be able to sing, and must be trained in a way of singing that is "operatic." (Just as the "interpretive" dancer may create any form of movement with or without music and accurately call it dance, but the ballet *danseur* must be trained in classical dance rules and with certain characteristics like aplomb, turn-out, et cetera, that qualify the ballet as an art form.)

If you dislike the human voice as an instrument you are unlikely to enjoy opera—however, many persons like the pomp and pageantry of opera even if they do not especially care for the art of singing. If you do like singing, of any kind, you will find opera singing fascinating of itself. Richard Strauss declared that the human voice was the most beautiful instrument of all and the one most difficult to play. The singer is his own instrument, one which is played by the singer, the opera composer and to great extent by the orchestra conductor. But as only certain sounds come from violins (different from the sounds that emanate from horns) so are voices limited to the human instruments, especially in range.

There are categories of vocal ranges common to ordinary human beings, which the opera singer develops to an extraordinary extent. But he is always set within his own range, with a few exceptions when he begins in one classification of singing and changes to another. "Light-baritones" may turn to tenors; sopranos into mezzo-sopranos.

In terminology for singing, there are three general classifications each for male and female voices.

The masculine range comprises: tenor, the highest; baritone, the middle; and bass (pronounced base) the lowest, deepest tone.

The feminine range comprises: soprano, the highest; mezzo-soprano, the middle; and contralto, the lowest, deepest tone.

To compare the human voice with the sounds of the piano keyboard, the ranges from high, light, clear tones to low, heavy, deep tones are approximately the same.

Since the human (as opposed to the mechanical means) of making music is a personal act, capacities and limitations affect opera singing. Three supernormal styles of singing are castrato, boy-soprano and coloratura. Equally rare is countertenor.

The *castrato* is now obsolete except by accident but his type was once considered the acme of singers. If we are to believe musicologists, a castrato voice is still unsurpassed. It was achieved for the male singer before puberty, when he underwent a surgical operation which severed the ducts in the testicles, resulting in these organs shriveling and the

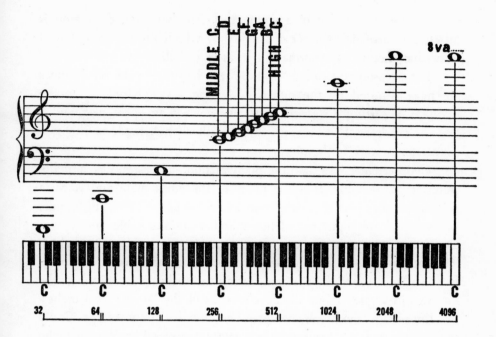

*Tenor* has a range of C below middle C to C above.

*Baritone,* generally G an octave and a half below G to F above.

*Bass,* from E two octaves below middle C to middle C and sometimes to low G.

*Soprano* is usually two octaves from middle C, and rising.

*Mezzo-soprano,* two octaves from A, sometimes reaching B flat.

*Contralto,* two octaves from F below C to F an octave and a half above.

male becoming incapable of siring children. Thereafter, his voice retained the sweet limpidity of pre-adolescence, sweeter, by far, than a woman's voice. *The Castrati in Opera* by Angus Heriot is a book devoted to the subject. A common error in thought is that the boys were made eunuchs by full castration. In fact, the *castrati* were gentlemen of potent charms and some of them were Don Juans of the restless ardor of Mozart's hell-bent Don Giovanni. In range, the castrato voice exceeded the tenor and soprano ranges.

*Boy-soprano,* as implied, is the range of a pre-adolescent male and occasionally a woman singer, of soprano range, is so classified, meaning she has the clear treble of a young boy. Another type of soprano is *falsetto,* an artificial manner of singing by which the larynx is forced to produce notes above normal pitch, as in yodelling.

For a reason best called "operatic" the higher, clearer voice ranges are most admired by the majority of composers, giving rise to the tradition of casting a soprano as the heroine of an opera plot, and a tenor as the hero. However, it is not a 20th century mode to choose a countertenor voice for heroic and romantic roles.

*Countertenor* is a natural phenomenon, as castrato is a deliberately contrived one. It is the range of the adult male alto voice; a voice which does not change at puberty but remains, in an adult male, as the clear, high-pitched, delicate and vibratoless voice of a boy. Musicologists say that it was the countertenor's lovely voice which brought the castrati into fashion, because a countertenor is very rare. It was a voice especially admired during the early opera era when the lute was in vogue, before the development of the large, varied orchestra. Lute-songs, madrigals, cantatas and folk ballads were specifically composed for the countertenor by early composers like Purcell (who was himself a countertenor) and Monteverdi, Bach and Handel. The parts originally written for the countertenors and castrati were later sung by contraltos.

Singing as countertenor is almost a lost art except that occasionally some natural phenomena produces new countertenors who revive interest in the voice. Most recently such revived interest has come from the voices of the American countertenor Russell Oberlin and the English countertenor Alfred Deller.

Musicologists say that there is no voice quite like that of the countertenor and no sound so intrinsically musical. Scholes says that it is chiefly cultivated in Britain where church music and glees provide compositions for its use. It is more often heard in the performance of oratorio and cantata than in opera.

Countertenor may be a freak of a voice but its possessor is not a freak as a man. It is not the voice of a transvestite or an abnormally sexed or undersexed male. Normally, at puberty, a boy's voice changes owing to the sudden and unequal growth of the various parts of the vocal cords and other parts of the sound-producing apparatus—and to ensure the boy's voice remaining alto surgery was formerly effected on his testicles. But it appears that in some instances a boy passes puberty without voice change and becomes a countertenor; he develops normally in every other way. Deller is a big man (6 feet, 2 inches tall and over two hundred pounds in weight) and the father of two sons and a daughter; one son, Mark, is also a countertenor. He accounts for his countertenor voice by the fact that he sang in the church choir from the age of ten to sixteen, that his voice was not trained and that it never "broke" or changed from boyhood.

*Coloratura soprano* is a voice in the soprano range which is trained to perform feats of song through pitch, resonance and control. This type of singer is a vocal acrobat, in the same way as the virtuoso ballerina is one in dance and their "feats" are pyrotechnical displays in opera and ballet. These artistes are prodigies and they have unusual charm for the opera and ballet audience because of the sheer excitement their performances generate. Opera history is marked by the era of the coloratura, as ballet history is marked by that of the virtuoso dancer. Neither artiste is very popular with orchestra conductors for opera and ballet, and some composers and choreographers abhor them and their gifts—but many a composer and a choreographer have made good use of these magnificent freaks and promoted entire careers on aptitudes for composing operas and ballets to show them off to best advantage.

The primary difference in operatic voices lies in the masculine and feminine ranges. A man's vocal cords are longer than a woman's, to begin with, and he is generally bigger physically. These differences matter a great deal because the human body is the living instrument of voice production or vocalization.

The physical aspect of singing extends through the demeanor or outward appearance of the opera artiste. He does not stand or move (any more than he speaks and sings) in an ordinary way (he is not "of the street" or common, daily life), but with the distinctions which make him an opera singer, even before he puts on the costume for the opera role he is singing.

The exercise of the operatic voice (with its ensuing exercise of the opera singer's whole body) sometimes develops a characteristic person. The figure, especially in the chest, back and throat, is more developed than the layman's. The extreme of this development is noted in Wagnerian singers because Wagner's operas require powerful voices, usually contained in powerfully built men and women. The modern vogue for slender divas has compelled opera singers, gender: female, to shed the excessive avoirdupois of divas from an older era, but the opera singer "look" is still a characteristic—just as is the ballet dancer's "waddle" or crotch-sprung gait from the ballet turn-out of hip, knee and foot.

An actor may "look the part" to be type-cast in a play. The opera singer must sound the part of the role in the opera. Composers have adopted a formula that we might compare to that of Western folk art in literature, painting or movies. In the "typical Western" the hero is manly and comely in person and of exaggerated chivalry in demeanor (if more to his horse than his lady love) whereas the villain is sour in mood and harsh in attitude. The way these two sound (when they speak or sing), as well as behave and look, impresses the audience's ear and eye—and the "typical Western" has practiced its formula so graphically that a "Western" movie, for example, barely requires dialogue for it to convey its meaning as plot and characterizations. Foreign language audiences attend English-spoken "American Western" movies with ease, unaware of every English word-meaning, but thoroughly able to follow the sense of all that is said and acted.

Composers tend to cast tenors as heroes and sopranos as heroines, against baritones as villains, and mezzo-sopranos as the "other" women in love triangles. Only infrequently is a contralto the heroine and the bass the hero of an opera—although the bass is often the voice for a heroic role. This is not a hard and fast rule but a generalization.[9] However, in *Aida* for example, this tradition is observed, and to the extent where the Pharaoh is a bass but the Ethiopian king (kings are usually bass), being of rather villainous bent, is a baritone—a good contrast, musically, with the high priest and the Pharaoh.

As composers are concerned with drama as well as musical composition the singer works in three correlated styles: in his voice range (more or less, his natural voice); in his school or system of training; and in the emotion or temperament of the role in the opera. The emotional or dramatic divisions in voice ranges are lyric and dramatic, generally pertaining to tenor and soprano. The classification of "coloratura" is emotional and physical. Italians break voice range and style into well-defined divisions and their meanings are the best definitions for the operatic voice.

*Tenor* (from Latin *tenere*: to hold) is the highest non-falsetto male voice with the lightest tone. *Leggiero* is a very high, light voice, suited to comic roles; *lirico* is light but not so high; *lirico spinto* clear and high but the heaviest of the three. The lyric tenor (of which type the two greatest 20th century singers were Enrico Caruso and Benia-mino Gigli) is the chief romantic voice and is distinguished by high, bright tones, and a liquid or fluid style which makes singing appear effortless and spontaneous. The *tenore robusto* or heroic tenor is even heavier and more dramatic than the middle tenor range usually thought of as "dramatic" tenor. *Heldentenor* is the term used in Germany for the tenor who sings with dramatic vigor and, usually, profound emotion.

Comparatively, the female voice as soprano has the four types of *leggiero, lirico, lirico spinto* and *drammatico,* the last being the dramatic soprano. In addition, the female singer may be *coloratura* as the acme of the soprano range and class.

*Coloratura* is literally "colored music or song." Color comes in part from the singer's natural voice and from its training. Operatic termin-ology classifies thin, dry voices as "white," meaning that such voices have little depth or feeling as "color." The "white" voice is inclined to be mechanical and is a "coloring" to be noted in the deaf, who speak from a mechanical mastery, not by ear. In short, a "white" voice does not have the resonance and the fullness of the voices which combine diction and expression so marvelously that voice has "color" as music has "color."

In every opera singers must "color" their voices for the role or characterization.[10] Singers can no more put into words what they *do* when they consciously color their voices than dancers can express to the layman how they manage, as it seems, to rise into the air and stay there long enough to turn around, beat their legs together, place their bodies in positions different to how they stood on the ground, and then, apparently with superhuman ease, descend (not fall down) after exe-cuting these pyrotechnics of dance. It is the artistic nature as well as the technical expertness which permits opera singers and ballet dancers to perform their work. And it is the mysterious affinity between these, inexpressible by the artiste and bewildering to laymen, which keeps the theatre truly magical, as it was from its start in antiquity.

"Coloring" is in effect all through operatic singing, in every voice range, but it is the *coloratura* soprano who is classed as the most brilliantly "colored" of all. *Coloratura* singing is wordless or usually wordless and is pure song as the symphony is pure music; it is generally utilized by the composer of the opera to embroider a theme or emotion. Originally, *coloratura* singing was extravagant frill or unnecessary ornamentation and a singer able to sing *coloratura* was apt to break into runs and trills and tricky twists and turns, musically, anywhere in a role, simply to capture the audience's attention and win applause from the claques.

Most of opera singing entails the pronunciation of words and therefore diction is a part of operatic training for the singer. This is not ordinary diction, either in the actual singing or the recitative, and in the "patter songs" which some composers employ for effect.

Pure musical notes are not enough in singing; the singer must properly enunciate the verse and he does so primarily by the pronunciation of vowel sounds. In ordinary speech, we require very little change in the movements of tongue and lips for the vowel sounds but in opera the singer must practice diligently to produce what is termed "pure vowels." Consonants do not play as important a part as vowels since they appear usually at the introduction or ending of a note. The vowels accompany notes throughout their lengths and a distortion of the *usual* or *ordinary* vowel sound is inevitable. For instance, the sound *ee* is not easily sustained on a very high note and a diphthong (with most of the breath and stress on the first part) is substituted, by which the sound *oi* (almost sounding like *aw*) precedes a very short *ee*. For this and other technical reasons operatic singing is not like the more ordinary forms of song and not at all like common or everyday speech. The way in which he is obliged to *speak*, as well as to sing, qualifies the opera artiste's voice when he performs for his audience.

Singers are to great extent the tools or instruments of the composer, although singers have tyrannized opera, just as dancers have subjugated the ballet. We are apparently in the epoch of the composer and choreographer, an era in which the artistes are compelled to obey the dictates of opera composers and ballet choreographers. This is a triumph of art over personalities, a turn of the wheel which may, one of these decades, turn full round and put the prima donna or the prima ballerina at the top of their contemporary theatre, where they have stood before now.

Composers are explicit in their requirements of singers, who are asked to sing in various ways—*affettuoso,* with passion; *amabile*: amiably, tenderly; *capriccioso*: in a humorous or whimsical manner; *dolce*: sweetly; *con dolore*: mournfully; *furioso*: stormily; *grazioso*: with grace; *maestoso*: majestically; *secco*: drily; *serioso*: seriously, solemnly, et cetera. These directions are not only applied to the musical technicalities but also to the emotional and dramatic expression. Thus, *vivace* means to quicken tempo and also to express vivaciously.

Usually, the composer relinquishes his opera into the authority of the director and the conductor of the orchestra. The singers are under as many as three chains of command. They are seldom tractable, always preferring to interpret a role according to their ideas instead of the composer's, the director's and the conductor's. An opera in rehearsal is apt to be *furioso* and *tumultuoso* rather than *moderato*: with moderation. Rows between singers and conductors or composers are legend, one of the oldest and most amusing being that between Handel and the prima donna Cuzzoni. She was very temperamental and Handel, none too even-tempered himself, had put himself out to write a special aria for her to sing in one of his operas. When she arrived in London she refused to sing it. Handel, exasperated, seized her and held her outside a window, declaring he would drop her unless she agreed to sing his aria. He made her writhe in mid-air until she did consent, whereupon he dragged her back inside. Cuzzoni sang the aria, but we are not told if she did so *piacevole*: in a graceful, pleasant manner.

Many a composer and conductor has cried that life would be happier without a tenor, said to be the most fractious of singers. But few operas can do without a tenor and no opera could be without its singers because opera is made to be sung.

# Notes

1. Opera's conventions, which include manners and speech, are as valid and viable as the conventions for Shakespearean drama. Actors practice a delivery and demeanor, and a manner of speech (in meters, et cetera) conventional to Shakespearean plays, and the "verse" in this kind of drama is not rhymed. It has, also, to be uttered in ways which make it speech within the Shakespearean dramatic form. Accept opera's conventions as true to opera, in the same way as you accept Shakespearean drama conventions as being true to that kind of play.

2. *La Bohème's* libretto is derived from a novel by Henri Murger: *Scènes de la vie de Bohème*, romantically describing the Parisian bohemians of the 1830's, artists and poets and their on-the-fringe world—a sort of "beat" generation. "Mimi Pinson" was the "Jane Doe" or archtypical Paris midinette, hence the pet-name of "Mimi" for Puccini's wistful heroine, whose name was really Lucia, because she earned her living sewing (embroidering flowers) for the rich. "Mimi Pinson" was a French colloquialism for any poor little young woman of the class of Puccini's heroine and the favorite topic of tavern songs by a tune-smith named Pierre Jean Béranger (1780–1857) whose ditties about "Mimi Pinson" were "pop" songs in Paris into post-World War I. "Mimi Pinson" lived "under the eaves with the sparrows" in the attic world of the romantic wretches who painted, wrote poetry and, as the Parisians said, "caught the Devil by the tail" in order to exist. Puccini and his librettists, Giuseppe Giacosa and Luigi Illica, caught "Mimi Pinson" and her world and imprisoned them in the drama in music that is *La Bohème*.

3. Also, every now and then a composer makes several characters stop what they have been doing and gather together to sing their surprise, indignation or delight about what has been going on, as Rossini does, to excellent effect, in *The Barber of Seville*, end of Act I. These tableaux or set pieces allow ensembles and choruses to punctuate the dramatic action, increasing emotional tensions either by making the comedy more risible or the tragedy more poignant.

4. Wagner tucked his orchestra away under the stage but when you attend Wagnerian opera you are likely to find the orchestra in the pit. Wagner built a theatre for the presentation of his works but opera houses are for all kinds of opera, not solely the Wagnerian. Modern opera, or theatre pieces that resemble the opera form, are not included in the span of this book but here it is useful to note that some contemporary composers like Igor Stravinsky and Arnold Schönberg made such extraordinary demands within their forms of opera that equal demands were made of the stage, with unconventional results. If you attend a performance of Stravinsky's *L'Histoire du Soldat* in a theatre you should

know that the composer created it to be performed at fairs or in barns and that its original primitive setting has to be deliberately assumed on stage. On stage will appear the cast, which is Narrator, Soldier, Devil and Princess, with the Narrator seated at a table with a glass and a bottle of wine and across from him, on the other end of the stage, the orchestra: violin, double bass, clarinet, bassoon, cornet, trombone and percussion. Instead of changing scenery to mark changes in scene a few props are shifted about. Stravinsky's *Renard* (The Fox) and *Les Noces* (The Marriage) are in pantomime and dance as well as in an "opera" form. But despite improvisations in form, opera's usual orchestral placement is in the pit, sunk in front of the stage.

5. It is unusual to hear two actors making separate statements together in a play but it is common in opera for two or more singers to sing simultaneously about separate things. Sometimes, they have the same vocal line but different words to sing; other times, ensembles sing the same words to different vocal strands—an example being in Verdi's *La Traviata*, before the heroine's death scene. *La Bohème, Act III*, has four characters singing simultaneously,  two pairs of lovers—one quarrelling jealously; the other madly happy and warbling sweetly. These divergent statements in opera do not confuse the audience because the total result is valid to opera. Moreover, its complexity enriches the scene, enhancing it dramatically and musically.

6. The chorus and ensemble in an opera may be used a great deal, to sing a lot of music and perform great dramatic services—or may be allocated small parts; all depending on the composer's design and also on the requirements of the libretto. In some operas, ensembles or chorus have only a few bars of music, at a time. But in many an opera the chorus undertakes a major obligation, as in *The Mastersingers of Nuremberg* when it provides a midnight brawl on a city street. In the sum of opera, ensemble and chorus are important parts, together with solo and duet.

7. Wagner, a positive man, elected to write his own libretti and in our time Menotti is notable for doing the same. Occasionally, a composer who writes his own libretto achieves the remarkable success of Leoncavallo with *Pagliacci*; more usually, the best achievement is in rapport between the literary and musical composers such as marked the relationships of Gluck and Calzabigi, Mozart and Da Ponte, and Verdi and Boito. Such rapport is rare and patience and toil are the next best means for the collaboration. Writing a libretto is not as easy as writing a play, since every word has to be sung as well as spoken. Hofmannshal, Richard Strauss' able librettist, was lauded by that composer in these words: "When I say that you are a born librettist, I mean it as the highest possible compliment, for I hold that it is far more difficult to write a good libretto than a good play." Operatic diction has to be characteristic and appropriate and of a sort that can be sung easily and well; it should make sense as it is uttered and it should have a certain subtlety as well as a lucidity or clearness of expression. A libretto is first composed on an idea or plot and then worked on or organized into acts, and also into solos, duets, ensembles. Throughout, the librettist is mindful of the fact that he must propel the dramatic action from start to finish. It is the composer who decides what kind of voice will sing each role or character's part and if he chooses he will have the same voice range for several

roles; in *Der Rosenkavalier* Strauss has three sopranos for leading roles. Together, librettist and composer work up to and then away from climax, because the opera is a theatre presentation and as such must be theatrically produced for best effects in its form—this form being that of drama in music.

8. The flamboyant conductor is a 19th century innovation in opera. Hans von Bülow (1830–1894), an associate of Wagner, was the first virtuoso, as personality and conductor. The 20th century has not yet produced one to match the towering figure of Arturo Toscanini (1867–1957) who for more than fifty years, before and after World War I, ruled Milan's La Scala as few kings then ruled realms. There he established standards for opera performances never again realized and, as conductor, gave Italy another golden age of opera. Between 1908 and 1915 he was conductor for the Metropolitan Opera in New York where he attempted to institute his own high operatic standards but gave up because of ceaseless battles with temperamental singers. His life (longer by two years than Verdi's) and times are a source of valuable reference.

9. Lady Macbeth, one of the wickedest women in theatre, is a dramatic soprano in Verdi's *Macbeth* as are Wagner's "good" girls Isolde and Brünnhilde in *Tristan und Isolde* and *The Ring*. The evil Queen of the Night in Mozart's *The Magic Flute* is a coloratura, and in *Rigoletto* Verdi's Duke, an utter cad, is a role for a tenor voice of exceptional sweetness.

10. This general statement must not be misconstrued to mean that any kind of voice can be "colored" to sing a role. The lower the voice, the richer the tone in the sense that the tone is "fuller." And roles are "interpreted" by different kinds of voices as well as different ranges of song. For instance, the role of Mimi in *La Bohème* requires a different sort of soprano voice than Cio-Cio-San's in *Madama Butterfly* and if the same singer is performing both roles in repertory she must change the emotional and, to extent, the actual sort of voice from Mimi's "fruity, quite a lot sexier" voice style (as a singer has told me) than the sweetly innocent voice for Cio-Cio-San. Read what Caruso had to say about his voice and how he colored and "interpreted" his roles, as in *This Business of Singing* by Pierre Key. Caruso describes himself as keeping several voices in drawers "And when I am to sing Radames, I take out of one drawer my Radames voice. It is heavy and dramatic in fibre." Caruso, another realistic Italian like Verdi, spoke realistically of "weight" and "color" in voice, making singing a physical as well as a musical fact. Caruso, incidentally, started as a baritone and changed to singing tenor, as did Jean de Reszke and Lauritz Melchior. Reversely, the American baritone Leonard Warren began his operatic career as a tenor.

# ❧ F I V E ❧

# Opera After Gluck

The centuries of opera tradition are divided into epochs, principally the baroque, classical and new or contemporary forms. Baroque is the term for music before Mozart, extending from the High Renaissance, about 1600, into mid-18th century. This music was in character polyphonic and its culmination occurred in two eras, one preceding the Camerata and the other issuing from Johann Sebastian Bach, contemporary of Handel and Rameau and in every way their peer—except that he did not write opera. It is of the Age of Bach that musicians speak, referring to the renaissance of polyphony.

Bach was born at Eisenach March 21, 1685, and died at Leipzig July 28, 1750, and is called the great Leipzig cantor. Some opera historians omit him from the story of opera. On the contrary, I believe that we should know as much as possible about him and the music he made the better to understand opera after Gluck and opera emanating from Mozart.

The famous sons of Bach were Carl Philipp Emanuel Bach, who was taken by Haydn as his master; and Johann Christian Bach (referred to as "the London Bach") who exerted influence on Mozart. With Bach's death in 1750 one epoch came to an end and another began, in which music assumed a form called homophonic.

The new mode of music and opera in the 19th century was called "classical," and is so differentiated from the earlier form called "baroque." In the 20th century yet another mode came into being, and this is what we speak of as being "modern" or "new" music because it is in and of our times.

The second important opera epoch, that called "classical," coincided with the development of German opera and is insoluble with German music *per se*. For an understanding of "classical" music the reader must research histories of music, there noting the developments of "the Mannheim school" in Germany and "the Viennese school" in Austria. For our purposes in this book it is necessary to note that the baroque yielded to the classical form in the 19th century and that an opera qualified as "new" to its times (the 19th century) was formed within and after the age of Mozart. Thereafter, the opera tradition fell into opera before Gluck, and opera after Gluck.

To discuss music not of our times as "old" and to describe it as "old-fashioned" betrays the utmost naïveté. And when you approach opera you must not think of it in these terms but as "pre-classical," before Gluck; as "classical" after Haydn, Mozart and Beethoven; and as "modern" where and when it changes from the Baroque and Classical forms into the forms atypical of the 20th century.[1]

Another, more valid name than "modern" will eventually describe this atypical 20th century music because it, in time, will recede into the past, there to stand with the Baroque and the Classical. For a thing is "modern" only while it is in and of its times and the thing assumes a title in order to be categorized among the records of the ever-accumulating past.

We are living in the 20th century and the arts that are created here and now, in our place and time, are "of" our world. When they are original or experimental in form and style they are authentically "new" and when they are in an older, known form and style they are of that form and style. An opera maker in the 1960's can produce a valid Baroque or Classical work simply by assuming a form and style of that period.

The materials of opera are music and drama and the formal "shape" of the sounds of opera rely on instrumentation and voice range and style. Basic concepts for music are melody, rhythm and harmony; tempo, dynamics and expression. This book is not an "introduction to music" and I will not attempt an explanation of musical terminology here, except to extract from it just sufficient information to show you how the *shape of sound* altered between the Baroque and Classical ages, affecting opera's formal musical structure. At the same time, you must conceive of the ideological changes which affected the meaning and style, and the actual verse or literary part of opera. Since music and verse are the absolutes of opera the opera makers must always work in both forms. And as fashions change and experiments are continuously attempted opera most naturally evolves from epoch to epoch. But what is strange and new in any time or "age" is, in its time, modern. Thus, Hindemith and Stravinsky were "modern," and, in his time, Caccini was "modern."

Comparisons are said to be odious and they are never more so, and more untenable, than in opera. It is not only wrong but also ridiculous to compare Monteverdi with Verdi for the reason that these two composers worked with different materials, essentially in different forms, to design opera.[2] The "materials" of opera are vocal and instrumental music. In *The Beginning* I briefly outlined the kind of opera that was made in the art's earliest tradition: that of the Camerata, the Venetian and the Neapolitan which we call the early Italian opera. This (as I have described in *The Beginning*) was the opera art that circulated through the Western nations (the Christian nations are the founders and developers of opera) and assumed some "national" forms or traditions. The first of these were French and German and the three oldest and primary opera forms are the Italian, French and German.

Between the 18th and 19th century, between the opera before and the opera after Gluck, there occurred a revolution in music by which opera altered from its baroque style and assumed a classical style. The "baroque" and "classical" appellations for opera are rather more than terms indicating periods of time; they are also terms which describe the outward form, the principles of opera as evidence of the inner or spiritual motivations of the two styles.

"Baroque" is a word of unknown origin, apparently nothing more than a mnemonic device for cataloguing art works of a certain style. But usage has to great extent deprived the term of its explicitness, since a "baroque pearl" is one of rough or uneven shape (however, still of authentic pearly lustre) and the "baroque" in architecture is a style in florid taste. The music that we call (since about 1818) Baroque was basically spare and pure of form. You have only to return to the operas of Gluck, stripped of the superfluous and inane, to resurrect the baroque.

I should like to give you some understanding of opera after Gluck, so that you know the basic principles by which opera changed from the baroque to the classical. Within the "classical" period there was an age or style called "romantic," of which more here, in due course. But if you are to understand clearly what opera was after Mozart you must know enough to compare it with music before him, and the opera as it was played and sung, constructed or "shaped as sound" and as a theatre art, before Gluck. For opera, like Medieval man, accumulated a past as well as a present.

In *The Beginning* you have a bare knowledge of the commencement and very early evolution of opera and you should, I think, relate opera's development and evolution to the historical eras in which these were formed, the better to understand how opera came to be, and why; where and when it was composed, by whom, and within what major influences. When Gluck died, opera did not come to an end but in the French Revolution (1789-1799) the world that Europeans knew when Gluck was born ended, never to begin again. Gluck, if he had been a philosopher as well as a composer (as Rousseau was) should have seen the ending of his world. Had he lived to hear of his royal patroness' death Gluck should have known without the shadow of a doubt that his world had indeed come to an end and with it old ideas and ideals, as a predominant one concerning the holiness of the persons of kings. And gods, as well as kings, were in disrepute.

Two tremendous civil revolutions shook the Western nations in one century (the American, 1775-1783, is romantically assumed to have inspired the French to their doctrine of the Rights of Man) and when the earthquakes ceased the world itself fell into new patterns, unfamiliar design in social castes, and in radical philosophies and "modern" attitudes and behavior. France, from the peak of absolutism under Louis XIV, moved through revolt by reason, and revolt of the *philosophes* against authority (Rousseau being the trumpet voice in his *Social Contract*) into, at length, revolt by anarchy. Could Gluck have conceived that a people as frivolous as the French, with such a love of wit and humor, so much sophistication—people who prided themselves on the virtue of being reasonable rather than being right—would turn into an unkempt mob which would drench France in blood for a decade?

The war between the French was an ideological as well as a physical one. The American and French revolutions were undertaken like crusades, by which the human masses made their hopes and purposes known to the few who had elected or had inherited positions of awesome power over the lot of the majority.

Wars of this kind, and especially the civil war of the French Revolution, changed the character of the Western world far more than the wars of the 20th century, which changed the geographical face of Europe.

Absolute power, as held by kings, vanished from France—and France had from the reign of Louis XIV set the mold for civilized European society. Even French vices become the mode. And although the French *philosophes* were originally inspired by foreigners, chief among them being the English Hume, it was the French philosophy which prevailed after the French Revolution and influenced all European society.

Louis XV, the strange great-grandson of Louis XIV (strange because his character was one of such complexities) foresaw the end of his world as did Mme. de Pompadour, who said: *Après nous le déluge*. The War of the Austrian Succession (1740-1748) and France's luckless Seven Year War (1774-1792) occurred early in the reign of Empress Maria Theresa (1740-1780), in time to indicate for the philosophers the approaching end of one world or sort of life and the beginning of another. We may be certain that artistes were then as now more engrossed in the arts than in politics, so that it is easy to understand how shockingly brusque the end of the epoch appeared to those who survived it. Autocracy was not entirely crushed in the age of "enlightenment," but while Maria Theresa was autocratically the Empress of Austria she was not the ruler of Germany—and her husband, Francis I, although Emperor of the Holy Roman Empire was not the Emperor of Austria. Austria was part of the Holy Roman Empire, but Croatia, Hungary, Transylvania, et cetera were not. These historical facts have to be recalled, to understand the new wave of "nationalism" in the arts and in opera, emergent in the "romanticism" of the 19th century. Religious arguments and schisms, and secret societies were part of the new epoch.[3]

If you wonder what these revolutions, physical and philosophic, had to do with opera, the answer is: everything. The revolution in society was matched by a revolution in the arts, and music and poetry, the materials from which operas are made, were radically altered. The poets Goethe and Schiller exerted powerful influences and directly on opera, for which both wrote libretti. Music underwent an enormous rebellion, the monophonic against the polyphonic form, and opera seemed to a great many persons (Rossini among them) to become so corrupted by "new" and radical styles that it was in danger of perishing as an art form.

Freemasonry, far removed as that might appear to be from opera, was near enough for Mozart's *The Magic Flute* to be taken as an operatic treatise on this secret society and the papal and empirical reactions against it.

"Nationalism" and "romanticism" are aspects of 19th century opera but opera is not isolated in these ideologies; they were symptomatic of the age for all the Western nations, for their philosophy and psychology, their theatre and creative arts.

The history books inform us that nationalism was the doom of three empires but the saviour of two nations, serving to unify Germany and Italy and institute political order among individual states. The liberal, democratic and republican climate of Europe after Gluck (and Marie Antoinette) bred individualism in thought and act. Ideally, the individual had freedom to create and express and this state of mind bred an aesthetically romantic estate. The "new" men of 19th century Europe (an "age" which began long before the year 1800 and may be said to have been in embryo in the mid-18th century) gloried in personal achievement. The age (particularly after the French Revolution and the Napoleonic wars) was that of the virtuoso, from which came Mozart and Beethoven, and, later, the unparallelled virtuoso pianists Chopin and Liszt (born exactly 20 months apart, Chopin, February 22, 1810; Liszt, October 22, 1811), the latter occupying the whole romantic period from Beethoven into Wagner, whom he survived by three years.

"Romanticism" was the underlying philosophy of what Victor Hugo called 'liberalism in literature,' and Heinrich Heine a 'reawakening of medieval poetry,' and both these writers were "romantics," as was Sir Walter Scott—and, also, as was the Shakespearean renaissance. In music, Beethoven was the preceptor of romanticism for composers like Berlioz, Weber and Wagner, and also for Franz Schubert, Mendelssohn, Robert Schumann, Chopin and Liszt.

The "classical" and the "romantic" eras overlapped to such degree that many musicologists use the terms as antonyms. For our purposes in understanding what they signified in opera let it be seen that the "classical" denoted a style more objective than personal; more universal as art than individual as expression.

The dominantly "classical" composers excelled in mastery of form and clarity of musical presentation. Their uses of musical idioms became the conventions of the "classical" mode. They were more restrained, emotionally, than the purely "romantic" composers.

Poets, philosophers, novelists and musicians of a totally "romantic" nature were uninhibited in expression—they may be said to be the "progressive classicists" in that they, too, invented new modes for expressing artistic ideologies, as the 19th century classicists did in rebellion against those preceding. The literary Romantics encouraged and even urged the music of their times to be "romantic" or emotionally free and expressive—the absolute opposite of being formal and restrained. Music was conceived as "the language of the emotions" and as such was the most eloquent one for the Romantic credo. Manners and mores had altered drastically and what would before then have been considered in bad taste was the vaunted style. The rage to express and to be heard or seen in their works, which moved 19th century artistes, was the same one which made Rousseau cry: "I am different from all men I have seen. If I am not better at least I am different."[4]

Allied with this striking sense of individuality was the universal romance of sensual love and all it betokened—chivalry, sacrifice, passion, et cetera, from the sublimest virtue to the basest vice. The "romantic" operas were essentially about men and women and their human characters, desires and deeds. It was also, in one branch, opera of the fantastic, drawing on folklore of the supernatural, returning to the deeply rooted belief of Medieval peoples that Elements, as well as spirits and earthly or corporeal beings, occupied the world. The 19th century Romantics treated this awesome idea with sweet and occasionally sickening sentiment; at its best, it created the charming other-worldly operas of Weber, who (after Mozart) is the creator of German opera. Both Mozart and Weber drew on the *Singspiel* for the evolution of a true German tradition, and Weber advocated poetry of fantasy and myth which gave his works a wholly different character from *opéra comique* or other styles "new" to the first, formal and Italian opera.

Weber was a pupil of Haydn and he followed Hoffmann, the eccentric genius of opera, and in his time Weber was an exceedingly important composer. Unfortunately, his pretty operas, of which the masterwork is *Der Freischutz* (The Marksman), are unfamiliar in English-speaking theatres but if you trace the development of German opera and the rise of the "romantic" and "national" movements in art you will find Weber an influential source for all three.[5]

Wagner, in his own forms and styles, elaborated on Weber's original principles, by composing operas in German libretti, turning to myth for inspiration and as the basis of his "Elemental" or symbolical dramas, and assuming a ruggedly "national" character for German opera. Wagnerian examples of "romanticism" of Weber's supernatural spirit are *The Flying Dutchman* and the operas from the Arthurian saga, and also *The Ring*; and, of Weber's tender if less dramaturgical expression of "nationalism," Wagner's *The Mastersingers of Nuremberg*.

While the "isms" (romantic and national, et cetera) were taking shape in opera, opera's means of shaping sound as music was undergoing enormous change through new, revolutionary techniques called "harmonics." *Harmonics* are artificial notes, partial tones, with delicate, vibrant sounds. They were made by avant-garde musicians on new instruments (like the piano and horn) and by daring innovations on older instruments, like the strings.[6] These new sounds in music were strange and they were controversial. They caused as much pro and anti discussion in 19th century music as has been caused in 20th century music. Music seemed new because the development of *harmonics* and other "unnatural" sounds were in theory and in *shape of sound* different than music of older epochs.

Before opera's richest evolution, in the 19th century, music was *polyphonic* and its culmination as a form is to be observed in the works of Handel and Bach. Homophony, or homophonic music, the antithesis of polyphony, and harmonics were the principles to which 19th century composers were dedicated, outraging former and older musical principles. Thus, a new kind of opera was made or shaped.

Monteverdi worked in the period of time and with the materials then available for early opera and all the composers within that epoch (the Baroque) were compelled to work within the physical limitations of their materials. I have shown something of the evolution of the orchestra so that you could understand the different means by which composers "shaped the sound" of music. I have told you how opera moved from the Camerata's concept (in chamber, *in camera*) to a public theatre, a specifically designed opera house—and in so doing acquired a greater volume in sound.

The very fact that singers had to sing louder, and instrumentalists had to make more noise or play music of greater volume, helped to alter opera. The countertenor and the *castrato* were singers developed for the Baroque epoch, during an era when stringed instruments were the vogue and the violin and the harpsichord the primaries of the orchestra. Recall that Lully worked in a court theatre where the king's 24 violins were primary in the orchestra and that in one era (into Beethoven's time) the conductor of the orchestra marked tempo on the organ or harpsichord, playing with one hand and beating time with the other. (Refer here, to refresh your memory, to pages 83-84, *The Orchestra* in *Opera: What It Is . . . .*) Some of the changes during Gluck's time and after materially altered the form of opera and the "shape of the sound" of music.

Gluck banished the harpsichord from the orchestra and placed therein these instruments: piccolo, harp, trombone, bass drums, cymbals, side-drum and triangle. Gluck was a genius at orchestration and he instituted the orchestra in a paramount role for opera, disciplined the role of the vocalist, and established for opera a continuity or flow of music. His principles refined the existing and prevailing mode, in which the Italian opera had assumed some of the most florid styles of art, chiefly out of the individual singer or instrumentalist striving in extemporaneous solo exhibitions. But Gluck was not an inventor; he was a reformer.

A new style of orchestral music, the new roles equated by Gluck for orchestra and singers, developed a new style of opera. For the plain reason that countertenor and *castrati* roles were no longer composed, singers were trained within the voice ranges conventional in 19th and 20th century opera. It was the simple reason of cessation in demand causing cessation in supply. Nowadays, when such 17th century operas are revived the roles composed for countertenors and *castrati* have to be performed by contraltos, women with a voice range deeper than soprano.

Gluck's reforms were not absolutely and abruptly instituted but gradually and most notably when Wagner championed their validity for opera, but Gluck is the composer who stands, conveniently, as a significant change in style for opera.

Mozart is in the next epoch and as he was a remarkably individual genius he is not considered to "descend from" another composer (Handel may be seen as a direct descendant of Scarlatti) nor to have started a musical dynasty as did Erik Satie (1866-1925).[7] Mozart occupied an epoch of his own.

What is necessary to note for opera is that Mozart and all who followed him in the 19th century possessed materials with which to make the "classical" opera tradition. Opera had been formed, the symphony orchestra (which is the opera orchestra) had evolved, composers had toiled to balance the merits of drama and music and unite them as one for opera art, and a social and philosophic revolution exerted influence on arts and artists. In short, the Baroque Age ended (the world of the Western nations changed) and opera after Gluck became the "classical" mode of the 19th century.

These, in brief, are the reasons why Monteverdi opera is different from Verdi opera, and why the shape of the sound of music altered between the Baroque and Classical epochs. When you continue to trace the course of music and opera you discover that there are reasons why the music of Mozart is different than the music of Gustav Mahler,[8] reasons as sound and explicable as why Gounod's opera is not in the style of Gluck's, although both composers were working in a musical art medium.

Accept the fact that composers are different and that epochs in art and society give way to other succeeding epochs, and for these reasons opera changes in form and style. Major changes occurred in opera, the chief of which we must now note.

Baroque music (like modern music) had freely flowing melody. Classical music laid out melody harmonically (harmony is a theory of chords). It was as though in musical architecture the style had changed; the structure or composition had assumed a new style. Melody, rhythm and harmony are three basic elements for constructing or composing music, qualified (when sung or played) by tempo, dynamics, expression, and so on. *Tempi* (measures of speed) indicate the speeds at which a piece of music is performed and the terminology (*allegro*, *adagio*) which is common to us in the 20th century was established by the Italians in the baroque epoch. When in 1812 a mechanic in Vienna invented an instrument for the exact determination of tempo, music acquired the metronome. Meanwhile, a number of instruments had come into use, undreamed of by the Camerata, and on these composers were shaping sounds, and constructing music which fell as strangely on the ear of late 18th century folk as some avant-garde 20th century music now falls on ours. The shape of sound was altered by harmonics, dynamics, et cetera.

*Dynamics* in music is a scale of volume of sound, ranging from *piano* to *forte*, meaning soft into loud. A terminology (also from the Italian) defines dynamic transitions, as *crescendo*: meaning to gradually become louder; and *decrescendo* or *diminuendo*: gradually becoming softer in tone. Abrupt transition, in what are called terraced or stepped dynamics, was characteristic of baroque music, as were contrasts of *piano* and *forte*, for echo effects. The dynamics of transition were inaugurated by composers of the Mannheim school about mid-18th century, and thereafter music had a subtler, more complex matrix.[9]

Think that the Camerata's composers made music to sing to lute and flute, gentle-voiced instruments; that the singer's voice could be gentle and still be heard in a chamber, where the audience sat very close to the performers. But in a large auditorium, removed from the audience and lifted up on a stage, the singer was required to sing much more loudly. In the orchestra, an immense volume of sound could be shaped as music. There were strings, exceedingly versatile instruments (the violin being four instruments with a common resonator); woodwinds, brass and percussion; instruments whose strings were plucked (in addition to the strings that were bowed: played with a bow), and instruments played by means of a keyboard, like the celesta, piano and organ.

Even the instruments evolved, the piano gaining more and more power until it became the superb instrument we know now; the organ growing larger, so that an organ from Bach's time is primitive compared to one played by Albert Schweitzer in our century. The greater the variety of instruments, the more subtle the nuances of music played. The larger the orchestra, the greater its capacity of sound in music. As orchestras became more complex, composers were able to build larger and richer designs in music.

Orchestras grew from the demands of opera, which was the major musical theatre art for several centuries. Its inspiration was vocal music, for which composers devised *homophony*: melody supported by chords. Major developments in harmony stem from this requirement and new instruments, new groupings of instruments, consistently developed the orchestra to its zenith. Music acquired idioms, one being "tone-color," a device by which composers selected and blended tone-color in music.[10] We have noted elsewhere the traditional use of the trumpet for scenes of pomp, as in marches; of the oboe as characteristic of profundity of feeling.

The architecture of opera changed when composers had at their command materials (like instruments) and idioms through which to express new ideas and define new principles. Beethoven's music, for example, came to be called "dramatic," although it is within the epoch of "classical" music. The best way of discovering the difference between the baroque and classical is to listen to examples of it, the first seeming "thin" in the music of Bach, as compared to music that is "thick" in Beethoven's more richly designed structures, his quartets, et cetera.

In the baroque era, small orchestras were the rule; large orchestras the exception even for opera of the scale of Handel's. Baroque music therefore sounds to our 20th century ears as though played on quaint instruments, by orchestras of "chamber" size, and as "thin" shapes of sounds. In the classical era, marked by the virtuoso as well as the large orchestra, instruments and groups of instruments were boldly defined and in the Romantic era the classical orchestra adopted more instruments (the harp and tuba) and increased the number or made permanent other instruments, all culminating in the giant orchestra, previously described.

While it is common to attribute the beginnings and endings of various eras to composers it must be understood that the evolution of opera, like that of the orchestra, was gradual, more or less spontaneous, and impossible to allocate in hard and fast dates. Every daring, known inaugurator in reality inherited or accumulated experiences and experiments made by other composers. When a composer is set up as the progenitor of a style he is, in actuality, named as the culmination of the work of many other composers (some of them forever anonymous) who provided him with the materials on which to base a genuine mode or form in music.

The epochs of the baroque and the classical are bridged by composers of the Mannheim school and of the Viennese school, the second notable to opera for having Mozart emergent from it—following Joseph Haydn and preceding Ludwig van Beethoven. In this brief and very condensed description of the change in music it is sufficient for our purposes here to know that Mozart's epoch occurred after Gluck and within Gluck's career (see *The Beginning*) and that Mozart occupied an epoch of his own, in which his operas are of two forms, Italian and German.

But Mozart, singular in his work, unique as a composer, is also emergent from a musical dynasty. He may be said to have inherited the world of music that Haydn made and to have, as Westerman remarks, transformed everything he laid his hand to. While Haydn was the master of the symphony Mozart (as he concerns us here) was the creator of human characterization and a new dramaturgy in opera.

This "new" and invigorating music came out of what was then Germany and Austria. There the symphony was evolved as the music of the 18th century. German musicians, chief among them Carl Philipp Emanuel Bach, evolved the sonata; at Mannheim, Stamitz inaugurated a new orchestral language; and in Vienna, where composers adhered to very strict rules of composition, symphonists began to incorporate popular as well as national music in their works. The French, meanwhile, had contributed the *ouverture* or overture in two-part form and the Italians were introducing vocally derived melody into symphonic forms. All these affected opera.

### The Age of Bach

Music made as music *per se* is, as everyone knows, distinguished as "concert music." By this term we understand that it is not music made for dance and opera, the other musical theatrical arts. Music made for dancing and singing is older than music made for concertizing; this sort of music-making came into vogue in the 18th century and the oldest known European concert group, the *Concerts Spirituels*, was founded in Paris in 1725. No one then realized how significant an art form had been inaugurated, nor how great a rival the symphony would become to the opera, then the greatest theatre art form, and the most popular theatrical entertainment.

Out of opera came the "suite," musical compositions for instrumental music without vocal accompaniment, designed by French opera composers for the ballets. These *interludi*, as we note in *The Beginning*, were lengthy and elaborate and so was the style of overture invented by Lully. Since the opera-ballet was ceremonial, music was written for every grand entrée and, we may expect, every grand exit. Given such opportunities for making instrumental music, the opera composers soon had whole forms from, say, an overture, seven or more *entr'actes*, and ballet *interludi*; *voila!* enough for a "suite" or related composition in itself for the orchestra solely, without need of vocalization. The musical form of the concert was thus begun.

*Concerts Spirituels* came into vogue in the Lenten season of the Roman Catholic year, when opera productions were frowned at as too great and greatly admired a worldly entertainment. Frenchmen "gave up" opera going for Lent, to discipline themselves by denials of the senses. But in Louis XIV's reign the *Violons du Roi* under Lully was the most famous orchestra in Europe, and 17th and 18th century Frenchmen could not be expected to forsake music entirely, even while performing the pious offices of the church. Opera makers resorted to music dramas with libretti based on Bible episodes, and, calling them oratorios, did not offend the ban against opera in Lent. *Sans* dramatic action and scenery, the "holy plays" were performed for the public as well as for the courts of kings and princes and other nobility.

The intervals between the music dramas were filled by music, some of it for voice and instruments; all of it for the orchestra. Soon the *concert*, from the Latin word *concertare*: to proportion and bring together in unity, was a vogue. Lesser creatures than kings could afford to patronize it, since it did not require the monstrous sums expended on costumes, scenery and stage machinery for the opera-ballet. In fact, a concert could be performed wherever and whenever players grouped themselves and this was the style of the concert for some time—*théâtre intime*, of the drawing-room and salon. It was also of the public theatre, because almost all audiences except the Italian fell in love with the orchestra, instituting it as the chief rival of the audiences' affections for opera. The Italians into the time of Verdi, as we have noted, were seriously concerned about the "German" trait for instrumental music, believing it the knell of vocal music and opera.

Vocal and instrumental music could both take "concert" form and (into our time) balance each other admirably for the audience's entertainment, thus avoiding the ennui which so plagued the French that their most successful artistes were obliged (as Wagner believed) to constantly amuse or titivate while "creating" works of art. This vice on the part of the French turned into an amiable virtue for music makers, as composers and as players, and gave rise to the virtuoso instrumentalist who composed for the instrument on which he excelled as performer. The violin and the harpsichord, and later the piano, were favorite instruments of the virtuoso composer-player.

A musical form as *concertante* (in 1730) came into vogue; this being a piece of music for orchestra in which there were parts for solo instruments; and/or a piece for solo instruments without orchestra. Other new forms were *concerto*: a composition for one or more solo instruments accompanied by orchestra (1730); and the full-fledged symphony, a larger form than the *sonata*: musical composition for instruments (not voice), which was the opposite of the *cantata*: the recitative or aria for single voice which had been the mode from about 1724. But all these forms, new in their times of origin, coalesced for music and opera after Gluck. Mozart stands at the start of the new epoch, "modern" opera stretching from mid-18th century into late 19th, which is the chasm between polyphonic music and the "new" 20th century polyphony. Mozart had a vocabulary which included the symphonic form; only a composer who knew this form could have written the music Mozart created for the opera *Don Giovanni*. And to know Mozart and the "classical" we must know Bach and the baroque.

Johann Sebastian Bach, dying in 1750, may be seen as the composer who created a renaissance for polyphony, and ideally balanced it and the newer, monophonic music. The music called *polyphonic*, many-voiced, was the form in which Palestrina, whom Verdi held up to the Italian opera makers as a guide, composed his *Stabat Mater*, circa 1590. In polyphony, the music of several voices (or instruments) moves independently. The antithesis of polyphony is *homophony*: a form of music in which one voice (or instrument) takes precedence and is accompanied by other parts, with harmonies. Distinctions of polyphonic and homophonic music are comparable to those of contrapuntal and harmonic music, see *Note No. 1*.

Medieval music was polyphonic and opera developed the monodic form; later, the homophonic form came into vogue and classical composers tended to prefer it to polyphony—although all major composers worked in both the principles of harmonic and contrapuntal music. Differences between polyphony and homophony are basic to the differences between baroque and classical music, and between the opera of the 18th and 19th centuries, respectively.

Bach's renaissance of polyphony brought the baroque to its apogee; he left no form excepting opera unexplored, so much so that any polyphonic invention after Bach is redundant. If a single mode must be chosen to illustrate Bach's genius it might be the cantata, whose primary examples today are the works of Bach. The cantatas for which Bach is famed were compositions with verse in arias, duets, recitatives and choruses; secular and sacred in themes. In these works the composer shows his gifts for characterizing personalities as varied as those of Jesus Christ and a father (in the *Coffee Cantata*) wild with anxiety about his daughter's addiction to caffeine. He could also depict, in tone-colors, events and episodes as diverse as the quarrel of the soldiers under the Cross over the disposal of the Saviour's robe, and villagers (in the *Peasant Cantata*) on a rustic jollification, saluting their feudal lord by quaffing free beer. We shall never know what Bach might have done in the form of a full-scale opera, because it so happened that his lot was cast in far humbler spheres than those granted to Handel in England and Rameau in France. Bach was largely unknown in his lifetime and for almost a century after.

For several hundreds of years almost all music and poetry were dependent on patronage. From the Camerata to Mozart the composer was obliged to sue for the favors of powerful and influential patrons of art, these usually among the nobility. A genius' work might be unrecognized (as was Bach's) without noble (even royal) favor if he happened to live in a city where the rich and fashionable patrons did not make a vogue of his music. But where there was a real craze for music then composers were discovered and encouraged and to such extent that sooner or later an authentic genius emerged from the musical society. It must be added that the most avidly admired composers in any musical epoch were composers who happened to work in the idioms or styles then popular.[11]

While Handel, at the pinnacle of his fame, was ruling an empire of music in England, composing one opera after another that caused audiences to rave over his genius, Bach was toiling as an unknown choirmaster, teaching little boys to sing hymns and trying out his glorious cantatas on feeble choirs.

He was from a Thuringian family of fifty musicians who contributed to German music. An orphan at ten, Bach was adopted by an elder brother who taught him to play the violin, organ and clavier. By the age of eighteen, Bach was earning a living as chapel organist in the small German towns of Arnstadt and Mühlhausen—and earning reprimands from church authorities for the "strange harmonies" he was prone to introduce into sacred music.

In Bach's era, a musician-composer was hired in both functions— to perform on musical instruments and to compose for them. There was no thought of a composer "creating" a composition which came from his inspiration and, being created, became his work. What a musician-composer made as music, whether it was played and sung, or literally made up as musical composition, was purely his job and this "work" belonged, quite legally, to his employer. A composer occupied a position comparable to that of a cook. As their employer might have looked at it, he provided the materials for his cook to turn out a banquet and it was his, the master's banquet. So did he provide the materials (choirs and instruments) for his kapellmeister, who was called on, simply, to turn out feasts of music for all occasions, including state banquets!

Rameau's works were known (and known as Rameau's) in his lifetime because Rameau worked in professional theatre and even though the Opéra's orchestra was recalcitrant it was obliged to play his music. Rameau could express himself and with fine, not to say sumptuous effects. He reached a large, sophisticated audience and was the peer of other known and successful composers of the day.

Handel in England had the splendid priorities that accrue to theatre when it is royally patronized and made fashionable by high society. And Handel enjoyed the absolute power of a pedagogue as well as the accoutrements of a richly appointed stage. Thus, Handel's fame was world-wide, within his world and time.

It was the rule for small orchestras to provide instrumental music for opera as well as for cantata and oratorio. Handel's operas and oratorios were not liturgical (as the major part of Bach's works were) but for theatre and concert. Handel addressed himself to an audience while Bach, whatever he may have dreamed of doing, spoke to a congregation. The physical instruments with which they worked were widely dissimilar, Bach having to make do with untrained voices and the most meagre of chorus and orchestra. Handel, meanwhile, in developing his undisputed gift for vocal musical idioms, commanded the greatest living singers for his arias and choruses, and orchestras that were extravaganzas for the day.

His *Water Music* composed for a picnic on the Thames in 1717 (George I of England and a party cruising on the river) is for twenty-five pieces played by fifty musicians. (They traveled on a barge alongside the royal yacht.) See poor Bach, now, setting his glorious cantatas for seventeen untrained voices and twelve instrumentalists, many of them poor players, and compare the artistic estates of these contemporaries. Yet what Bach wrought he wrought exceedingly well (to be disclosed only about seventy years after his death)[12] and although both he and Handel worked "on call," supplying music for specific occasions, his works are characterized by an exquisite musical logic, the foundation on which he laid his improvisational music.

Handel had an altogether different ideal and precept (remember, both men were governed by their employment: Bach in the church, Handel in theatre) and his objective was to charm an audience. Handel's operas alternate in quality between compositions of genius and ones of compromise, urged on him by haste to meet deadlines and deliver pieces for certain occasions and also, winningly designed to please a fashionable audience.

Handel spoke in simple, direct musical terms, and was a conscious imitator of the Italian mode in opera. Bach, who composed in every kind of music except opera, brought all the precedent and contemporary forms to a nucleus and while he was a major theorist (his noted treatise is *The Art of the Fugue*) he possessed an amazing gift of virtuosity. He could, we may say, take the old and make it new and do it with such apparent spontaneity that it seemed improvisation.

He wrote a great deal of music for the organ and because he was a master of this instrument his compositions are works of great difficulty for players. He is thought of as being invariably serious, and his music as being "cold" and this wholesale categorizing maligns him. The huge body of his work cannot be described here but the serious opera goer does well to investigate Bach and the works of Bach, if only to know how the conventional contemporary forms of the baroque epoch were brought to a state of perfection.

The Brandenburg Concertos, which Bach wrote for the youngest son of the Margrave of Brandenburg (Elector Christian Ludvig) are examples of polyphonic music—and in them are to be descried the dramatic development that was to qualify later music. The *concerto*, a form in music, derives from the Latin word *concertare*, to compete, and Bach's work in this form was an important contribution to instrumental music. The term was operative, in Bach's time, for players designated *concerto grosso* (a large group) and a smaller group called *concertino*, and was on stringed instruments, the solos being rendered on violin. Bach was among the first composers to introduce the harpsichord as a solo instrument and as part of the *concertino*. His development of concerto is one form in which polyphonic texture and dramatic development are to be observed. And Bach strongly but delicately balanced the principles of polyphony and monophony, establishing himself as a musical signpost of an epoch.

When we know that Bach worked in obscurity, with pitifully inadequate materials by which to express his music, and under pressing need to please his employers (he had twenty children) in order to survive, it is incredible that his enormous productivity did not force him into consistent banality. How many men, working in small German courts (they were not at all of the sophistication of the French court, or the society common even to ordinary folk in the Italian metropolis) might have barely earned their pay instead of creating a musical legacy at once brilliant and majestic. Bach turned music as a commodity into music as genius, and on materials which seem very limited by comparison to those of the 19th century orchestra.

His vocal works (as in choral compositions) are considered the major part of his genius but his instrumental music is equally important. The organ on which he composed had thirty-five stops and no mechanism for gradual adjustment of volume, so that tonal changes were brusque and in strong contrasts. The variety of stringed keyboard instruments were divided into those whose keys could be struck, like the clavichord (which had four octaves) and those whose strings could be plucked, like the harpsichord, which sometimes had two keyboards, and had "couplers," mechanical devices that caused corresponding notes in different octaves to sound simultaneously.

The harpsichord (which was not, as is sometimes assumed, the crude origin of the pianoforte, now called the piano) was precise, able to provide varied tone color, and, in the hands of a master, could be brilliant.

Bach wrote compositions that are designated as "Clavier Music"— the word clavier, German, is generic of the stringed keyboard instruments of his time: the clavichord, harpsichord and the piano, with which "new" instrument Bach was unfamiliar until 1747. It is recorded that he disliked it and found its music (in its early, unevolved state) unpleasant.[13]

The atypical 18th century music (which you should know in order to appreciate 19th century music) is in Bach's six *French Suites*, six *English Suites*, and seven *Partitas* (the Leipzig Partitas). In the 16th century, when opera was embryo, polyphonic music was in brilliant apogee. It is this apogee in music that Bach resurrected and to which certain 20th century composers returned. Old scores bear the cryptic information: *Apt for voices or viols*, as though man or instrument would do equally well for making the music. 19th century music, on the contrary, was passionately individualistic or "romantic."

Bach, in many ways, was closer to 20th century composers than to the classicists and romanticists of the 19th.

Absolute music was the mode of the middle Renaissance; drama in music was the new music, the *stile rappresentativo*, the mode of the High Renaissance. Modern music is closer to the baroque in principle than to the classical form and the romantic ideal. Some music, after Richard Strauss (whose music is an example of this), could be made by instruments substituting in the parts for human voices. In this, contemporary music has the same dispassionate "absoluteness" of ancient music, a more disembodied, far less personal kind of music than that made in the 19th century.

Bach's instrumental and vocal works together realize all that went before him, and since so much of his composition was for sacred music (as it had been during the Renaissance) he draws even closer to the root style than his compeer Handel. He wrote for the harpsichord (although nowadays many of these compositions are transposed to the piano), for combinations of instruments, and for combinations of instruments and voices. In Bach's time, the harpsichordist served the role of orchestra conductor and played a sort of musical shorthand called "figured bass," described as "filling in" the harmonic structure of the piece. (Bach's music requires this *continuo* to be authentic; however, it is often omitted from contemporary performances of his works.) Haydn rejected this method of harmonic "filling in" and by writing precise music in place of the old *continuo* Haydn established a new rule.

Bach employed a diversity of chorale styles, one using the soprano voice for the melody, and he experimented with melodies of descriptive and symbolic characterizations—all, as we later find, to become the nature of opera. The influences that Bach indirectly exerted on Haydn and Mozart of the Viennese school were through his sons (famed harpsichordists in their time), and Bach, a prophet largely unknown in his place and lifetime, was a herald of new music while seeming to be solely the loving preserver of music that was "old."

While his most primitively formed recitatives can drag (one example being the *St Luke Passion*, which is dubiously accredited to him but may be by another composer of the period) his arias have a rich if antique beauty. The language of the verse is, of course, from an older time and its figurative and imaginative context is not a mode now used. Yet Bach's music and some of the words of the arias are wholly convincing, entirely beautiful, as in the tenor aria "Ah my soul, ah whither wilt thou fly?" (following Peter's three denials of Christ in the *St John Passion*). A major episode occurs in the argument of the soldiers under the Cross over the division of the crucified Jesus' robe, in which the whole chorus participates, and from which the contralto part takes Jesus' final words "It is finished."

For the *St Matthew Passion* Bach had an experienced librettist, one Picander, who accepted and followed the composer's instructions. The result was a masterwork; the arias in the form of *da capo aria*, the thematic line constantly preserved, and recitative and aria bound within the textual content.

*Passions* refer to chorales, motets and especially oratorios based on the Passion of Jesus Christ as related in the Gospels. It is a subject which lends itself ideally to the fugue, of which Bach was the great master. *Fugue*, from Latin *fuga* for flight, is a musical composition in which a single theme is worked on for two or more parts or voices in strict imitation. Usually, a fugue begins with a single voice singing the theme, which is called the *subject*. This is then repeated by a second voice, in the dominant key—but a fifth higher or a fourth lower, and this second voice is called the *answer*. While the second voice is singing, the first voice continues, in a contrasting counterpoint which, within the fugue, is called the *countersubject*. And if the fugue is in three or four parts, the third and fourth voices enter, in succession, as the first voices continue to develop additional countersubjects in free counterpoint. After all the voices have sung the theme in its first section, the section called the *exposition* is completed. The fugue continues, three sections being its whole form. Mozart, Beethoven, Strauss and Bela Bartok (all of whom wrote opera) were composers of the fugue. Bach was so great a master of it and of oratorio that we must always regret he did not write opera. It seems he never thought of composing one, while Handel, a German and one born the same year as Bach, only stopped making operas when he could not get audiences for them. Yet these two, one in a little backwater, the other in the glittering public view, worked at the same time towards the same end: the glory of music and of German music, too. Incidentally, Bach, like Handel, died blind.

Bach was exceedingly happy in private life, twice married, with ten children who survived him. Handel remained a bachelor. Although he had sons who were accomplished musicians Bach did not inaugurate a "school" and left no emulators. He said all that needed to be said about the fugue, restated the polyphonic apogee, and in the *suite* (which came to be called *lessons* in England, *ordre* in France, and *partita* in Italy and Germany) helped to affirm the orchestral form of music begun in the French opera-ballet.

The development of this musical form, essentially from dance music, is one whole and consistently evoked style in opera—dance music culminating in Offenbach's *opéras bouffes* and the operettas of Strauss and others. The Gallicized names of such dances (*allemande, polonaise, anglaise*) are indicative of the utilization of them by the French; they were, as is obvious by their names, dances of other European origins. Weber and the waltz opened a whole musical vista[14] and, a considerable time later, Westerman was to note that in the 20th century's "new" music, strongly influenced by rhythm, the dance would become more the vogue than opera.

But as Bach's era came to an end opera was still paramount among the musical arts, and the virtuoso performer and composer in concert music was yet to come into his zenith. The Viennese Tonkunstler Society, the first public concerts, did not commence regular performances until 1771—and then it was to raise funds for the widows and orphans of German musicians. Italy, which had a lively concert stage from the 17th century, was independent of court patronage but the German and Austrian composers remained almost feudally bound to their patrons. The major difference in national music and opera lay in Italy founding academies and public theatres and other countries, Germany and Austria for example, maintaining the arts from social patronage instead of in an academic source. Nevertheless, the Mannheim and Viennese schools emerged from such societies, the latter producing Haydn, Mozart and Beethoven.

## The Viennese School

Joseph Haydn (1732-1809), master of the symphony, was one of the marvelously fecund composers in which the 18th and 19th centuries abounded. Emotional intensity varied with fresh, almost childlike themes are hallmarks of his style. He commanded gracious variations and naïve or droll musical ideas. Notably, he made rich counterpoint, played off themes against each other and in combinations, all with great skill, while maintaining an air of engaging simplicity. His major symphonic achievement was the "Salomon Set," in which the Surprise Symphony is a famous musical joke.[15]

Haydn composed some operas (as related in *The Beginning*), with Italian libretti but in *Singspiel* style. And he started his career as a singer, choirboy in St. Stephen's Cathedral in Vienna, far from his birthplace in a village in Lower Austria. Here he was taught to play violin and clavier and sang for nine years, until his voice broke, when he was dismissed. In 1749, aged eighteen, he determined to teach himself composition, although he knew little harmony and counterpoint. He lived in a draughty attic, supporting himself by giving lessons to students on an old clavichord he owned, and playing the violin at nocturnal concerts, a musical entertainment then in fashion. Unable to study under teachers, he taught himself from the writings of two men he admired, Bach's son Carl Philipp Emanuel, and Johann Joseph Fux, an Austrian opera maker who excelled in the Italian modes.

Establishing an arduous discipline for himself, Haydn mastered the principles of composition, aided by natural talent. In 1761 he obtained a good post, assistant kapellmeister for Prince Paul Esterhazy at an estate in Eisenstadt, near Vienna. The prince died the following year, his inheritance passing to a brother, Nicholas, who was much taken with Haydn and put him in full charge of the music at Eisenstadt, an excellent orchestra of fourteen performers. As safe and secure in his appointment as Bach had been in his (and as poor Mozart should never have the good fortune to be) Haydn was launched on an agreeable career under a genial master. Nicholas Esterhazy was a true patron of music and encouraged by this prince Haydn composed a large number of works, which were published and brought him honor and fame—and commissions from Paris and London. He worked in a benign influence far different from Mozart, with whom he became great friends during a visit to Vienna, remaining attached to the younger man until Mozart's death. He said of Mozart (to the latter's father): "I assure you before God, as an honorable man, your son is the greatest composer that I know personally or by reputation; he has taste and in addition the greatest knowledge of the technique of composition."

Haydn is a historical link between the polyphony (brought to its apogee) of Bach and the "new" opera. He did not invent new opera forms but crystallized existing symphonic ones, and since he was very well known in his lifetime (he lived in London and Vienna, after Nicholas Esterhazy's death) he exerted a wide influence. His idiom was essentially a homophonic one, and its chief nature was melody of intrinsically instrumental form. He liked folk music and employed actual dance tunes. (Bach, it should be noted, employed older, graver forms of dance music in his French Suites, like the *allemande, corrente, sarabande, polonaise, bourrée, minuet* and *gigue*.)

For the orchestra, Haydn's major accomplishment was the stand-ardization of instrumentation; he demonstrated in one hundred and four symphonies the possibilities of combinations of instruments and did this so efficiently that it stands substantially as the mode of today. Later composers merely added more instruments, but Haydn's "classi-cal" orchestra stayed the foundation of 19th and 20th century music. His orchestra while comparatively small was treated so masterfully, its "color" handled so inventively, and in a harmonic idiom so fluent and eloquent, that it was no longer necessary to "fill in" the gaps formerly left to the harpsichordist, who vanished from the orchestra, with his instrument, after Haydn.

Vienna at the end of the 18th century was the third European city, capital of an empire made up of several racial cultures. The city was an important commercial and political center and noblemen, tradi-tionally the most generous of art patrons, had palaces in and outside Vienna. All these maintained orchestras (liveried in a uniform like the other retainers of the household, under kapellmeisters who were conductors as well as composers. The dynasty that was being founded here in the Viennese school was one for German opera, about to come to fruition in Mozart's *Singspiel* and in a German opera both grave and gay.

The composer may have occupied a socially inferior position in such a society to the one he conventionally occupies in ours today, but he at least had the assurance that when he wrote music it would be performed for an audience, a certainty the new, unknown composer does not have in our society. And composers were fortunate to be living in an age and in a city where the craze was for new music; there was no hero-worship of dead and gone composers, no desire to treasure their works. Instead, high and low demanded new music in a continuous supply. It was a mode to tax the creativity of a lesser composer, and inspire that of a greater talent.

In addition, the Hapsburg rulers of Austria exerted a strict censor-ship to prevent the radical political and social ideas of the wicked French from corrupting their people, closing out the Revolution and all that it engendered as "freedom" for the individual to the extent of rebellion against authority. But the chief influence to be noted for Haydn (who was a mild-mannered man, not a revolutionary) was the pervading one for new music, in abundance. Not only princes bought or commissioned music (and in batches, so that Haydn would deliver six symphonies at once) but tradesmen as well. Haydn would be required to turn out half-a-dozen quartets for a merchant who wanted them performed for the entertainment of his customers. Thus, making music in abundance and making it surpassingly well in his style, Haydn died (of old age) in 1809, leaving to the world of music his own estimable contribution, and his prophetic statement about Mozart, who predeceased him but who, in musical history, is seen as following Haydn in the Viennese school.

Theatre goers tend to dismiss all opera before the 19th century as archaic but this applies only to pre-Mozartian opera of the baroque style. Mozart is timeless because he was not a stylist and is therefore incorruptible in his pure forms. His great operas are genuine works of art, impossible to disqualify in music. He reformed a concept and defined an evolution in opera by altering it from the baroque and *buffo* or slap-bang comic styles and in so doing developed something as important as *dramma per musica* itself.

The early accomplishment for opera was in learning how to develop drama through music, and it was a major evolution when composers mastered the technique of relating numerous songs and instrumental passages into a series of orchestrated and vocal "numbers," and later turned this method into a dramatically logical and musically conceived form. The form of music and drama in simultaneity was enriched and made virtuoso by several composers, as briefly described in *The Beginning*.

Mozart's concept of drama in music was to alter the idea of music as accompaniment or underscoring of action and make the action and music indissoluble as well as simultaneous—and he did not do this here and there, or now and then, but continuously. Opera's nature of drama and music in simultaneity grew in Mozartian maturity to one which could perhaps be explained as dramatic music. This is a clumsy way of expressing Mozart's accomplishment but the approved musical semantics are too obtuse for a layman.

Think of Mozart as a matchless juggler of human emotions and actions, the inner and outer worlds of his characters; as a sort of musical psychologist who works hand in hand with the juggler; and, beyond being these things, as a musical genius—if you visualize him as this trinity you begin to understand the opera maker he was, and to understand that Mozart made music psychologically true. He was never merely apt but always certain and right. He did not need to interject a bit of "color" to underline a point in the drama, the drama was instinctive to his music, as your senses are instinctive to your nervous system. A study of the music for *Don Giovanni* should make clear and explicit the techniques of Mozart and his formidable accomplishments. An authority on this composer, Sir Donald Tovey, is a good source of reference; he is considered unconventional by musicians but he uses language that a layman speaks and offers explanations on music that a sensible opera goer can come to terms with, as about Mozart for example.[16]

Wolfgang Amadeus Mozart is a solitary genius, unique in that he occupies an epoch to himself, self-created. He is one of the great romantic enigmas in art. Born January 27, 1756, at Salzburg, Austria, he had a short and miserable life. Yet, like a diamond, he is fixed in music, appearing there as an incandescent light in the central era of opera evolution, between the baroque and classical.

Scarlatti, from whose era the first international opera is to be traced, composed one hundred and fifteen operas; Mozart a total of fifteen works of which only four are in the permanent active repertory; a fifth in the German opera repertory.

A child prodigy, he was fated to make enemies because of his genius. When at the age of eleven and on the invitation of Emperor Joseph II, the boy Mozart composed *La Finta Simplice* his much older compeers did everything in their power to prevent the work from being performed. It eventually was, in Salzburg in May, 1769. Gluck was one of the envious musicians who intrigued against Mozart, whose most fanatical enemy was one Antonio Salieri, a composer who slavishly imitated Gluck with great commercial success in the European theatre, was conductor at the Viennese court and well able to connive against Mozart. Salieri worked industriously to prevent Mozart's music from being played and sung and, when it was, managed to ruin the productions. Anti-Mozart claques made it a practice to disrupt performances of the composer's operas and one giant anti-Mozart rally, planned to abort *The Marriage of Figaro* at its première, had to be forbidden by the Emperor himself in order to have it called off. (When *Figaro* proved an enormous success, Mozart's enemies put on a rival comic opera *Una Cosa Rara* by Martin y Soler at another theatre in Vienna and divided the audience so successfully that *Figaro* closed after nine performances.[17])

Despite these and many other grievous wrongs done to Mozart in his lifetime, he is known and loved today while his enemies and a great many of his compeers are forgotten. It is poetic to say that Gluck is the father of modern opera but it is Mozart's operas which represent the start of the new era after Gluck. Mozart invented a new type of opera, and laid the foundation of romanticism, on which the 19th century opera matured.[18]

### The "German" Opera

The stage was now set for a new kind of opera. The age shared by Handel, Rameau and Bach (with Bach still an anonymous contributor to it for European music at large) gave way to that of Gluck. And in Germany, from the Viennese school of which Haydn is the first of the trio of Haydn, Mozart and Beethoven, came the nucleus of German opera. It was the epoch of Mozart. But the contributions of these three famous men are not the sole foundations of "German" opera. Collectively, as the Viennese school, they stand as a signpost from which to view the panorama of opera in the 19th century. In this era, German opera surged to the forefront to stand with the French and Italian.

German opera came into being as soon as it was proven that German could be sung as well as spoken and written as poetry. One poet, Gotthold Lessing, defined opera as a divine unity between music and poetry and urged that they live harmoniously in opera; in the aria, poetry must be the auxiliary art, in the recitative, music took a secondary role. Johann Herder, a Prussian pastor and philosopher, saw opera as the "unreality of a dream" and on this inspiration opera of fantasy and allegory throve, with Goethe's *Faust* inspiring innumerable composers and librettists. For Mozart, music was the supreme and perhaps the sole reality, and out of music he created true characters for opera. But he was not the first composer to attempt opera out of *Singspiel*.

A Nationaltheater opened in Mannheim, 1776, and German arts

(encouraged by the Elector Karl Theodor) flourished where until 1770 Italian opera had been the vogue. Here, in 1777, Anton Schweitzer's *Gunther von Schwartzburg* became the first opera with a theme taken from real life. In 1782 Schiller's *Die Rauber* was hailed as epochal and in the same theatre a Bohemian composer, Georg Benda, produced theatre pieces with songs, dialogue and musical accompaniment. Mozart admired Benda (but did not think much of Schweitzer's work) and his first *Singspiel* opera owed a debt to the Mannheim school, whose innovations appreciably influenced German opera.

In the age-old way of artists, Mozart borrowed and adapted inventions made by others, while perfecting his own principles and instituting a new style for opera—a style which other composers would borrow to great profit not only in Germany but internationally for the opera form *per se*.

Mozart, with his creation of an opera out of *Singspiel*, is the father of German opera. Had he done no more than this, he would be immortal. But Mozart did much more, in establishing a human character for opera roles, in treating what the "precious" considered silly themes with musical seriousness, and in bringing to opera its truest international veracity. For this composer, who wrote excellent "German" opera, also wrote operas in the "Italian" form, with the delightful airs and graces of the best Italian school.

Mozart's earliest extant opera, *Bastien and Bastienne*, is charming—and has some historical interest for the new opera goer. Its libretto (by Favart) is a satire on Rousseau's *The Village Soothsayer*.

Mozart was born into a musical family, and his father (Leopold Mozart) toured Europe with his two small children, Mozart and his sister Marianne, arranging concert performances for them. Before Mozart's time, concert singing and playing were not the mode; they came into vogue and at their height glorified the virtuoso performer like Chopin and Liszt.

In his travels and from his own great natural intelligence, Mozart became sophisticated at an early age. He was not the most cultured or best educated of composers (Verdi should never have described him as erudite) but he knew all he needed to know to make beautiful music, and some marvelously entertaining operas.

He was an incorrigible comedian and one of the most masterful men of the theatre who has ever lived. He seemed able to visualize a work in its entirety and when he was able to influence a lesser librettist or to enjoy the collaboration of a truly great one, he shaped his works with consummate skill and artistry. His first famed work (among the extant Mozart operas) is *The Abduction from the Seraglio*, which he composed in 1782 for the Vienna National Singspiel Theater. His librettist Gottlieb Stephanie (called Stephanie the Younger) accepted considerable help from Mozart and as a result the musical and dramatic scenes have unity, the dialogue leads naturally into the vocal ensembles.

*The Abduction from the Seraglio* put musicologists in a quandary. It was not an opera of either of the approved forms (Italian or French) and on this fact it was unacceptable to the "precious" as an opera. But it was simply too good to be dismissed as just another *Singspiel* or "pop" musical play. The predicament was solved by calling it a "German" opera.

The verse was sung in the vernacular and Mozart's audience, coming into the theatre off the street (in 1782) found the tenor and soprano singing in their own common, everyday tongue instead of the Italian that was *de rigueur* for opera. Moreover, the composer cracked jokes and in general had a high old time—his relish for the improbable characters and the implausible plot is irresistible even today, nearly two hundred years later.

Mozart's *Abduction from the Seraglio* deals with bodily assault (the heroine, Constanze, is abducted and carried off to an illusive Oriental state ruled by Pasha Selim) and the threat of rape. But it is a deliciously comic work because while all the characters take themselves very seriously, we in the audience are not expected to take them so— least of all the pivot of the opera: the abductee, fair Constanze. Mozart did not make her into a woman but into the *species coloratura soprano*. She is a mere paper doll, but one cut out of a fragile paper doily. We can see clear through her but her frills and furbelows (the trills and runs Mozart gives her to sing) endow her with a special character.

The closest resemblance she bears is to the Victorian heroine, the impregnable virgin forever chaste and chased. The role is one of the coloratura soprano's show pieces and Mozart composed it expressly for a friend, Katherine Cavalieri, as a bravura piece, interjecting into *Singspiel* a characteristic of Italian opera. Mozart was just then betrothed and about to be married to Constance Weber and he gave his beloved's name to the heroine in his new opera. It was a smash hit from its première and Constanze's *adagio* aria in *Act I* is still, in theatrical parlance, a "show-stopper."

Had the Vienna National Singspiel continued to prosper Mozart might have worked thenceforth solely in the *Singspiel* form (he had previously composed some Italian operas) but Viennese society with a capital S favored the foreign to the native opera and Mozart bowed to the audience's tastes.

Mozart wrote twenty-five theatre pieces: operas, operettas, intermezzi. He dealt in novelties but his music is not ephemeral; a great deal of it sounds as though it were freshly minted. A composer of his great facility could have decorated all his operas with glittering filigree, and Mozart could imitate any style; but he did not, preferring to enlighten the audience rather than bedazzle it.[19] No composer before or since has had a greater gift for characterization. For a man with a zesty not to say racy sense of humor he had enormous compassion and understanding for the human race; his people are not crudely drawn but subtly, and none more so than the fools and the rogues.

Emotionally, he could run the gamut from the sublime to the ridiculous, from a zany or pompous "villain" out of commedia dell'arte to a character in *The Magic Flute* singing music (as has been said) that might have been put in the mouth of God. And he was the master of depicting idiosyncrasies in music, so that the opera goer who knows Mozart knows his characters as though they were living beings.

The extant operas are *The Abduction from the Seraglio* and *The Magic Flute,* in German verse; and *The Marriage of Figaro, Don Giovanni* and *Cosi Fan Tutte* in Italian. Except for *Cosi Fan Tutte* these operas were successful at premières but Mozart earned little by his music. He was reduced to eking out his paltry stipend (in the poorly paid posts he was given in his country) by borrowing and begging small sums from friends. He died a pauper, and is buried in an unmarked grave. In terms of material success, Mozart is at the lowest scale and his predecessor, Haydn, and the Italian Rossini, who came after Mozart, are at the highest. The irony of his life and death lay in being the darling of the civilized world from the age of six, and the victim of it from about sixteen. Mozart died a month before his thirty-fifth birthday and may never have achieved his peak as a composer, since the majority of the great composers reached theirs after forty. Nevertheless, Mozart is the most versatile musical genius of all time, who produced masterpieces in every genre—the larger number being of a crystalline or "sparkling" quality.

Unlike Haydn, Mozart was well trained and as a very young child, almost an infant. His father was assistant kapellmeister to the Archbishop of Salzburg, a prince of the church, and taught the child to play clavier and violin. Mozart showed his gifts at once. He was playing the harpsichord at three, composing for it when he was five. His first piano concerto was written at age eleven and he was acknowledged as the finest pianist of his day. Twenty-seven piano concerti, the last (*Concerto in B-flat major*) written in the year of his death, are among the music Mozart left us.

His childhood was a magical time. At twelve, on an extended tour with his sister, Mozart stayed for fourteen days at Versailles, enchanting this most worldly court with his performances on the violin, the harpsichord and the organ, astonishing it with his phenomenal ability to transpose songs and accompany them on sight, and by his uncanny aptitude for improvisation. In London, he made an equal sensation, amazing J. C. Bach, himself a famous harpsichordist, and the teacher of the Queen of England. Two years later, taken by his father to Italy, Mozart became a legend in Rome, when after his first hearing of Gregorio Allegri's *Miserere*, a work for nine voices in two choirs, the fourteen-year-old boy wrote the whole from memory. Still in his teens, Mozart's Italian-style operas were being produced and hugely admired in Italy. Up to 1773, when Mozart was seventeen, it seemed that life must be a halcyon one for this darling of the gods. In his short time, there was nothing in music that he did not attempt, and nothing that he attempted which did not surpass its genre, into his great *Requiem*, written on his death bed and, in 1792 (when it was performed in Vienna) standing so high above all others that Haydn declared on this one work alone the composer deserved immortality.

But Mozart, never physically strong, was the most luckless of composers in a time ruled by patronage. He went to work, as his father had done, for the archbishop of Salzburg and this man, new to the post (by name Hieronymus von Colloredo) treated Mozart with contempt.

He was considered a menial, subjected to personal abuse, and so checked and constrained that his post was intolerable. Mozart was refused permission to perform at benefit concerts (one of the few means of a composer's earning money) and demurred; the archbishop discharged him and Mozart made the inevitable break with his native city which used him worse than any other town has ever used a genius in music.

He went to Vienna, one of the few great musical metropolitan centers, and was most kindly received there by the Emperor. But in the same city where the child Mozart had incurred so much enmity from other composers (Gluck among them), the man Mozart found ill luck still dogging his heels. Here he met his implacable enemy, Antonio Salieri. And here he died in 1791, believing himself to have been poisoned.[20]

The part of Mozart's music that sparkles, that is often almost riotously gay, gives him the reputation of being a sunny-tempered composer. This is a kind sentiment, and a compliment from the Mozartian fans who are fond of "happy" music.

For the acme of his jubilant musical nature go to the overture of *The Marriage of Figaro*, a torrent that begins like a fountain (with a cheeky, chuckling bassoon, to quote Westerman) and then gushes forth in such power that one must listen carefully, resisting the lovely flooding whole, for the happy dance rhythms of the *sforzati*: sudden accentuations of individual notes. The overture to *Cosi Fan Tutte* is even more uninhibited—and quite different from *Figaro's*. The first has something stronger, sterner ("a Bacchic maelstrom of the life-force in flood," says Westerman) and the second an almost frenetic gaiety, suitable to the satirically comic situation devised by fickle and amorous debutantes who "carry on" like all women, or so the opera insists as its theme.

Mozart had a dark as well as a light side and in this mood his diamond-like beauty is captured in the heart of the musical jewel, blinding in the prismatic color which suffuses his emotional profundities. One example of this mood is the *Piano Concerto in B-flat major*, K. 456, which Mozart wrote for a blind pianist, Maria Theresa Paradis, a pupil of a rival Viennese composer, Leopold Kozeluch. Mozart wrote church music which may have signified the beginning of a monumental

accomplishment in that genre. His last work, the *Requiem in D minor,*
*K. 626,* unfinished at his death, was completed by a friend and pupil,
Franz Sussmayer. But when we consider Mozart as the opera maker he
seems spirited and almost antic, the happiest of men as well as the most
charming, the most human of opera composers up to his time. His
radiance, at its most brilliant, warms as well as illumines the spirit, so
that a very young child, explaining his feelings about the world of
opera, declared: "I have Wagner on Thursday because it is Thor's day
and he thunders, and Mr. Gluck I keep for Sunday because he is pure.
But Mozart I have every day to play with and be like my brother."
Mozart opened people's hearts to music and gave a whole new dimension to opera.

There was no more a rigid form as *opera seria,* to divide a serious
musical art from the "pop" *Singspiel* form and *opera buffa.* There was,
now, opera which in subject might be grave or gay. Mozart and Gluck
are the two major opera reformers but their reforms were of different
natures. Mozart humanized opera and enlarged its dramatic scope and
he seems to have had little care about disciplining singers and orchestra,
as Handel and Gluck toiled to do (but then, these were conductors and
were involved in opera production as well as composition). Mozart, even
when he had to use a libretto of rococo style, animates characters in
principle as well as in song. Characters out of Handel and Gluck are
either too horrifying or too lofty of ideal to countenance as "real," and
the Italian composers of *opera buffa* caricatured real life in the "types"
of the commedia dell'arte. But Mozart's people are entirely natural and
"true" in every event of his operas—if their actions or vocal parts surprise us, it is because Mozart intended these usually as a joke.

Composers had made singers perform as characters in opera.
Mozart's "people" sing as other people breathe; it is natural for them
to sing, it would be unnatural to them if they did not. Mozartian opera
is as simple, and as complex, as this riddle.

In *The Abduction from the Seraglio,* the least "likely" of events
fly by as sheer "action," and as such become "true" in themselves; a
reality. Mozart utilizes commedia dell'arte stock characters (saucy servant girl; gullible, foolish lackey; madly amorous villain; heroically good
and naïve hero and heroine; the whole rag-bag) but who is more
"human" than the maid, Blonde? And what character could be a
better flesh-and-blood foil for her preposterous mistress, the cardboard

Constanze? The essential frivolity of this improbable plot, with its implausible characters, is underlaid by an irony towards the "upper classes" that Mozart shows again in *Cosi Fan Tutte*, *The Marriage of Figaro* and *Don Giovanni*. He had a wit as delicate and sharp as a needle.

The miracle of Mozart is that he travels to the brink of burlesque but never falls into superficiality; he dances across chasms on air; in fact, in music.

For his three Italian operas Mozart had the benefit of libretti by Lorenzo Da Ponte, one of the three great librettists in opera (the other two are Boito who worked with Verdi and Hofmannsthal who worked with Richard Strauss), a most gifted writer who dashed off *Don Giovanni* in two months.

This opera, which is sometimes assumed to be a morality play, is Mozart's masterwork and Da Ponte's as well, being neither wholly comic nor entirely tragic, and yet something of both. The Don Giovanni of the opera is based on the Spanish Don Juan, most legendary of libertines, who is unrepentant for his wicked deeds, dares the devil and defies the dead and goes to Hell—a fine, flaring Medieval Hell, with flames licking the walls of his castle and the Don vanishing through the floor into the abyss.

The opera ends ludicrously, with a sextet singing righteously to the Don: *Sinner pause and ponder well*, but soon turning to their own mundane affairs; whereupon they decide to dine together, marry, hie to a convent and find a job, according to their dispositions.

The music is glorious! One of the most famed passages is the ball at Don Giovanni's castle (*Act I, Scene V*) when Mozart makes three orchestras play simultaneously: a solemn minuet, a fast waltz and a graceful quadrille, blending music in ¾, ⅜ and ¾ times. There are a number of famed airs, one being Leporello's (the Don's valet) "catalogue aria" about his master's rapes, assaults and seductions (2,065 all told) and the ladies his master pursues: young and old, thin and fat, tall and short, and especially those who are virgin.

And Mozart makes fun of Mozart by introducing into *Don Giovanni* a song from *Figaro* (*Non piu andrai*), so that the impudent valet, Leporello can comment: "Well, I can't say I think much of that tune."

To make the point quite clear in *Don Giovanni*, Da Ponte called it *dramma giocoso*: gay drama. Despite its serious characters, like the ghost of the Commendatore, killed in a duel with Giovanni, fought to avenge the honor of his daughter, the opera has a rollicking spirit— that it is one tinged with ominous colors like death and violence, sin and hell, makes *Don Giovanni* more than a superb *opera buffa*; in short, a superb opera.[21]

*Cosi Fan Tutte* (Women Are All Alike) was the least successful of Da Ponte's libretti and has been less successful than Mozart's other two Italian operas. The adverse critical opinion is that *Cosi Fan Tutte* is so artificial as to be false. Perhaps a knowledge of how the opera came to be written puts it in better perspective for the opera goer.

Joseph II, then emperor, is said to have asked Mozart to contrive a theatre piece on a current scandal at the Viennese court, when two army officers determined to test their fiancées' fidelity by pretending to leave the city on maneuvers then sneaking back in disguise to find out what went on in their presumed absence. They are alleged to have found the young ladies less faithful than fair.

Mozart's opera follows this episode: two sisters in love with and beloved by their fiancés, are discovered to be the ficklest of their sex when the lovers put them to the test. Disguises, mistaken identities, a conniving maid and riotous antics are all true to commedia dell'arte. But instead of being in the broad country humor of the artless, natural style *Cosi Fan Tutte* affects the stylish vaporings of the society it mimics and satirizes. It is no wonder the opera seems artificial; the real life characters it was based on were in themselves comic operetta types. Mozart, in fact, parodies *opera buffa*, which originally parodied *opera seria*.

There is seldom a carping word uttered about *Figaro*, however, the oldest comic opera extant in repertory. The libretto by Da Ponte was adapted from a play by Beaumarchais, ridiculing the nobility, which had been banned by the Emperor in Vienna for being danger- ously inflammable to the revolutionary element of society. Da Ponte tactfully overcame the Emperor's prejudice and to such a degree that (as has been said) Joseph II made personal intervention to assure the opera's première. *The Marriage of Figaro*, in proper sequence, follows the events in *The Barber of Seville*, but was composed thirty years before Rossini's *Barber of Seville*.

These two operas, one by an Austrian, the other by an Italian, are not at all alike musically—it is the drama which unites them as two parts of a whole. One of the piquant puzzles of opera is pondering what Mozart might have done with a young Almaviva and Rossini with an aging Almaviva. For although the "barber," whose name is Figaro, holds the title roles of both operas he is not the only character developed in the double drama, nor indeed the most important one. Count Almaviva is both romantic and pathetic, while Figaro is chiefly comic even when he is involved in a romance of his own. Almaviva is the provocative "human" study.

In Rossini's opera, *The Barber of Seville*, Figaro is a footloose and fancy free town barber in Seville, officiously officiating in every intrigue, especially the romantic ones of the city. This finger-in-every-pie charlatan (barbers were also dentists and surgeons, scribes and marriage counselors) undertakes to unite a love-sick gentleman, Count Almaviva, with the object of his affection: Rosina, the young and beautiful ward of an old curmudgeon named Dr. Bartolo. This tyrant keeps the fair Rosina under lock and key, intending to marry her and thereby keep her fortune at his disposal, but meanwhile provides her with the education of a lady, including music lessons from a *maître* named Basilio. This Basilio, on the side, works as a marriage broker and Bartolo enlists Basilio to make up a marriage contract between himself and his ward. Basilio warns Bartolo that the handsome young nobleman, Almaviva, has an eye on Rosina—but guarantees to demolish this gallant with such calumny that Rosina will never pay attention to his suit. Almaviva, meanwhile, serenades Rosina from the street, where he confides his infatuation to Figaro—and that he wishes to be known to Rosina as "Lindoro," an ordinary young man, so that she will not be swayed by the fame of his station and fortune nor repelled by his bad reputation as a roué!

Figaro arranges for Almaviva to substitute for a supposedly ailing Basilio and while giving Rosina a music lesson Almaviva makes hasty love to his adored one under the nose, so to speak, of her guardian—whom Figaro insists on shaving while the music lesson (and love affair) is progressing, regardless of whether the good Doctor wishes to have his cheeks lathered or no. The lovers make plans to elope. Dr. Bartolo is not as foolish as he seems because he suspects the elopement and while "Lindoro" is off making arrangements to steal Rosina away,

Bartolo tells her that her suitor Lindoro is in the pay of the notorious rake, Almaviva, and intends to hand her over to the depravities of that nobleman. The pure Rosina is horrified but Almaviva turns up soon thereafter, swears that his intentions are honorable, reveals his noble identity and begs her to marry him. Dancing with impatience, Figaro urges them to fly at once but the lovers waste so much time assuring each other of their mutual adoration that Bartolo, accompanied by Basilio with the marriage contract, arrives on the scene.

The opera comes to a happy ending when Almaviva ardently declares that he loves Rosina for herself alone (as she him for himself alone) and that for all they care Bartolo can keep his ward's fortune. Bartolo is easily consoled for the loss of fair Rosina (his housekeeper is his mistress, we later discover) and in a capital good humor changes his name to Almaviva's on the marriage contract, giving the lovers his blessing.

The Barber presides over this idyl, a sanguine and roguish Cupid.

Mozart's opera takes a stride into time and sets us back among the familiar personalities, with a few additions. Rosina, now Countess Almaviva, has a maid, Susanna, with whom Figaro (who has taken service with the Count as his valet) is in love. The gay and feckless barber nostalgically recalls his hectic past but he has found the girl whom he adores and is willing to settle down. He needs his master's official consent and this is withheld, because Figaro (deeply in debt to this lady) has signed a marriage contract with the Countess' housekeeper, a matron named Marcellina. She had formerly been the housekeeper of Bartolo (euphemistically, he had been her "patron") and this good friend (and his good friend, the music teacher Basilio) plan to force Figaro to keep his contract and marry Marcellina—plus, repay the loan he borrowed from her.

Cherubino, the Count's page, is madly in love with the Countess—he is a silly boy, rather like a girl (no wonder, since his role is for a soprano). What is more serious is that the Count (whose amorous ways were not cured by marriage) is infatuated with Susanna and is determined to exercise the *droit du Seigneur*, the right of a nobleman to sleep with a virgin bride in his employ on her wedding night. Figaro is appalled when shrewd Susanna tells him what she suspects Almaviva will demand of her.

The opera begins with a very funny scene—Figaro is measuring the space in Susanna's bedroom where their bed will be set. The room, incidentally, is very close to Count Almaviva's suite. Susanna explains what will happen some morning—the Count will send Figaro on an errand "din, din" to the peal of the bell. Then he will ring for Susanna, "don, don" with another peal of the bell. Because, says Susanna, the Count is looking for love at home—but not from the Countess. It's the countess' maid he's after.

Rosina, Countess Almaviva, sings of her husband's infidelities, which have made her so miserable (she still loves him) and begs the god of love, *Porgi Amor*, to restore his passion for her. Figaro and Susanna decide to make the Count jealous of the Countess, to revive his old love, and the Countess consents to help. Susanna pretends to agree to a meeting with the Count, but she and the Countess dress the boy Cherubino in girl's clothes to send him off to keep the rendez-vous, so Almaviva will be caught and made ashamed of his folly.

While they are doing this, the Count comes to see his wife who will not let him in until she and her maid hide Cherubino. When Almaviva enters and finds a locked door in his wife's suite (which in great agitation she refuses to open) he suspects that she is hiding a lover. In a fury, dragging his wife with him, he goes to fetch tools to force the door open, whereupon Susanna quickly changes places with Cherubino, making the page climb out of the window into the garden. The Count finds Susanna behind the locked door and is about to apologize to the Countess when his gardener, Antonio, appears to say that someone has jumped out of the Countess' window. Figaro claims it was he but his heroic stance is spoiled when Marcellina, Basilio and Bartolo choose this moment to appear and demand that he satisfy the signed contract and marry Marcellina.

Soon after, in the countess' ballroom, Susanna agrees to meet the Count in the garden. He is determined to have her (and angrily sings: *Must I forego my pleasure while a serf of mine rejoices*) and things look black for Figaro. Magically, they clear up, for in the legal hearing that takes place to force Figaro to keep his contract with Marcellina it is revealed that she is really his mother (and that Bartolo is his father) so it is impossible for him to become her husband, contract notwithstanding.

The Countess sings of her happy past, the love she once knew with Almaviva, in an aria: *I remember days long departed*, and dictates a love letter to Susanna, with instructions to give it to the Count.

Susanna, fond of her mistress and of Figaro, intends to lead the Count back to the Countess' arms with this letter. She fastens it with a pin and asks him to return the pin as a sign that he will keep their rendezvous. Now that Figaro's affairs are in good order (the marriage contract with Marcellina cancelled, his debt dismissed) the Count cannot refuse consent to his valet's marriage. General rejoicing takes place and a bevy of pretty village maidens arrive for the wedding feast, Cherubino among them and still disguised as a girl. The Count has meanwhile ordered him off to take up a commission in the army but the love-sick young man cannot tear himself from the Countess. While Susanna strums her guitar Cherubino sighs and sings: *Come, fair ladies, instruct me in love*, for which Mozart provided this charming air:

The Count returns the pin (he is elated!) to Susanna by way of the gardener's daughter, Barbarina. She loses the pin and while expressing her worry and fright is surprised by Figaro and his mama, Marcellina. When Figaro learns that Susanna has made a rendezvous with their master he suspects her of planning to deceive him, and loudly laments, raging against the perfidy of women in general and his fiancée in particular.

The Countess and Susanna come into the garden and exchange their cloaks, so that Almaviva will mistake his wife for her maid. Susanna, truly in love with Figaro, sings of her "heart's delight," and Figaro, stealing upon her, pretends that he mistakes her for her mistress—he, in fact, knows it is Susanna. Now a fine piece of histrionics begins: Susanna in a temper boxes Figaro's ears because she thinks he thinks she is the Countess, and she becomes jealous at his fancied infatuation for Rosina. Figaro cannot resist teasing her and insists she is the Countess.

At length, Figaro stops the joke by taking Susanna in his arms and "forgiving" her. She consents to "forgive" him, also. The Count comes on them in their embrace, recognizes his wife's cloak, and accuses his supposed Countess and his valet of a love affair. In his rage, he calls all the servants in the castle to note what he has discovered— in comes the Countess, there stands Susanna, meek and mild in Figaro's arms. Made to look like a fool, the Count apologizes to the Countess and begs her to forgive his unjust suspicions. She gives him this forgiveness so sweetly that Mozart's music leaves no doubt as to her compassion for this pathetic figure—an aging Don Juan who pursues the glitter while ignoring the gold in his possession. Susanna is the jubilant girl who gets the famous Barber.

Both operas are delightful experiences in the *opera buffa* style and Mozart's is more sophisticated, and enriched by the most inventive musical characterizations. There are four sopranos, Rosina, Cherubino, Susanna and Barbarina, and (though it is difficult to express in words) in fact these four voices are as different and separate as the four women whose roles they signify. The Countess is a lovely, mature woman; Susanna is a coquette who enjoys flirting with danger; Cherubino is a love-sick boy; and Barbarina is a scatter-brain. Nothing could better describe a scatter-brain than Mozart's music for Barberina, when she had lost the fateful pin:

To this, feckless Barbarina rushes about, wringing her hands and wailing: *O, how dreadful! have I lost it? O, wherever can it be!*

Mozart's Figaro is a mellower chap than Rossini's irrepressible general factotum, and sings a bachelor's dirge on the eve of his wedding: *Say goodbye now to pastime and play, lad; say goodbye to the girls you have known!*

all very much in the mood of Mr. Doolittle in *My Fair Lady* on the eve of *his* wedding.

Mozart's Count Almaviva is pitilessly drawn as an aging roué, still stirred by passion, singing of his planned seduction of Susanna with more fervor than he sang to Rosina in his youthful ardors.

Count Almaviva in *The Barber of Seville* and *The Marriage of Figaro* is the remarkable study of a man (unwittingly undertaken in collaboration by Mozart and Rossini) from young manhood into late middle-age. The two halves of a rake are put together in the operas, and the man himself wholly contained in the characters who sing (in Rossini's *Barber of Seville*):

> *Pace e gioia sia con voi*
> Peace and joy I bring with me

and (in Mozart's *Marriage of Figaro*):

> *Mi sento dal contento pieno di gioia il cor*
> All my desires to obtain with joy beyond expression

In the first Almaviva is masquerading as a music teacher, come to give Rosina a lesson and here he is in a sympathetic role, the young gallant stealing the young ward from her ugly old guardian, Bartolo. But in the second opera Almaviva, no longer young, is pursuing his wife's maid and is it love of Susanna or love of his lost youth that pierces him? He is a comic Faust, and one we can understand very well—and understand, perhaps, the private devils that inhabit the hell he makes for himself in Mozart's opera.

In 1791, Mozart's last opera was created as *The Magic Flute*, undertaken on commission from Emanuel Schikaneder, actor-playwright and impresario, and an old friend of Mozart from Salzburg. He operated the Theater-auf-der-Wien in Vienna and was very successful in presenting popular entertainment to the Viennese. He wrote the libretto of *The Magic Flute* for Mozart to compose a *Singspiel*, with German text and dialogue instead of opera recitative. The plot was almost burlesque in Good versus Bad elements, with characters that were allegorical rather than human, and the object was to make attractive young persons fall in love and then complicate the romance with every trick the audience would accept and the collaborators, Mozart and Schikaneder, could contrive. But Mozart did not contrive a hack job; instead, he composed a marvelous opera.

In form, it is deceptively simple: musically, the opera comprises twenty-one numbers, two of these finales, varying in length from one to seven minutes each. The dialogue of the libretto is sometimes several pages long, so that it is almost a play with music. In the music Mozart introduced popular song and dance tunes of the day, as well as fancy Italian touches like coloratura. But he also put in *glockenspiel*: music made by ringing bells, like the carillon, a kind of "country music" of the time and place—much as though a 20th century opera composer might introduce a banjo or a ukelele into a serious composition. Mozart entered into Schikaneder's plans for a gala entertainment (for the Viennese audience en masse, the general public) with such gusto that he never stopped to think that he must play "down" to the public. But then, he was not a composer who fawned by playing "up" to persons he conceived to be his social superiors. As a result, he made of *The Magic Flute* a masterpiece, and in no other of his operas is the full range of his genius so strongly evident.

Because Mozart and Schikaneder were Freemasons and *The Magic Flute* has an interplay of demonic and angelic forces, some have transposed the opera into an allegory, seeing Maria Theresa as the wicked Queen of the Night because the Empress was against the liberal ideas of Freemasons. In this construction, the romantic pivot of the plot, an appealing pair of lovers named Tamino and Pamina, persecuted by the Queen of the Night, represented the Austrian people. Monostatos, a Moorish servant of the high priest Sarastro, was taken for the Jesuits or the Roman Catholic Church, another faction opposing radical or liberal behavior. But the opera was chiefly construed as the "Masonic opera" because of the element of mystery and the ritual in rhythms, which were believed to have been copied from the Masonic lodge ceremonies.

Whatever hidden meaning the opera may have held it was and remains a wonderful fairy tale as well as a wonderful opera. In style it is "magic opera" in a form that was exceedingly popular in Europe, examples being Weber's *The Marksman* and Franz Schubert's *The Magic Harp*.

But in Mozart's music the elementary subject of a fairy-tale becomes the mysterious theme on which to build an extraordinary composition, with arias that are beautiful beyond compare, and passages of grandeur, like those given Sarastro, the high priest. Yet never did Mozart flinch from the job in hand: a comic opera. Therefore, he wrote some of his most charmingly apt and cleverly characterized music for the antic moments of *The Magic Flute*, these being chiefly for Papageno, a bird-catcher.

Mozart had a childlike wonder (he was superstitious and believed in the supernatural, this belief apparently hastening his death while writing the *Requiem*)[22] and obviously adored fairy-tales. Also, he delighted in libretti which gave him opportunities for being a comedian, and for pairing and yet contrasting themes, persons, et cetera—a kind of musical interweaving and accentuation at which he was especially adroit and inventive.

We see him throwing himself with relish into *The Magic Flute*, where ceremonial pomp is seriously undertaken, and, also, the most flagrantly antic affairs. Yet throughout the opera a noble fundamental idea prevails, almost melancholy and somber by reason of the majestic beauty and awesome genius of the music and the composer.

That such a man would put his art wholly at the service of a pretty fairy-tale, that he would utilize "popular" song and dance tunes and a commonplace instrument of contemporary use like the glockenspiel, and that into this one work he could so happily infuse the diverse styles of *Singspiel, opera buffa, opera seria* and music drama (thus uniting in one great work all the contending but contributing forms of international opera) makes Mozart the undisputed master of modern opera, the great energizing, liberal and human force with which opera moved into the 19th century, and into an even greater popularity with audiences than it had known before Mozart.

Schikaneder was no poetic genius and his aims were dictated by theatrical effects, so that he piled Ossa on Pelion, caring not a whit for "psychological" truth or even probability. Yet, thanks to the music, the sheer theatricality of the piece emphasized its mystery and the *volte-face* which the apparently inimical High Priest makes (he turns into a benign providence for the lovers) enhances the supernatural aspect of the plot.

Of all the gems in the opera, the aria of the wicked Queen of the Night is said to be the most exacting for the coloratura soprano—indeed, some sour critics of our time say there are no living singers able to perform it as Mozart wrote it. Of all the musical passages in the work none is more apt than Tamino's flute solo. Tamino is the hero, in the serious romance; Papageno, a sort of German Harlequin, is the comic hero of the other romance which runs concurrent with Tamino's.

The scene in front of the High Priest's temple (*Act I, Scene III*) is in the sublime scale of Gluck's musical drama, and the precursor of Wagner's. This composer, inheriting the German opera tradition founded before his birth in 1813, recognized his debt to Mozart, writing of *The Magic Flute*: "Germany can never pay enough tribute to this work. Before it German opera hardly existed: this was its moment of creation."

For Mozart it was a swan song. Nine weeks after the première of *The Magic Flute*, which brought Schikaneder fame and fortune, the composer was dead.

Ludwig van Beethoven (1770-1827) was the great symphonic composer who hankered to be an equally great opera composer. His one and only essay into the genre was made when he was thirty-five: *Fidelio* (1805), for Schikaneder's theatre, Theater-auf-der-Wien in Vienna. It was a most inauspicious timing for the maiden effort, as the French army had entered Vienna that week and the theatre-going public had, in the majority, prudently quit the city. The opera was performed three times and not enthusiastically received, which made Schikaneder withdraw it. The next year, shortened to two acts and with considerable rewriting of the music by Beethoven, it received two performances only. It was not until its revival in 1814 (at another theatre, the Kartnertor in Vienna) that *Fidelio* was recognized as a success; this time, it received twenty-two performances.

It is a work in the form of French opera, a style inaugurated by Gluck and followed by an Italian, Cherubini, who admired Gluck and worked in France, living through the regimes of the Revolution and Napoleon I, in the latter of which he fell out of favor. Beethoven was a great admirer of Cherubini.

*Fidelio* is in the *opéra comique* form: spoken dialogue and not recitative connecting the musical airs for soloists and ensembles. The libretto is arranged in the manner of German *Singspiel*. But as the theme is serious enough ("Fidelio" is a girl in disguise, this masquerade undertaken so that she can free her husband from the jail where his enemy, Don Pizarro, has imprisoned him) the opera is not *buffo* but serious.

Beethoven apparently had great difficulty composing for opera and altogether lacked Mozart's great facility for integrating the common *Singspiel* with grandeur. Beethoven's shifts in musical mood, as from a wonderful aria for Lenore ("Fidelio" is really Lenore) at the climax of *Act I*, to that for the jailor (Rocco), are undertaken as though the composer were ever conscious of the lady and her station in life—and that Rocco and his aria is bourgeois *Singspiel*. It is as though where Mozart could fly on music from the sublime to the ridiculous, and wing between these two wide apart points with the ease of a great, soaring bird, Beethoven had to trudge downhill from his sublime moments to find the less-than-sublime ones. He did not have Mozart's sense of humor nor Mozart's incorrigible desire to make operatic characters into *persons*.

And Mozart was married, while Beethoven was a bachelor, which may explain the labored clichés of *Fidelio's* love scenes. Lenore and her husband Florestan are not real lovers, in the sense of Mozart's and Verdi's. Mozart's people in love, like Tamino and Pamina in *The*

*Magic Flute*, and Rosina and Almaviva in *The Marriage of Figaro*, are superlatively drawn on the ardent infatuations of youth and the ironic passions of middle-age.

Beethoven composed four overtures for *Fidelio*, the most beautiful (and famed) being the *Lenore Overture No. 3*, which is played before the dungeon scene *Act II*, but, in other styles of production for this opera, appears between the two scenes of this act. Both arrangements are attributed to Mahler and the best position of *Lenore No. 3* in *Fidelio* continues, in this era, to furnish argument for international opera buffs.

Of these three titans of the Viennese school (Haydn, Mozart and Beethoven) Mozart was the most important opera composer. Haydn's works are in the category of comic opera and (composed for the Esterhazy castle theatre) were not well known and influential on European opera. Beethoven's *Fidelio*, not lacking merit as an opera (and sometimes described as a perfect opera by the most dedicated Beethoven fans) is an isolated and largely experimental work by this great composer. But Mozart, in the time when instrumental music for orchestra, as in the symphonic form, was achieving a popularity which threatened to outrank opera, was both a titan of instrumental music and of opera. Even if he had been incapable of creating the marvelous and beautiful music he wrote for operas his individual and instinctive approach to opera, the "humanizing" influence he instigated for it would have made him esteemed among the opera makers.

The marvel of Mozart as an opera composer is that his music was created spontaneously but with a craftsman's exacting discipline, good-humored intent and workaday or businesslike economy directed to the job in hand. For it is Mozart who set the unexampled tradition for the music in opera, saying: "I like an aria to fit a singer as perfectly as a well-tailored suit of clothes."

In this one man, a lyric and a dramatic musician, there was genius enough to please and move audiences, to create an inexhaustible new and novel world for opera, and still to make out of his operas masterpieces of its form in art.

Little success as Mozart had, personally, German opera thereafter became extremely successful, developing along with the important musical trends inaugurated and advanced by composers in Austria,

1. Anselmo Colzani
as Falstaff

2. Tito Gobbi
as Scarpia
in *Tosca*

3. Teresa Stratas
as Mimi in *La Bohème*

4. Eleanor Steber
as Donna Anna
in *Don Giovanni*

5. Licia Albanese
   in the title role
   of *Madama Butterfly*

6. Anneliese Rothenberger
   as Sophie and
   Hertha Toepper
   as Octavian in
   *Der Rosenkavalier*

7. Tito Gobbi as Scarpia and
   Maria Callas in the
   title role of *Tosca*

8. Fernando Corena
   as Leporello
   and Cesare Siepi
   as the Don,
   from *Don Giovanni*

9. Renata Tebaldi
singing the title
role of *Adriana
Lecouvreur,* with
Franco Corelli
as Maurizio

10. Minnie, *The Girl
of the Golden West,*
is sung by Dorothy
Kirsten, with Richard
Tucker as Johnson

11. Cesare Siepi as Figaro and Elisabeth Söderström as Susanna, in *The Marriage of Figaro*

12. Rigoletto with his daughter Gilda, as sung by Cornell MacNeil and Giana d'Angelo

13. William Dooley
as Jokanaan and
Birgit Nilsson
in the title
role of *Salome*

14. Joan
Sutherland (Violetta)
in the final scene
of *La Traviata,*
with Sandor Konya
as Alfredo and
Lynn Blair as Annina

15. Elisabeth Schwarzkopf
as the Marschallin
in Der Rosenkavalier

16. Anna Moffo
as Violetta
in La Traviata

Germany and their related states. The Teutonic peoples were by nature inclined to music of grandeur as well as robust comedy; to sentiments for which the fey and supernatural made strongest appeal, and to a heroic concept, a familial or ancestral worship, that preserved myth as saga. Culminating in Wagner, music and drama reached an apotheosis for opera and is therein (in its Wagnerian form and styles) one whole aspect of opera. But there was also the important aspect of opera issuing from Hoffmann and Weber, the German "romantic" opera, whose creators commenced a dynasty for the art.

### The Nineteenth Century Opera

Up to Mozart, it is comparatively easy to follow the chief opera composers in a sort of "family tree" and to trace their distinct influences in opera. Past the Mozartian epoch, the tree, as it were, is too thickly overgrown and entwined with its enormous crop of fecund composers, whose works are of varied forms and styles. A bare understanding of the opera hierarchy is to be seized from dividing the national opera traditions, as "schools" and theatres, between, say, the Italian, French and German. Yet, recognize that between these and within the entire international opera tradition, there is a relationship between opera composers, and between certain forms and styles of opera, through which opera itself is unified and strengthened as art.

Epochs in opera are, for example: early French opera, of the time of Lully; opera in France of the Italian mode of *opera buffa* resulting (after Rousseau) in *opéra comique*; French opera of the 19th century, revolutionary in character and in influence, like Daniel Auber's *Dumb Girl of Portici* (1828), and opera of two well-defined categories as grand opera and *opéra comique*, the difference in these being that grand opera was marked by grand display and serious theme, something of the class of the older, sumptuously produced opera tragedies of an earlier French epoch. Thus, grand opera, coming to its apogee in French theatre in the works of Giacomo Meyerbeer (1791-1864) was a form in which several composers worked, the Italian Rossini being one in his *William Tell* (1829).

At the same time, Hector Berlioz was trying to develop his own ideas for opera, ranging from a grand opera like *Benvenuto Cellini*

(1838) to a dramatic work in cantata form as *The Damnation of Faust*, first performed as a concert piece (1846), then staged as a theatre piece (1893), neither style ever carrying the work to the popularity of Gounod's *Faust*, created in 1859.

After this period, Bizet's *Carmen* (1875) ushered in a whole new epoch; that of the realistic or *verismo* opera. *Carmen* in itself was the most important French opera of its period.

A great deal that occurred in French opera during and immediately after the Wagnerian period in the 19th century is attributable to pro- and anti-Wagner feeling. This composer influenced composers who admired him (as did Berlioz) as well as those whose principles were opposite to his, as were Debussy's. *Leitmotiv* became a characteristic, with Bizet making good and individual use of it in *Carmen*.

French opera has always been a decidedly national development, suited to the national temperament and taste. The Paris Opéra's repertory is markedly different from those of the New York Metropolitan and London's Covent Garden Opera but it, like the Metropolitan and Covent Garden houses, has always represented French opera tradition.

French opera of the 19th century was principally composed by Daniel Auber (his *Dumb Girl of Portici* in 1828 being a significant work); Hector Berlioz; composers of romantic works, such as Adam; Gounod and Bizet (immortalized through their *Faust* and *Carmen*); Camille Saint-Saëns (whose *Samson and Delilah* is an oratorio-opera); and Jules Massenet, perhaps best known for his *Manon*. The German composers of the period included Weber and Robert Schumann at the commencement of the "romantic" period; Flotow and others as masters of the comic and romantic opera; the titan, Wagner and his emulators; and Humperdinck. Two composers who might have been within the German hierarchy, except that they made their names in French opera, are Meyerbeer (son of a Berlin banker) and Offenbach (son of a synagogue cantor in Cologne). These two were eminently Gallic in temperament for theatre and Meyerbeer established *grand opera* for the French, while Offenbach became the father of the classical operetta. When the satiric and bitter-sweet romanticism of Offenbach became the vogue, a Viennese school picked it up and exploited it in its own style—the leaders being Johann Strauss the younger, already a world-famed composer of waltzes. His *Die Fledermaus* (The Bat) in 1874 inaugurated the Viennese epoch of light opera. Few emulated him with greater success than Franz Lehar, immensely popular in his day and beyond it, as testified by his works—of which *The Merry Widow* (1905) is the prime example. Such opera mode, culminating on one branch in the American "musical" of the 20th century, grew out of *The Beggar's Opera* and *Singspiel*, and the fruits of their grafts.

While these and other events were occurring in French and German opera, Italian opera tradition continued to grow, not so much on radical styles as on the old, enduring national love of opera. In Italy, from its inception, opera was thoroughly understood and ardently loved by the Italian people—quite ordinary people, the general public, as well as the rich and noble. Italian opera tradition has its epoch of greatness, called "golden eras," but it has, primarily, a steadfast course in theatre arts.

As far into the past as Palestrina, (and as close to the present as Gian-Carlo Menotti, the American composer of Italian birth and antecedents) composers of opera music and song have come in a steady stream from Italy.

Pergolesi and Paisiello were masters of *opera buffa*, and so was another gifted Italian, Domenico Cimarosa (1749-1801), whose *The Secret Marriage* (1792) based on the *The Clandestine Marriage*, David Garrick's London play, was a great favorite of Leopold II. The emperor liked it so well that he requested an encore the first time it was performed in Vienna.

While the ambitious European nations were fighting each other (and in between rioting internally) Italy spent the 16th, 17th and 18th centuries consolidating its theatrical status at home and abroad, its native composers becoming the most famed and influential opera makers. When Gioacchino Rossini was born in 1792, it was just in time to inherit a handsome tradition. And Rossini was just the man to ornament it.

After composing five works which made no stir, Rossini's *Tancredi* in 1813 (premièred in Venice) made him one of the most admired composers. At twenty-one, coming of age as a musician, he found himself in possession of a great gift for music making and a sound sense of theatre, and living in an era to which his style was perfectly suited. His *Barber of Seville* was composed in thirteen days, the time allowed him by the Roman theatre (Teatro Argentina), which commissioned it for an opening in 1816. Rossini delivered the score in time—rather, as he wrote it, page by page, it was snatched from his pen, passed to the copyists, and circulated among the opera house's performers, so that they could as rapidly study their parts.

Giovanni Paisiello (1740-1816) was immensely popular in Rome and his version of Beaumarchais' *Barber of Seville* was well known and well liked. Incensed that the young upstart, Rossini, would use the same libretto for his opera, a Paisiello claque staged a demonstration at the première, for which Rossini played the piano accompaniment of the recitatives. All manner of things went wrong on that first night: a cat stalked across the stage during the performance, the singer in the role of Almaviva broke the string on the guitar he was supposed to play in a scene, and the singer in the role of Basilio inadvertently fell into an open trapdoor. Rossini, meaning to encourage the luckless cast, rose to his feet in the orchestra after the first act and applauded—this was taken as an exhibition of bad manners and egotism and the audience joined the Paisiello claque in the second act, whistling so loudly that not a note of the singing could be heard. Following the debacle, Rossini went home and to bed, where he stayed through the second performance, next day, refusing to return to the theatre.

But his friends arrived after the second performance with jubilant news—*The Barber of Seville* had proved an enormous success, as it was thereafter to remain. The Romans forgave Rossini for taking Paisiello's libretto to make an opera; Rossini's suited them so much better that it eventually totally eclipsed poor Paisiello's. Time would establish Rossini's *Barber* as fit companion for Mozart's *Figaro* and make it more universally popular because of its lighter vein and the romantic character of young Count Almaviva.

Three comic operas by Rossini are extant: *The Barber of Seville*, *The Italian Girl in Algiers*, and *Cinderella*, more commonly called *La Cenerentola* even in English-speaking countries. His grand opera, *William Tell*, was his last work and his greatest disappointment—having pleased audiences throughout Europe so well that critics complained he was too facile a melodist, Rossini in *Tell* pleased musicians and critics but not the public which had adored him for sixteen years. *William Tell* was an artistic success and a financial failure.

Rossini (like Mozart and Verdi) had enormous contemporary appeal for audiences. By temperament a hack, he could churn out music with astonishing facility and was intellectually lazy, never bestirring himself to work out new ideas when it was easy and convenient to take up an old one. He not only made use of poor material and let other and lesser composers insert their works in his operas but he even reproduced his own works instead of seeking more original themes. In spite of these faults, he was a creative genius and an innovator, and some of the precedents he set became operatic forms.

Until Rossini, it was the custom for a leading singer to improvise his *cadenza* (the virtuoso passage that occurs at the end of a solo) but Rossini composed his and thereafter this became the rule rather than the exception, requiring the soloist to sing what the composer had created instead of going off into flights of improvised and spontaneous song. He developed a crescendo which still bears his name, and he was a pioneer in using string instead of piano accompaniment for recitative.

His opinion of a good singer was that he "must be only an able *interpreter* of the composer's ideas, seeking to express them with all his skill and investing them with the brilliance inherent in them. In addition, players need only be faithful *executants* of the score as written." He complained that not infrequently this "execution" was distorted, "often spoiling the ideas of the composers, robbing them of that simplicity of expression which they should have." From this, we gather that Rossini felt somewhat like Gluck about the artistes (singers and instrumentalists) on whom the composer had to depend. He defined creativity as "to *extract from nothing*" [as the composer did] and maintained that "the singer, on the other hand, certainly works on something, that is to say, on poetry and on music which are not of his creation."

So much was made of his laziness (people simply could not understand how one man could turn out so much music with, apparently, so little effort) that Rossini capitalized on it as a virtue instead of a vice.

A composer asked his advice on the best time to compose an overture; Rossini's reply is his most celebrated remark: "Wait until the evening before opening night. Nothing primes inspiration more than necessity . . ."

His own procrastination maddened his employers and one, Domenico Barbaja, locked Rossini in a room with a plate of spaghetti and the threat that he would not be allowed to leave the room alive until he had written the last note of *Otello*.

For another opera, *La Gazza Ladra*, which he had not provided with an overture up to the day of the première, Rossini was again locked up in a room by the theatre manager, this time under the surveillance of four stage-hands. As he wrote the music, a stage-hand threw it down, page by page, to copyists waiting below a window, so that it could be transcribed into parts for the players. "In default of pages," confessed Rossini, "they were ordered to throw me out of the window bodily."

The same Barbaja (the most important impresario in Italy and director of La Scala) hired Rossini to direct two opera troupes in Naples and write works for them. From his first opera, *Elisabetta*, he claimed the prima donna Isabella Colbran for his wife. She was a very popular Italian singer and Rossini wrote several works for her. His contract with Barbaja allowed him to accept commissions and it was for one such that he dashed off *The Barber*.

There was no time to compose an overture for *The Barber* (into which Rossini crammed music from earlier operas) so he tacked on to it the same overture he had used before, for *Aureliano* and *Elisabetta*. "The public was completely satisfied," Rossini remarked sanguinely.

But he could create most difficult music, all the same, and his *The Italian Girl in Algiers* requires a splendid coloratura technique of the mezzo-soprano title role (whose name is Elisabetta—for like Molière, Rossini had the distracting habit of using a name over and over for his characters).

Aged thirty, he adventured out of Italy for the first time—to find himself a household word in international opera, where *The Barber* and his other works had made him the most celebrated of composers. He was feted in Vienna and in 1824 went to live in Paris, where he became the director of *Théâtre des Italiens*, and was given a contract by the king (Charles X) to write five operas a year for a decade, thereafter to be pensioned by the government. Under this princely agreement, Rossini wrote *William Tell*—and nothing more, retiring from the theatre and spending the next twenty years of his life in litigation over his contract.

At the age of thirty-seven, but with nearly forty more years to live, the famed, wealthy and well-loved composer stopped working and devoted himself to caring for his health (he suffered from neurasthenia), and to his passion for Olympe Pelissier, whom he married in 1855, after the death of his first wife.

A worldly, witty man, the most charming of companions, Rossini was an important figure in the cultured life of Paris, where he and Olympe lived in great style, noted hosts and society leaders. The French buried Rossini at Père Lachaise, Paris' famed cemetery, then at the request of the Italian government exhumed the body and sent it to Florence to be reburied at Santa Croce.

While it is usual to think of Rossini as a glib, facile composer the fact is that he worked hard enough in his productive years, turning out two or more works a year for nearly twenty years; sometimes as many as four a year. And not since Monteverdi had an Italian composer made such rich use of orchestration, and developed the orchestra with such expressiveness and variety. *William Tell* in itself was a monumental achievement, a new genre for the composer and one in which he worked well enough to cause Bellini, his compatriot, to say it reduced all other operas of the day to pygmies; Wagner to state that it antici-pated his own dramatic ideas and stylistic modes. A work in the grandest grand opera ideal, *William Tell* requires six hours for its full production. Had Rossini persevered in working, he might have become the peer of Verdi.

In this felicitous time for melody, Rossini's two contemporaries Donizetti and Bellini were only scarcely less gifted than Rossini, and Donizetti enjoyed fame and fortune in his lifetime as the elder did—he (Rossini) being the first composer to become wealthy writing operas.

Gaetano Donizetti (1797-1848) wrote Italian and French operas, was as popular in Paris as in Italy, and had a Gallic elegance as well as a native gusto for music. His two masterworks, *Don Pasquale* and *Lucia di Lammermoor*, are stunning expositions of one theme, turned upside down to create a comedy that ranks with *The Barber of Seville* and a tragedy that compares with Bellini's works—these all in the tragic vein.

The theme is one much used in theatre: young lovers thwarted by their elders or by persons in power who wickedly abuse that power to keep the lovers apart. Don Pasquale is a kind of Dr. Bartolo and the lovers are his nephew, Ernesto, a tenor, who is threatened with disinheritance of his uncle's fortune if he persists in marrying a pretty little widow, the soprano Norina. It is a variation on *La Serva Padrona* but very wittily undertaken, with grace and considerable skill for the coloratura role of Norina. Besides, it has a novel chorus in *Act III*, where the servants sing: "What perpetual coming and going . . ."—a number that still brings down the house in the jaded 20th century.

*Lucia di Lammermoor*, based on Sir Walter Scott's romance, is almost a Sicilian vendetta, the sort of love affair in which any Italian theatre man would feel at home. Lucy's mad scene is one of the plums in the dramatic soprano's repertory—especially as she is also expected to be a singer in the *bel canto* style. The opera is revived, together with Bellini's *Norma*, only when a qualified singer comes along—as, in the present era, the Australian Joan Sutherland and the Greek-American Maria Callas have come.

Donizetti wrote sixty-seven operas, of which *Don Pasquale* (created for *Théâtre des Italiens* in 1846) was the last major success. He apparently suffered from brain damage, possibly tumorous, had violent headaches and aberrations and was committed to an asylum for the mentally ill. Leaving there to live with his brother in his native Bergamo he died shortly thereafter, but for half a century more his works remained in style and today (with *Don Pasquale* and *Lucia di Lammermoor*) he is still treasured among the best-loved composers. His fine *opera buffa The Elixir of Love* returned to the English-speaking repertory in mid-20th century.

Vincenzo Bellini (1801-1835) was a composer of passion and melody and in this characteristic is the precursor of Verdi. He enjoyed the collaboration of a good librettist, Felice Romani, with whom *La Sonnambula* (The Sleepwalker) and *Norma* were composed. These are two of Bellini's greatest extant works, although he considered his last (and eleventh) opera, *I Puritani*, his masterpiece.

*The Sleepwalker* and *Norma* (both created in one year, 1831) are distinguished by grand emotion and a melting lyricism in song. The Sleepwalker is Amina, to whom Bellini gave lovely arias which deify this rustic beauty among the principal soprano roles in the lyric hierarchy. An opera in one act and four scenes, it is set in Bellini's time (early 19th century) and is of the natural and romantic genre.

For *Norma*, Bellini and Romani reincarnated the Druids of the first century A.D., in a setting in early Gaul, and caused the romantic conflict to occur between Norma, a Druid priestess, and a Roman consul. Norma is somewhat like Medea, and like Aida and Radames, Norma and her Roman lover are sacrificed for religious and political principles and die together, in sublimely ecstatic music and mood.

*I Puritani* is one example of how opera evolves its own forms and makes its own principles, holding poetry as its handmaiden, not as its mistress. Bellini, a man about town in Paris and the idolized composer of the era, frequented the salon of a society lady, Princess Cristina of Belgiojoso, who was admired by Heine and Chopin and kept a salon for men of letters as well as of theatre arts. Here Bellini made the acquaintance of Count Pepoli, a refugee from the Austrian occupation of Italy, and invited him to furnish a libretto for a new opera. Pepoli was a minor poet but altogether inexperienced in writing for theatre. He proposed several ideas for libretti, Bellini eventually choosing one on the Puritans in the period of Britain's Civil War between Royalists and Roundheads. Charles I's widow, the French Queen Henrietta, appears in the cast. It is yet another opera of the thwarting of love between a soprano, Elvira, and a tenor, the Royalist Sir Arthur Talbot.

Bellini brought his considerable knowledge of theatre to the making of *I Puritani*, which has a "mad scene" for the soprano (as does Donizetti's *Lucia*), and every other sure-fire adjunct of romantic drama: political intrigue, civil war (always more disturbing than war between two separate nations), heroic demands of the tenor (he has to choose between loyalty to the Stuarts and sensual love: Henrietta or Elvira), heart-rending anguish of the soprano (her father and lover are Royalists; she is obliged to marry a Puritan general—another tenor, which makes the music interestingly complex).

Pepoli, a poet concerned purely with his verse, insisted on correctness above dramatic and emotional nuances in the libretto and the making of *I Puritani* was a vexation for its contending collaborationists. However, its première was a triumph, and Bellini had to take a curtain call from the overwrought audience, which wept unashamedly (at *Théâtre des Italiens*) when Elvira sang her *Qui la voce sua soave*—Yes, t'is here, where once so brightly fell those accents that breath'd my name . . . With a crown of roses on her dishevelled hair, like Ophelia, she crazily enacts the marriage ceremony she has been denied with Sir Arthur.

Bellini kept his head amidst the wild adulation after the finale, writing to a friend in Milan: "It is unnecessary for me to describe the duet for the two basses; you must have heard it where you are!"

His correspondence (with his closest friend, Francesco Florimo, with whom Bellini shared student days at the Neapolitan conservatory) shows how seriously and astutely Bellini worked to perfect *I Puritani.* Florimo advised the composer to end the opera with a big scene for the prima donna (a customary exhibition which pleased the public and delighted the soprano if not the tenor) but Bellini decided against this, writing: "You advise me to finish up my *I Puritani* with a big scene for the prima donna. I did intend to do so, but, in consequence of some very proper changes in the second act, the singer's scene comes in the middle of this act, a situation rather like that quator of *Nina* [one of Paisiello's operas], but with a different setting, passing through phases of melancholy, gaiety, dimness, and ending in a vigorous *agitato.* So another scene at the end, perhaps misplaced, could only injure the whole—I have decided to close it with a little duet, graceful or passionate, between the tenor and the prima donna, like that in the first finale of *La Sonnambula.* It would be preceded by a *largo* concerted between the two basses, the tenor, the soprano and the chorus, as in *Norma.* I think it will go pretty well, the situation being interesting during the whole performance." Incidentally, he was quite right!

The soprano of the hour was Maria Felicita Garcia-Malibran, called Malibran, daughter of the celebrated singer and composer who created the role of Almaviva in *The Barber of Seville* at its Paris première. In April, 1833, while Bellini was in London, he heard her sing *La Sonnambula* and determined to have her create (for its Neapolitan première) the role of Elvira in *I Puritani,* writing to Florimo: "Yes, certainly I will do a new *cavatina* [a short aria] for Mme. Malibran . . . Lastly, tell her that I will arrange and adapt *I Puritani* for her voice, and she need not fear the part as it is as passionate as *Nina,* and the situations spoken and acted in prose by her would by themselves be tremendously effective."

Malibran was a dramatic soprano and a tailored role for her by Bellini was most attractive—but she was destined not to sing it, nor Bellini to hear her. In 1835, following the première of *I Puritani* in Paris, the composer began work on two other operas, contracted an intestinal fever and died in delirium, believing that a performance of

*I Puritani* was taking place in his bedroom. Malibran was in Milan, looking forward to going to Naples to sing Elvira, when the news of Bellini's death reached her. He had died September 23, 1835. The prima donna burst into tears, exclaiming: *Sento che non tarderò molto a seguirlo* (I feel I shall soon follow him). As she did, to the day, herself dying on September 23, 1836.

Bellini was not versatile in comedy and tragedy like Donizetti, nor a facile genius like Rossini, but he had a great gift for composing arias and he was invariably lyrical throughout all the dramatic and emotional scenes of his works. He is buried (in his native Cantina) under a stone inscribed with the first notes of Amina's *Ah! non credea mirarti*—Scarcely could I believe it! from *La Sonnambula*. It was a romantic age.

The 19th century was dominated by the "romantic" influence in opera and the thesis of Wagner's music-drama. Wagner's principles were not immediately accepted but when they were they became almost total, extending into Verdi's Italian works, and into French opera. In this period, the Paris Opéra rose to superlative status in the international opera, losing its pristine place only at the end of the century, The French composers obviously influenced by Wagner, and those advertising themselves as against his theories, alike added to the prestige of French opera.

The comic opera, once entrenched in a national tradition, never again yielded its popularity.

"Romanticism" and "classicism" are qualifying attributes of 19th century theatre, especially manifested in opera and ballet and emergent from poetry and music, and from painting and other arts. In "romantic" works the accents were more on color and mood than on form and design—but, of course, it was (and is) possible to combine all these characteristics and contain in a single opera (or a ballet) color and mood, form and design, thereby producing a work that is both romantic and classical. Adam in France was a leading romantic composer (writing thirty-nine operas and fourteen ballets) but as a musician he was not the equal of Germany's leading romantic composer, Robert Schumann (1810-1856), who wrote only one opera: *Genoveva* (1850), yet is known as the genius of the romantic genre. Like Weber and Berlioz, Schumann was a journalist as well as a composer (indeed Schumann in his lifetime was considered more the former than the latter) and his opinions and dissertations are valuable for the reader desiring a first-hand idea of what is so mysteriously labelled "romanticism."[23]

"Romanticism" in opera terminology refers to the formal structure of an opera, and to the style of expression—which is free and "emotional" (sometimes extravagantly so) rather than, as in *Pelléas and Mélisande*, restrained. The "natural" style (which is briefly described in *The Beginning*) culminated in romanticism and the subject matter of romantic opera (its characterizations and the events in which human principals are involved) is realistic, and always of strong emotional expression. These are the operas in which *feeling* is interpreted with large gestures, rapid action, vivid visual details and, almost invariably, grand roles for singers' interpretations.

The plots are apt to be melodramatic because melodrama is a 19th century characteristic. To sustain the drama, the action is paced to achieve a series of climaxes ending in a grand climax: the finale. When a triumph of stagecraft combines with beautiful music and singing then we have the greatest type of romantic opera, of which Verdi's *Aida* and *Otello* are the finest examples in the Italian style.

These operas are distinguished (as is almost all authentic Romantic opera) by strong dramatic tensions and sequences of tensions (climaxes building towards the final climax), all swept steadily (we may say, inexorably) through music and action to the great clause or theme of the opera. Passion and poetry are inextricably blended, especially in *Otello* which is based on Shakespeare's verse. In addition, these operas have the formal trappings or accoutrements of "Romantic" opera: several changes of scene (four acts in seven scenes for *Aida*; four acts in as many scenes for *Otello*), and large casts. The visual or scenic aspect is never less than grand—far, far removed from the bare "abstractions" of 20th century theatre, in which opera and ballet are stripped of all save essential properties in staging. Consider the palace and temple scenes in *Aida* and know that in *Otello* the action is set in a 15th century castle overlooking a harbor—allowing the opera's staging to include a storm at sea, a great bonfire on the shore, and a populace as great as the massed Egyptians and Ethiopians of *Aida*.

Claude Debussy (1862-1918) was the last of the independent

romanticists and although he wrote only one opera, *Pelléas and Mélisande,* he is a historical personage, standing at the end of the great tradition of French romantic opera. He was motivated by impressionism, the same element that transformed the era's painting and poetry, aesthetic principles directly opposite to the dramatic. Following Debussy, but moving into the 20th century, came Maurice Ravel (1875-1937) and Manuel de Falla (1876-1946), a Spaniard who is counted among the French composers because of his debt to this school.

In German opera, Wagner had several emulators and successors, among them Engelbert Humperdinck (1854-1921) whose *Hansel and Gretel* is an imperishable if simple musical joy.

The classical operetta is a subject omitted entirely from this book (like "grand opera") save to note that operetta in its apogee under Jacques Offenbach (1819-1880) is a sophisticated descendant of Gay's impertinent and merry *The Beggar's Opera.* Offenbach wrote more than one hundred operettas and by his masterful handling of his subject deserves (and requires) far more than a passing glance. The same applies to Johann Strauss the Younger (1825-1899) who became in Vienna the personage that Offenbach was in Paris. Strauss' *Fledermaus* or *Bat* mingles quite respectably in opera repertory and is as popular as Richard Strauss' *Der Rosenkavalier.*

This Strauss (Richard) is the most important composer in late 19th century German romanticism, his life span being 1864-1949. He was the foremost German composer after Wagner, and was a famous composer-conductor of his time. In 1919-1924 he was principal conductor and co-director of music for the Vienna State Opera, conducted at musical festivals in Munich, Bayreuth and Salzburg, and (as orchestra conductor) worked in the United States in 1904 and 1921. He wrote several operas, the best-known in America being *Der Rosenkavalier* and *Arabella.* His small opera *Ariadne auf Naxos* is derived from *Le Bourgeois Gentilhomme* (Molière-Lully) and is a tour de force, presenting a serious and a comic opera simultaneously. His *Capriccio,* an opera about opera, takes up the argument that has always raged: which is the more important in opera, the poetry or the music?

*Capriccio,* Strauss' last opera (composed in 1942) is set in 18th century Paris, the period of Gluck's reforms in opera.

If you begin with Gluck and come to Richard Strauss you have made a great circle, and in Richard Strauss, traveling through opera history from Mozart, the art stands in almost perfect ellipse.

At least, up to the beginning of the 20th century!

The 20th century established a new ideal, with new principles for art as well as life and 20th century opera contains the genuine "American opera" and a new if tentative flowering of British opera which may trace itself to Purcell and even farther back in history, if it chooses.

The modern opera, like Medieval man, has a present that is founded on its past. Whatever its future is to be will, in great degree, come from its present—eventually, to join the past.

Opera's romantic past is vividly alive in the international repertory, where the major works, the "classics," almost all date fifty or a hundred years before mid-20th century theatre. And this past is vivid, also, in the memories of the opera makers.

We see them in the records that have accumulated since the latter half of the 16th century, in part in their own words and in part through the descriptions, friendly or inimical, of others in their times.

Look back, with an imaginative eye, and see a Florentine, aged about sixty, dressed in the clothes of his time and his station (a not inferior one) explaining earnestly why he had invented a "new" music. This fellow had a beautiful voice and quite naturally wished to make the most of it; he was Giulio Caccini, one of the Camerata, and his ideal was to elevate the solo voice in the monodic style; the *stile rappresentativo*. Counterpoint had come to its most fruitful expression; it was now voted over-elaborate and "old" by the avant-garde poets and musicians, sympathetically encouraged by the intelligentsia among the rich and noble "patrons of the arts." Soloists were not yet the vogue because a solo part would have been thought extraneous and tasteless in the vocal mode or form of that day. Music was polyphonic and vocal ensembles were at their zenith in counterpoint. Caccini now, as we look back, seizes on the idea of extolling the human voice in an individual or solo form, and produces a great novelty, "new" music to alarm and shock the traditionalists and their conventions. He composes songs for solo voice accompanied (in chords) by stringed instruments. In defense and explanation of his theories, Caccini writes (in *Le Nuove Musiche*, printed in 1614): "Returning to Florence I observed that at that time musicians were setting certain songs to vulgar words which, to my mind, were neither appropriate nor well regarded by people of taste. It then occurred to me to compose a few songs in the style of an aria [an air, or melody] to be played with several stringed instruments in order to lift the spirits of the listener."

'Lift the spirits of the listener' is what Caccini proposes to do and it is in this proposition that all the great opera makers thereafter engage their art and craft. Drama through music, hereafter, will stir us to laughter or to tears.

The Italians do this with such brio and eclat and do it so well in a theatrical character that the new art called Opera flies around the Western world and is adopted and adapted by every society rich and fashionable enough to take it up. Where, in such societies, there were native men of genius, "national" opera traditions developed. The individual romances or histories of national operas are fascinating.

The Sun King and his court, the most splendid in Europe, dance (as an acid critic has remarked) like marvelous clockwork figures across the pages of French history. They dance with such physical adeptness and grace that one might think they did nothing else, although Louis XIV also hunted, made love and commissioned the arts of painters, sculptors and architects for the embellishment of royal palaces and public places of la belle France. Theatre was burgeoning in its professional estate and although the Roman Catholic Church did not allow actors to receive the sacraments the *Comédie Italienne* had a special papal dispensation and actors describing themselves as "musicians" could be baptized and given Extreme Unction on their death beds by amenable priests.

It is at this historical point that French opera comes into being, through the diabolical energy and ambitions of a Florentine scullion, raised by the King of France to the most omnipotent position in French arts. Nimble and fleet of foot, grimacing like a monkey, every nerve and sinew impregnated with the verve and wit of commedia dell'arte, his blood gushing in the passionate stream of Italy's music, Lully springs on the scene. By the time he has cavorted across it he has changed opera in France and given to the art a new form: opera-ballet.

How perfectly we see this dark-visaged, grinning creature, a common opportunist and a wickedly ruthless negotiator of his musi-

cianly ends. A monster of egotism who found a way to make himself
indispensible to Louis by keeping him entertained (by knowing how
to lift Louis' spirits), Lully drives poor Robert Cambert into exile and
turns the householders of the Académie Royale out of their home in
the Rue Mazarine, and even succeeds in gaining exclusive copyright of
opera-ballets which were half Molière's, by which Molière suffered
considerable financial loss.

His rapacity is described by La Fontaine in *Le Florentin*: "He's
a libertine, an all-devouring, all-grabbing, all-hoarding mongrel with
a triple throat. Give him anything, stuff him with it, the glutton
demands more; the King himself would have trouble in appeasing
him."

Scarcely until Wagner would an opera composer inspire such
detestation but seldom has an artiste been so highly esteemed by a
patron as Lully was by Louis, who declared to the minister Colbert
that he could not resist the demands of his master-maker of *divertissements*—and Lully, whenever he flew into a temper from being crossed,
would threaten to leave Paris and return to Florence. Yet how could
even his enemies help but applaud him for his feats in grand entertainments, the *Menus Plaisirs* he cooked up like an inspired chef? See him
as the Mufti, wearing an enormous turban with candles blazing on it,
performing a pseudo-Turkish dance of his own choreography, and
shouting *Hou la ba, ba la chou, ba la ba, ba la da,* in Molière's *Le
Bourgeois Gentilhomme*. Or (in his most celebrated feat) as Molière's
Dr. Chiachiarroni in *Monsieur de Pourceaugnac,* cavorting across the
stage in a leap that cannot have been surpassed by Nijinsky, straight
into a harpsichord, smashing it to bits.

He cared not a jot that no one loved him save the king, and least
of all La Fontaine (again from *Le Florentin*):

> Sa femme, ses enfants, et tout le genre humain,
>    Petits et grands, dans leurs prières
>    Disent le soir et le matin;
> 'Seigneur, par Vos bontés pour nous si singulières,
>    Délivrez-nous du Florentin!' *

* His wife, his children, and the entire human race, great and small, pray
night and day; 'Lord, of Your singular goodness towards us, deliver us from the
Florentine!'

And because he cared about no one save himself and about little else save music Lully founded the tradition from which all the French opera makers come. It was a singular achievement for any man at any period of history, and despite making life a hell on earth for several of his compeers the detestable Lully doubtless winged his way to the special heaven reserved for opera makers, hymned there by the final song he industriously composed on his deathbed: *Bisogna morire, peccatore.*

Not too far away in time from the Florentine father of French opera we come to the great philosophic dilettante, Rousseau, who had a great deal to say about music, writing a volume on the subject as *Ecrites sur la Musique* (it was here he defended the Italians in the *Guerre des Bouffons*) and maintaining with his characteristic pedagoguery that Italian was a better language for singing than French. How piquant, then, that Rousseau is the father of a peculiarly French opera form, the *opéra comique!* His *The Village Soothsayer* (1752) is the signpost that, romantically, marks the new way of making opera: with spoken dialogue interpolated between musical passages.

Opera in Germany during the baroque period had a golden era during the reign of Charles VI (1711-1740) and if we imagine ourselves attending a performance in the Vienna Imperial Theatre, of a work by Johann Joseph Fux, we might expect to find the music of less importance than the scenery. From a taste cultivated on the works of Italians (like Cesti's *Pomo d'Oro*) the Viennese opera was more musical extravaganza than the austere art the Camerata had evolved for music and drama. Fux, a celebrated composer of the time, was considered the equal of the Italian masters he emulated, and with the Imperial treasury to assist him he was able to produce a masterpiece like *Angelica,* the second act of which featured a lake on which two flotillas of battleships (painted in gold) engaged each other.

Johann Adolf Hasse, an admirable composer in the esteem of the Italians and the Germans, wrote an opera, *Solimano,* which required live elephants and camels, a fully panopolied Turkish camp, a replica of the Gardens of Babylon, and ships "sailing" on a river. And his *Ezio* actually included a march of four hundred soldiers with one hundred horses, the latter being requisitioned from the Imperial stables— the march consuming twenty-five minutes of the opera!

Opera was ruled not by the composer in this era but by the poet Pietro Metastasio who from Vienna exercised an incredible dictatorship over opera everywhere. It is not surprising that a scenic designer named Servandoni was more famed and wealthy than most composers—or that he took himself so seriously that once, when an accidental fire destroyed a temple he had built for a musical extravaganza, this fellow drew his sword on an English duke out of pure pique.

It was a time when music was made for kings and queens, and at the command of emperors and courtesans; for every purpose from a cruise up-river to the commemoration of a political treaty. The Peace of Aix-la-Chapelle in 1748 ended the war of the Austrian Succession and required, at George II's command, a display of fireworks and a significant musical remark from Handel. So he wrote *Music for the Royal Fireworks,* with a pause after the Overture (before the Bourrée, Largo, two Minuets, et cetera) for a salute by one hundred and one cannons.

Dancing with impatience for the show to begin, his Hanoverian Majesty changed his uniform every two hours and no gentlemen have ever been so pleased to hear an overture as the unfortunates who had to dress and undress the excited monarch. Forty trumpets, twenty horns, sixteen oboes, sixteen bassoons, eight pairs of kettledrums, twelve side drums and equal numbers of flutes and fifes played for the gala. Handel in music was as great a king as George in England and Alexander Pope saluted the composer thus:

> Strong in new arms, lo! giant Handel stands,
> Like bold Briareus, with a hundred hands;
> To stir, to rouse, to shake the soul he comes,
> And Jove's own thunder follows Mars' drums . . .

The giant fell and his crash was hardly heard in the laughter roaring out from the theatre where *The Beggar's Opera* was making Gay rich and Rich gay . . .

Then, amidst these vivid shades, comes Gluck, bold enough to challenge Metastasio's absolute rule. After traveling about Europe for twenty years (making operas in the styles of Hasse, Handel and Rameau) he meets Calzabigi. With Marie Antoinette as his champion and the Paris Opéra stage as his arena, Gluck fights for his principles and wins, defeating not only Metastasio but Piccinni as well.

Shedding superficial decoration, opera here returned to the ideal the Camerata had visioned but already opera was stronger, more complex, altogether a greater art.

In the epoch of Mozart the architecture of opera changes, music assuming a flexible, dynamic form, drama becoming infused with vitality and human reason and feeling.

After Mozart and the "classical" age we reach the romanticists, those passionate individuals who in music were like Byron and Shelley in poetry. How better to understand those possessed young men than to know Berlioz's story? Aged twenty-six he fell in love with an actress whom he had never met, an Irish girl named Harriet Smithson. Perhaps autobiographically, he wrote his *Symphonie Fantastique* (1829), describing the score in his own words: "A young musician of morbid sensibility and ardent imagination poisons himself with opium in a fit of amorous despair. The dose, too weak to kill him, plunges him into a heavy sleep accompanied by visions. The beloved woman has become for him a melody which he finds and hears everywhere."[24]

Many 19th century people deeply distrusted this sort of music, Rossini among them. In a letter to a friend, Leopoldo Cicognara, dated February 12, 1817, Rossini wrote: "Ever since the five notes were added to the harpsichord [he refers to the extension of the harpsichord keyboard from 4½ to 5 octaves, *circa* 1750] I have maintained that a dire revolution was brewing in our art which, at that time, had reached perfection; for experience has shown that when we wish perforce to achieve the best, we fall into the worst."

Rossini had by then created *The Barber of Seville* and *La Cenerentola; William Tell* and some other important operas were still to come from his pen. His letter continues: "Haydn had already begun to corrupt purity of taste by introducing strange chords, artificial passages and daring novelties into his compositions, but he still preserved a sublimity and traditional music which would seem to excuse his deviations . . . finally, Beethoven, with his compositions lacking in unity and natural flow and full of arbitrary oddities, corrupted taste in instrumental music completely. And now, for the simple and majestic styles of Sarti, Paisiello and Cimarosa, [others have] substituted in the theatre [their] own ingenious but vicious harmonies in which the main melody is strangled in deference to the new German school wherein all the young composers have set out to write theatre music.

"Many of our singers, born outside Italy, have renounced purity of musical taste which never found roots beyond the confines of Italy, and have adopted the impure style of foreigners to please the capitals of Europe. They have then returned, bringing back and spreading here the germs of bad taste.

"Warblings, leaps, trills, jumps, abuses of semitones, clusters of notes, these characterize the singing which now prevails. Therefore meter, the essential part of music, without which melody is incomprehensible and harmony falls into disorder, is ignored and violated by singers. They astound rather than move the public, and whereas in the good old days players sought to make their instruments sing, now our singers endeavor to handle their voices as if they were instruments. The populace, meantime applauding such bad style, makes of music what the Jesuits made of poetry and oratory when they preferred Lucan to Virgil, Seneca to Cicero.

"These are my ideas on the current state of music, and I confess to you that I have little hope of seeing this divine art emerge from the corruption in which it is submerged without the total overthrow of existing social institutions and, as you see, the remedy might then be worse than the disease."

I have quoted this bitter diatribe against 19th century harmonics because it might have been written today by a man of our times about the "new" music which by being altogether strange and foreign to 19th century "classical" music appears to some of us to be "impure," full of "oddities," with melody that is incomprehensible, harmony in disorder, and of such "bad style" that the traditionalists now believe that unless the divine art of music emerges from the corruption in which it is submerged music will perish altogether. Every age has its conventions outraged, its traditionalists shocked. The new and the strange, the avant-garde is suspected as a derangement of reason, an offense against form, in every era. There never was an ideal defined, a principle established without contention and dissension.

Rossini's view was shrewd. As he foresaw, the Germans did not rest until they had learned to handle voices like instruments, as witness Richard Strauss. Yet in the newest and most revolutionary form the oldest verities were evident, and antique styles in ellipse became the mode.

In its rebellion against the "classical," 20th century music moved back towards the Renaissance style and the polyphonic form was revived in place of the monophonic. In drama and poetry and music "reality" was so abhorred that fantasy and caricature were points of departure for "theatre of the absurd."

Before the new century was twenty years old it had known a world war (with an encore to come before another twenty years) and another revolution: the Russian.

The mood as well as the form of music had changed; life was grimmer than it had seemed for the gay Venetians and the gay Viennese. The waltz, for instance, was considered effete (and, also, erotic) and a new sentiment, as well as a new music and drama, had to express the scepticism, doubt and anxiety of the 20th century. What had seemed fresh, vital and valid in the 19th century, what had been elegant was naïve and passé. All the romantic and narcissus-like geniuses who had affronted Rossini at the beginning of the 19th century (when that was new and they were modern) were dead and buried, and their works in disgrace.

A utilitarian (and Freudian) age now took the place of the more leisured 19th century era. Opulence was superseded by a sparse economy. The kind of theatre created in the 20th century had no place for operas of five to seven acts, and opera was everything but "grand" in the new art epoch. The radical musicians, composers of "new" music, were hardly interested in opera because 20th century ideas proselyted against extravagance, either of expression of feeling or as dramatic spectacle. Rather than a stated theme, themes were understated, cryptic and deliberately obtuse. Obscurity in art was an important philosophic element and for many artists materialism became decadence; they required art to be obliquely viewed or viewed in strange perspectives.

The concept of music drama, on which opera was founded, was altered in 20th century music. The form of the opera was discarded; the large-scale opera shrank to one-act musical plays. Opera seemed as fluid of form as the world on the day of creation and sheer chaos existed, seemingly, until valid principles and a sense of order emerged to create a recognizably "new" music, and a new way of shaping sound as music for opera. But that is a subject for another time, another book.

# Notes

1. Atypical of 20th century music is the radical break with "Romanticism" in musical philosophy and form. In brief: modern composers today eschew tradition as a rule in reaction to the "classical" form. The fundamental change in 20th century music is in the reformation of stylistic elements of melody, rhythm, harmony, tonality and meter. Melody has been altogether altered from that of the romanticist 19th century music. Harmony, which was the most important development of the classical mode, has been negated. "Contrapuntal" music is also called "horizontal" and "linear" music, and may be described as the simultaneity of various melodic lines. "Harmonic" music is thought of as harmony recognizable in "vertical" sections of a composition; it was as characteristic of "classical" music as contrapuntal or horizontal music is characteristic of the "modern" form. Rhythm, in modern music, generally holds a primary position over melody and harmony, a development in part through American jazz, which introduced rhythmic innovations and syncopations. *Polyrhythm*: various and different rhythms used with simultaneity, is a virtuoso feat of modern music, itself characterized by its disregard for metrical constancy. In this, modern music breaks a fundamental law (the regularity of a certain number of beats in a bar of music). Another law which modern music has broken is tonality (the retention of one tonality, one key). Modern music is *atonal*: meaning music with no central key. These are some but not all the qualifying forms of "modern" music.

The result in a great deal of 20th century music has been a return or retardation to 17th century music in strict contrapuntal forms of the *fugue*, *canon*, *toccata* and *passacaglia*, which the interested reader should research, as in Scholes' *Dictionary of Music* to which I referred in *Opera Lingo*.

2. A more reasonable comparison than Monteverdi and Verdi is one between Mozart and Beethoven. So as not to appear to be implying that the greatest range of instruments is the best guarantee of major composition, let me note here than Beethoven had a larger orchestra, a bigger harmonic "palette" and a wider range of forms to work with than did Mozart. But an opinion, to which I subscribe, esteems Mozart more because he achieved superior music within his more limited compass in proportion to what Beethoven composed within an enlarged one.

3. Generally, philosophic thought takes a very gradual course before it becomes influential on society, or the audience en masse. The revolutionary age saw a hastened or accelerated consummation of the new philosophy. It went by a variety of names: Deism, the "natural religion" which propounds that man by

reason alone, and without authority, can come to a knowledge of right and wrong and of eternity; Materialism: that matter is all and nothing is the spirit, an idea by which the inspirational motive of the Bible was denied and the Church was subject to the state or its ruler; Scepticism, the philosophy of David Hume, through which men lost their sense of certainty, including faith in religious tenets; the Philosophy propounded by anti-Christian Frenchmen like Voltaire, aided by the "rationalists" Diderot and D'Alembert, and fiercely and didactically instituted by Rousseau.

In 1776, The Order of the Illuminati, a secret society designed to reform the world according to "new" doctrines, was formed by Adam Weishaupt, a professor at Ingolstadt. A wave of the new rationalism swept German art and letters and two poets, Schiller and Goethe, and the philosopher Immanuel Kant, championed the new era of freedom and enlightenment.

For about two hundred years the Jesuits and "The Society of Jesus" had attempted to maintain the Roman Catholic Church's authority in Europe by opposing "rationalism" and its various cults and philosophies. The Church itself was weak and irresolute but resisted the demands of the Bourbon family (members of which ruled France, Naples and Parma) to suppress the influence of the Jesuits. Clement XIV at length acceded and in a harsh papal letter (*Dominus ac Redemptor Noster*) in 1773 dissolved the order and the Jesuits were expelled from Spain, France and Portugal, and from the Italian states of Naples and Parma. A large number of European princes and statesmen had meanwhile become Freemasons, aligning themselves with a secret society founded in 1717. In the Masonic order of "lodges" Freemasons were divided into grades as in guilds, the Masonic society being copied from the Medieval guild of stone-workers, free masons. It was believed to be a society inimical to the Roman Catholic Church and in 1738 membership in a Masonic lodge was punished by excommunication.

4. It is this premise, that to be "different" is all, regardless of whether the difference increases or decreases the worth of music, which is the most singular of the radical philosophies in modern music. A number of composers have entirely alienated themselves from audiences for the reason that they do not communicate and are unable or wilfully are resolved not to be articulate. There is, in fact, nothing like "progress" in arts but only innovations and reforms or reaffirmations of certain values from which styles are made valid. 19th century man's belief was that "change is progress" and for better or worse our restless contemporary society (living in what has been called *The Age of Anxiety* by a poet, W. H. Auden, a composer, Leonard Bernstein, and a choreographer, Jerome Robbins) requires something "new and different" at all and any costs. The classical composer worked in the idea of becoming more and more the master of his material and that material (the thesis of Western music) had been defined by the ancient Greeks. Chief of these is the primary harmonic fact that women generally sing an octave higher than men, and that the art of music is a form of specific, organized notes as sounds; this latter discovery explored and defined by Pythagoras. A radical 20th century composer works only in the Rousseauian ideal that to be different from all other men, all other composers, is his finest destiny. Since opera is an art form requiring dramaturgy as well as music, and a prevailing sense of order and design is part of theatre, these most

radical 20th century musicians do not work in opera form. They are to be encountered in the concert hall as "performers" where some of them may not actually and actively perform at all, as in the instance of a serious and seriously accepted American composer whose compositions include a "work" in which the lid of a piano is lifted, the "performer" or pianist sits down at the instrument, perfectly still and silent, for three minutes, closes the piano lid and completes the "work." This composer, whose name is John Cage, is an undisputably "different" composer, well known as a concert performer and as a collaborator of modern dance choreographers.

5. If you begin with Mozart's operas and continue into those of Richard Strauss you will have a panoramic view of romanticism in opera, and how it was interpreted by Italians, Germans and French opera makers. You will note that out of the "romantic" period there emerged a strong "national" development in opera—and, if you like, you can diverge and investigate the true "national" opera form as it was created in various countries. The Scandinavian and Slavic countries have their own opera traditions, and Slavonic music has inspired some important works.

Like almost all the national operas Russian opera began with Italian troupes (in 1730 the first such troupe performed in St. Petersburg to celebrate the coronation of the Empress Anna Joannovna). Paisiello, composer of the first *Barber of Seville*, worked in St. Petersburg as did Cimarosa and others, and the Imperial Russian Opera engaged the finest Italian singers, making opera almost as great a mania for the sophisticated Russian nobility as ballet was for the French. *Opéra comique* (in this form) was introduced in Russia at the end of the 18th century and the idea (which was one opposite to *opera seria*) was converted to a sort of Russian *Singspiel*: pastoral drama of Rousseau's philosophy set to Russian folk music. No real "Russian" opera was conceived until Glinka (1804–1857), whose best known work is *A Life for the Tsar* (1836). The famous "Five," the Russian composers who developed national music free of Western European influences, contributed to "Russian" opera, among which the most notable works were Mussorgsky's *Boris Godunov*, Rimsky-Korsakov's *The Golden Cockerel* and Borodin's *Prince Igor*, all extant in Western opera repertory. Tchaikovsky's well-known operas are *Eugene Onegin* and *The Queen of Spades* (Pique Dame).

Czech music is also an important contribution to opera and if you are drawn to German *Singspiel* opera you will delight in the works of Smetana, while Janáček is a fine exponent of the fantasy or fairy tale opera.

6. The piano, originally called pianoforte, is the invention (in 1709) of an Italian, Christofori, whose name for it was *gravicembalo col piano e forte*— "heavy harpsichord with loud and soft" tones; the words *piano e forte* thereafter becoming the name for such an instrument. Famous piano makers like the Germans Silbermann, Stein and Streicher, and the English Broadwood (who invented the piano's damper pedal in 1783) elaborated on Christofori's invention. A Frenchman, Erard, invented the contemporary double-escapement action of the piano in 1823.

Horns belong to the instrumental group called "brass"—for which reason the *cor anglais* or "English horn" is not a horn at all, since it is an alto oboe.

The oboe belongs to the woodwind family. *Cor anglais* is neither English nor horn. It is a French invention as an instrument and bears exactly the same resemblance to the oboe as does the viola to the violin. But the true horns of an orchestra are an expressive group, exceedingly difficult to master and therefore a great accomplishment or forte for the gifted player. Into Beethoven's era the common orchestra horn was related to the old French *cor de chasse* and the German *Waldhorn* (forest horn), used in the hunt or "chase." This sort of instrument is called a "natural" horn to distinguish it from a later development which came about by interchangeable parts called "crooks." The length of the horn tube was altered by changing sections or crooks and in Mozart's operas horn players were busy people, continually changing crooks of their instruments between their musical passages. About 1830 a better means was invented: brass instruments were made with a mechanical device enabling the instrumentalist to lengthen the range or make a shift in the harmonic series. The device is called "valves" and can be added to or removed from the instrument. Three different lengths of tube (each with a valve to cut in or out of the main tube or horn) can be used in combinations for every note of the chromatic scale, or scale of half-tones. The mere addition of valves to the brass afforded the 19th century orchestra "color" in a range and subtlety impossible to have been imagined by 17th and early 18th century musicians. Hence: a larger "palette" was created for horns alone, in "tone-color" idioms of music.

Strings are the most versatile group in the orchestra, superior to all others in purity of tone, dynamics, and "color." Each string of a violin, for example, has a different tone-color; therefore the violin is four instruments with a common resonator. The richness of the strings has enabled composers to create works for them alone, or for their primary performance. Examples include Bach's 3rd and 6th concerti in the *Brandenburg* series, and (among modern composers) Honegger's *Symphony for Strings* (1941) and Stravinsky's *Concerto for Strings* (1946). The violin as it is today was the substantial invention of an Italian, Antonio Stradivarius (1644–1737) but the violin's bow was not perfected for a century after—by a Frenchman, Tourte (1747–1835). There are generally 36 violins, divided into two groups as "first" and "second" violins, in a contemporary symphony orchestra. When you hear them know that while there have been developments in techniques for playing the violin it and its relatives are unique among musical instruments in that they are structurally the same as the instruments on which musicians played two centuries ago. Modern composers have made semi-divisions in the primary divisions of "first" and "second" violin grouping, Wagner among them as with the passage for violins in *four* parts (instead of two) in the *Prelude* of *Lohengrin*. The bowing technique of the violin is a determinant of its "color-tone" and various ways of applying the bow (which is an instrument fitted with taut horsehairs) to the strings results in certain musical forms. Up-and-down, rapid movements of the bow on the strings produces *tremolo*; plucking the strings with the fingers in precisely sounded short notes produces *pizzicato*. The latter style is very familiar in Delibes' ballet *Sylvia* (1866), and in its famous "persistent" melody of Tchaikovsky's *4th Symphony: Pizzicato Ostinato*. Addition of a "mute" gives the violin a different sound. There are many other variances and string techniques, the sum of which makes the "strings" of an orchestra powerful harmonic and melodic entities in themselves. The reader desiring a greater knowledge of *harmonics* should note that when the left or "holding" hand of the player is applied very lightly to certain places of a violin string, and that string is bowed, the type of note produced is the ethereal tone called a harmonic. One such exercise for the violin in 53 measures occurs in the Russian composer Borodin's *In The Steppes of Central Asia* (1885). A painter who is an amateur composer has explained to me that there is aesthetic similarity between *harmonics*, which musicians think of as "thin, ethereal but vibrant and delicate tones" and the abstract but realized "shimmering" light or "quivering space" between objects in modern painting of the style of Monet.

7. Erik Satie (1866–1925) was a radical composer of satiric temperament and the artistic progenitor of the philosophies of *Les Six*: the "modern" composers Georges Auric, Louis Durey, Arthur Honegger, Darius Milhaud, Francis Poulenc and Germaine Tailleferre. Of these, Auric, Honegger, Milhaud and Poulenc became front rank composers. The musical revolution for which *Les Six*, Satie and Debussy are held chiefly responsible is comparable to the revolution in painting by *Les Fauves*, "the wild beasts" Derain, Friesz, Manguin, Marquet, Rouault, Puy, Valtat, Van Dongen, Vlaminck and, above all, Matisse. Because the gifted composers were great individualists as well as great musicians, they were not entirely united in theories and styles. The revolution of *Les Six* was directed against the tradition of romanticism, which the French composers saw as a pernicious German influence. However, Honegger admired Wagner, whom Milhaud despised. They were also against impressionism (and therefore turned away from Debussy instead of following him). They were intent on establishing a national French style in music of the 20th century, and took Satie as their point of departure from "hypertrophied chromaticism." (*Chromaticism* is terminology for the use of notes progressing in semitones and chromatic music is opposed to the diatonic scale.) Satie favored simplicity in melody and harmony, and other elements of music, but he had an eccentric not to say grotesque imagination and was influenced by jazz. He had, also, a perverse sense of humor which discomfited his admirers who have never known exactly when or how far to take Satie seriously. His influence on modern music, into Stravinsky's neo-classicism, is incontrovertible.

8. Gustav Mahler (1860–1911) was a composer equally famed as a conductor. He belongs to the German "line" of composers descendant from Anton Bruckner (1824–1896) while Richard Strauss is of the "line" after Johannes Brahms (1833–1897), all emergent after Wagner.

9. *Dynamics*, the scale of volume in musical sound, are indicated by:

| | |
|---|---|
| *pianissimo possibile* | soft as possible (*ppp* in music) |
| *pianissimo* | very soft (*pp*) |
| *piano* | soft (*p*) |
| *mezzopiano* | half or medium soft (*mp*) |
| *mezzoforte* | half loud (*mf*) |
| *forte* | loud (*f*) |
| *fortissimo* | very loud (*ff*) |
| *triple forte* | loud as possible (*fff*) |

| | |
|---|---|
| *crescendo* | grow gradually louder |
| *decrescendo* | grow gradually softer |
| *sforzato* | sudden accentuation of individual notes |
| *marcato* | bring out, by playing louder, some individual notes in the musical context |
| *morendo* | dying or fading away in volume of sound |

*Dynamics* were introduced by composers of the Mannheim school in mid-18th century. These are the direct predecessors of the Viennese school of classical composers, famed for its three individual geniuses Haydn, Mozart and Beethoven.

10. This idea, in its mechanical sense, is alleged to have been realized by a Jesuit, Louis-Bertrand Castel, with a color harpsichord invented in 1725. Just what this color harpsichord was and what it did, musically, is unknown. It is the subject of a sarcastic diatribe by André Grétry in *Essays on Music*, 1914. Grétry and others refute the probability of such an instrument; Rousseau did not.

11. For example: Rossini's facility to compose melodic music that contained catchy or singable tunes and military marches accelerated his recognition in his era, one of European wars and consequent hysteria and sentimentality. Rossini is often accused of being too entertaining but had he written less melodious operas it is doubtful whether his operas would have drawn such enthusiastic throngs to the theatre. Or that his extant works would be preserved for us today.

12. Felix Mendelssohn, in conducting Bach's *St Matthew Passion* in Berlin in 1829 (the works first performance following Bach's death), is credited with introducing Bach into the musical mainstream of the 19th century. As the majority of his compositions were not published in Bach's lifetime they were hardly known, then or until the Bach renaissance. And it is believed that many of his compositions have been lost. These lost works may fall into both categories of Bach, as described by Debussy (who was a reviewer for periodicals as well as a composer): ". . . he [Bach] is unbearable except when he is admirable," and when "unbearable" (again to quote Debussy) "from his insistence on turning to account any old idea, no matter what the price."

13. Bach was the originator of the harpsichord concerto, and, from that, of the piano concerto. Until his time, concertos were for violins or a solo violin and the harpsichord was essentially an accompanist, not a solo instrument. Westerman propounds the logical idea that Bach used the harpsichord, in numerous arrangements of his own works and the works of other composers, to show off the talents of his two eldest sons (who were exceptionally gifted players of the harpsichord) and also to provide material for performances by the Telemann Music Society which he organized in Leipzig. His seven known harpsichord concertos are arrangements of older compositions, mostly for violins. Those in *D major* and *G minor* are the most frequently heard today. His most famed concerto for two harpsichords is the *C major Concerto*.

14. The waltz originated in the Austrian landler and some characteristics drawn from another dance, the weller; these two dances, merging at the end of the 18th century, became one dance: the waltz. It was the rage of European society by 1815, and the scandal of it, since it was a dance in which strangers of opposite sex embraced each other publicly, and swayed to the abandonment

of aphrodisiac melodies. Mozart, Beethoven and Schubert used the landler more than the ballroom waltz, with stiff rhythms and skipping steps that were true to the country dance from which it derived. But Carl Maria von Weber made the waltz romantic and sophisticated, of smooth, floating rhythms and enchanting tunes. His great innovation for the dance in symphony and opera was to take five waltz tunes and arrange them between an introduction and coda, calling it *Invitation to the Dance* in 1819.

Johann Strauss the Elder (1804–1849) and August Lanner (1834–1855) elaborated on the waltz until it became a cult. Lanner, to quote Hanslick, scented his with violets and if young ladies pined for unrequited love and died of consumption, more favored romances bloomed to the glide of the waltz. Fully orchestrated by the elder Strauss, the waltz was extended in contrapuntal and harmonic music by Chopin; Liszt and Brahms and Berlioz and Tchaikovsky developed it in the symphonic form.

The waltz was known in opera from 1670, in the works of a composer called Draghi, and those of another, Soler, about 1786; it is not too surprising to find a waltz in Mozart's *Don Giovanni* in 1787. Goethe admired the waltz so much that as a student (in 1765) he set himself to learn it and in his novel *Werther* he put the hero and his Lotte to waltz together, describing them as having "rolled about like the spheres." The landler's melodies are evident in the minuets of Stamitz, Haydn and Mozart, and landler and waltz melodies in Schubert's music. The range of the melodic dance steps accented the first beat of a measure and this corresponds with the development of music which passed from the polyphonic to the homophonic form. It contrasted with the former linear concept, emphasizing a harmonic up and down (vertical form) in a sequence of dissonance and consonance.

15. The *Surprise Symphony*, a nickname for Haydn's *No. 94*, is derived from the joke Haydn perpetrated to wake up an audience which had fallen asleep. The piece begins with a theme in *piano* and *pianissimo* and then, quite unexpectedly for the listener the first time it is heard, contrives a great bang on the drum. The "Salomon Set" (as Westerman notes) is the most perfect embodiment of Haydn's genius, each one a masterpiece in its own right.

16. For the most illuminating insight into Mozart, read his letters. In these he writes of his own music and that of other musicians of his times and his vigorous style of expression makes him one of the most fascinating of musical correspondents. The gay atmosphere of Vienna, the very frank mode of letter-writing practiced in his day, and Mozart's own rapport with his correspondents make these letters the most engaging collection of their kind. They were translated into English and collected with others of his family by Emily Anderson: *The Letters of Mozart and his Family*, 1938.

17. Salieri's fanatical hatred of Mozart was the bitter enmity of a lesser man for a greater one. But any musician-composer of Mozart's times would have been strained to practice virtues of friendship for the prodigy, who towered over them all, including Haydn, for whom Mozart had such deep affection and respect. There seemed nothing in music that Mozart could not undertake, and no instrument (of the times) that he did not master. The "London" Bach, revered as harpsichordist and organist, was enchanted by the child Mozart, as Haydn

(twenty-four years Mozart's senior) was by the man. The violin, the favorite
stringed instrument of the time, and the clavier in all its forms, were equally
the servants of Mozart's skilled fingers as performer. But beyond this faculty to
make music instrumentally was the astonishing one to compose or literally make
music *per se*. From infancy, Mozart's capacity to assimilate what he was taught
was phenomenal, and as the son of a capable composer and excellent musician
this natural talent was developed to the finest accomplishments. Leopold Mozart
gave Mozart his first lessons and devoted his life thereafter to promoting Mozart
and his sister, endeavoring through their performing tours to bring them to the
notice of affable patrons who would recognize the gifts of these two and cherish
them. The elder Mozart strove to get his son placed in the best circumstances
then available to a musician: under private and powerful patronage. That he
was unsuccessful was Mozart's bad luck but not his father's fault by neglect—or
envy of a son who was so brilliant a musician that his diamond brightness made
lesser composers pale with fury and despair. It should be noted that in Mozart's
time audiences expected solo instrumentalists to be composers and it was normal
for the soloist, appearing with an orchestra, to write concerti they had themselves
composed for the occasion. It was not until Liszt that an instrumentalist sat down
to his instrument (usually, the piano) and engaged the attention of his audience
without the collaboration of the orchestra. Therefore, Mozart had as a matter of
course to write whole works in order to play a part in them as a concert performer. Moreover, his audience (surely one of the most exacting and stimulating
that music has ever been made for!) expected him to be a master magician,
extemporizing cadenzas and launching into pure improvisations that were pyrotechnical feats in themselves. Mozart could perform these exciting feats with the
greatest of ease. He was a marvelous musical trapezist who could take a theme
from one of his own works, or the works of another composer, and airily
extemporize and improvise the original until it became a new and glittering
work. His one human vanity was his small, well-shaped hands and he is reputed
to have loved to show them off on piano and violin. In his tragically brief career,
he composed 52 symphonies, 27 piano concerti, and about 25 instrumental
concerti, and more than 30 serenades and divertimenti, and wrote a great deal
of dance music—most of the dance tunes being commissioned for masked balls
in Vienna. He was fond of the *landler*, a folk dance in ¾ time, which later
became the *waltz*, and was turned into *valse* by the French. Mozart's serious side,
expressed in music as majestic as Beethoven's grandest works, is more in his
instrumental works than the vocal and instrumental music he composed for his
extant operas and should be known to the serious opera goer to realize the full
dimension of this composer. His *opera seria* works *Idomeneo* (1781) and *The
Clemency of Titus* (1791) are seldom revived.

Mozart's fame in his lifetime, especially among his compeers, was in his
ability to compose whole works in his head. It was customary with him to
develop a piece mentally and then do the actual writing at the last minute—
a drudgery he never enjoyed since the entire composition, intact, already existed
for him. As Mozart was one of the greatest masters of melody the world has ever
known, and worked in the homophonic style but also with great fluency in a
very complex polyphonic idiom, even a non-musician must recognize the magni-

tude of his gift: to create works which he heard only with the mind's ear and which were then laboriously put down on paper, in the form of notes and other musical memoranda, for instrumentalists to play; these being pedestrians in the world where Mozart soared.

His letters (see *Note No. 13* above) and the memoirs we have of him from his contemporaries indicate that he was of a critical but generous disposition. He was the most impractical of men, whose purse was opened so easily if it were full (and to the least deserving mendicants) that it was little wonder he could not subsist on the beggar's dole he earned. It may be said that he worked himself to exhaustion: in the posts he held as concertmaster (first violin), court organist, hack composer (music was ordered from him like cloth by the yard), and teacher of young students. All these endeavors brought him pittances as pay; his great opera successes (all save *Cosi Fan Tutte*) made money for others but appear to have made little difference to Mozart's finances.

The romantic tragedy of a life in music is written in the word "Mozart," and the history of a man who for the early part of his life seemed to have led Dame Fortune by the forelock but later (after 1773) been so plagued by bad luck as to seem cursed by the gods. He appears to have been naïve to the point of saintliness in avoiding envy. Haydn he addressed as *caro amico*, dedicating a group of six quartets to the older composer and in every way deferring to him as the maître—and, apparently, never stopping to think what his own lot might have been with an Esterhazy for a patron, and the sinecure of Haydn's position. Salieri's cabal was only one more injury in a career blighted before it was well begun but, nevertheless, a great and memorable one.

18. *Romanticism* is a characteristic of 19th century art, relating to a style and now evocative of a period in which the style was predominant in the arts; music, poetry, painting and also opera and the novel. It signifies a free or un-inhibited expression of emotion and in this genre Rousseau's *The Village Sooth-sayer* may be said to be "romantic" and the reverse of "classical." But 19th century opera and music were both "classical" and "romantic," as has been stated. When *Singspiel* achieved an opera form Mozart and his compeers proved that German could be sung; as Rousseau proved that French could be sung. Benda, the composer of the *Singspiel* music-plays Mozart admired, was of the "Mannheim school." Here, from 1770, the Italian opera domination was broken and German arts encouraged to the extent that in 1776 a Nationaltheater opened and flourished. The Elector Karl Theodor, a genial bon vivant, presided over this evolution and the "Mannheim school," under J. Stamitz, developed what is the foundation of today's orchestra. The Mannheim orchestra comprised:

| | |
|---|---|
| 2 flutes | first violins |
| 2 oboes | second violins |
| 2 bassoons | violas |
| 2 horns | cellos |
| 2 trumpets | double basses |
| 2 kettledrums | |

With the addition of two clarinets this was the orchestra for which Haydn and Mozart composed; with the horns increased to four and trombones added, it was the orchestra of Beethoven's time, and the one for which Rossini, Verdi and Bizet wrote, and, also, Schumann, Liszt, Brahms, Grieg, Dvořák, Franck and Sibelius.

19. He wrote, in a letter to Leopold Mozart: "I can more or less adopt or imitate any kind and any style of composition."

20. Salieri, but without proof, is depicted as the poisoner of the composer in Rimsky-Korsakov's opera *Mozart and Salieri* (1898), based on the poem by Alexander Pushkin.

21. In the 19th century, *Don Giovanni* was bowdlerized in performances for English-speaking audiences, and the end was altered, omitting the sextet and the hypocritical finale. The Don was therefore seen as consigned to hell with a metaphorical *Amen*. This is altogether contrary to Mozart's intentions and to those of Da Ponte. The latter, Italian-born Emmanuel Conegliano, had to leave Venice because of scandal and became the favorite poet in Vienna of Joseph II, over whom he exerted great influence. Mozart's *The Marriage of Figaro* probably owed its own success to that which Da Ponte had with the emperor, first in obtaining permission for the ban on Beaumarchais' play to be lifted and for the emperor to intervene and forbid the anti-Mozart claque's demonstration at the opera's première. Da Ponte was, to say the least, a worldly Italian, well versed in commedia dell'arte and fond of satire and intrigue. Commedia dell'arte is obviously the basis of some events in *Don Giovanni*: the beating administered by the Don to a character named Masetto, the crude tricks and disguises which would not fool a child, and the general exaggeration of emotion and gesture for all the characters that the librettist, tongue in cheek, makes out to be gullible fools. Not *Don Giovanni* but *Pagliacci* is the cuckold's opera.

22. A stranger of mysterious mien appeared at Mozart's house one evening and commissioned him to write a requiem, making it conditional that Mozart must not inquire his identity. Mozart was then dying and at his lowest financial ebb, and came to believe that the stranger was Death himself, who had in fact commissioned him to write his own requiem. On his death bed, Mozart tried to sing the *Lacrimosa* from the requiem with friends who had called to see him. Overcome, he broke down and the music had to be laid aside. It was completed after Mozart's death by one of his pupils, Franz Xavier Sussmayer, with whom he had discussed the work in great detail. The man who paid Mozart in advance for a Mass for the Dead, and in so doing may have frightened the composer to death, was a living person, an eccentric dilettante named Count Wallsegg who used to buy music and pass it off as his own composition. Walsegg actually transposed Mozart's music into his own hand, in an attempt to claim it as his original composition.

23. See Robert Schumann's *Of Music and Musicians,* edited by Konrad Wolff, translated into English by Paul Rosenfeld.

24. *Symphonie Fantastique* was premièred in 1830, and Berlioz wrote a sequel: *Lelio,* premièred in 1832. He now met Harriet Smithson, pressed his courtship and these two were married on October 3, 1833, despite strenuous opposition from their friends who knew the lovers to be thoroughly incompatible. They separated a short time after and Berlioz's friends said that Mme. Berlioz had proved in life to be the incarnation of the Witch her husband made her into, in the *Witches' Sabbath,* the last movement of his *Fantastic Symphony.*

# ✿ S I X ✿

# *Aida* for Example

Schopenhauer said that we stand before a picture as before a prince, like the sailor at sea, able to plumb the depths only so far as the length of the line will allow.

For the new opera goer, opera is a great flood of music which pours out of the radio and off phonograph records, bearing overtures and arias, ballets and choruses on its crest. In the torrent we cling to familiar airs like rafts and buoys, as we are borne on the current that sweeps an opera through acts and scenes to its finale. And many a theatre goer, in the opera house for the first time, almost drowns in the musical flood, emerging aghast at the difficulty of getting his bearings. It seems, then, that opera is too strange, and too tedious to know about, simply to enjoy for pleasure in our leisure. Then: turn to Verdi, *Aida* for example.

In four hundred years, no composer (whether of opera or symphony) has communicated so vividly with so many audiences as Giuseppe Verdi. He did not reform opera as Gluck did but he reformed the idea about opera (that it was a diversion for the rich, and for "high" society or the "intelligentsia") which barred the "average" listener or audience en masse from enjoying opera. He was a man so full of life, and a composer of such genius that in his operas (as D'Annunzio spoke his epitaph) "he wept and loved for us all."—*Piange e amo per tutti.*

*Aida* is the first work on the list of "best known, best loved" operas—and this is not a list composed by the business managers of opera companies or the publishing houses of opera libretti, but made from the statistics compiled from figures of audience attendance in opera houses. The list is comparatively short, when we think that the opera repertory dates to 1600 and that all the major Western nations are represented in opera repertory by national opera composers. Yet, despite the thousands of operas that have been produced only a few are among the "best known, best loved" and in this list Verdi is represented with more works than any other composer. Of all his popular works *Aida* is most popular, one of the few "perfect" operas and in style "Italian" opera of high caliber. It is a 19th century opera with a melodramatic plot, the principals being two women and one man. The man loves and desires the girl he cannot have, and he dies of his dilemma.

This is a stock situation in theatre as well as a "human situation" of real life, a conflict that is colloquially described as "the eternal triangle." Its plot could occur in a cheap "thriller" as a book and in "soap opera" on radio and television, and a certain kind of movie. The music by Verdi and the complexities of the drama, as well as the forms in which the drama is expressed, make *Aida* a masterwork.

The plot is not solely about two girls and one man but also about their gods and demons. One girl's demon is pride and the other is bedevilled by pity, which makes her weak and yet exalts her. The man, the least complicated character of the three, is one whom the gods will not destroy even if he angers them. He is protected from personal demons because his heart is pure.

The drama is in the music—hence: *Aida* is an opera.

It is probably the best example you could have for what a traditional opera is, in its form and style, and it is an opera with a well-constructed plot, exciting action, marvelously defined characters . . . all the aspects of drama which make an opera interesting. Therefore, *Aida* is a good example for what an opera is about.

When I am conducting "Arts Appreciation" lectures in opera, and use *Aida* for example, I suggest a method for the group by which we observe some ways and means for "discovering" *Aida*, in preparation for "experiencing" *Aida* in theatre. If you prefer to be surprised rather than prepared, then you may skip over this portion of the book. If you like a degree of preparation, especially for *Aida* in the original Italian libretto, then you can adapt this portion of the book to your interests or requirements. It is a good procedure for teacher-student uses, and for a group working with a correlator in opera appreciation.

Begin with the drama, the dimension of the opera you will be most at ease in: know what *Aida* is about. There are numerous books of "stories from the operas" but if you are the teacher working with a class, or a correlator with a group, be careful in planning the dramatic aspect of *Aida*. While all books give the facts about the plot, many printed accounts are not suited to being read aloud. And a few are written in language that stupefies the imagination, especially of young or new opera goers. For my part, I recommend the best results as narration. Familiarize yourself with *Aida*, know it as you know a favorite play or novel, until it has come alive for you—then, relay this experience in words to your group, as though you were relating (not "narrating") events in which you have a great interest, about persons whose affairs interest you, whose characters you know and know well. You may think that you lack the quality of a story-teller— but if you were witness to a quarrel or a murderous attack, if you saw one person save another from drowning or a blazing pyre, you would find words to relate what you experienced. This "experience" is in what you heard and saw and also in what you felt when hearing and seeing the events.

It is not sufficient only to relate what happened to the people in *Aida* without making your listeners in the group understand who these people *are* . . . and if you employ present tense you make the events urgent and immediate, as they will be for the group or individual experiencing *Aida* in theatre. Do not stop at a bald statement about *Aida* as an opera with a cast. Think of the cast of characters as persons, know that they are the reason for the opera of *Aida*, which is concerned with their affairs and feelings and acts. "Color" the opera by personal insight into the characters, to the extent of making the group know that it, collectively and in its individual parts, will also have insight from personal observation or "experience" of *Aida*. In short, make *Aida* true as well as operatic.

Don't make a report on *Aida* as though you were a policeman or you will turn *Aida* as cold as a corpse. Whatever you do, allow the characters to remain alive. Otherwise, you are half-way to killing *Aida* for the group.

To go about this experiment with opera (*Aida* is only an example here, a good one to "break down" for our purposes) think of *Who, as persons,* the opera concerns. Make the intellectual effort of focusing the characters in the plot and then (perhaps we should call this an emotional effort) "see" them in the mind's eye not only as corporeal beings but as beings whose inner world you also perceive, and as doing what, and where, and when, and why . . . as Verdi thought of *Aida.*

The place is Egypt, the time that of the Pharaohs, and with poetic license Verdi establishes the here and now of *Aida*—the teacher or the studious reader will recall that the era of the Pharaohs was approximately 5004 B.C.-A.D. 381. The present Pharaoh (whose name is not given) has a daughter, Amneris. Like all pharaohs (the title was applied to male and female rulers) the princess is sacred in her symbolic person, one with the gods. Chief arbiter between Egypt and its gods is the oracle in the temple of Vulcan (in the opera, called Phtha), a priestess who makes the god's will, and the will of the goddess Isis, known to the people through the priests. Ramfis is the high priest.

A young soldier, captain of the royal guard, named Radames, is chosen to be general, by decree from the temple, to command the Egyptian army in a campaign against the Ethiopians. When the drama begins we know that the two nations have been at war, Ethiopians have been captured and enslaved and one of these, a young girl of beauty and gentle bearing, has been made servant to the Princess Amneris. She is Aida.

But Aida is not what she seems, desirable as that is in the eyes of Radames. She is in truth a princess like Amneris, daughter of Amonasro, King of Ethiopia. Aida in great misery of homesickness and humiliation (Amneris is a cruel mistress) carries also the burden of her secret which she keeps even from Radames. She dares not divulge her true identity and make her rank known to the Egyptians, who would hold her as hostage and use her as a pawn against the king, her father.

So much for who these are; now as to what they are. And for that the teacher may refer to history—not without good reason, as the plot of *Aida* is reputed to be derived from archaeological fact.

The Egypt of the pharaohs was, on the whole, a priest-ridden, god-obsessed era on one hand, and a society of the most remarkable emancipation for the woman. Amneris is a woman of her time—bold, sensual, free to express herself on any topic. No civilization then or since has allowed females the freedom comparable to that possessed by the woman in antique Egypt. She did as she pleased, making advances in love, proposing marriage; in public no less free than in private. Her society was far from prudish. Into their teens, male and female children went nude, save for cosmetics and jewelry, and the Egyptians placed prurient literature with the dead, to while away the tedium of the long journey to "the fields of food." In these elysian fields they were greeted by Osiris, the god of the dead, who questioned them from the *Book of the Dead,* the first book of etiquette. When in doubt as to the veracity of the candidate's statements, it was Osiris' habit to weigh the heart on a scale against a feather.

The woman in Verdi's opera who is called Amneris is a theatrical tour de force; she is represented truly as what she is: an Egyptian woman of high rank. And to this valid concept Verdi adds a depth of perception which gives Amneris psychical dimension that makes her more real than many a real-life woman. Bear in mind that Amneris was a princess whose person was as sacred as a goddess, and as goddess she is amoral and imperious, and the slightest defection from her will and way constitutes not only lese majesty but also a sort of sacrilege. She is impervious as a princess but fatally vulnerable as a woman. And it is the princess' final discovery that she is a woman which pierces her to the heart.

Observe (in *Act III*) that when Amneris is enraged she is *outraged,* and responds as a pharaoh—it is later (in *Act IV*) that her torment as a woman begins. And she is in character more a child of Ramfis than her own father, a king existing in a matriarchal, religious society and cowed by it.[1] Verdi makes him a bass but compels him to sing in one octave (*Act I*), making him musically simple, almost a figure-head.

Ramfis, on the contrary, is a powerful man in love with power. With the impregnable gods at his back (and at his cunning behest when he wishes to summon them) he has all Egypt on its knees. In any event, no Egyptian stood upright in the presence of the gods; the religious intent was to diminish the stature of the human being and obliterate meaning or identity in this life. Egyptians existed solely to die and death was the preoccupation of their splendid empire.

All Egyptian art was dedicated to the awesome power of the gods and to this end pyramids, sphinx, statues and tombs were of gargantuan size, by comparison shrinking the worshippers. To comprehend the Egyptian approach to religion we need only contrast Egyptians with Greeks—the Greeks made gods in their own human image, and played, made love and quarrelled with them as one race. When the Greek gods changed shape, it was by magic (often, the better to pursue sensual love affairs) and on occasion a Greek defied a god even if he were cursed for it. Radames behaves like an Egyptian and not like a Greek—he dies with sublimest calm, almost with pleasure. Death was not deprivation and loss but the promise of bliss and material pleasures. The tomb, to the Egyptian of Radames' time, was a wayside station, a kind of immigration depot on the border of hereafter. Death was the point of departure for "the fields of food," where an Egyptian or an Egyptian's slave could expect to be happy forever, provided he had studied the *Book of the Dead* and knew his etiquette.

These concepts of death have great meaning in Verdi's opera and are clear if you make Amneris the intellectual as well as the emotional crux of the drama. For Amneris is as important to the drama as Aida. Verdi said that he loved Amneris above all others in *Aida* but he did not make her lovable, for she was not. Yet she is lovely and fascinating —fearless, ruthless, proud, passionate. It is Amneris who fills the plot with an intensity and what Verdi doubtless thought of as reality. When the curtain falls we know for certain that the lovers will expire, in a quite terrible sort of death, but we cannot forget Amneris—what becomes of her? How is she to bear the knowledge which, until the last act of the drama, entirely escapes her—that Radames is not temporarily separated from her by his infatuation for the abhorred rival, Aida, but that Radames never was and never could be possessed of a love for her such as had possessed the princess for Radames. Verdi makes us know that even if Aida had not existed, even if on order of the Pharaoh Radames had married Amneris, he would have been a consort in name and deed, perhaps, but never at heart.

*Aida* is an opera of passion, Amneris' passion for Radames is the troubled waste in which the lovers are lost; Ramfis is the rock against which Amneris destroys Radames, Aida and herself. Amonasro provides the tide of deceit which sweeps Radames and Aida onto the rock.

As the drama begins, Ramfis and Radames are in conversation about military affairs. Ramfis is high priest and politician as well—a sort of combination pope, secretary of state, chief justice and vice-president. The routed Ethiopians are known to have rallied and Egypt must move quickly against them; a new commander is to be named (it is Radames, in short order) and the people of Egypt are all for it; they want war. The Pharaoh, accompanied by his Messenger (an aide who is nameless, lending more anonymity to the king of Egypt), puts his royal stamp on the pre-arranged affair and off to war goes Radames, leaving a seething feminine cauldron of jealousy and fear.

For Amneris, coming on her soldier soon after his chat with Ramfis, had found him singing with great rapture, behaving altogether like a man taken quite out of himself—more elated than he should have reasonably been at that moment, as he had not yet been confirmed in his hoped-for promotion as army commander. Amneris, very intelligent and sharp-tongued, immediately says to him: What is the reason for this extraordinary behavior? (In the opera, she sings: *Quale insolita gioia*—What unaccustomed joy.) Thereby, we know that Radames is not given to such outbursts, melodic and emotional, and it is natural that the Pharaoh's hawk-eyed daughter takes note of his rapture.

Soon enough, she fixes on Aida as the reason and ruthlessly sets out to prove it. After Radames has gone to war and a suitable time elapsed, Amneris pretends to sit down and have a cosy chat with her little maid, addressing her familiarly (only Aida would be taken in by the silky manner and dulcet tone) as a friend (*Vieni, o diletta*—Come here, dearest one).

Amneris then tells her bad news—Radames has been killed. This plunges Aida into an abyss of grief. Amneris, watching Aida intently, now says: it's not true, she has deceived Aida—Radames is alive. Aida is lifted up to heaven with joy. The Princess now knows beyond a doubt that Aida is in love with Radames and having plumbed, as she thinks, the mysterious Ethiopian's whole secret, Amneris mocks her cruelly—how dare a slave compete with the Pharaoh's daughter? Does Aida realize who her rival is for Radames? It is the Pharaoh's daughter! As Radames is in fact victorious and on his way to Thebes with a caravan of prisoners, Amneris, the Pharaoh and Ramfis will go to meet him and give him a hero's welcome. In pure spite, Amneris takes

Aida along, so that Radames will see servant and mistress together—then, says Amneris cruelly, Aida will know which woman Radames has eyes for!

But what Verdi knew and Amneris did not is that men like Radames always fall in love with women like Aida. Radames is a good man, a valiant soldier, with one fatal weakness—his heart rules his head. And Verdi gives us warning that it does, for Radames pleads with the Pharaoh to free the prisoners the Egyptians have taken from the beaten Ethiopian army. Radames is an odd man for his times, while Amneris is a true woman of them. An ordinary Egyptian soldier would not have brought a train of prisoners to Thebes, he should have lopped off a limb and the phallus of each of the prisoners to offer to Pharaoh as evidence of his prowess in the war. Radames is compassionate and a girl like Aida is bound to attract him.

Aida is Oriental, submissive and seductive, a captive who moves her master to tender pity—or a mistress to ferocity—by her sweet languor. Aida is the catalyst by which the best, the most human part of Radames is summoned up, and the worst of Amneris.

Verdi does not tell us what gods Aida worships but he makes her call to heaven (in a terrible dilemma, should she pray for the safety of her lover or of her father?) when she sees Radames go off to war against her people. Yet we feel that Aida does not really expect help from heaven; she is resigned where Amneris is passionately determined, gentle where Amneris is bold. These two women are both lovely, Amneris beautiful in the way of a great ruby, darkly smouldering; Aida like a pearl, softly gleaming. Verdi loved rubies above pearls but he was a good jeweller and he set both gems with equal skill and care. Yet Radames loved the pearl more.

The action is briskly launched, never again to abate until the horrifying climax. The drama begun in Memphis now moves to Thebes and here Amonasro, Aida's father, enters it, in chains, one of the wretched Ethiopian prisoners brought before Pharaoh. None of the Ethiopians will divulge his identity and the first thing the old man does is whisper to Aida to protect him, keep his rank secret, or the Egyptians will have him executed—knowing that if the Ethiopian king dies then the Ethiopian army will indeed be vanquished.

Impulsively, Aida throws herself on the old man's bosom, calling him "Father!" Unwittingly, she convinces the Egyptians that Amonasro is what he makes himself out to be (an Ethiopian soldier, nothing more) for it has never occurred to any Egyptian that Amneris' servant is herself a princess.

After a touching scene with his child (during which the old king shows us how quickwitted he is) Amonasro relates that he has seen (with these very eyes) the King of Ethiopia dead of his wounds (lying at these very feet) and Amonasro tells Pharaoh that since Ethiopia is vanquished, will he not be merciful, as the Ethiopians are helpless to harm proud Egypt, will Pharaoh strike off their chains and let them go home again, miserable and beaten but, at least, free? Amonasro makes his plea with clever psychology: *Ma tu, O Re, tu signore possente a costoro ti volgi clemento*—But you, O King, in your power transcendent, spare the lives on thy mercy dependent.

Radames is moved by the old man's plea and adds his own entreaty, saying to Pharaoh that if, indeed, Pharaoh wishes to show gratitude for Radames (who has been called the saviour of Egypt) will he release the Ethiopian prisoners and let them go home again? Ramfis protests, solemnly warning that the gods have delivered Egypt's enemies into Egypt's hands and to set those enemies free will anger the gods. But Radames persists and the Pharaoh can deny his young general nothing (especially as he has just named him his son-in-law) and releases the Ethiopians. Ramfis is conciliated only on one point— Amonasro and Aida, the Pharaoh orders, must remain in Egypt as hostages to ensure that the Ethiopians do not rally and again attack the Nile country.

Amonasro is freed of his chains but compelled to stay at Thebes, and Aida with him. Amonasro has now entered the drama and joined the plot, and has a plot of his own working. Alert to every glance and word, he has absorbed something of everyone and more than a little of circumstances—we may believe that Amonasro has taken the measure of all his enemies, even while they look and listen to him with pity for his grey hairs and wretchedness, all save Ramfis, who perceives very quickly that Amonasro, far from seeming beaten and terrified, is twice the man and three times the king that Pharaoh is. It is not surprising to discover, later in the story, that Ramfis has Amonasro watched wherever he goes, and all his actions and words noted.

Equally suspicious and angry is Amneris, who, coming to place her hand in Radames', when the Pharaoh announces her the bride of his victorious general, has intercepted a look of love and anguish between her fiancé and her maid. It is inconceivable (at least, to an Egyptian) that Radames would allow his infatuation for a servant girl to come between him and the dazzling future now opened to him! If Radames were to dare refuse Amneris and the position promised to him by Pharaoh he would be judged a traitor—or a madman. Amneris takes her reluctant lover's hand and leads him away to her suite in the palace, dismissing Aida, as though to allow the slave some time with the father with whom she has been so surprisingly (if sadly) reunited.

Seeing these two together, in their splendor so far removed from her, Aida falls into her father's arms and clings to him in such shocking grief that it cannot take this old fox long to smell out the truth . . . that the Egyptian general is beloved by his daughter. And, is she his beloved? Aida is certain to admit this, or to give Amonasro good reason to see through her transparent suffering and jealousy. . . . Aida is the simple soul Amneris put to the test to discover did she or did she not love Radames in *Act I*.

Aida is the same simple soul, but a soul beginning to be transfigured by personal tragedy, at the beginning of *Act III*. Picture a moonlit night, the stars coming out, the desert landscape stilled in a listening hush—and Aida stealing through moonlight and shadow down to the river bank, to keep a rendezvous with Radames. The shadow that is cast on this scene is from the temple of Isis, in a grove of palms, where Amneris has gone in religious retreat. Dedicated to Isis, she must pray to the goddess before her marriage ceremony with Radames —and Ramfis is here, too, invisible but omnipotent, like the gods themselves keeping watch and listening to all that transpires.

Aida goes to the rendezvous sure that it is to be her last with Radames, and behind her, unknown to her, follows Amonasro, waiting his opportunity to persuade his daughter to spy on the Egyptians for him, so he will know what the general plans, the better to be advised for *his* plans—for Amonasro has never ceased to be king of Ethiopia and commander of the army, and he knows that the army is already rallying, that the prisoners released by Pharaoh have sped homeward, meeting their comrades on the way and giving them news of the ruse by which Amonasro has saved his army and himself. The old king knows that this army will hide and wait for word from him, certain, from long experience, that while he is alive he will be plotting to resume the war against Egypt.

Amonasro, knowing his army to have suffered grave losses in the last battle, to be capable of, perhaps, one last herculean stand, racks his brain for the means to ensure an Ethiopian victory over Egypt. Aida has presented him with such means, by having as lover the impressionable, kind-hearted young general of the enemy's forces!

And Amonasro, always more the King of Ethiopia than father to Aida, listens to his child singing her heart out, homesick for her own country, and cares little for her grief—except to discover in it one means of making her do as he wishes.

Going to her, he appears to comfort her, promises her that she shall, indeed, go home again, he and she and all their poor people—all she has to do is to find out which road Radames' army will take the following day, so that the Ethiopians will know in advance of the march. And, as even the guileless Aida knows, this is not so that the Ethiopians can avoid the Egyptians, but so that they may ambush them.

Aida refuses, because she loves Radames too much to make him betray his honor as a soldier—an honor she knows, somewhat sadly, to be dearer to him than life. But Amonasro insists, rejecting her if she refuses, describing to her, pitilessly, the bloodshed of her people and the fury of the spirit of her dead mother, all resulting from Aida's stubbornness and selfishness—and Aida, weak and submissive in all things, at length assents and promises to seduce Radames. Not for her father (who in principle treats her like a soldier rather than a woman, whose idea is that what is good for Ethiopia is good for Aida) but for her country she will betray her lover. These two great passions vie in her heart and she murmurs: "Ah, my country, what you have cost me! (singing it as *O patria! quanto mi costi!*)

Satisfied that she will do as he has commanded, Amonasro conceals himself to listen as Radames comes hurrying to the rendezvous. Aida's despondency, a trait associated with her character from *Act I*, has become embittered—she is jealous of Amneris, guilty of premeditated treachery, unhappily in love. In this mood, and like a woman, she receives Radames' affectionate greeting with such coldness that one would think she hated him. He, on the contrary, is warmly loving and, moreover, ebullient—he tells her that he has made up his mind to have a man-to-man talk with the Pharaoh and make him know that his, Radames', dearest wish is to have Aida for his wife—and only Aida, his celestial Aida.

Clear as glass (he has not a single complex fibre) Radames tells this to his beloved with a shining face, already certain that all will be well with them—confident that the impulsive, extravagant promise of a king (the word of a king) will bind the Pharaoh to the letter and line of that promise. Has not Pharaoh offered his victorious general any favor he demands? Then, the favor will be this: release Radames from his engagement to the Princess, let Radames have Aida and Radames will ask of Pharaoh nothing more—no titles of honor, no prizes as wealth. Surely this will be a small thing for Pharaoh to grant! Unthinkable, for Radames, that he shall be denied this request!

But here Aida extinguishes the bright flame of his confidence, bitterly reminding him of who she is—a woman of another race, a different color, an enemy. Radames must know their marriage would be impossible in Egypt, for even if Pharaoh, bound by his promise, allowed it, Amneris would persecute them until they were too miserable to endure life in her country. No!—cries Aida, if Radames loves her, if indeed he will give up all the honors Pharaoh has heaped on him to marry *her*, then they must run away together, far from Egypt, this inhospitable land . . .

Everything she has endured as slave in Egypt, every hurt she has suffered at Amneris' hand and tongue, colors her voice, as she speaks to Radames—of the green meadows and rivers of her own country and, above all, the cool forests. How happy they two could be, in her own country! Will he come with her, leave Egypt and all his life behind him, to be with her? Is she truly, as he has called her, his "celestial Aida" and thus able to make a heaven wherever she is with him?

Passionate as he has never seen her, Aida moves Radames' impressionable heart as nothing before has stirred it. The able strategist, the valiant soldier, the Egyptian patriot, all that Radames is within these three parts of himself, ceases to be. Aida has always seemed mysterious to him, unattainable in her gentle melancholy, her unyielding pain, and he has seen her spirit as a radiant one—something like an angel's. Poor Radames, he cannot have been well read beyond his book of etiquette, the questions and answers that, sensibly, he must have learned from the *Book of the Dead* so as to pass Osiris' test. Had he read an ancient Egyptian poet he should have been advised: "Beware of the woman from abroad . . . Look not upon her when she comes; and know her not. She is like a vortex of deep waters, whose whirling is unfathomable."

But the general impulsively agrees that he will go away with his love, he will leave Egypt and all his honors, his rank, even the promise Pharaoh has made him—that in time, he, too, would be Pharaoh. Deserting all earthly things, and even his country, he will go with Aida and they two will live in ecstatic happiness in her forest far away.

Aida falls back into her old timidity and asks how shall they go, how will they be sure to avoid the Egyptian army?—for what if they are caught running away! Lovingly, Radames assures her that she will be in no peril, he will lead her safely out of Egypt—he knows a safe way, where the Egyptian army (which he so lately led to victories against the Ethiopians) will not be encountered. Aida knows that the *other* way, the way the Ethiopians will march, is what her father means to discover. So she innocently asks Radames: by what road will the army be traveling? And Radames at once replies: "The Pass of Napata."

He hears a voice repeat the exact words. "Who's there?" he shouts, and Amonasro emerges from hiding, saying proudly that he is King of Ethiopia and father of Aida. He proposes that Radames join the Ethiopians, throw in his lot with them . . . and Radames, to his horror, realizes that he has betrayed his own army. Before he can get an account of her perfidy from Aida, Amneris' ringing voice cries out an accusation: "Traitor!" She and Ramfis, witness to what appears to be Radames' treachery, have heard Amonasro declare himself. Radames is caught in his guilt and the furious Princess no longer sees him as the man she loves but as a defector, who has betrayed his gods, his pharaoh and his people in the arms of the foreign woman Aida.

Amonasro, equally furious that Amneris has interrupted his conversation with Radames, draws a dagger from his clothing and springs at her; Radames throws himself between them, loyal Egyptian that he is, to protect the Princess. And, like the lover he still is, he shouts to Amonasro to run, and take Aida. They go and Radames yields his arms to Isis, and so gives himself up, and is taken prisoner.

Ramfis and his priests now bring Radames to trial in the temple to determine if he is guilty as charged, and if he is judged guilty, for Ramfis to invoke punishment from the gods he interprets for the Egyptians. Radames is calm, prepared for his fate whatever it will be, But Amneris is not.

The woman is uppermost, the princess forgetful of her rank, as she implores him to save himself, protect himself from the accusations in court, try with all his nerve to explain the circumstances in which he was caught with Aida, so that his seeming treachery will be excused —so that he will not be put to death as a traitor. She reasons with him, saying that Aida has escaped, Amonasro has been killed, and that there is no further need for Radames to torment himself over Aida—by now she is safely home again and already beginning to forget him. Now Radames must think of himself, and fight to live—he *must* live, because she, Amneris, wants him to live.

Radames would rather die because life on earth without Aida is without meaning. At his trial, where Amneris is helpless to intervene, he is three times accused as traitor, three times stays silent, and by his silence seems to admit his guilt. So he is condemned to death by entombment. He will be buried alive under the floor of the temple.

Into this crypt he goes calmly. Amneris, powerless now to save him, turns ranting and raving on the priests who have condemned him and in condemning him taken him away from her forever. For to Amneris Radames in this death is totally lost. She will some day be buried in state in her own tomb, surrounded with her treasures, her favorite pets and even her favorite friends, in effigy. As a royal lady, she will travel to "the fields of food" and there reclaim her true identity, to live as a princess among her own set. Radames, interred without honors, without signs of the high rank he has sacrificed, will arrive in the hereafter like a slave, but as a slave be admitted by Osiris if he knows all the right answers to the *Book of the Dead*. This is the rule of the Egyptian gods.

And, as it happens, it is a rule which blesses Radames in his tomb for there, awaiting him, is Aida, longing to atone to Radames for her deception and betrayal—willing to share his death when she could easily have escaped the Egyptians by fleeing back to her own people. For with her characteristic pessimism, her fatal sense of doom, Aida knows that Radames cannot escape this most dreadful of deaths—burial alive, alone, without food for the long journey that must be undertaken by the dead, without trinket, toy or armor, with nothing to identify him as a great and valiant hero. Thus, she has found her way into the crypt by its dark labyrinth, in dread and shrinking, but in love.

And so they die, together, and together go to the Egyptians gods who (as we must be sure Radames knows) accept Egyptians and their slaves, receive those who come together from a shared tomb—and set these (as Aida and Radames will be set) to live together, safely, securely, in eternal pleasures.

This, in brief, is the romance of Verdi's *Aida*.

*In brief, this is my method with a group for "discovering* Aida*":*
I treat *Aida's* story and characters as I would those of a play or novel, or events and persons out of history.[2] When the group knows the characters by name and nature and all their involvements with each other, only then do we listen to Verdi's music and I prefer to listen, first, to orchestral music without the vocalization. Allegedly, music does not "say" anything but of course we know that music has enormous expression and, moreover, summons up feelings in listeners. It is my aim now to make the group hear *Aida* in the music, just as it has learned to "see" *Aida* in the mind's eye out of its drama. And Verdi has a superlative score for listening in *Aida*.

No attempt is made to analyze the music as music. If my approach has been successful the group has now reached a phase where drama and music are indissoluble and *Aida* is in the music . . . this is not music to be treated as music *per se* or as accompaniment to staged singing and acting. The teacher need only maintain suspense to create interest—*Aida* is a great deal more exciting than the "pop" radio and television "soap operas" to which thousands of Americans are said to be addicted.

As *Aida* is full of wonderful melodies it provides an infinite number of rafts or buoys on which to launch the new opera goer. There are splendid marches, as the procession at Memphis in *Act I* (the investure of Radames as leader of the army) and the grand march at Thebes in *Act II,* a celebrated composition for trumpets. Verdi's best ballet music is in *Aida,* and several choreographers have excerpted the *Dance of the Blackamoors* and the sacred dance of the priestesses to turn into "ballet from *Aida.*"

The first aria is Radames' *Celeste Aida* and the opera ends with *O terra, addio*—the dying lovers' tender farewell to earth. In between are several famous airs for solo, ensemble and chorus. Aida has a great *romanza* (a type of aria) in *O patria mia*—My fatherland, and Amneris, *Morir mi sento,* her soul-searing cry when she cannot save Radames because he will not save himself for her sake. But far over and beyond these separate compositions is the opera as a whole in which all the music and the drama are as one, and one of the best and most important examples of what an opera is. When Verdi sealed the stone in the temple over the crypt of Radames and Aida (in eight bars of music in reiterated low Ds) he was preserving forever a work of art.

*Aida's* text is in Italian, of which there are English translations. Get hold of the printed text and also of the vocal score; try and get a vocal score that has stage directions and other elementary notations. After you have told your story of the opera (excitingly, so that the group is entertained by it, is responsive to the drama) use the libretto as you would the script of a play. I use it to the extent of allocating parts, which we read exactly as we read a play, with vocal inflection and "expression," but without action.

We separate the "play" into acts and scenes, observe the stage directions and the information about bits of theatrical by-play, and discuss the "action" itself and how its cycle rises and falls, and flows, from act into act, and scene into scene, from start to close.

We come now to the characters, who have become personalities with motives and natures, real people. We know who's who and we find out, in what we have read out of their mouths in the opera's plot, why they behave as they do, for what purposes, from what motivations, toward what ends. We trace them individually and together, where they proceed, and when and how and why, within the opera, and we analyze acts and emotions so that the inner and the outer world of the opera's people are known to us.

Then we revert to the preliminary treatment of the opera as a form, as having parts and a sum, and we "take the opera apart in pieces" as some students say, to examine it of itself and within the design. We have ceased to think of the opera as having skeleton and flesh and look at it now as having design and color. The drama is the design or shape; the music is the color or emotion. We have progressed to treating opera as form and spirit.

*Aida's* prelude lasts three minutes but in that short time states a tender theme for Aida and the heavy bass theme, fraught with doom, that is Ramfis and his priests. It is almost as though Verdi pits the real protagonists against each other for us to know, at the opening, how the cards are stacked in *Aida*. She is the heroine in a romantic concept and has the title role but Amneris, her rival, is her equal, dramatically and musically.

Verdi took great care to balance these attributes so that both women have important lines of action, both women have dramatic strands of music, and these knit them into the plot. An example of the exquisite balance Verdi achieved is in Aida's appeal to the gods, *Act I*: *Numi, pietà,* and Amneris' appeal, in the same words, *Act IV*: *Pietà, Numi, pietà.*

I think that Verdi here manages to convey the whole sum of Amneris' role. For the opera begins with Amneris the princess, Aida the slave, and ends with Aida freed by the Angel of Death and Amneris broken rather than exalted by love, crying for pity as Aida did in the beginning.

The opera's form is *drama through music* and the group must discover the musical natures of the characters as they at first discovered the dramatic natures of *Aida's* people from the plot. The preliminary knowledge of these musical natures is obtained from knowing the kinds of voices, or voice-range, cast in the opera. The cast is as follows:

| | |
|---|---|
| *Ramfis*, the high priest | bass |
| *Radames*, the young general of the Egyptian army | tenor |
| *Amneris*, Pharaoh's daughter | mezzo-soprano |
| *Aida*, an Ethiopian slave, servant to Amneris, beloved by Radames | soprano |
| The Pharaoh of Egypt | bass |
| *Amonasro*, King of Ethiopia, father of Aida | baritone |

The group at this point begins to listen to the music of *Aida,* and the more familiar it becomes to the ear, *as music,* the easier it will be to relate the sung or vocal parts of the score within the orchestral or whole of *Aida.* The easiest means of relating the vocal parts to the orchestral score is to use "highlights" or highly dramatic and musically expressive parts of the opera as a map or guide-line—one such, in brief, is provided on pages 201-202.

The verse and music can now be put together, but first we return to the libretto, and one where the English as well as the Italian verse appears. In actual production, opera's action may drag (it sometimes does because this is a major production problem) but the music and singing continue and the audience needs to be attentive or it will miss the nuances of mood and subtleties of conversational exchanges. If the sense of the singing is known to the new opera goer he will carry through fairly well. But when he can actually recognize the singing in recitatives, arias, et cetera, then he has a better grasp of the opera and can appreciate the performance more—or be more critical about it. Above all, he will be at his ease, not his unease.

We do not attempt a literal transposition from Italian to English for *Aida* but we observe the phonetics of the arias and choruses and such of the verse that attracts the group's attention—for example the curious duet in *Act I,* where Radames sings with magnificent maleness (the operatic term is *grandioso*) and Aida sings in an altogether different vein of her anguish—beloved of a man who is the enemy of her people, she is understandably quite miserable while Radames is exultant over the war. This is the sort of emotional counterpoint, more delicate and intricate than fine needlework, which excites the new opera goer's admiration—*when* he knows enough to appreciate the artistry of it.

If you match the great arias in verse in English-Italian (or, for other operas, in English-French and English-German) you discover that the phonetics are recognizable when you hear the verse sung. The arias and recitatives are usually the best verse for doing this; verse for the chorus may be somewhat more difficult to follow but it can be heard and recognized, with practice.

After these preliminaries, we hear *Aida* in the full score, taped or on phonograph recording, and whenever possible I attempt to provide such recordings of the opera with different casts. Tebaldi and Callas

are two different women, two different singers, two different Aidas.³
Who is the superior Aida? This is for you to decide, for it is you who,
like Schopenhauer's sailor, are plumbing their depth. You will plumb
as your line or knowledge allows and after that you will decide which
singer moves you more. If you listen and look through several *Aidas*
you will eventually find your favorite as an opera buff.

When the group undertakes listening to a fully recorded opera it
discovers itself to be a great deal more sophisticated than the average
theatre goer. We have not studied the Italian language to be able to
converse in it but the language of *Aida* is not entirely strange. We find,
as we hear *Aida* sung, that we have a degree of knowledge (through
knowing the drama and the music and through having absorbed some
of the Italian phonetics as they relate to the meanings of the verse).
We are able to relate the sound of the singing to the sense of *Aida*.

*Act I, Scene I* does not present a medley of incomprehensible
solos by three but the three persons (Radames, Aida, Amneris) singing
simultaneously and revealing to us worlds within that are secret from
each other: Radames exultant as a soldier and lover, Amneris amorous
but agitated as the princess who suspects her lover of being enamored
of her maid, Aida oppressed by her secrets—she is enemy as well as
beloved of Radames, and is helpless against the cruelty and malice of
her mistress. She thinks of her father, pledged to attack Egypt with his
army to set her free and when, at Thebes, she sees him a captive, in
chains, she throws herself in his arms in grief and horror. It is logical
for her to behave like this, after *Act I*.

This "eternal triangle" from first to last has validity in the music
because Verdi set firm, delicate imprints for each: Aida seductive and
sweet (her *O patria mia* is to oboe *obbligato*), Radames stalwart (his
singing is *grandioso*), and Amneris proud—so proud that her love is
like fire. A passionate, sensual woman as well as a princess, Amneris
sings *Ah vieni vien', amor mio, m'inebbria*—Ah, come love, come love,
fill me with rapture, because she rejoices to be possessed by love, and
she fiercely intends to possess Radames. Compare this nature with
Aida's, who mourns her state (that she dare not claim father as king,
Radames as lover): "Never on earth was a heart torn by more cruel
agonies." And at the height of the jubilation when Radames is cere-
moniously hailed as hero at Thebes, Aida sings (against the great chorus
*Gloria all'Egitto*—Glory to Egypt) that nothing is now left for her, only

oblivion and tears for her hopeless love—while Radames has glory from his military victories and the throne, when he marries Pharaoh's daughter. Aida is a born pessimist, a girl with a fatal sense of doom. She invites disaster because she believes that this alone is her lot.

Some opera buffs complain that Verdi did not make Aida "great enough" but I do not think Verdi wanted her to be "great" as a saint or genius is great—he meant her to be Aida, a girl with a mortal dilemma. We may be certain that Amneris, enslaved in Ethiopia, would behave in a different manner to Aida enslaved in Egypt.

Radames is the just foil for these two, stout-hearted if a bit wooden-headed, the perfect knight blundering into the role of traitor and crying out for his dishonor as though he had been stabbed to the heart. In that scene (*Act III*) Verdi tells a truth that is quite terrifying—the weak can be the most dangerous of friends, our true enemies. Radames was a general, seasoned in campaigns, an ambitious soldier, and he was betrayed by a girl who was frightened (as Amonasro frightened her) by the threat of her mother's ghost. It is not Amonasro who betrays Radames—it is Aida.

Verdi sets the treachery at an emotional point when music and drama have carried us (and Radames) to a climax. The great duet in this scene is between Aida and Radames: *Là tra foreste vergini, in estasi, la terra scorderem*—In the virgin forest grove, in ecstasy, the world forgotten, sung when Aida has persuaded Radames to leave Egypt and go away with her.

*Aida* is a great love story and Radames a heroic lover. Descending into his tomb (*Act IV*) his heart eagerly bounds to *mia dolce Aida*— my sweet Aida! Radames has an unearthly patience and kindliness— there is nothing he will not forgive for love.

A group should be encouraged to assess an opera after experiencing it in performance but should first be guided to understand that assessment is made from contributions of knowledge, plus individual taste— and that taste is subject to the same prejudices we each carry as solitary burdens into every experience. Assessing a performance is a valuable exercise for the opera goer, for comparison through successive performances.

This assessment may be approached in several ways, from theme paper to conversational debate—the latter in the social-cum-cultural group doing "Arts Appreciation" more for pleasure in leisure than as class assignment. But the assessment must be recognized as being in parts, any one part of which may alter the quality and quantity of the sum.

Your valid basis of assessment is the opera's form, qualified by the *style* in which it was created by the composer and librettist, and the *style of production* chosen by the opera company. The style of production, added to the standard of production (the staging, musical rendition, quality of singing) must be further qualified by the *performance* which you experience. You will know opera (*Aida* for example) in these ways: as it was created; as it is produced in the theatre; and as it happens or is performed when you see and hear it.

A valid assessment of an opera is the sum of all these factors, and if, for example, you experience numerous *Aidas*, in different productions, by different casts, then the assessment can be made on broader, deeper values, all of which remain valid for Verdi's *Aida*.

As I consider theatre performances by the persons on stage to be "experiences" for the audience, I recommend that you keep a record or theatrical diary of your own impressions and responses to opera productions, performance by performance, noting the singers in the cast, the company which presents the opera, et cetera, and making your own "critique" or résumé opinion of the opera performance. Such a diary, kept over a long period (I was made to keep a theatre diary from childhood and have found the fruits over a lifetime to be infinitely well worth the task) will inform you about a great deal in opera—and about yourself, as to tastes, intellectual analyses, emotional responses, and power of observation. In short, it will make you a critic of discernment, Schopenhauer's sailor plumbing the depths as far as the length of your line will allow. And theatre itself is a liberal classical education.

My lectures in "Arts Appreciation" for opera, *Aida* for example, are generally directed towards the group experience of *Aida* as "live" production or as filmed version. The productions vary from professional to amateur and it is impossible for me to know what *Aida* you will see, by what company, in what kind of production, so I can make no further "guide" for your experience of *Aida*. I resist, on principle, telling the individual what to look for and what to listen to beyond offering a means of guidance as to how to go about looking and listening . . . and I, again on principle, do not "recommend" any cast and opera house production since *Aida* is constantly in theatrical production and performance.

If you are interested in that aspect of opera history which records the highlights of operas and opera artistes then you will enjoy reading about *Aida's* romantic aspects, its origins and creation, its various presentations around the world, and the *transubstantiations* (changes in substance while remaining substantially unchanged) of which *Aida* seems capable.

Some examples of the transubstantiation process are described in this book, and are of general interest to the teacher or to the reader working in amateur non-commercial aspects of opera. They are included here not as a literal guide of how to make a theatrical presentation of *Aida* but as examples of some contemporary approaches, from groups in educational curriculum, to an opera—*Aida* for example.

You are fortunate in living in America if you want to experience *Aida* "live" within the opera house. This is a favorite American opera, maintained by the Metropolitan Opera and constantly refurbished through the employment of new stage directors, scenic artists and choreographers and, of course, new casts. In ten years, 1950-1960, the Metropolitan performed *Aida* 78 times.

If you are very lucky (if, as the Italians say, you "hold your mouth right" when you pray for a miracle) you will experience *Aida* in the opera house as it might have leaped from Verdi's hand, immaculate and true, Minerva from the head of Jupiter. I promise you, this is a thrilling experience—as when, in the dark theatre, a curtain lifts between you and Pharaoh's Egypt and there is Aida, in the person of Leontyne Price, a beautiful Negress who is a lovely soprano.

### Highlights *from* Aida

Casts for operas are usually stated in order of the appearance of the characters in the dramatic action. The principals in *Aida* are:

| | |
|---|---|
| *Ramfis*, the high priest | bass |
| *Radames* (Rah-da-*mace*) | tenor |
| *Amneris* (Ahm-*nair*-ees) | mezzo-soprano |
| *Aida* (Ah-*ee*-dah) | soprano |
| *Pharaoh*, the King of Egypt | bass |
| *Amonasro* (Am-oh-*nas*-roh) | baritone |

and the Pharaoh's aide, called the Messenger, is a tenor.

The opera is in four acts and seven scenes, and omitting intervals between acts (intermissions in the theatre) is approximately two and one-half hours long.

*Act I, Scene I* is a hall in the Pharaoh's palace at Memphis; *Scene II* is within the Temple of Phtha where the invocation by the priests is *Immenso Phtha, noi t'invochiamo*—Almighty (Immense) Phtha, we invoke you. As *Aida's* characters call on "God" frequently, know that the word *Nume* means god.

The first aria is Radames' *Celeste Aida, forma divina*—Heavenly Aida, of divine form, and the first duet is between Amneris and Radames. They are agitated for different reasons, he embarrassed because she comes on him singing about Aida, she because she is pricked by sudden jealousy which causes her to sing *O, guai*—Oh, woe. The first trio is between the rivals for Radames' love and Radames. Amneris rages how she will make Aida *Trema*—tremble; Aida bewails her fate: *Piango*—weeping; and Radames, aware of what his love for Aida is likely to bring them both, sings *Guai*. When the Pharaoh announces the campaign against Ethiopia, Aida cries *Mio padre*—my father. The first great chorus in *Aida* is the praise of the people of Egypt for their country and their response to Pharaoh's demand if Egypt shall go to war against Ethiopia—the people cry *Guerra* (war) and sing of their beloved Egypt. Within this jubilant chorus Aida sings her melancholy lament for her unhappy love, her unhappy fate. Amneris, the princess, in the *Ritorna vincitor*—Return victorious, addresses the general in a cry of triumph or exaltation, not as a prayer for his safety in the war. Aida sings her aria, about her unhappy love for Radames: *E l'amor mio*—And my love, which struggles against her love for her father, and entreats the Gods to let her die to end her dilemma (she is being torn apart between Radames and her father) in the *Numi, pietà, del mio soffrir*—Gods, have pity on my sufferings. All the foregoing occurs in the first scene.

The second scene is comparatively short. A chorus by the priests and a dance (the first ballet) by the priestesses marks the beginning of the ceremony in the temple where Radames is consecrated and receives his arms. His head is veiled by a silver cloth and Ramfis prays with him, for strength to obtain victory in the battle. The whole first act, with the prelude, lasts about one half-hour.

*Act II, Scene I* is set within Amneris' suite in the palace, where she is being dressed by her servants. She has a large suite of attendants, among them little blackamoors, Moorish children, who perform for her entertainment the *Dance of the Moors*. Thinking of Radames, Amneris sings *O vieni, vien', amor mio*—Oh, come, come, my love. Amneris suggests to Aida that if she had a lover her pain might be eased, she would not pine for her country, mourn her people's defeat. Aida bursts out that love is both a boon and a curse, forgetting for the moment that she is a slave. In the duet between the rivals, Amneris puts Aida to the test and discovers her secret love for Radames by the ruse of saying he is dead, then that he is alive. Aida again prays to the gods for deliverance from her miseries while Amneris, richly dressed, goes to join the triumphal procession at Thebes, which occurs in *Scene II*.

At Thebes the grand spectacle or finale of *Act II* comprises a huge gathering for chorus, the priests and Ramfis (there occurs a second ballet and this one an opportunity for a choreographic frenzy as exciting as the bacchanal in *Faust*), a parade of armed troops, the disposition of the beaten Ethiopians and entry of Amonasro and his aria: *Ma tu, Re*—But you, King. The entreaty of Amonasro, supported by Aida, to which is added Radames' plea for mercy; the protests of Ramfis, the conciliatory statement of the Pharaoh, Amneris' burst of jealousy at the looks exchanged between her fiancé and her servant, and other utterances (as by the priests insisting the Ethiopians must be sacrificed, and the people, stirred by Amonasro and Radames, begging for mercy for the prisoners) make this passage extremely rich in vocalization. There are twelve to sixteen different voice parts as one in this scene, then sudden silence and Radames asks the Pharaoh to grant clemency to the prisoners.

In the chorus is heard Aida bewailing her fate against the prisoners rejoicing at their freedom, Pharaoh betrothing his daughter to the general (with Amneris triumphant, Radames terrified that he may lose Aida), Amonasro plotting his vengeance, and Ramphis invoking the gods—a chorus and sextet, or vocalization by six. *Act II* is approximately 40 minutes.

*Act III* (the easiest to see with the mind's eye) is in one scene: the bank of the Nile river. Amneris goes into retreat in the temple, Aida comes to keep a rendezvous with Radames who has sent her a message to meet him at this place, and sings her aria *O patria mia*—Oh my country. There follows the duet between father and daughter. Aida's refusal to seduce Radames is *No, no, giammai*—No, no, never! And, as she soon breaks under her father's harshness, she again cries *Pietà*— Have pity, as in *Act I, Scene II* she cries it to Amneris.

The exchange between the lovers is musically and dramatically a study of Aida, the eternal woman. *Va*—Go, she says to Radames, telling him to return to the embraces of the princess. But Radames woos her all over again, telling her of his plans to defeat the final stragglers of the Ethiopian army, finally dispel the threat of harm that lies over Egypt from the Ethiopians, and, returning victorious, demand of Pharaoh the redemption of the promise that Radames may have anything he asks—and ask for Aida.

The denouement follows the confiding of Radames to Aida that the army will attack by the Pass (or gorge) of Napata, and when Amonasro appears, Radames says: *Tu! Amonasro . . . tu . . . il . . . Re!*—You! Amonasro . . . the dead king! And then Radames cries: *Io son disonorato* —I am dishonored! There follows a trio, Aida trying to placate her lover, he wild with despair at what he has done, Amonasro urging him to throw in his lot with Ethiopia. Amneris' great cry is: *Traditor!*—Traitor! *Act III* consumes about 30 minutes, *Act IV* about the same time.

*Scene I* (of *Act IV*) is after the final battle between Egyptians and Ethiopians in which Amonasro has been killed. Amneris is raging within herself, princess and woman struggling for domination. The princess wishes Radames, the traitor, dead; the woman argues that he is not a traitor, that he has only been seduced by the foreign woman. She hates him and she loves him and she finds she loves more than she hates. *Io l'amo, io l'amo sempre*—I love him, I shall love him always. And in their duet she begs him to save himself, he having assured her that he is not a traitor—she believes him and begs him to help himself, promising that she will beg her father to save his life. He accuses her of having Aida killed but believes her when she denies this, and rejoices that Aida is free. Live for her, the princess implores, live because Pharaoh's daughter loves him. Radames replies: *non posso* —I cannot, and tells her that without Aida death is a blessing. When he goes, Amneris cries, like a desolate child: *O chi lo salva?*—Oh who will save him now? And, humbled at last, she prays: *Numi pietà*—

Gods, have pity. She sobs the prayer three times more as Radames is accused and judged guilty, saying: *Pietà, Numi, pietà.*

The end of this scene is the princess' cursing of the priests, a tirade that is emotionally and musically taxing, and one of the great histrionic episodes in all opera.

*Scene II* is the famed "double chamber" scene, in which the audience sees the temple above, in the upper part of the stage, and the crypt below, where the lovers are reconciled. Radames' aria begins: *Morir, si pura e bella*—To die, so pure and lovely. Aida's aria is addressed half wonderingly to the Angel of Death (faint with hunger after three days in the labyrinth, she has begun to have hallucinations). The great finale is *O terra addio*—Oh earth farewell, as a duet. Verdi invokes in this last scene the *Celeste Aida* music from the first not merely as a reprise but richly, in the form of two arias and the wonderful duet, the *Addio.*

All these "highlights" are easily recognized when hearing the opera sung.

### Aida's *Composer*

Giuseppe Verdi was rich, famous and middle-aged when he created *Aida.* Adored by Italians of all classes, respected throughout the world as a great composer and worshipped by two women (his wives, both of whom pre-deceased him), he was to end his private life in loneliness but to know, before he died, that he was already legendary.

"I will grant opera to be a world art," an Italian opera buff has said. "Because of Gluck and Mozart and a few Frenchmen. But what would opera be without Italians, beginning with Monteverdi and ending with Verdi? In opera Italians are the substance of the Greeks in drama."

Indeed, Verdi's operas are in idea very close to Greek drama and poetry, he had a Grecian turn of thought about death—of which he seemed always aware, of the brevity of life and awful chance of death (like Gilda's in *Rigoletto*), the fatality of coincidence (again in *Rigoletto* and also in his *Otello*), and of life itself as Pindar saw it: "a shadow's dream." (Radames' and Aida's "vale of sorrow.") Verdi made his creatures superior to imminent death; they never lose their taste for living until and unless death offers something more glorious than life. And he deals with matters of life and death as though they were commonplace, as being common to the human estate—it is his *human beings* that Verdi lifts above the commonplace.

Again, in the choice of his plots, the events and circumstances remind me of an aspect of Greek literature: the attitude towards tragedy. Verdi thought of tragedy as poetry, not as spectacle—he was a self-avowed realist but he did not interpret death as, for instance, it was interpreted in the Hamburg opera. No one is more sincere and urgent than Verdi, and he is a composer of passionate vitality, never afraid of grappling with emotion; no one is less "mannered" in a nice, neat, style of composition or expression; yet it is Verdi who defined death (*Aida*) for his librettist as lyrical and elegiac, warning Ghislanzoni that he wanted no "death pangs" or signs of physical suffering because (as Radames sings) *Morir, si pura e bella*—To die, how pure and beautiful.[4]

Yet in his tragedies he never spares us any more than he spares his characters. We are witness to most monstrous and appalling deeds and, it must be admitted, we enjoy them dearly—for what else makes Verdi's operas so universally loved, so popular but the audiences' enjoyment of them?

Pain, sorrow, catastrophes of grief and loss and humiliation are endured by Verdi's people but these sufferings are never depressing, they never become sordid and what happens to Verdi's people are not pitiable disasters but sheer tragedy. You and I do not dare pity these people—for how could we dare, when they exalt us? And Verdi is a connoisseur of suffering; he shows us suffering by the innocent (Aida or Gilda) and suffering by the damned (Amneris or Rigoletto).

This composer's career, his whole life, is the richest source of information about the creative aspect of opera. Whereas some opera composers (Purcell, Rameau, Gluck, Mozart, Wagner) came to their work by way of an inheritance or through an environmental influence in arts, Verdi is of the other sort—the kind that appear suddenly and as by the whim as well as the will of God, destined to make music. Nothing in Verdi's antecedent history prepares us for Verdi, who began his life October 10, 1813. His life may be seen, in retrospect, as a search for how to make opera, and then for the best means of expressing in the form of opera what he thought about life and music.

In his youth, when he was a passionate national idealist, his operas were "political" and revolutionary, and he contrived dramatic situations and composed music for them as the means of expressing his republican opinions. He was a fiery patriot, a revolutionist, who fought for Italy with music as Italy's famous soldier Garibaldi fought with arms.

His first success was the opera *Oberto*, his first triumph the opera *Nabucco*. These, with *I Lombardi, Ernani, Atilla* and *La Battaglia di Legnano* are all "political" operas from his first period, while in his second compositional period the "political" operas are *The Sicilian Vespers* and *The Masked Ball*. He was a revolutionist first and an opera composer perhaps second until 1859, the year in which Italy was unified under Victor Emanuel, King of Sardinia. He remained passionately devoted to Italy, maintaining a large property, Sant'Agata, chiefly to provide employment for the villagers from the district where he was born (La Roncole) so that they would not be tempted to emigrate to the United States of America.

In 1847, with *Macbeth*, an opera with libretto (by Francesco Piave and Andrea Maffei) based on Shakespeare's play, he showed a change from his earlier period, of which *Nabucco* and *Ernani* were the most important works. His biographer Francis Toye describes *Macbeth* as Verdi's search for an expressiveness, "an acute delineation of the human soul, never before realized," such as he achieved with Amneris in *Aida* and with almost every character in *Otello*. With *Ernani* (based on Victor Hugo's drama *Hernani*, in a libretto by Piave) Verdi became internationally famous—perhaps because it was censored in Italy, where the Austrian government required the libretto to be extensively revised and disapproved of the opera because of its inflammable nature. Performed in Paris, *Ernani* became a *cause célèbre*, a source of argument between young French romanticists, who called it a masterpiece, and classicists, who were repelled by Verdi's overwhelming emotion. From a critical viewpoint, the uninhibited feeling of Verdi's music is suited to the melodramatic poetry of Hugo—but Hugo was one of the Frenchmen who disliked Verdi's *Ernani*.

*Rigoletto* (1851) marked a new period for Verdi, in which his genius for an apparently inexhaustible lyricism was enhanced by drama. His works assumed a form in which music, characterizations of genuine humanity, dramatic climax, and construction as opera, were superb examples of theatrical art. *Aida* belongs to the period commencing with

*Rigoletto* and may be said to terminate this second period of the composer's career, if *Otello* and *Falstaff* are thought of as being within the
third and final period.

*Aida, La Bohème, Carmen* and *La Traviata* are the world's most
popular operas and of these Verdi's *Aida* is said to be the "most perfect"
and his *La Traviata* the most often performed, for the reason that it is
immensely popular and also requires a smaller cast and orchestra than
the other three operas. In the thousands of operas composed and the
hundreds in permanent repertory, these four represent examples of
extraordinary response by audiences—and two of these four are Verdi's.

*Nabucco* is still maintained in Italian repertory, where it has great
sentimental associations. It was the opera chosen to reopen La Scala
after World War II. The best known Verdi operas are *Nabucco*—1842,
*Ernani*—1844, *Rigoletto*—1851, *Il Trovatore* (The Troubadour) and
*La Traviata*, both in 1853, *Les Vêpres Siciliennes* (The Sicilian Vespers)—1855, *Simon Boccanegra*—1857, *Un Ballo in Maschera* (The
Masked Ball)—1859, *La Forza del Destino* (The Forces of Destiny)—
1862, *Macbeth*—1865, *Don Carlo*—1867, *Aida*—1871, *Otello*—1887 and
*Falstaff*—1893.*

His first opera was composed when he was twenty-four and his
last premièred when he was eighty. He lived a long, productive life,
eighty-eight years, which was as well for opera because his early times
were not like Mozart's, an infant prodigy who wrote his first opera at
twelve, and who composed minuets at five, a sonata at seven, a symphony at eight; from the age of six was an accomplished harpsichordist,
and died at thirty-five. Verdi got off to a later start but lasted longer. He
was born fifty-seven years after Mozart's death, and was exactly thirty-
five years older than his compatriot Puccini, the composer of *La
Bohème;* fifteen years older than Bizet, the composer of *Carmen.* He
was born in the same year as Richard Wagner and these two present
the perfect examples and perfect contrasts in "Italian" and "German"
opera.

He came from poor, ordinary folk, born near Busetto in Parma,
and from a child he loved music inordinately. His father, despite real
poverty, bought him a spinet and paid for music lessons. Verdi was

* The dates given are the premières of the works; *Macbeth*, in its revised
version.

schooled in Busetto, whose townspeople raised funds to send him to the Milan Conservatory of Music in 1832.

The Conservatory refused Verdi admittance because he was too old (he was nineteen) and too poorly trained (by the town organist in Busetto) and he returned to Busetto after studying privately under a teacher, Vincenzo Lavigna, in Milan.

In Busetto he became the town organist and conductor of the Philharmonic Society (but was subjected to many humiliations in that post), married (Margherita Barezzi) in 1836, and wrote his first opera, *Oberto*, which was accepted for publication and produced at La Scala in 1837. Its reception was good enough for La Scala to commission three more works from the young composer.

Verdi, at twenty-seven the father of two sons, and a loving husband, composed as his second work a comedy: *King for a Day*, which was produced at La Scala in 1840. It was an abject failure. In this same year, Verdi's happy family life was destroyed by the deaths of his wife and two little boys within a few months of each other. He composed no more comedies until *Falstaff*.

His second commissioned work for La Scala (his third opera), premièred March 9, 1842, was *Nabucco*, based on Nebuchadnezzar, the Biblical character who led the Jews out of Babylon—as Verdi burned to lead Italy out of the Austrian yoke. The opera had a chorus: *Speed your journey, my thoughts and my longings,* which stirred the emotional Italians, who seized it as a freedom hymn. They sang it in the streets with such brio that the opera's fame spread— to the Austrians, like a dangerous bonfire. Overnight, Verdi became famous; dishes of food and articles of dress were named after him. *Nabucco* also brought him a new love, Giuseppina Strepponi, the Abigail in the opera. She was Verdi's mistress from 1849 and he married her in 1859, when his work as a "revolutionist" was completed; Italy was again unified and whole! His only excursion into politics was as a member of the new Italian parliament, memorable in that it was during this period (1861-1865) that he composed *The Forces of Destiny*, a melodramatic opera of the finest "Italian" style.

Even his name leaned to political propaganda, the letters VERDI standing for those of *Vittorio Emmanuele Re d'Italia*, to which wily patriots added VIVA! *Viva d'Italia!* (Long live Italy!) was forbidden by the Austrians. Italian patriots demonstrated against their oppressors by shouting and scrawling the words VIVA VERDI! with impunity, pretending that they were applauding their beloved composer. He soon became a legendary figure in Italy and his fecundity as an opera composer preserved his popularity after the Italian revolution. The Paris Opéra as well as La Scala commissioned works from him, and Ismail Pasha, Khedive of Egypt, invited Verdi to compose an opera for the opening of the new Italian Theatre in Cairo.

The Khedive sent Verdi the plot of *Aida*, which had been suggested for an opera by Mariette Bey, a French archaeologist, a noted Egyptologist, who undertook to design the production. He recreated for the theatre ancient Memphis and Thebes, and the palace and Temple of Phtha, as well as the costumes for *Aida*. Verdi was asked to name his fee for the opera and requested 150,000 francs, a sum of much greater value then than now.[5] At first, he was not especially taken with the idea of *Aida* but when his price was met he set to work with characteristic energy—which meant working as well and as hard as he was able. Characteristically, too, he never undertook what he could not achieve, setting himself within limitations which he freely admitted—but which few would have dared to set him at that phase of his career.

To the Khedive, *Aida* was more than an opera, it was part of a splendid historical occasion—the celebration of the opening of the Suez Canal. Not only Verdi benefited from this auspicious occasion but also the dressmaker Worth, who furnished the Empress Eugénie and her ladies with hundreds of elegant gowns and accessories which the Frenchwomen wore to match the Oriental splendor of their welcome in Egypt.

The Empress and her suite with all their belongings safely made the trip to Egypt and home again—the last grand occasion in the reign of Emperor Napoleon III. Verdi was not so fortunate when *Aida's* luggage had to make the same trip. The Italian Theatre opened in Cairo in November, 1869, but not with *Aida* (which did not turn up on stage until Christmas Eve, 1871). Its scenery and costumes, having been executed in France, had to stay there until the end of the Franco-Prussian War.

Verdi was customarily on hand for the openings of his works (he generally conducted the opera in première) but was afraid of the long sea voyage and stayed home in Busetto, where *Aida* had, in fact, been launched or created.

This is how it was done: the composer was sent the rough plot of *Aida* and he and his friend Camille du Locle, formerly the director of l'Opéra Comique, drafted the libretto, du Locle writing in French (but afterwards saying that Verdi took great interest in the libretto in all its details, making several suggestions and devising the "double-chamber" scene for the finale).[6] The opera was blocked out in four acts and seven scenes and a well-known Italian librettist, Antonio Ghislanzoni, began to write the text in Italian. He and Verdi were geographically apart and *Aida* was created in collaboration by correspondence. Nevertheless, Verdi was never far from Ghislanzoni's elbow. On at least one occasion, he metaphorically snatched the pen from his librettist and furiously scribbled his own verse, to make sure he got out of Aida's mouth what he was putting into it, musically.

Ismail Pasha and Mariette Bey foresaw *Aida* as a splendid production; Verdi was concerned with the people in *Aida*, and especially with Amneris on whom he lavished not only great music but burning intensity. In *Scene II* of *Act I* where the Princess dupes her slave into admitting her love for Radames and then cruelly tells Aida *she* is her rival, Ghislanzoni rendered the declaration in four lines of operatic verse. Verdi wrote: "Abandon rhyme, rhythm, stanza. Forget it all!" He wanted only *la parola scenica* (the dramatic word) and not fanciful operatic phrasing. And this is what Amneris tells Aida (Verdi's own words): "You love him but so do I! Do you hear me? I am your rival! I, the daughter of the Pharaohs!"[7]

Ghislanzoni had written more than sixty libretti before *Aida* and, skilled in his craft, provided the traditional *cabaletta* (to which Verdi was very partial) in *Act III* for the exchange between Aida and Amonasro, where the king coerces his daughter into betraying Radames. Verdi liked little about this verse but Ghislanzoni's sneering repudiation by Amonasro stands in the opera: "You are not my daughter, you are the Pharaoh's slave!" when Aida at first resists his command about Radames. Broken-hearted, Aida appeals to her father (if he deserts her, whom has she left?) and Ghislanzoni provided her with a *cabaletta*. Verdi seized his pen to write: "No *cabalettas* here! In her state of terror and moral depression, Aida cannot possibly sing an extended melodic passage. Just give me a few broken words that she can utter *con voce cupa*, in a low, hollow voice." Ghislanzoni obliged.

Again they clashed over Amneris, in *Act IV* when the Princess tries to persuade Radames to plead his case before his judges, to exculpate himself. She pleads as though she were her own client, she pleads like a veritable Portia from her energy and wit (this is the sort of woman Amneris is: intelligent and energetic, bent on the object of her desire with every fibre, never mind if the object is good or bad). Verdi complains to Ghislanzoni that he has made Amneris talk like a jurist; he, Verdi, does not know how he will find appropriate music for her to sing such words! But Verdi finds the music and writes quickly to Ghislanzoni: "Under these words of a lawyer there beats the heart of a woman, desperate with ardent love. Only music can depict what goes on in her soul, hidden behind her words."

So it was that wherever *Aida* went from Verdi's keeping, and however it was caparisoned (and it has had productions with armies, ballets and live elephants on stage) its people had such integrity that they were always vital, always viable.

Verdi was then aged fifty-seven, his reputation already made, but he worked like a madman, or a composer who was about to make his name, intending that *Aida* should be his swan song. He planned to retire from theatre and live at Sant'Agata with his second wife.

*Aida* won its first great esteem in Cairo, where its production featured (among other splendors) three hundred singers and actors in the triumphal march at Thebes, *Act II*. The great chorus, *Gloria all'Egitto* (Glory to Egypt) so moved the Egyptians that their government adopted it as the national hymn—as the chorus from *Nabucco* had become the Italian revolutionary anthem.

*Aida's* second première was at La Scala in February, 1872, and this time Verdi was present to conduct the opera, receiving an ovation which recalled him thirty-two times, an ivory baton, and diamond star (a decoration) with *Aida* in rubies and *Verdi* in other precious gems.

Every capital was clamoring to produce *Aida*, the Paris Opéra among other theatres, but *Aida* traveled all the way to America, to appear, on its third première, in the New World. It was produced at the Academy of Music, New York, November 26, 1873 and Kobbé, (to whose *Complete Opera Book* I have referred readers) attended the performance, reporting that its brilliancy was never surpassed, if, indeed, equalled from that occasion.[8]

The opera reached Paris in April, 1876 (it was presented at the *Théâtre des Italiens*) but the Opéra did not produce it until March, 1880—and here lies an anecdote about Verdi, who like Rameau and Gluck had trouble with l'Opéra's temperamental orchestra.

In 1855, when the Opéra was producing *The Sicilian Vespers* (it is set on a plot laid in 13th century Sicily and a revolt against the French occupation forces) Verdi had trouble getting the orchestra to follow his explicit instructions. He eventually took offense (he believed the chef d'orchestre had deliberately insulted him) and putting on his hat, left the Opéra without a backward glance. The failure of his *Don Carlo* in 1867 to thrill the Parisian audience did not especially endear the French to him and he made the Opéra wait five years for *Aida*.[9]

Once he assumed a responsibility, he never faltered and he worked to make *Aida's* Parisian debut a success, as it was—overwhelmingly so. In response, Verdi was honored at a banquet by the President of France, who created Verdi a Grand Officer of the Legion of Honor.

Believing that the Wagnerian style of music drama would now eclipse other opera styles, Verdi retired (except to make some attempts to write an opera on *King Lear*) and composed nothing for the next fifteen years except his *Requiem* (1874), minor works and the revision of *Simon Boccanegra*.

He could now look back on a long career and analyze its fruits. When he was forty he wrote: "My long experience has confirmed me in the beliefs I've always held concerning dramatic effect, though in my youth I didn't have the courage to put them wholly into practice. (For instance, ten years ago I wouldn't have risked composing *Rigoletto*).[10] To me our opera nowadays sins in the direction of too great monotony, so much so that I should refuse to write on such subjects as *Nabucco*, etc. They offer extremely interesting dramatic situations, but they lack variety. They have but one burden to their song; elevated, if you like, but always the same."

His great gift for lyricism was thought too facile by some, who criticized him as being tritely melodious—but when the melodies are left in context within the operas (dramatically and musically) they cannot be faulted for what they are: expressions that suit the mood and the moment, true to the characters who utter them. If he was not always well suited by the librettist at least his music rang true. Imitators, lacking his genius, and his self-discipline, slipped into banality and what a musicologist has called "fatal sentimentality."

Once he had mounted a work, Verdi was impervious to criticism. From one of his letters: "As to the newspapers, does anybody force you to read them? And as to the public, when your conscience tells you that you have written something good, never mind if it is abused (sometimes it is a good sign). The day of justice will come, and it is a great pleasure for the artist, a supreme pleasure, to be able to say: 'Imbeciles, you were wrong.'"

While he was working he tried to make sure that everything was right but in *Aida* he scored in a new way, so avant-garde that he had no idea what it would sound like and begged Bottesini, the conductor for the Cairo première, to let him know how a passage came out when it was played by orchestra. This was the music he conceived for Aida to see the Angel of Death, sung within Radames' *Morir, si pura e bella*, which is set to muted violins *legato* and other strings, harp, flute, two clarinets, bassoon and horn.

He did not try to adapt Egyptian music or to employ Egyptian instruments but colored the temple music by employing (as Kobbé informs us) certain intervals peculiar to the music of Eastern peoples: the interval consisting of three semi-tones. When the invisible priestess invokes Phtha, he used the broken chords of harps.

His musical characterization of Amneris is of such towering stature that it tends to dwarf Aida for the musician (unless this person can withhold judgment and see Aida as Verdi saw her and makes some of us see her: the woman she is and therefore in the image Verdi created her). He said that Amneris was the one he loved above all others in *Aida*, and he made her sing as he believed she must: *con agitazione, animando, con espressione*, as she pleads with Radames to save himself; vituperative as a fish-wife, not a princess, when she curses the priests for having condemned him to death.

Wagner, born the same year as Verdi, and born, like Verdi, to dominate 19th century opera, had meanwhile brought his music drama to fruition, building a theatre to house it according to his ideas. Verdi appreciated Wagner's work and while he did not apply the *leitmotiv* technique to his own work Verdi developed his own and rather comparable ideas of musical "representation." To generalize: in the Wagnerian operas the *leitmotiv* is bold (and sometimes rather blatant) and will literally guide the opera goer step by step through an opera, identifying each role and the nature of the character, as well as something he wears (a ring, a sword), or some element with which he is connected, like the Fire theme for Loge, the Curse theme for Alberich, et cetera.[11] Verdi, now, is not so authoritative, he does not identify person, place and thing or feeling with the hard and fast musical motif, and he does not try to lead the opera goer step by step through the opera (perhaps he cared less about impressing the audience with what was said and sung, as Wagner impresses it). Instead, Verdi repeats musical phrases and fragments of them, not always identical to the original phrase, and this thematic repetition (the repeated phrase used with symbolic intent) is infinitely subtler, so much so that in comparison it coarsens some Wagnerian symbolism.

If you like melodic music, you will admire Verdi; if you are of a dramatic bent, you will respond to Wagner and you will also admire Verdi. As musicians, of course, they were quite unlike and no two sentences spoken by their people sound the same, especially as Wagner wrote his libretti, and in German verse that reads with archaic pompousness in English translation. Verdi was a flexible, elastic personality, with a mind which never stopped growing and exploring. When he came out of his self-imposed retirement after *Aida* it was to create *Otello* (on Shakespeare's theme of the Moor of Venice) for La Scala, where the opera received its première in 1887. Ranked by some musicologists as a music drama, it was not "German" in form—a triumph of technique by Verdi kept it "Italian" opera in that it was dramatic but preserved the continuous melodic line.

Taking the Italians' beloved aria as his starting point, Verdi extended and explored operatic melody, from the vocal into the orchestral strands. *Otello* is notable for its choral and ensemble sections, and Verdi chose to make the music feverish in temperament except for the love-duet between the Moor and Desdemona, which he expressed in a lovely tranquility. Verdi raised Iago above Shakespeare's man, a mere man filled with evil and ambition, and turned him into the supreme Medieval idea of Evil, the Demon Himself. The character is Mephistophelian.

Verdi had the benefit of working in *Otello* and *Falstaff* with the librettist Arrigo Boito, himself a composer, whose verse particularly suited Verdi—always to the point, poetic and imaginative within *la parola scenica*. How *right* it is for a contemporary ear like yours and mine to hear the theme of jealousy in *Otello* sound thus:

*The Merry Wives of Windsor* was the Shakespearean drama Boito chose for his next libretto and this work was premièred at La Scala in 1893, when Verdi was eighty years old. It astounded the world because in the consideration of some *Falstaff* exceeded *Otello* as a masterwork. The amazement over the old man's genius was excited by the fact that he had turned here to comedy, that the "whirling" score (as Westerman describes it) of *Falstaff* was as clever as it was musically beautiful.

Here, in what for lesser men should have been the twilight of life, Verdi found new melodic ideas, in a theme he had eschewed—that of the Comic muse—from the first trial in *King for a Day*, his comic opera that held for him nothing but painful memories, of the year 1840.[12] He had lived a lifetime since and gained more of enduring worth than what he had lost—for Verdi would have been realistic enough to admit that the world would scarcely shed a tear to hear of the deaths of his wife and children a century after, but that Aida's horrifying fate (buried alive) and Rigoletto's anguish (as the murderer of his own daughter) would never be lightly taken.

How grand the old boy is in *Falstaff* (I am speaking of the composer, not the subject) and how sophisticated and polished! A clumsier hand might have made the humor heavy as unleavened dough—the genius Verdi kept it elfin, turned the old rascal Falstaff into a real charmer (as well as kept him the vain philanderer he is). Verdi had not forgotten the sweetness of sensual love, for he composed a delicate love refrain which recurs often—even while he laughs and jokes quite heartily, as in Mistress Quickly's caricature *Reverenza.*

Westerman points to the wonderful fugue of *Falstaff* as its crowning glory and calls *Falstaff* itself "a genial, understanding smile" from Verdi at the world in which he had lived so full and rich a life.

From that world, one by one, rivals and lovers were departing but Verdi stayed for eight more years, moving to a hotel in Milan after the death of his second wife (in 1897), away from Sant'Agata, the property to which he had retired to live like a country gentleman after writing *Aida.* Wagner was gone, drawing from Verdi this quick, warm response (in a letter to his friend and publisher, Ricordi): "Sad, sad, sad. Wagner is dead! When I read the news yesterday, [the letter's date is February 14, 1883] I may truly say that I was completely crushed. Let us not discuss it. It is a great personality that has disappeared. A name which leaves a mighty imprint upon the history of art."

And what about the imprint of Verdi? Wagner extolled his own genius, was a boor and one of music's great monomaniacs. Verdi expressed himself as being a realist; he never fell into the social trap which lies in wait for the artiste and which, once it snaps shut, turns the artiste into an "arty" character. Verdi, who had the capacity to invoke the most melodious music, to move a heart of stone (rather than to bludgeon the sensibilities, to shock the mind, like Wagner) was subtle as composer, down-to-earth as a man. "Please don't think that when I speak of *my extreme musical ignorance* I'm merely indulging in a little *blague.* It's the truth, pure and simple. In my home there is almost no music, I've never gone to a music library, or to a publisher, to look at a piece of music. I keep up with a few of the best operas of our day, [the letter is dated March 4, 1869] not by studying them, but only by hearing them now and then in the theatre. In all this I have a purpose that you will understand. So I repeat to you: of all past or present composers I am the least erudite. Let's understand each other—I tell you again that this is no *blague* with me: I am talking about *erudition,* not about musical *knowledge.* I should be lying if I denied that in my youth I studied long and hard. That is why my hand is strong enough to shape the sounds as I want them, and sure enough for me generally to succeed in making the effect I have in mind. And when I write something that doesn't conform to the rules, I do it because, in that case, the strict rule doesn't give me what I need, and because I don't really believe all the rules that have been taught up to now are good. The schoolbooks of counterpoint must be revised."

If you want to search out the heart of Verdi's work, look to the melody of it and know that his style in melody was one of exquisite modulations, with, as example, the operas *La Traviata*, *The Forces of Destiny*, and *The Masked Ball*, all of which have torrid not to say melodramatic plots. Look for an infinite variety, and extraordinary lucidity in the depths of his characterizations in music—and the man's will to have his own way, to make things over in a "shape" that he created, as he did with *Otello*. Here Desdemona, still as gentle and doomed as Shakespeare made her, nevertheless in Verdi's opera dominates her world, the Moor, and the devil, Iago. Know that Verdi was a realist, that, indeed, there was no *blague* about him. He was also, in a derogatory opinion, what could be called a "hack" in that (*Aida* for example) he created on commission or wrote to order for a fee, a happy capitalist who extorted the best price he could get for his work. In short, a man of the times, his times and our times.

Know, also, that Verdi was inventive and resourceful, that he had scruples and took pains but was too much the realist to blight his life with seeking perfection beyond his control—he never made anything over except the concepts which he took as his own. Unlike Handel, he did not tyrannize over singers. When he could not get a singer that pleased him in a role he had composed, he was philosophic: "So-called vocal perfection concerns me little; I like to have roles sung as I wish, but I am unable to provide the voice, the soul, that certain something which should be called the spark—it is usually described by the Italian phrase 'to have the Devil on your back.'" For Verdi, what a dear Demon his Music was, how it possessed him, and how ardently he responded to it! That he might be free of it, he wrote it down, "shaped" it into works that now belong to those of us who know them.

He lived, as they say in Latin countries of such a man, until he died; complaining for some months that his eyes and ears were failing, and his legs and arms no longer obeyed him, as though these were unruly members of his household that he would have to dismiss and engage new ones instead if they did not mend their ways. He suffered a stroke and was helpless for five days; dead on the sixth, the date being January 27, 1901, the first month of the first year of the new century.

Verdi stands on the threshhold of *verismo* opera, opera of the "realists" like the Italian Mascagni and Leoncavallo. Verdi was imaginative enough to use realism without allowing the writ or legality of the word to abuse his inspiration: "It may be a good thing to copy reality; but to invent reality is much, much better." And he was a liberal. "In the matter of musical opinions we must be broad-minded, and for my part I am very tolerant indeed. I am willing to admit the melodists, the harmonists, the bores—those who want to be boring at all costs, as is smart [he means: as is the vogue, the musical fashion] I appreciate the past, the present, and I would appreciate the future, too, if I knew anything about it and liked it."

In his correspondence, he shows a caustic impatience with "vogues" while remaining the most tolerant of men. Complaining about the penchant in his own people, the Italians, for following a vogue whether or not it was suited to their style, he wrote [to Clarina Maffei] April 20, 1878: "We are all working, without meaning to, for the downfall of our theatre. . . . To give all the reasons would take up too much time. But why, in the name of all that's holy, must we do German art if we are living in Italy? Twelve or fifteen years ago I was elected president of a concert society, I don't remember whether in Milan or elsewhere. I refused, and I asked: "Why not form a society for vocal music? That's alive in Italy—the rest is an art for Germans." Perhaps that sounded as foolish then as it does now; but a society for vocal music, which would let us hear Palestrina, the best of his contemporaries, Marcello, and such people, would have preserved for us our love of song, as it is expressed in opera. Now everything is supposed to be based on orchestration, on harmony. The alpha and omega is Beethoven's *Ninth Symphony*, marvelous in the first three movements, very badly set in the last. No one will ever approach the sublimity of the first movement, but it will be an easy task to write as badly for voices as is done in the last movement. And supported by the authority of Beethoven, they will all shout: "That's the way to do it . . ." Never mind! Let them go on as they have begun. It may even be better; but it's a "better" that undoubtedly means the end of opera. Art belongs to all nations—nobody believes that more firmly than I. But it is practiced by individuals; and since the Germans have other artistic methods than we have, their art is basically different from ours. We cannot compose like the Germans, or at least we ought not to; nor they like us. Let the Germans assimilate our artistic substance, as Haydn and Mozart did in their time; yet they are predominantly symphonic musicians. And it is perfectly proper for Rossini to have taken over certain formal elements from Mozart; he is still a melodist for all that. But if we let fashion, love of innovation, and an alleged scientific spirit tempt us to surrender the native quality of our own art, the free natural certainty of our work and perception, our bright golden light, then we are simply being stupid and senseless."

And he was perspicacious, writing [in a letter dated February 2, 1883]: "Our music differs from German music. Their symphonies can live in halls [meaning: concert halls]; their chamber music can live in the home. Our music, I say, resides principally in the theatre."

Aware of the economy or financial conditions of the Italian theatre at that time, he commented, too: "Now the theatres can no longer exist without government subsidy." For Verdi saw that the end of private patronage, such as had come from the de'Medicis and their compeers, might mean the end of theatre, however popular theatre remained with the public, the audience en masse, simply because the costs of theatre were always higher than its commercial profit or box office take. He foresaw that government subsidy of theatre arts alone would provide economic subsistence for theatre.

What he said in his music remains equally true and real for us today, and in almost every verbal statement Verdi made he might be addressing us in our time, speaking to us as makers of music and as audiences to music. We can apply almost everything he says about the Italians and opera to Americans and opera, for example . . .

But, above all, what makes Verdi modern is his spirit, for see what he undertakes to do. He will appreciate music in the future, he says, meaning our music today. He undertakes to listen to it, to think about it—but he reserves the right to know it and determine whether he likes it. He treated music with great love but with utter realism, writing: "In a word, melody, harmony, coloratura, declamation, instrumentation, local color (a word so frequently used in most cases only to hide the absence of thought): all these are only means. Make good music with these means, and I will accept everything, and every genre."

At Verdi's death, the leading conductor of the era was Toscanini at La Scala. On the day of the composer's funeral La Scala scheduled an evening performance of the opera *Nabucco*, that work which contained the chorus Italians found so thrilling: *Va pensiero, sull' ali dorate—* Speed your journey, my thoughts and my longings, under Toscanini's baton. Toscanini himself led the chorus during the funeral procession. A quarter of a million people stood in the streets of Milan, in the wintry air, to honor the cortege for the composer who had lived just one decade short of a century, leaving his mark on a century to come.[13] Verdi had so freely and clearly stated his ideas about life and music that there remained little to "interpret" about this man whose only mystery was the enigma of genius. He had been attacked for being overly fond of melody, accused of being a lyricist, as though the miraculous faculty for melodious harmonies were a degrading super-ficiality. This, at least, could be noted to vindicate Verdi: he never wrote a vulgar air, however sweet, because there was in him, as in Mozart, not a vulgar note and never a note of vulgarity.

*Aida* for example.

# Notes

1. Verdi disliked priests and *he* was not woman-ridden; his second wife was an opera diva who abandoned her professional career to devote herself to making a home for her husband.

2. *Aida's* plot was treated as being from ancient Egyptian history until recently, when the Mexican writer F. Perez de la Vega propounded that it is from Metastasio's *Nitteti*. However, it is factual that the Egyptologist Mariette Bey collaborated on the production and Verdi's contemporaries accepted the statement that Mariette Bey had suggested the story of *Aida* to the Khedive for an opera for the Cairo opera house. Detractors of Verdi ridicule the notion that Aida is near death after three days awaiting Radames in the tomb. I do not know why this appears so incredible as to destroy the artistic connotations for the opera. I know that the ancient Egyptians believed that, if they were rejected by Osiris (if they failed to pass the examination he set them out of *"The Book of the Dead"*) they were banished from "the fields of food" and were forced to return to the tombs where they had been interred upon their corporeal deaths. There they stayed, very miserably, thirsting and hungering and being attacked by crocodiles. This implies that there was a way in and out of the tomb—and it is perfectly credible that the Temple of Phtha had a labyrinth or maze, which the priests shut tight when they chose (as when they interred Radames alive). Then, why not assume that Aida knew the way into the maze and voluntarily entered it, knowing that she could not get out again? If it took her three days to reach the crypt, just in time to die with Radames, that is not only artistic premise—it is also logical. I have no compunction in treating the characters in *Aida* in a realistic or historic sense, because Verdi is especially "true" even when he invented instead of copying reality. I have found *Aida* excellent for practical use as theatre arts in education and never more so than now, in the decade when Egypt is ambitiously modernizing its nation—while other nations are troubled about the threatened loss of Egypt's antiques. Several nations have contributed $36 millions to UNESCO in an attempt to preserve the statues and temples raised by the pharaohs, in that part of Egypt now being inundated by water from the Aswan Dam.

3. Two recordings of *Aida* worth your attention are a *London* LLA–13 with Renata Tebaldi as Aida and Mario Del Monaco as Radames, Santa Cecilia Chorus and Orchestra, and an *Angel* recording, 3525, with Maria Callas as Aida and Richard Tucker the Radames, La Scala Chorus and Orchestra.

4. Compare the deaths of Radames and Aida with the demise of *Stortebecker*!

( 222 )

5. Verdi was paid 150,000 francs, which has been estimated as having been worth at least $200,000 of our currency—and he did not have to pay income tax. He only sold the rights to perform *Aida* in Cairo for this sum (which was contracted to him before he had written a note of music) and the royalties from publication of the libretto and performances of the opera elsewhere accrued to the opera makers, the larger share being Verdi's. In Rossini's day, the composer had no copyright on his work, and when an opera was produced it thereafter belonged to the opera house or impresario for two years, after which it belonged to anyone who wished to make use of it—it became public property. Rossini received the equivalent of $500 and (so that he would do the opera house credit when he conducted) a nut-brown suit with gilt buttons, as pay for his *Barber of Seville*.

6. The "double chamber" scene in *Aida* is famed in opera production and that Verdi suggested it proves how he grasped dramatic situation and visual effects for theatre. The scene always occurs in professional productions of *Aida*, thereby requiring considerable stagecraft and good physical facilities for the two-in-one effect—literally, this is the appearance of the temple, the priests and priestesses, and Amneris, in the upper portion of the stage, and the tomb, with the two lovers, in the lower part. In amateur productions of *Aida*, where there are inadequate stage facilities, it is common to show only the crypt and the lovers, and to have the temple scene "believed but unseen," with its singers singing in the background.

7. Ghislanzoni had offered:   *I love him also, do you hear*
                                  *I love him, hear and tremble!*
                                  *You are my rival, that is clear,*
                                  *It's useless to dissemble!*

8. We may be sure it was better than the Metropolitan Opera's first production, November 12, 1886, when *Aida* was sung in German, the language of its Aida (Theresa Foerster of the Vienna Court Theatre, who was the wife of the Met's first cellist, Victor Herbert) and its Ramfis (Emil Fischer, a celebrated interpreter of Wagner's Hans Sachs in *The Mastersingers of Nuremberg*). The critic from the *New York Times* was less than elated; he declared that the labors of almost all the artistes in the performance lacked refinement in feeling and expression, and urged the necessity of obtaining a different cast for Italian opera.

9. Verdi never enjoyed working with the Paris Opéra, although he composed two operas for that house: *The Sicilian Vespers* and *Don Carlo*, often referred to as his "French operas." His revised *Macbeth* (which is the version extant) is an opera he arranged (with a ballet) for the Paris audience in 1865; its original production was in Florence in 1847. *The Sicilian Vespers* and *Don Carlo* are in the genre of "grand opera," the forte of Meyerbeer, and comparing them shows how astute and quick Verdi was as a composer—he learned from the *Vespers* what it might have taken ten consecutive composers to discover and use in *Don Carlo*. Restricted in *Vespers* by the requirements of "grand opera," and embarrassed by the libretto (which insulted the French by a French massacre of Sicilians, and infuriated the Italians because of Sicilian treachery in the plot) Verdi felt this work to be plagued with bad luck. Indeed, it was one of his lesser works. During rehearsals for its première the prima donna, Cruvelli, a soprano,

disappeared—throwing all concerned with the production into panic. Francis Toye, Verdi's biographer, records that she went off on a trial honeymoon with a baron whom she later married. She returned in time to sing the role of Elena, but the opera was not an unqualified success. The French libretto was later translated into Italian and Elena's *bolero* became a well-known operatic air. You may hear it as *Merce, dilette amiche* or *Merci, jeunes amies* but in either event it will be lively. Verdi worked hard on *Don Carlo*, having mastered the "grand opera" technique, and was better pleased with the libretto, which was by his friend du Locle and François Joseph Mery from Schiller's drama of a princess unfortunate enough to be loved by the son of her husband in the time of the Spanish Inquisition. Verdi did not like the French production well enough to maintain it; he revised the opera to an Italian text by Ghislanzoni. The première production of five acts and a ballet was discarded for a shortened version which omitted the first act and the ballet, and a third version (now more often re-created than Verdi's) restored the first act but shortened the length of the opera by extracting parts of the later acts.

10. *Rigoletto* was severely criticized in its early premières because Victorian audiences thought the hunchback in the title role to be in bad taste—sensitive opera buffs were shocked to see a physically deformed opera singer, although their sensibilities were unharmed by, for instance, Shakespeare's misshapen Richard III or Dumas' hunchback of Notre Dame. But Verdi was even more daring two years after *Rigoletto*, when he chose as heroine of his *La Traviata* the real life character (from Dumas' *La Dame aux Camélias*) of a famous prostitute.

11. All appearing in Wagner's epic *Götterdämmerung*, or *The Ring of the Nibelungs*, in which the parts are *The Rhinegold*, *The Valkyrie*, *Siegfried* and *The Twilight of the Gods*, this fourth title being, literally: *Götterdämmerung*. The four music dramas were described by Wagner as being a tetralogy, a prelude and three main works, and he intended them to be performed consecutively, for the same audience. Towards this, Wagner built his theatre at Bayreuth, in Bavaria, Germany, where the "Ring" cycle was performed in 1876, to an audience including the composers Saint-Saëns, Grieg, Gounod, Tchaikovsky, and Anton Rubinstein. Wagner's operas and his principles for music drama are too complex to be related in this book. The most recent recording that I know of *The Ring* is (as *Götterdämmerung*) by the Vienna Philharmonic Orchestra conducted by Georg Solti, with two well-known contemporary Wagnerians: Birgit Nilsson as Brünnhilde and Wolfgang Windgassen as Siegfried, on a *London* recording; total listening time 4½ hours. The opera goer will find it advisable to familiarize himself thoroughly with Wagner's plots before experiencing the operas in performance. Those of *The Ring* cycle, four stories or operas in all, are extremely complicated and are based on German myth and Wagner's concept of Nietzsche's Superman.

12. We know that Verdi admired *opera buffa*, especially Rossini's *Barber of Seville* of which he wrote that it was "the finest *opera buffa* in existence." [May 2, 1898] "Like you," his letter to Camille Bellaigue continues, "I admire *William Tell*, but how many other magnificent, sublime things are in various of Rossini's other operas."

13. Many foreigners were shocked at the use of the *Nabucco* chorus, associated with a revolutionary theme, for Verdi's funeral. At the time a young Englishman doing his "grand tour" of the European capitals as part of his education recorded his own and the impressions of some others. Referring to the *Nabucco* chorus as the elegy: "The English think it should properly have been the *O terra addio* from *Aida* and the Germans, sensibly enough, suggested the old boy's own *Requiem* [which Verdi had composed for the death of his friend, the novelist Manzoni] while the French, not surprisingly, thought something particular to the occasion should have been commissioned from a French composer. But the Italians seemed to think *Nabucco* quite the thing and made good capital of it and sang *con gusto* and sped the dear old fellow on his 'journey' as though they had been kissed by Apollo and nursed from the cradle by Polyhymnia. It would never do in Piccadilly but I must tell you the Milanese do this sort of thing with style. For my part, I wish the dear old boy had done one more job but then that's because I find I can't bear to part with Verdi." Italy mourned him as a national hero. For himself, Verdi had asked in his will: "I direct that my funeral shall be very modest, at dawn or at the time of the *Ave Maria* in the evening, without singing or music." It was said, after Toscanini's death (in New York, January 16, 1957) that Toscanini had admired only one man in his life and that man was Verdi. The composer's definitive biography is by Francis Toye, *Giuseppe Verdi, His Life and Works*. His collected letters, which better than any other writing reveals the man and the musician (together with a short biography by Franz Werfel) were printed in *Verdi, the Man in his Letters*, edited by Werfel and Paul Stefen, English translation by Edward Downes and Barrows Mussey.

# ❀ S E V E N ❀

# Overture

"My reason for insisting on the importance of all lovers of art being able to form their own opinions is obvious, when we consider that our music public is obliged to take everything on trust."

EDWARD ALEXANDER MACDOWELL:
*Critical and Historical Essays, 1912*\*

Learning to like opera and ballet is rather like acquiring a taste for avocado and caviar. If you grow up in a family where exotic food is common fare you are likely to accept it as part of your normal diet. Environment has a great deal to do with developing tastes for cuisine and music. Dishes are particular to peoples and places, and nowadays we hygienically plan good eating habits for a child so that he will be healthy and well nourished as the man. Music is "national" in expression as song and dance and by particular kinds of instruments, and in its evocative responses no other art arouses the human spirit or touches the heart as readily as music.

Theatre should exert an early influence if it is to be of "cultural" benefit in society. If you are resolved to become an opera buff you must make attendance in the opera house habitual, not occasional.

As a new opera goer you are in the enviable situation of being able to prepare yourself sufficiently to know what opera is, the better to discover the joy of experiencing what opera is about . . . this you

---

\* Excerpt from this American composer's lectures at Columbia University, 1896.

find out by attending operas of all styles, and by noting and comparing the performances you attend so that you gradually form your individual critiques, your sense of discernment. Knowledge, compounded by experience, and qualified by individual response eventually creates taste.

A theatrical piece is presented with or without taste, by which is meant that it is produced in a style, to a standard, that makes a performance good or mediocre—and in professional theatre if a performance is mediocre it is, simply, bad. But the audience's taste, collectively and individually, is not styled and standardized because it is emotionally motivated—even when it attempts to be intellectually so. Get used here to the fact that you will like certain kinds of operas and dislike certain kinds, and that in opera as in everything else subjected to "taste" there is truth in the adage that one man's meat is another man's poison.

Young, inexperienced opera goers are usually without prejudices and are the most impartial about "classical" and "modern" works—by which terms the 19th century opera is defined as being different from the contemporary opera of the 20th century.

Your easiest way of determining which kind of opera you will enjoy is for you to analyze the kind of music you most admire or are most responsive to.

Note that I use the phrase "most responsive to . . ." and that I suggest you analyze your musical preference. I have nowhere in this book suggested an analysis of opera since that is not within the contents of this book. From all that I write here and including this chapter: *Overture* (which means "introduction" to opera) you should know that I conceive art to be a medium of expression, but not a medium without expression or interpretation. In the theatre, I expect art to express or interpret.

Many writers define an art solely in its medium, as the art form, and concern themselves with an analysis of that form, an exposé of examples which exactly adhere to or, variously, are divergent from, the principles of form.

Such writers express their convictions (refrain from calling these their "feelings") and make detached but authoritative statements on the art and certain physical emanations of the art. The best kind of writer of this sort is the practicing performer of the art (a dancer in dance, a singer in opera, et cetera) and/or a creative artist who commands the medium, such as an opera composer and librettist or a choreographer, et cetera.

Writing as a member of the audience, as I do, I am not concerned with the science of a medium (although I believe that I must know its essential or fundamental form, as I know the form of opera, for instance) but with the artistic expression or interpretation; in one word: the *communication*. This book is written from that point of view, and in this chapter: *Overture*, I am suggesting methods and disciplines (the chief being a resistance of "expert" authorities with dogmatic views) by which you can cultivate your own approach or point of view for opera.

As a reader of this book you are not a "precious" opera buff but a member of the theatre audience en masse—from which strata the American opera audience is drawn, and to great extent draws the means of its subsistence.

What prevails on us, you and me, to buy a ticket at the opera house's box office? It is not an intellectual intent to analyze the opera in performance, or to consider (as impresario or entrepreneur) the quality of the production and the standard of the singing. We go to the opera, as a rule, for pleasure in our leisure and therefore the primary intent is to enjoy opera, to receive a stimulus to which we respond. The opera's subject might be serious and its theme tragic; or it might be of the operetta form, light-hearted and comic. It does not matter what emotion is stirred, but that emotions *are stirred*. It is by being moved and touched, by being made to feel or experience emotions that we enjoy theatre, opera for example. Theatre arts are sensual communications or pleasures.

The audience's role in theatre is not passive because it is an actively responsive one. We, in the theatre, serve the function of the sounding-board or reactor for the stage. In order to play this role we must go into the theatre and participate in the "live" or "legitimate" theatre—as opposed to sitting at home to enjoy "canned" theatre by way of television, or going to the cinema to see a filmed version of an opera, a ballet or a play which was designed to be staged in the traditional theatre.

The process by which the audience responds allows the audience to evaluate theatre. This evaluation determines the popularity of theatrical works, since we reject, usually with apathy, what does not touch or move us, and welcome, even in repetition, what does. You, in the audience, become a part of opera tradition because you communicate with the art and respond in your personal communication to the feeling evoked by an opera in performance.

Mathematics are exact systems which we approach with logic. Art has no rules and is by nature audacious, experimental, rebellious and inconstant, wholly concerned with the selfish if occasionally selfless creative impulse. Art is not at all concerned with hard fact; art is not logical and has no morals, although artistic creators, *artistes*, develop principles as well as techniques. You must accept opera as an art form, you should know enough of its techniques to respect its mode of expression (drama through music) and to recognize its varieties as styles. But you must be prepared to tolerate the medium, to allow the opera to express in its own language—not require it, for instance, to resemble a play. You must, as it were, cultivate a way of thought, a state of mind about opera, which is art and therefore artificial, a communication not natural or ordinary in itself.

The arts have techniques and media and there are two basic means of expression in art. The artist may present, in painting, an object as it is visually observed, as it is physically seen. He will divide a picture in chiaroscuro sharply between light and dark, depicting what he sees in the light and obliterating in shadow what he does not see or choose to see in the dark. His eyesight and his point of view may differ entirely from ours and what the canvas shows is both an objective and a subjective view. When the artist paints from an entirely non-objective view then he is said to be dealing in "abstraction" but, if you think about it, all art is abstraction since art works are created by individuals, with individual points of view. If you apply this generalization to theatre arts you will be more tolerant and sympathetic towards their communicative forms of expression, and more discerning of their styles.

Opera is various in style and sometimes in its form, although this is intrinsic as drama in music. The two primary forms are operas that are, in concept, within real life (at its extensive, this is *verismo*) or impressionistic—the style in which ideas, intangibles, are more important than actions. And it is general to divide opera into the "classical" music (emergent from about Mozart's era) and "modern" music (the 20th century music after Richard Strauss). 20th century art is sometimes neo-classical and has principles and characteristics of its own. All art has ethics, which is a different thing, altogether, from morality. It is artistic ethics that we must respect.

The true opera goer goes to theatre for love of opera; some go to cultivate a knowledge of this musical art, and others to cultivate a "cultural" status as patrons of the opera. However you choose to go, do not go laboring under the false ideal that you will better yourself. To acquire such virtue, go to church or go to school.

The stage is not a rostrum or a pulpit; it should not lecture or preach—these are not theatre's functions. But theatre, very often, compels us to think and almost always makes us feel or respond because theatrical arts are presented with the object of making effect, which might be described as attempting communication.

Familiar phrases about art include the ones that describe some artistic expressions as "obscure." Obscurity in art is itself ethical because the creative artist expresses what he feels and thinks, in ways which are possible to him, and by means which he deliberately chooses. The creative artist is not at all concerned with how the spectator feels, as the audience looks and/or listens, because the creative artist is not engaged in painting or drawing for an advertising poster, nor does he make up tunes and lyrics as "commercial jingles" to sell someone's manufactured product. When the artist creates in such media he moves outside art and into the selling of artifacts, where the total effect, the absolute communication, is far more important than the "artistic" expression—sometimes, more so than the artifact on sale!

The ethics of opera are musical ones and opera is sung in the ways that have been described here in *What Opera Is* . . . But when composers work, when they create, they are primarily concerned with expressing themselves; no composer worth the title ever gives a fig for whether or not the audience will approve of his work, or "like" his characterizations, or "understand" what the opera is about. The composer takes the rather truculent attitude, after he has created his brainchild, that there it is—it might not be as perfect as he imagined it, it may need tinkering with here and there, but it's the best that he could do and, for the moment, *he* must make the best of it. He sends his naked child out into the world, to be buffeted by chilly winds of adverse criticism, or to be warmly welcomed, extravagantly praised and raised to such prestige or held in such affection that the "child" will be immortal—it will never die or go out of fashion but will outlive the composer and all the audiences within his own lifetime and after. No composer, nor singer and musician, hopes for more than to be known, and to be remembered. And an opera is known only if it is produced; remembered by succeeding singers and audiences only if it is maintained in repertory.

An opera's continual success, the status it acquires as being among the "best loved" in repertory, accrues to it only in part from its own worth. In part, an opera survives from its rapprochement with audiences. This is never so true as in our kind of theatre, the commercial, non-subsidized opera. It is unjust and really quite cruel that works of art are neglected to the extent of being forgotten, as is the case with the works of Hector Berlioz, an early 19th century French composer. He, too, wrote an opera on Goethe's Faust but it is Gounod's that is famous. Berlioz's masterwork *Les Troyens* (The Trojans) is a monumental opera but is almost never staged because of its particular theatrical requirements—nevertheless, Wagner's works, which also require rather special stage properties, are preserved with better than fair consistency.

It seems that many major composers lack the mysterious ingredient in their works which opera requires to charm the audience. When that charm is present the opera survives epochs and styles and becomes one of the few "best known, best loved" works in the tradition. Puccini's *Tosca* is one such, in spite of being sneered at by many opera buffs as being merely a musical melodrama instead of a work of art. The four all-time, all-round favorites are Verdi's *Aida* and *La Traviata*; Puccini's *La Bohème*; and Bizet's *Carmen*. The roles in these operas are the bread and butter of singers.

These four operas have at least two common denominators: all the plots are focused on love, unhappy, even tragic love; the pivot of each plot is a woman, not a man. And except perhaps for the Ethiopian slave, Aida, these girls are not the sort a nice young man dares take home to tea with mama because they are exceptionally careless about their morals. Mimi is pensive and gentle, where Carmen is brittle and haughty, but they pass, with equal facility, from one lover to another and with little happiness at the end. We may assume Aida to be pure although loving (Radames makes her seem more beloved than in love) but there is no doubt about Violetta, "la traviata" or "the frail one," whose sobriquet does not refer to her delicate health (she, like Mimi, is a consumptive) but to her character and reputation. Violetta, as the Victorians had it, is "one gone astray" or, as described by an opera buff at her London première in 1856: "a Fallen Woman; in fact: A Whore."

I am secretly amused when I hear someone who is not an opera buff, and intends never to become one if he can help it, declare that opera is "dull" because it is "artistic" and "high-minded." Opera is all sorts of things in the treatise of what *opera is about* . . . and is solely responsible, as ethics in art, in being a musical art. As I have said before (it is worth saying again) opera is not only a musical art but is also a theatrical art. You will find, I think, that the opera makers who communicated most eloquently with audiences were composers who were also men of the theatre. In this category, none exceeds the matchless combination of musical genius and dramatic perception of Mozart and Verdi.

Of these two, Verdi is more popular and this is not because he exceeds as a composer the genius of the 18th century Mozart, but because Verdi worked in an age of richer orchestration, bigger, more versatile orchestras, and composed for instruments whose sounds are familiar to our 20th century ears. If you begin your opera education with 19th century composers, especially with Verdi and Wagner (the latter was partial to mammoth orchestras) you will risk being disappointed by Mozartian opera, which sounds "tinkly" to some theatre goers who are used to larger, richer orchestrations. But if you begin your opera going with Mozart (preferably, begin with Monteverdi!) then you will accustom your ear to the infinite subtleties and gradations of opera orchestrations—and you will, I hope, know and love Mozart for what he is: as radiant a creator as Gluck, as "pure" a maker of music, but with the incomparable gift of *humanizing* music, of making operatic persons such realities that never again, after Mozart, would audiences countenance shadows instead of flesh and blood in opera.

Thus, when composers like Debussy willfully reneged from the gross materialization of music drama (and Debussy was seriously aggravated by Wagner's penchant for turning symbolism into corporeal images) opera of the "impressionistic" kind was thought of as "inhuman" even when, as in *Pelléas and Mélisande,* it was, in style, dubbed "romantic."

Faced with the startling paradox of an "impressionistic" and at the same time "romantic" opera you may quail at the thought of "understanding" opera. Be of good heart and keen mind and you shall gradually, and happily, fathom these operatic mysteries.

As an opera goer, you do not need to worry over the "style" of an opera while it is in performance—and even if you are approaching opera more studiously than for entertainment I think you are well advised to accept the opera in performance as a theatre piece, and at a later or earlier time (as preparation or recapitulation) study it for form and style.

A good idea is to keep your own diary, a theatrical journal in which you record the operas you attend and note your responses. If you do this frankly and self-analytically, you will, over the years, accumulate the most personal and valuable idea of what opera means to you. Note the opera company, the principals in the cast, and the type of production (as in Shakespeare, opera producers change décor from time to time, and while it is not a regular practice it is not a *verboten* one to transfer plot and personnel into a new time and scene). If you keep your opera journal with a collection of "opera books" (the glossy souvenir books put out for a season of opera) and performance programs you will compile a valuable collection, something you will be proud to maintain and to pass on to your heirs or to a library as a private collection of opera notes and memorabilia. Such private collections are the treasure trove of historians, for they enable a contemporary writer to perceive how an opera or an opera artiste seemed to *you,* in *your* day—something that no writer, however astute, can extract from either reason or imagination. (For instance, it was interesting for me to know how one man, present on the scene, felt and wrote about witnessing Verdi's funeral, before I was born.)

These intimacies with composers make them very real and human to us, emphasizing what for me is a cardinal aspect of opera: that it is made by human beings for human beings, and is, thereby, a form of human expression or communication as well as "Art."

We cannot deny our own humanity in theatre, and the geniuses of theatre capitalize on this trait—Verdi for example. And in the opera house you never need to be informed of the mood of the opera. It will be tragic or comic or something of both and, if you are not suffocated or bound by authoritative "rules" for opera going, you will respond accordingly. You will not, for instance, hesitate to laugh if an opera is antic in fun, because it is a work of art by a great composer, Mozart for example.

If you are a parent or a teacher, try attending Mozart's operas with a bright child (if you are not a parent or a teacher, then borrow a child from somebody who will lend you one). Quite young children of intelligence and warm emotional responses understand Mozart perfectly—and adore him. But Mozart is too often considered, by opera goers, to be merely a "great composer" and his hallowed estate in music obscures the very element of his work in opera.

As a child, I knew his operas through small German and Italian troupes who performed them faithfully if not famously—they were not decorated (and top-heavy in artistic balance) with famous stars. But in my adolescence, when I attended performances of Mozartian opera in London, I was astonished to find myself in audiences that sat without a flicker of animation, except to politely pat hands together at curtain fall. In the United States, I observed the same peculiar attitude towards Mozart and when, as often happened, I burst out laughing at a familiar Mozartian joke, persons close to me turned their attention on the fool among them instead of on the professional fools on stage.

I saw that English-speaking audiences did not laugh at Mozart because Mozart was a "great composer" and the idea was that "great" meant "serious." Mozart was, indubitably, a great composer (some believe him to be the greatest who ever lived) but he was also a great comedian and all his extant operas, every one of his masterworks, is in the comic medium. He was the inspired creator of modern comic opera, a style far subtler and more aesthetic than the older one derived from commedia dell'arte and of the *buffo* genre. Mozart is the true father of German opera, recognized by Wagner as the towering genius whose precedents, in two "German" operas, formed the basis for the German national opera tradition.

Genius is thought to be a melancholy state (it sets the creative genius apart from his fellows) but Mozart, despite the fact that his real life condition was miserable, was inveterately comic, even when he was sending a man to Hell, as in *Don Giovanni*. The 18th century Italians perceived this about Mozart and described him as a comedian who was "sinfully fond of music." He loved music so passionately that he composed some of the finest ever written.

In the opera house, meet the opera in performance on its terms and as the composer's creation. While opera is of different styles these styles were not scientifically formed on theories propounded by logicians but were spontaneously created by composers. It is true that a rebellion against Wagnerian principles motivated both Bizet's *Carmen* and Debussy's *Pelléas and Mélisande* but we may be certain that even if Wagner had not run counter to the ideas of Bizet and Debussy these two creative persons should have found their own modes for expressing in opera language. Wagner happens to handily provide a basis of comparison by which to estimate Bizet and Debussy—in observing Wagnerian music drama and comparing it to the realism of *Carmen* and the impressionism of *Pelléas and Mélisande* we note how these operas differ, what they are as well as what they are about.

This does not require a herculean intellectual effort but a normally alert one, such as an intelligent theatre goer makes as a matter of course. Consider that Wagner's operas all have a romantic theme of some kind and that Carmen and Mélisande are romantically involved—Carmen with a pair of rivals for her affections, which she is in the habit of strewing as she fancies between the soldiers camped in the square, the bandits who hang out on the environs of the town, and a popular hero, a bullfighter, or as Bizet called him, a "toreador." Mélisande, naïve but (mystically) a *femme fatale,* has the bad luck to attract as passionate admirers two men, brothers. This is as unfortunate a contretemps as Wagner's Irish Isolde precipitates, by inspiring fervor in the breast of Tristan, who has come to collect her as the bride of his king and uncle, Mark of Cornwall.

Attacking what are intrinsically three illicit and tragic love affairs, three composers handled the material in altogether separate ways—

Debussy in a form that might be called ethereal (he was concerned more with the spirit than the flesh, the Word and not the act of love), while Bizet was intent on creating the flesh or reality—Carmen is, veritably, the great strumpet of opera, a woman of fire who inflamed men while her own vanity coursed like ice water in her veins. Wagner propounded, somewhat ponderously for Debussy's taste, the intangible tangibly—behind all his creatures stand symbolic spectres or "morals," which when related to the man's own affairs, in his life story as well as his career, are construed as Wagner's "redemption" theories. He was generally bent on idealizing virtues like Continence, Sacrifice, Unselfishness, Heroism, et cetera, and some uncharitable detractors (people either adore or detest Wagner; he is not a composer who inspires reasonableness in opera buffs) maintain that it was his sore personal need of virtues that persuaded Wagner to extol them in opera.

In the structure of these three widely divergent styles of opera you will also note that while Wagner's opera is, on the whole, large-scale (*Tristan and Isolde* has a cast of eight singing or solo parts) Bizet's opera really has one principal character: Carmen. Everyone and everything is subsidiary or emanates from her. Indeed, when a perfect *Carmen* is sung the diva dominates the entire opera and you realize that the persons you are seeing and hearing in and around Seville would simply not exist but for Carmen.

Debussy's (and Maeterlinck's) concepts in *Pelléas and Mélisande* are not in the earthy, sensual tones of Bizet's *Carmen*, nor, again, in the ecstatic idea (sensuality overlaid with a patina of suffering) explored by Wagner for *Tristan and Isolde*. For these reasons, *Carmen* can be experienced only on its own (and unrivalled) level, as reality in passionate hues; *Tristan and Isolde* on at least two levels, as the reality of its human lovers or as symbolical idealization; and *Pelléas and Mélisande* may be experienced on several levels, depending on your point of view, your affinity for the dramatic implications—and, also, on the production itself.

Some operas are wholly the composers'—Wagner required every word of the verse and stage direction to be followed, as well as every note of the score played. Other operas are "producers' works," easily re-arranged in form (as is done, regularly, to Gounod's *Faust*) or

"interpreted" by shades of meaning and, sometimes, substantially altered implications—as in a production of *Pelléas and Mélisande* when
she became a mysterious homeless boy found in the forest by Golaud,
instead of (as Maeterlinck portrayed her) a mysterious homeless girl.
In that production, retaining the music by Debussy, the producer
achieved a tour de force, forcing the audience to interpret as it would,
*honi soit qui mal y pense.* Some offendedly or sentimentally took this
as a homosexual diversion; others accepted the "boy" Mélisande as a
corporeal form of Truth and Innocence, a kind of symbolic Element
which brother Golaud found and wanted to keep, and that brother
Pelléas sought as purely as the Grail.

With these and many, many other plots in opera, some frank and
free and ringing with noble words, others shadowed with double-
entendre and lighted by "human" passions, opera repertory defies the
"precious" authorities who contend that the audience must treat opera
as "Art" and not as entertainment. Very often, one reads a book or
hears a lecture from an opera authority who shames our common tastes
and spontaneous responses to opera. Even Kobbé, sound chap that he
is in his *Complete Opera Book,* occasionally adopts a schoolmasterish
tone, as when he comments that some persons regard *Tristan and
Isolde* "merely as a form of amusement" rather than as "the greatest
setting of a love-story for the lyric stage." If your taste is for love-stories
then opera is your dish—a dish served in great variety, with love as it
is experienced in several parts of the world, from the age of myth,
through ancient history, and into our times. These operas present
the composers' individual conceptions of love, by way of the characters
employed in the opera roles, and the situations in which they are
involved, as the opera's plot or drama. I believe that no "expert" or
authority has the right to infringe on your taste, and your point of
view as the opera goer. You are, in the opera house, Schopenhauer's
sailor at sea, bound to the length of your line—to your knowledge and
experience, and to your nature or turn of thought and attitude; your
manners and mores. You will know what the composer knew and was
able to relate—and what your own faculties are able to fathom.

Your state of mind, and the extent of your preparedness, will
determine the degree of your enjoyment in the opera house. Remember
that you share a dream experienced by the opera makers (the librettist

and composer) and interpreted by the performers (the singers and instrumentalists). Dreams can have an intensity in emotion and a vividness of scene greater than actions and places in real life. Theatre sometimes achieves the dimensions of a dream, dependent on the communicative power of the theatre piece and the ability of the players to reach the audience.

Never try to like an opera because you have been informed that it is admirable. Be prepared to pick and choose, to cultivate your taste. It is natural for you to dislike some things that others adore. You cannot expect to admire every book you read and picture you see, no matter how worthy these objects may be of aesthetic appreciation as works of art.

If you leave yourself free to enjoy theatre, it is more than likely that in the pleasure of theatre you will find that there is more than enjoyment alone. Now that you know how to cultivate a state of mind about opera let us find out what kinds of opera you are most likely to enjoy.

Thoughtfully choose your first season's repertory of opera because this, to great extent, will determine your ease in the opera house and your future feelings about opera. Then, as you become a seasoned opera goer, experiment. Choose operas with subjects that you believe will not appeal to you, with music of idioms that are unfamiliar. Judicious experimentation will extend your knowledge and widen your scope of experience; it is very likely to develop your tastes in opera.

You already know some famous airs from operas even if you have never known an opera itself. The arts, whether we note this or not, are within our lives; not mere frills of "culture" on society. This is one indestructible verity about art.

Poets and playwrights consistently impress their images on the language, in metaphor and simile, adage and proverb. We make common usage of Aesop and of Shakespeare, as well as of the Bible and an old poet like John Byrom, who from twitting Handel and Buononcini gave to us the inimitable if nonsensical term of equating Tweedledum with Tweedledee: sameness in form or style.

Music has a similar influence and opera, being a drama in music, makes vivid impression. All Western peoples have a tradition in opera art and as a baby you may have had this lullaby sung to you:

It is not, as many new opera goers surmise, a simple hymn or pious nursery rhyme but the theme of the overture and three scenes from an opera called *Hansel and Gretel* by the composer Engelbert Humperdinck (1854-1921). This is a famous opera based on a fairy tale, and Humperdinck also composed another "fairy tale" opera: *Königskinder* or *The Royal Children*.

The particular forte of making fairy tales into operas is a German genius and was exceedingly popular in the *Singspiel* form, of which Carl Maria von Weber's works are archtypes. Weber, trained in theatre music, and a brilliant conductor, founded the Dresden opera and helped establish "German opera" in his country to the eclipse of the "Italian." The German romanticism in opera began just after the French Revolution, as though Europeans wished to turn brusquely away from "realism" and the Reign of Terror to unrealistic, airy themes. The subjects of the new operas and ballets were ethereal in form, supernatural by nature, whence come the faërie creatures of sagas and legends, and the mysterious Oriental personalities of that theatrical epoch.

E. T. A. Hoffmann (1776-1822) expressed his thesis in 1813 within an essay, *Poet and composer,* saying: "I believe romantic opera is the only genuine opera, for music belongs in the realm of romanticism alone." All who admire romantic opera and ballet support Hoffmann's ideal; those alien to it side with the composers and choreographers, predominant in the 20th century, who take another view of music altogether. Hoffmann composed *Singspiel,* musical dramas and operas, was the conductor for the opera house at Bamberg 1808-1811, and wrote the first "Romantic" opera: *Undine* (1816), based on a libretto by the poet Friedrich de la Motte-Fouqué, who derived it from his own famous short story about a nixie or water nymph.

You could take up the "Romantic" opera at this point and trace it through examples into its rise and decline in popularity—noting that Wagner's *The Flying Dutchman* is in the supernatural category, as are several other famed works.

Wagner's music is very familiar to us, even when we do not know his operas. Brides who pace the church aisle to the Wedding March from *Lohengrin* are following the steps of Elsa of Brabant, the lady who fell in love with a mysterious knight who arrived in a boat drawn by a swan. *Lohengrin* (1850) is a romantic opera in the style of a mystery drama. In Wagner's work, it represents the point at which he achieved a consistent musical line—an achievement begun in *The Flying Dutchman* (1843) and in *Tannhäuser* (1845).

Westerman calls *Lohengrin* Wagner's transitional point from the romantic opera instituted before Wagner, into Wagner's own realized form as music drama. It occurred at a transitional emotional point for the composer, who was involved in revolutionary politics in Saxony and fled to Switzerland in 1849, traveling with forged passport and under an assumed name. During his exile (when he lived in Zurich), Wagner began composing *The Ring* (November 1853), strongly influenced by the philosophy of Schopenhauer—and passionately but miserably in love with a woman who was the wife of Wesendonck, his friend and patron in Zurich.

Wagner is considered to have composed *The Valkyrie* (in which fire consumes love, metaphorically) as evocation of his consuming passion for Mathilde Wesendonck; to have imagined the ecstasy of fulfilled love with her in *Tristan and Isolde*; and to have renounced his love for the lady (figuratively, as Hans Sachs) in *The Master-singers of Nuremberg*. Wagner was one composer who wrote music in heart's blood.

Wagner is inescapable in our society and for the opera goer with the patience and inclination to unravel his complicated plots (almost all of which have to be traced into classical or legendary literary origins) his operas are a wonderful treasure of drama and music. He has provided what may be an inexhaustible repertory for band concerts and he is the composer beloved by the brass section of orchestras. In one of his softer moods he composed "The Evening Star" for *Tann-häuser*, which became a famed concert song. Its singable quality persuaded a dance band conductor to rearrange it as a "pop" tune, in which style it flourished briefly during the era of "swing" music.

Perhaps the best known opera air in the United States is the overture from Rossini's *William Tell* (1829), grand opera in the French opera style. It is a brisk march, with a sparkling rhythmic quality, and it was acquired as the "theme song" or signature tune of a popular radio and television melodrama: The Lone Ranger.

One of the most commonly known arias is from Rossini's *The Barber of Seville*, when that general factotum (who has no mean opinion of his indispensable self) sings, *allegro vivace*, Act I, Scene I:

Room for the city's factotum, room!

Equally familiar is the famed air by the Duke of Mantua, the rake in *Rigoletto*, who is not lacking in nerve or humor as he reproaches women for being fickle; *Act III*:

Woman so changeable, swayed like a feather

The first time you experience the double bill of "Cav and Pag," you are sure to recognize the overture (church bells ringing on Easter morning) and the beautiful Intermezzo from *Cavalleria Rusticana*; as well as Canio's bitter irony in *Pagliacci*:

On with the motley, and the paint and the powder

continuing into the heart-rending anguish of *Ridi, Pagliacco*—Laugh then, Pagliacco, with which the clown mocks his rage and anguish over his wife's infidelity.

Almost all the music from Bizet's *Carmen,* and especially the Toreador Song and the Habañera, are familiar; the overture and the prelude from *Act III,* the latter an occasion for flute, clarinet, English horn and bassoon, are frequently played.

If, like most new opera goers, your first inclinations are towards dramatic and melodic works, then you will find numerous examples to enjoy in the permanent active repertory for international opera. The three and a half centuries old opera tradition is represented by comparatively few composers in this repertory; Mozart, Rossini,

Gounod, Bizet, Wagner, Verdi, Puccini and Richard Strauss being the chief. The list of "best known, best loved" (one description qualifying the other) includes representative operas by these composers, for example: Mozart's two "German" and three "Italian" works; Rossini's superb *opera buffa: The Barber of Seville;* Gounod's *Faust* and Bizet's *Carmen;* a great deal of Wagnerian opera and Verdi's and Puccini's; some works by Strauss, most especially his *Der Rosenkavalier.*

Eight composers might seem very few to represent opera styles but these eight among themselves will offer you examples of the national opera (Italian, French and German), opera of traditionally serious theme and *opera buffa,* and styles ranging from the most classical romanticism into *verismo* opera. If you add Debussy and his opera *Pelléas and Mélisande* to the popular repertory complied on works by Mozart, Rossini, Gounod, Bizet, Wagner, Verdi, Puccini and Strauss then you will compile a repertory in almost perfect ellipse— because Debussy is the last independent romanticist, and *Pelléas and Mélisande* represents the close of the great French romantic opera tradition.

These traditions, seen as "national" opera traditions and also as operatic eras, are interlinked and often overlap each other but some idea of them may be seized from scanning the life-spans of the composers and setting them within their representative epochs.

In *The Beginning* I have briefly outlined the origins of opera. To recapitulate: it commenced within the Camerata and for about a decade was almost exclusively a Florentine art. Secondly, it was a Venetian one, with a form and style that was arbitrary for about half a century. Then followed the Neapolitan tradition, in which the innovations and developments of Scarlatti became universal for opera. From here, as opera assumed national traditions, we can trace its evolutionary styles through the works of famed composers.

FRENCH OPERA—DEVELOPMENT OF OPERA-BALLET

| | |
|---|---|
| Robert Cambert—c. 1628–1677 | Pomone (1671) |
| Jean Baptiste Lully—1632–1687 | Alceste (1674) et cetera |
| *tragédie lyrique* | |
| André Campra—1660–1744 | Fêtes Vénitiennes (1710) |
| Jean-Philippe Rameau—1683–1764 | Les Indes Galantes (1735) |
| *tragédie lyrique* | Castor et Pollux (1737) |
| | Zoroastre (1749) |

GERMAN SINGSPIEL—EARLY FORM
    Reinhard Keiser—1674–1739 and his compeers

ENGLISH OPERA
    Henry Purcell—c. 1659–1695     Dido and Aeneas (1689)
       (native genius)
    George Frederick Handel—1685–1759  Alcina (1735), et cetera
      *opera seria*, Italian style
    John Gay, poet—1685–1732
    Johann Christian Pepusch—      The Beggar's Opera (1728)
      1667–1752             satire on *opera seria*

COMIC OPERA—DERIVED FROM ITALIAN *comedia dell'arte*

Italian *opera buffa*
  Giovanni Battista Pergolesi—1710–1736  La Serva Padrona (1733)
  Niccolo Piccinni—1728–1800       La Buona Figliuola (1760)
  Giovanni Paisiello—1740–1816      The Barber of Seville (1782)

French *opéra comique*
  Jean-Jacques Rousseau—1712–1778    The Village Soothsayer (1752)
  Egidio Romoaldo Duni—1709–1775; André Modeste Grétry—
                         1741–1813 & their works

German *Singspiel*
  Johann Georg Standfuss— ?–1756     The Devil Is Loose (1752)
  Joseph Haydn—1732–1809        The World on the Moon
                           (1777)

Modern Opera—evolution and reform
  Christoph Willibald Gluck—1714–1787  *opera seria* works
  Wolfgang Amadeus Mozart—1756–1791  his works, in total

    This is not a list of opera composers. It is the barest glimpse into the early contributions to opera, up to Gluck and Mozart. Before them and beyond them lie the whole history of opera.

    You might see the composers as belonging to a gigantic family tree with the most convoluted kind of growth, branching into several directions, growing back towards the root or entwining with a trunk or limb. If you are able to see opera in this "banyan" concept you will see that music and drama are the roots and the continuing source, but that the fruits, the operas themselves, are of the richest variety in shape or form, and style.

*The Flying Dutchman*:
George London as
the Dutchman,
onie Rysanek as Senta,
iorgio Tozzi as Daland
Belan Amperan as Mary

18. Franco Corelli in the title role of *Andrea Chenier,* with Eileen Farrell as Maddalena

19. *Cosi Fan Tutte*, with, l. to r., Rosalind Elias, Richard Tucker, Roberta Peters, Donald Gramm, Theodore Uppman and Leontyne Price

20. *Don Giovanni:* Teresa Stitch-Randall as Donna Elvira, Leopold Simeneau as Don Ottavio, Cesare Siepi as the Don, Lucine Amara as Donna Anna

21. *The Magic Flute:* The Queen of the Night (Anna Moffo) is confronted by Monostatos (Nicolai Gedda) while Tamino (Andrea Velis) is held captive

22. The Mad Scene from *Lucia di Lammermoor,* with Anna Moffo as Lucia

23. *The Barber of Seville: Rosina* (Roberta Peters) weds Count Almaviva (Cesare Valetti); at left, Cesare Siepi as Dr. Bartolo and Robert Merrill as Figaro

24. *Der Rosenkavalier:* Octavian brings the silver rose to Sophie while the Marschallin watches

25. A scene from *Martha* showing, l. to r., Giorgio Tozzi, Richard Tucker, Victoria de los Angeles, Rosalind Elias and Lorenzo Alvary

26. Faust (Nicolai Gedda) and Marguerite (Gabriella Tucci) with Mephistopheles (Cesare Siepi) and Martha (Gladys Kriese)

27. Leontyne Price as Aida and Mario Sereni as Amonasro

28. The Triumphal Scene in *Aida*, with Aida, Amonasro, Radames, Pharaoh, Amneris and Ramfis in the foreground

29. La Bohème: the Cafe Momus, with Andrea Velis as Alcindoro, Heidi Krall as Musetta, Calvin Marsh as Marcello, Mirella Freni as Mimi and Gianni Raimondi as Rodolfo

30. The attic: the death of Mimi

31. A scene from *Carmen* with Joy Davidson in the title role

32. *La Cenerentola*: Cinderella (Sylvia Frederick, Don Magnifico (Arnold Vokelaitis) and the Sisters (Mary Beth Peil and Ellen Berse)

By mid-20th century an estimated 42,000 operas had been produced.

Of this number, less than one hundred are maintained in the international opera repertory.

National opera traditions have individual repertories, largely determined by opera production facilities and also by the availability of opera artistes (and the economy or financial status) in opera houses. But of the approximately one hundred internationally known operas only about fifty may be classed as "best known" and these are the operas that may also be described as "best loved."

An opera that is produced regularly, about twenty times in a decade, may be said to be maintained in active repertory by an opera house. One opera will have an almost continuous production record; another opera may disappear from the repertory for ten years at a time, to reappear in the eleventh, thereafter to be maintained in active repertory. There are differences between "permanent" and "active" repertory but the permanent productions are, it may be said, always active or ready to be reactivated or mounted as seasonal repertory. A good idea of how a repertory is maintained is to scan an opera house's record over a period of several decades.

In this list compiled from the Metropolitan Opera's repertory are operas mentioned in other portions of this book, by composers described in chapters: *The Beginning* and *Opera After Gluck*, which see. Most popular repertory at the Metropolitan 1883-1960:

| *Opera titles in alphabetical order* | *Number of Performances* |
| --- | --- |
| Aida (1871) | 441 |
| The Barber of Seville (1816) | 178 |
| La Bohème (1896) | 387 |
| Madama Butterfly (1904) | 278 |
| Carmen (1875) | 372 |
| Cavalleria Rusticana (1890) | 284 |
| Faust (1859) | 340 |
| Lohengrin (1850) | 327 |
| Lucia di Lammermoor (1835) | 202 |
| The Mastersingers of Nuremberg (1868) | 220 |
| I Pagliacci (1892) | 310 |
| Parsifal (1882) | 162 |

| Opera titles in alphabetical order | Number of Performances |
|---|---|
| Rigoletto (1851) | 275 |
| Siegfried (1876) | 164 |
| Tannhäuser (1845) | 250 |
| Tosca (1900) | 285 |
| La Traviata (1853) | 304 |
| Tristan and Isolde (1865) | 289 |
| Il Trovatore (1853) | 209 |
| The Valkyrie (1870) | 282 |

Every one of the operas named above received more than one hundred sixty productions in the ninety-seven year period listed.

The dates are the years of the operas' premières or first performances as theatre works.

In 1903 the Metropolitan elected "the greatest opera composers" (in an inscription over the proscenium) as Gounod, Verdi, Wagner, Mozart, Gluck and Beethoven. Gluck's *Orfeo* was very popular at the Metropolitan during the period 1908-1915, when it was performed oftener than *Carmen, Don Giovanni, The Marriage of Figaro* and *Rigoletto,* these four being among the most popular operas. Beethoven's *Fidelio* is the only opera he composed, and it has never enjoyed universal popularity. The Metropolitan accolade to opera composers omitted Rossini and Puccini and Bizet. Nevertheless, when we scan the Metropolitan Opera's records of performances in its first century of existence Wagner is represented with seven operas, Verdi with four, Puccini with three, and (one opera to each) Rossini, Donizetti, Mascagni, Leoncavallo, Gounod and Bizet alone with Wagner, Verdi and Puccini rank as composers of the twenty most often performed operas.

The acid test of an opera's popularity is its success at the box office because few big opera companies can afford to invest in controversial works over several seasons—the public simply will not "buy" or attend theatre that it does not want to patronize. The public's taste changes, and sometimes radically, and often through the insistence of an expert opera company manager. *Pelléas and Mélisande* was not performed at the Metropolitan until 1925 but in the period 1925-1960 was sung 52 times, exactly the same number of performances given Wagner's most popular opera: *The Flying Dutchman,* which has been in the repertory since 1889.

The record appears like this:

*The Flying Dutchman,* premièred at the Metropolitan November 27, 1889, was performed 19 times in the period 1883-1908; not at all, 1908-1915; 9 times 1915-1935; 8 times 1935-1950; 16 times 1950-1960. *Pelléas and Mélisande,* premièred at the Metropolitan March 21, 1925, was preformed 29 times in the period 1915-1935; 13 times 1935-1950; 10 times 1950-1960.

The period 1908-1915 when *The Flying Dutchman* did not appear in the repertory coincides with Toscanini's era as conductor at the Metropolitan.

The Metropolitan, because of its scope and international prestige represents the chief American opera tradition, as the Covent Garden opera represents the English one. There are, however, several other very important opera companies in the United States, one being the opera troupe at New York City Center theatre. Opera festivals in annual seasons present whole series by a composer (for example, a Mozart Festival), there are numerous "regional" opera groups, and some troupes specialize in staging opera for young audiences which are especially good for new opera goers of all ages, since they are sung in English translations and include a narrator on occasion.

As an opera goer you are not bound to company "policies" and you should, if I have succeeded in reaching you in the foregoing pages of this book, be prepared to rid yourself of prejudices. Instead of joining the aesthetic quarrels of the more precious buffs you are better advised to make your choice of a favorite opera repertory.

The 20th century aesthetic argument is over the "old" and "new" forms of music, tonality versus atonality. Opera arguments often generate around the "conservative" or traditional form and the "controversial" or avant-garde ones. There are still perennial "national" quarrels in opera, as the German contention that Beethoven materially influenced opera because Wagner succeeded Beethoven, and did [materially influence opera]—but Beethoven composed only a single operatic work. The Germans also claim that Gluck and Mozart are "German" composers, while international opera buffs know that Gluck composed in the Italian and French styles, and the *Singspiel* operas which are the "German" expression of Mozart are fewer in number than Mozart's "Italian" operas.

The only limitation on your repertory (the operas you choose to collect as your favorites) is in your proximity to an opera company or opera companies. If you are a theatre goer to whom opera going is a new experience then you probably live outside the largest metropolitan areas where opera going is habitual. In that event, you will probably have to depend on a big touring company or a "regional" troupe to give you opportunities for experiencing opera in theatre.

As a rule, you will find the larger, more opulent companies' repertory to be predominantly 19th century works, while the smaller companies are more apt to specialize in the lesser known operas (in revivals) or in very new and possibly avant-garde styles. Composers are continually adding to the repertory of some 42,000 works recorded and it may be your privilege to know operas in premières, as new and revelatory to audiences today as the Camerata's *dramma per musica* was new in 1600.

All you need to take with you into the opera house is the knowledge that opera is drama in music. This is a point that many writers fail to make for readers. Musicologists tend to regard opera solely as a musical art; drama critics tend to apply the essential standards of dramatic theatre to opera; and writers of both these categories appear to treat opera as the step-sister (a bastard sibling, at best) of Music and of Drama. The chief reason I attempted a book like this one for the new opera goer was to state the fact of Opera as an art, *per se*. It is a qualified art form and *its character is drama in music*.

Never lose sight of the fact that opera, from its inception under the Camerata, was made to be performed; that its form of drama in music is intended to present the word and meaning of verse (with intonation, mood, movement, gesture, costume and scenic design) in a musical estate. An opera is shaped from sound, vocal and instrumental, and opera is a musical art but different from the art of the symphony, which is an orchestral or purely instrumental one.

Not every composer was an opera composer, nor did great composers always succeed in becoming major influences in opera. The great opera composers, Mozart and Verdi and Wagner, are so not only because of being musicians but because of their gifts for composing drama in music. The Camerata's description of opera has never been better expressed. *Dramma per musica* is not music only but drama through music.

This is the first requirement opera makes of the audience: the knowledge and the recognition of what opera is, and it is sufficient to itself. It is not a disreputable relation of music, as some "precious" persons maintain—from the prudish notion that since opera is so pleasurable for the audience, through visual "effects" and its "theatrical" nature, it is reasoned that opera is not as great as music which is approached with an intellectual appreciation rather than an emotional one.

The attitude or approach may be intellectual and emotional but it is the creative genius which makes an art form truly great. Do not accept a ruling on art which arbitrarily divides the heart and head, the "feeling" and the "mind" of self. Approach opera, if you choose or if you wish to make a "study" of it, as scientifically as you approach mathematics. There are considerable similarities between music and mathematics, but the *difference* is the most considerable truth about these—music, unlike mathematics, will move the heart and exalt the spirit.

As to what opera is about, this you will discover through experiencing opera in performance, in its theatrical state. Three and a half centuries of opera tradition lie before you, from which you can choose, as many opera goers do, your favorite repertory. Singers have to learn roles in order to compile repertories; we in the audience collect our favorite repertories simply by knowing and loving certain operas best of all.

In the next chapter of this book I list some operas as examples. They represent forms that are Italian, German and French, and styles that are categorized as romantic, impressionistic and *verismo*, in themes tragic or comic. They have only one thing in common, beyond their character of being drama in music—all are in the Mozartian opera ideal and this ideal is best described in Mozart's own words: "music . . . must never offend the ear; it must please the hearer; in other words, it must never cease to be music." It seems on the evidence of the international repertory of best-known, best-loved works that Mozart's concept for music is the universal concept for opera. But it is not and never has been the only one because opera is composed by individuals, out of the impulse and egotism that is true "creativity." Every genius makes his wilful way, has his personal say, however strange this way and utterance may be within his place and time. Debussy, for example.

*A Basic "Sampler" for the New Opera Goer*

**"Italian" opera**

Cosi Fan Tutte ✗
Don Giovanni ✗
The Marriage of Figaro ✗
The Barber of Seville ✗
Don Pasquale ✗
La Cenerentola ✗

Lucia di Lammermoor
Rigoletto
La Traviata
Aida
La Bohème
Tosca
Madama Butterfly

**"French" opera**

Faust
Carmen ✗
Pelléas and Mélisande
Samson and Delilah
—opera-oratorio

**"German" opera**

The Abduction from the Seraglio
The Magic Flute ✗

The Flying Dutchman
Tristan and Isolde
The Mastersingers of Nuremberg

Salome

Der Rosenkavalier

Die Fledermaus ✗
—classical operetta

If possible, see *The Barber of Seville* first; *The Marriage of Figaro* second in a season of repertory when both works are available.

✗ *Often done in English.*

# What Opera Is About

Is everything!

When it is comic, it can be broad and coarse but brilliantly satirical—like Mozart's *Don Giovanni*, which flails the skin off a society while having great fun with some representatives of it. Opera is sometimes a tragedy of manners, as in Verdi's *La Traviata*; or a tragedy of mores as in his *Rigoletto*. And a comedy of manners, like Mozart's *Cosi Fan Tutte* and *The Marriage of Figaro*; Strauss' *Der Rosenkavalier* and Johann Strauss' *Die Fledermaus*. When opera is tragic its woe is utter, and anguish of the heart, or of the spirit, is a common resonator for the sound of such opera. The color of tragedy is of earthy hues in the romantic sufferings of operas like *La Bohème, Madama Butterfly, Carmen* and *La Traviata*, all of which are concerned with a deeply personal love, an intensely personal longing. But love and desire and the personalities these involve have a somewhat different tinge of color in operas like *Aida, Salome* and *Samson and Delilah*, for here, beyond the commitments of sensual love, the opera makers essay principles of racial and religious prejudices, and of war's inviolable patriotic rights which violate all human sentiments.

Opera can be real, vital and valid and actually true to life, as it is in Wagner's *The Mastersingers of Nuremberg*—set in a city famed for its guilds and *meistersingers*, a milieu to which Wagner's drama and music are exceedingly faithful, even to recreating the cobbler Hans Sachs. And opera can be mystical to the point of obscurity in art, in Wagner's *Tristan and Isolde* and Debussy's *Pelléas and Mélisande*. Opera's materials are equally the stuff of hard fact and of the most gossamer fancy. Rossini made reality out of Perrault's fairy tale about

( 251 )

*Cinderella;* Mozart made magic out of a *Flute,* and Wagner a mystery of love out of the legend of the *Flying Dutchman* (who is also the Wandering Jew seeking rest and salvation). Gounod in *Faust* invoked the premise that age is ugly, youth is so valuable a possession that a man who covets it willingly suffers the loss of his immortal soul. And opera is allegory and moral, in its dramatic duels between diabolical and angelic forces as in *Faust* and *The Magic Flute.* Almost invariably, opera is about love and it may be a love like Senta's for the Dutchman, which saves and exalts, or like Salome's for Jokanaan, which damns and destroys. Love has a lithesome grace, a wayward charm, a bitter-sweet taste in *Der Rosenkavalier's* affaire of the lovely, aging Marschallin with her young darling, "Quinquin," and a nostalgic, melancholy beauty in Rosina's conjugal love for Almaviva in *The Marriage of Figaro.*

Opera is epic, and (in love or out of it) opera is antic. Opera is sometimes authentically "grand" à la Meyerbeer; or consciously simple in the "natural" style of the pastoral and *buffo* varieties emergent after commedia dell'arte in Italy, an English poet named John Gay, and a French revolutionary named Rousseau. Opera is a funeral dirge or something evanescent, as sugary and light as delectable Viennese pastry —and when it is of that sort it is in the Viennese mode of classical operetta, from an era when the Viennese were as frivolous as the pleasure-mad Venetians of the 17th century. But the sardonic Offenbach's *opéras bouffes* have a poisoned kernel of wit.

Opera is deliberately "national," as Wagner's *The Mastersingers of Nuremberg* is both national and romantic. It is "contemporary," or of its time, so that when you know *Cosi Fan Tutte* you know, also, how people dressed (and, therefore, how they moved) in Mozart's own day. Such opera halts time and holds up a glass to the street.

Opera will invoke the faërie and supernatural (there is even an opera about a vampire, 1828) from Weber's *Oberon* to Gounod's demon, Mephisto, and Mozart's ghost of the Commendatore who takes Don Giovanni to meet his Satanic Majesty. Yet opera will also dress and compose scenes from life as it was lived day to day—say, in Verdi's *La Traviata.*

The tragic mold, impressed with the spirit of a woman who loves not wisely but much too well for her own peace of mind, is nowhere better revealed than in Verdi's *La Traviata* and Puccini's *Madama*

*Butterfly.* Nor are two women more unlike each other in or out of opera than the Lady of the Camellias in Paris and Cio-Cio-San in Nagasaki.

In *La Traviata,* a young man of family, Alfredo Germont, falls in love with a woman who is not of his class. He violates social mores when he thinks of marrying her—she is named Violetta and she is a beautiful and charming creature. We meet her in her salon, at a ball, and (when she is dying) in her bedroom—and we never again forget her! She is a woman kept in luxurious circumstances like a lady of culture and high fashion and if only she had become this as the daughter of a respectable and wealthy parent (or as the widow of an equally respectable and wealthy husband) she would be a perfect peach to be plucked by the Germonts. Alas, Violetta is kept by a series of lovers, gentlemen like the Germont father and son, whose manners and customs permit (more; *encourage*) them to keep a mistress on the side while courting and eventually marrying a lady of quality with an unsullied reputation.

The Germont predicament (as the father explains to Violetta) is that what Alfredo does and is reputed to do, affects the whole family, and especially affects his maiden sister's marriageable chances. In the society of Paris, 1850's, the performers and audiences of Verdi's opera found the theme perfectly true, credible in life and in theatre.

Verdi's librettist, Piave, adapted a famous novel for the libretto of *La Traviata.* The original: *La Dame aux Camélias* (The Lady of the Camellias) by Alexandre Dumas *fils* was considered "a shabby little shocker" by the prudes of 19th century society. (The title is alleged to refer to the lady's custom of wearing white camellias in the evening to inform the gentlemen who visited her salon that she was available for love-making that night; and red camellias on occasions when, for reasons of feminine hygiene, she was not).

Dumas based his novel on a real life character, Marie Duplessis, born January 15, 1824, who died of consumption (tuberculosis) February 3, 1847. By the age of twenty-three, little Duplessis (who was familiarly called "Camille") had become a lady in manner while losing her virtue to titled gentlemen. The country girl whom Dumas called "Marguerite" in his novel was the toast of Paris, a sensual, amoral young woman who had a sensitivity and simplicity rare in a creature of her class. She was famed, a contemporary writes, for her breeding and tact as well as for her sweet and obliging nature. Certainly her lovers were more than a little attracted, none more so than a very rich old count, Stackelberg, who at the age of eighty became so enamored of Duplessis (who was then in her teens) that Dumas (also one of Duplessis' lovers) said he sought her not as Oedipus sought Antigone but as David coveted Bathsheba.

Duplessis also included among her lovers the piano virtuoso Franz Liszt and the Duc de Gramont, and (in 1846) married a French vicomte, De Perregaux, in London. When she died, Perregaux, her young husband and Stackelberg, her aged "patron," walked side by side to her grave at the funeral. If you are in Montmartre Cemetery you will find her last resting place marked with a stone on which her real name is inscribed as *Alphonsine Plessis*. As *du* is a generic title ascribing the holder as being "of" a house or clan one assumes that the little unornamented nobody admired the attributes of French nobility— perhaps so well that she would have agreed with Dumas and Verdi on *la traviata's* fate; renunciation of her *grande amour,* subsequent "decline" and death from the poetic disease of the century: tuberculosis.

You will note that *La Bohème à la Puccini* has its heroine, Mimi, romantically expiring of "consumption," which popularly affected all young persons suffering with broken hearts in the 19th century. Although frankly carnal, Victorian romance was also "ethereal" in idyl.

But where *La Bohème* epitomizes the casual or "beatnik" ways of its times, *La Traviata* pitilessly enforces the mores of the time (that a woman of "light" or easy virtue before marriage is altogether unsuited to marriage with a man of good family) as does, in its own way, Puccini's *Madama Butterfly*. Here a racist propriety is defined, exactly as a social moralistic ideal is preserved in *La Traviata*.

Madama Butterfly is Cio-Cio-San, a Nagasaki maiden who is married in a "Japanese" ceremony, a marriage good only in Japan while the husband chooses to recognize it. Her temporary husband, whom she is unlucky enough to love for life, is a crass young American Navy officer, Lieutenant Pinkerton. The marriage is arranged through the nominal Japanese "marriage-broker" (a character named Goro) and Pinkerton enters the marriage thinking (and singing) of it as a lease which can be terminated with one month's notice. His cynicism is emphasized by remarking (in English, as an aside to his friend, the United States Consul at Nagasaki, Sharpless) "America forever!"

The opera is set in the year 1904, in a time when "mixed marriages" between Occidental and Oriental peoples were socially taboo. Pinkerton leaves Japan for duty elsewhere; Cio-Cio-San bears a child, a boy named "Trouble" or "Sorrow," according to the production; three years pass (Trouble is aged two years and some months when the audience sees him) and although Cio-Cio-San and her faithful maid Suzuki pray to the gods Pinkerton does not return. Cio-Cio-San never doubts that he will and tells Suzuki (in one of the loveliest of all arias):

One fine day we'll notice a thread of smoke arising on the sea
And then the ship appearing

Then, Cio-Cio-San thinks, Pinkerton will be so glad to see her, his wife, and Trouble, his blond-haired and blue-eyed son, that he will never again leave Nagasaki.

But when Pinkerton does reappear (Cio-Cio-San and Suzuki decorate the house as a bower of flowers for his visit) he has a white American wife, Kate, who is prepared to adopt Trouble and bring him up as her own. Cio-Cio-San quits the scene where she is an undesirable person, by killing herself in the Japanese manner of hari-kari. She does so very discreetly, behind a screen, giving the child Trouble an American flag and a doll to amuse himself with while she is busy dying.

Pinkerton returns to absolve himself from the charge of being the callowest lover in opera, and cry *Butterfly! Butterfly!* as she dies, to the poignant "Oriental" air that recurs whenever death or heartbreak affects the mood of the opera.

Puccini diligently incorporated an "American" character in the first part of the opera. The music for the conversation between Sharpless and Pinkerton is rationalized as "westernized" and the mood is ebullient, breathing masculine righteousness and national superiority. When Butterfly comes into the story the mood changes and the music becomes subtly Oriental. Thereafter, the opera is concerned with Cio-Cio-San and not with the detestable Pinkerton.

"For my part," wrote the composer (April 23, 1902), "I am laying stone on stone and doing my best to make Mr. Benjamin Franklin Pinkerton sing like an American."

Puccini made him sing like a tenor, and in a plot that Puccini found to be true to life.

"I have had a visit today from Mme Ohyama, wife of the Japanese ambassador," he wrote to a friend in 1900, when he was researching material for *Madama Butterfly*. "She told me a great many interesting things and sang some native songs to me. She has promised to send me some Japanese music. I sketched the story of the libretto for her, and she liked it, especially as just such a story as Butterfly's is known to her as having happened in real life."

The piteous fate of the Nagasaki maiden who loved not wisely but well left the audience at La Scala unmoved; the première of *Madama Butterfly* was a fiasco. But Puccini revised the score and got it produced three months later at Brescia, where it was then and thereafter a great success.

Stylistically, *Madama Butterfly* is not *verismo* opera like Mascagni's *Cavalleria Rusticana* and Leoncavallo's *Pagliacci*—or Puccini's own *Tosca*. But Puccini (who was apt to stretch theatricality beyond the bounds of good psychology) worked hard to create a true nature for the music, listening to hundreds of Oriental melodies before he began to compose. He worked mostly in a single line, pentatonically, with occasional harmonic developments, and achieved some novel instrumentation for the exotic mood of the score. *Madama Butterfly, La Bohème* and *Tosca* are his masterworks and any one of these three is sufficient to have immortalized Puccini's name.

Puccini, supremely a man of the theatre, was never afraid of melodrama, choosing his libretto for *Tosca* from a play by Victorien Sardou for Sarah Bernhardt. The play itself was performed three thousand times (on the count of Sardou) and Verdi and a composer named Franchetti tried to get the rights to it for operas of their own—Puccini won them in the final round, persuading his good friend Ricordi, publisher for both Puccini and Franchetti, to get these rights from the original owner, Franchetti. The librettists Luigi Illica and Giuseppe Giacosa translated the text into Italian with such fidelity that the torture scene in *Act II* raised a furore disputing Puccini's artistry versus his theatricality.

It is set in Rome, 1800, with Napoleon (as he was then thought to be) the archangel of political freedom and all who idolized him classed as rabid revolutionaries of their states. One such is Angelotti, the friend of a painter named Cavaradossi who is in love with the beautiful prima donna Floria Tosca. She, coveted by every man in Rome, loves only Cavaradossi and with a tempestuous passion easily tormented by jealousy. The enemy of these three ardent young creatures (the revolutionist Angelotti and the lovers Cavaradossi and Tosca) is the wicked Chief of Police, Baron Scarpia. As he madly desires Tosca it is with the greatest pleasure that he imprisons Cavaradossi on suspicion of harboring Angelotti, an escaped prisoner of the state.

The plot pits a woman's wit and wiles against a man's lechery and lies. Scarpia makes a bargain with Tosca: if she gives herself to him he will arrange a mock execution by the firing squad, with blank shot, for Cavaradossi, who will then be secretly released. Tosca has already betrayed Angelotti's hiding place (the well in the garden of Cavaradossi's house), being unable to bear her lover's agony when he is tortured. She expresses herself beautifully and truly in her great aria *Vissi d'arte*, a woman who lives only for love and music; it is for the first of these great forces that she agrees to sacrifice herself to Scarpia's lust. But when Scarpia comes to collect his reward for saving Cavaradossi, Tosca plunges a knife in his heart saying: "Thus it is that Tosca kisses!"

Cavaradossi, consigning himself to death, has sung his aria *E lucevan le stelle*—The stars were shining brightly, when Tosca, as though come to say goodbye, whispers to him of the bargain she has made with Scarpia and shows him the safe-conduct she has for him from the Chief of Police. She tells him that she has killed Scarpia: who lies in his palatial suite, on his breast a crucifix placed there by pious Tosca, and two candles beside his head, illuminating his dead face.

But Scarpia has the last, unholy chuckle—never intending to spare Cavaradossi, he has not changed the order for the firing squad, and real bullets are shot into Tosca's lover. She is mourning over his dead body when the soldiers, going to report their work to Scarpia, find him murdered. But before they can seize Tosca she leaps onto the parapet of the castle and flings herself down to the ground below to rejoin Cavaradossi in death. This leap has been carrying divas to fame ever since!

Following *Tosca* and *Madama Butterfly*, Puccini composed *La Fanciulla del West* (The Girl of the Golden West) in 1910, making a horse-opera into a real opera. The original was a play by David Belasco, a melodrama about poker-playing stakes for a man's life and a woman's (snow-white) body in the classic terms of 19th century melodrama. Puccini was fascinated by America when he visited it in 1905 and especially by the wild and woolly West with its bandits, Indians and gold miners, all of which he found in Belasco's play. Everything about the West was pure romance in 1850, the time in which *Girl of the Golden West* is set. Even a Wells Fargo Transport

Company man, an ordinary mail and freight carrier, was bathed in the luminous colors of wonder which painted the American West for Europeans well into the 20th century. In this golden hue, Puccini attempted to create the love story of Minnie, owner and chief operator of "The Polka" saloon, Jack Rance, the sheriff who loved Minnie, and Ramirrez, alias Dick Johnson, the bandit Minnie loved. Despite the resemblance this plot bears to that of many a successful "horse opera" on movies and innumerable television serials (of which *Gunsmoke* is the most notable) Puccini's *Girl* remains a respectable opera, classed with the most noble themes in repertory, appearing side by side with Beethoven's *Fidelio* and Mozart's *Don Giovanni.**

---

* In spring, 1966, for the now historic final season of the New York Metropolitan Opera, immediately before it moved to Lincoln Center from its original site downtown on Broadway between 39th and 40th streets, *The Girl of the Golden West* was featured in a repertory including *Fidelio* and *Don Giovanni*—and, also, featuring Puccini's own *Manon Lescaut, Tosca* and *La Bohème*, Verdi's *Aida* and *The Masked Ball* and Strauss' *Salome*. One performance of *Girl of the Golden West*, in this season, was a special student matinee at 1:00 p.m. February 8 with the soprano Lynn Owen in the title role. And another performance, earlier in the season, has become memorable for all of us who attended it. As a memento of the old Met., beloved home of American opera from 1883, I include the anecdote here for readers who are young in 1966 and others who, in years to come, may look back at 1966 as a time before *their* times.

The soprano Dorothy Kirsten had been scheduled to sing the role of Minnie—when her appearance was cancelled, due to an indisposition, Eleanor Steber was substituted opposite tenor Franco Corelli as Ramirrez. He, as it happened, was suffering with bronchitis but all backstage at the Met. hoped for the best on the night of the performance.

The curtain rose and "The Girl of the Golden West" herself got a rousing ovation—slenderer than she had been in previous seasons (and experienced in the role from having performed it in Florence, Italy, and in Chicago and Red Rocks, Colorado) Miss Steber appeared at the top of the stairs of "The Polka" saloon, fired off Minnie's pistol and got the affair off to a good start.

As for Corelli, although not in best voice, he managed to give a good account of himself. It is to be noted that Puccini makes comparatively little demands of the tenor in the first act. But offstage at intermission Corelli's doctor pronounced him unfit to continue and another tenor, Gaetano Bardini, was rushed into costume. It was not Corelli's costume, one may be sure—these two could never by the wildest chance fit into each other's clothes, however well they might fit their voices into the same role.

Franco "Legs" Corelli is a strapping figure of a tenor; Bardini is diminutive. Minnie of this Golden West, therefore, was faced with the difficulty of

*The Girl of the Golden West* has a constant charm as being one of the few operas of its time set in an American scene, and also for its chronological place in the composer's career. For many musicologists, *Madama Butterfly* ends the fecund period of Puccini's particular genius and *The Girl of the Golden West*, which was followed by *Il Tabarro* (The Cloak), *Suor Angelica* and *Gianni Schicchi* (all these, incidentally, receiving world premières in New York, 1918) has never been considered the equal of *La Bohème* or *Madama Butterfly*. And *Girl* marked a dismal chapter in Puccini's private life.

Returning to Italy from the United States to compose the opera, he went through his usual agonies with librettists (whom he hired and

---

being wooed by a lover who, seemingly, shrunk between acts, since Steber sang up to Corelli (who is taller than she is) in the first act, and, quite literally, sang down to Bardini in the following acts—Bardini being noticeably shorter than herself.

The poor man, knowing himself at a physical disadvantage, heroically ignored the audiences' titters and fixed his eye on the conductor, wisely singing to him (Jan Behr) instead of the imposing figure of Minnie. She, understandably, took the opera in her hands and magnified Minnie in dramatic power, pacing the stage like a lioness—or, as a critic unkindly remarked, like a misplaced Tosca in a blue night-gown.

When Bardini was wounded and had to crawl across the stage, looking piteously child-like, an irreverent voice from the stalls urged Steber to pick him up and carry him. Perhaps overcome by the ludicrous physical change in her tenors, Steber sang with an ill-concealed tremolo. There were moments when one wondered if she was going to burst out laughing or crying. Perhaps she was trying to regulate the volume so that in voice as well as stature she would not overpower her lover. Bardini, singing as creditably as ever an Italian tenor did, needed a smaller girl friend as badly as Miss Steber required a more stalwart boyfriend.

The Metropolitan audience took the proceedings like good sports with uncommon restraint for the blunders and short-comings and appreciation for the better points made in the evening. In fact, the audience deserved a rousing cheer from the stage for behaving beautifully in a situation that could easily have turned into an operatic fiasco, had this odd-sized singers' production been treated with less than kindly forbearance and good manners. In jolly mood, perfect strangers beamed at each other as we trooped out into the foyer, commenting that it would make a good story in decades to come when we spoke of "the old Met. on Broadway," with the familiar affection of members of the family—the opera audience in America, circa 20th century. For opera, like real life, is precariously balanced between pathos and bathos, the grand manner and the prat-fall.

fired in fine frenzy) and suffered from what his friends stoutly maintained to be the false accusations of his wife: that their maid was his
mistress. Mme Puccini, almost demented with jealousy, made accusations in public and so persecuted the poor servant girl that she committed suicide; a scandal shook Italian society and the parents of the
dead girl brought a legal suit against her employers. Mme Puccini
was tried and found guilty, the case was appealed—and perhaps settled
quietly out of court, as the dead girl's family suddenly withdrew the
suit, allowing the case to be dismissed. But the Puccinis were marked
for life by the scandal and, as they appear to have been in love with
each other, their long, miserable separation and eventual reconciliation
left them broken emotionally in middle-age. Puccini had just turned
fifty; he died at sixty-six, leaving his *Turandot* uncompleted. Finished
by his pupil Franco Alfano (from drafts left by the composer) it received its première at La Scala in 1926, during which, halfway through
the final act, Toscanini laid down his baton, turned to the audience and
said: "Here the Maestro laid down his pen."

*Turandot*, like *Tosca*, was based on a stage play, this time by
Carlo Gozzi, and is laid in the exotic scene of legendary China where
Turandot is a princess of such icy hauteur that she cannot bear to give
herself in marriage, even to a prince. She sets as her price the solving
of three riddles and the loss of the suitor's life when, having guessed
the enigmas incorrectly, he is proved unworthy of her.

Puccini has always been an especial favorite of American audiences. He came to the United States in 1905 at the height of his fame,
lauded as Verdi's successor, and in 1907 returned to advise the Metropolitan Opera in setting his *Madama Butterfly*. His *Girl of the Golden
West* was commissioned for this theatre, where the première, December 10, 1910, became one of the highlights of its history. He was a
perfect master of the opera of his time: lyrical, melodramatic, human,
with conscious elegance of style. And some of his harmonic compositions and instrumental colorations were daring and novel. A worldly
man, he was both honest and realistic, saying of himself that he made
music about small things—meaning: of human events and characters
that he could easily understand and interpret.

He was the prey of that new and engaging monster, the automobile, in one of which he was seriously injured in 1903, suffered from cancer of the throat and died of a heart attack, in a personal drama of love and anguish which would make a tolerable libretto for an opera *à la Puccini.* He was strongly aware of his times as evidenced by his masterful grasp of the poignant relationship between Cio-Cio-San and Pinkerton, which, more than an unhappy love affair, is a striking dissertation on social mores. Not for half a century after the première of *Madama Butterfly* would its theme of racial prejudice lose its pathos, and our conventions accept marriage between Oriental and Occidental lovers.

Verdi in *Aida* explores the same dilemma of love versus race and religion, and here the racial and religious conventions which separate the lovers are complicated by the theme of the "beloved enemy"— lovers divided in loyalties to their countries as well as to their races and their gods. Opera makers have made good use of the heart-breaking theme, Rossini's *William Tell* rising to epic character in the patriot of the title role. Camille Saint-Saëns' *Samson and Delilah* and Richard Strauss' *Salome* are also tinged with politics, race and religion, for while Delilah and Salome are reprehensible girls, fiendishly alluring, their murderous acts have the perverse logic of racial and religious vanity as well as (especially for Salome) female cruelty. They consider themselves superior to the men they desire—it is this which makes them two frightful, fascinating harpies. To Delilah, Samson is a despised enemy to be spied upon, seduced and traduced and the ends serve the means, without compunction. He (like Radames) is ruthlessly betrayed by love, and when Delilah has a twinge or two of conscience as a woman (she has none as a Philistine for Samson, and for his Israelites) Saint-Saëns puts it to good account in a lovely aria:

O Love! come to aid my weakness
Pour thy poison through Samson's heart!

Samson has his eyes put out and the opera follows, with more or less fidelity, the episode recorded in *Judges 16* of the Old Testament. The opera is set in the city of Gaza and the valley of Sorek near Gaza, *circa* 1136 B.C.

Salome, as everyone knows, thirsted for the lips of the prophet, John, while her stepfather Herod thirsted for her. This brought about the contretemps by which Salome danced for Herod and he awarded her her vengeful heart's desire: John the Baptist's bearded head in lieu of his lips, which he denied her except to shower her wanton name with curses.

Strauss made excellent use of this Biblical episode, with one of the most remarkable libretti in 20th century opera, a text by Hedwig Lachmann, based not on the Bible's version but on Oscar Wilde's play *Salome.*

Salome's musical theme (macabre and yet seductive) is like the serpent of which the ancient Hebrews used to warn men (as they warn Samson, literally, in the Bible), that appears in the guise of a lovely woman. Salome's shimmering dance music is famous, as is her abandoned desire in this air:

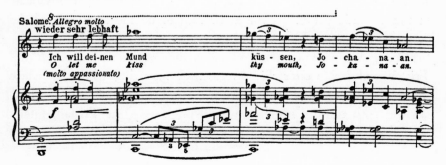

The final act, somewhat repellant to a queasy opera goer (Strauss is not as inhibited about gory details as is Puccini in *Madama Butterfly*), features Jokanaan divested of his body. This severed head is handed up to Salome from the pit where the execution takes place on stage. Seizing it, she kisses the mouth which in life was too scornful of hers even to speak a hypocrisy that could have saved Jokanaan's life.

Her ferocious passion costs Salome her own life. Disgusted by her act of kissing the decapitated prophet, Herod orders his soldiers to kill the princess. She is crushed beneath their shields, a scene as ominous and many times more gruesome than Verdi's entombment of Radames and Aida.

Strauss' music for *Salome* is so resplendent, such a work of genius, that the opera is, like *Aida*, a work of art.

So, too, are Bizet's *Carmen* and Wagner's *Tristan and Isolde*, and nothing that this Frenchman and this German created became them better or added more luster to their names. But while Bizet derived his opera from a torrid novel by Prosper Mérimée, Wagner went to Medieval mythical romance for the tragedy of Tristan and the two Isoldes, as Wagner also went to romantic legend for his operas *The Flying Dutchman, Götterdämmerung* (The Twilight of the Gods in the *Ring*), *Lohengrin, Parsifal, The Rhinegold, Siegfried, Tannhäuser* and *The Valkyrie*.

The Tristan legend exists in several versions, the best known to English-speaking peoples being that of the Arthurian saga. Tristan is the "myth of the hero" and he is also one of the great tenor roles in opera, in a work where death is glorified as life (and love) everlasting. In this respect (an Oriental or Eastern concept of love and death) *Tristan and Isolde* has some thematic likeness to *Aida*. But whereas Verdi, the realist, shapes his opera in very direct style, Wagner adopts an elusive, fathomless style that for the sake of clarity we call "mystical" in this operatic genre. (It might be said to be the antithesis of the corporeal.)

From the romantic point of view, the tragedies of *Carmen* and *Tristan and Isolde* offer this contrast: Carmen dies when José stabs her; Isolde, who cannot bear to live without Tristan, "breathes her last" (as the 19th century novelists were wont to say) as Tristan, fatally wounded by a sword, expires in her arms.

Wagner's operas are called "mysteries" by some musicologists and in that category *Parsifal* and *Tannhäuser* become "mysteries of faith" while *Tristan and Isolde* is a "mystery of love." So, too, is Wagner's *The Flying Dutchman*, which is also "supernatural" through the introduction of an abstract entity not of this world.

*The Flying Dutchman* is an accursed sailor who, for defying God, is condemned to sail for eternity unless he can win a selfless love to redeem his lost soul. Senta, a tender-hearted girl, gives him such a love and her life, in the bargain. But *Faust* is ordered on self-love, the avidity of an aging, unsuccessful scientist to live again in the body of a young and ardent man, and with money to burn while living a second existence. He makes a bargain with Mephisto, an exceptionally suave demon. It is incidental to Faust and to Mephisto that Faust seduces a pure young girl named Marguerite, who commits the sin of murdering their unwanted child when it is born. It is not incidental to Gounod, for he gave Marguerite such a plum of a role that indignant German opera goers declared the opera a travesty of their great poet Goethe's epic and insisted on calling it *Margrethe*, not *Faust*.

One of the most famous airs in *Faust* is Marguerite's "Jewel Song" as she plays with the gemmed trinkets in a casket presented by the demon to tempt her virtue. *Faust* shows the influence of Wagner's *leitimotiv* techniques on French opera; Debussy's *Pelléas and Mélisande* (yet another opera with a "supernatural" theme) is the antithesis of Wagnerian principles for music drama. The supernatural element in Debussy's opera is drawn from Maeterlinck's play (which is the literal verse of the opera), itself allegorical and symbolical; mystic and mysterious as poetry. And another opera of allegory and symbolism (as defined by some authorities) is Mozart's *The Magic Flute*.

If ever an opera was of divers content this is it! On the surface, and as the young and artless see it, it is an enchanting fairy tale about Tamino, a young prince of (more mythical than antique) Egypt, and Pamina, the good and lovely daughter of the wicked Queen of the Night. It is also the story of one of the most engaging little wretches in opera: Papageno, a bird-catcher, who avows himself more than willing to catch a girl instead. He makes do, with great bonhommie, with a little old woman who offers herself to him to be wed—his good nature is its own reward: the little ugly crone is transformed, magically (and before our eyes in the theatre) into an entrancing young bride, named Papagena. The entire opera is occupied by the efforts of these two pairs of lovers to live happily together, two by two, forever after.

As related in *Opera After Gluck*, there are various definitions for *The Magic Flute*, one being that it is a treatise by Freemasons on their times (Mozart and his librettist being fellow-members of the same Masonic lodge in Vienna). Another is that the hero, Tamino, is Everyman, and his trials and tribulations in the opera plot are a Bunyanesque progress through life. Knowing that Mozart's librettist, Schikaneder, was a man of the theatre and that, into the bargain, he wrote the story to be produced for his own theatre and to attract the biggest public audience, it seems safe to believe that from first to last *The Magic Flute* was intended to be a gala entertainment for theatre goers—as it is, indeed!

I have seen it performed as the opera it was created to be, as an opera-ballet and as a ballet with the Narrator or Speaker in the cast taking the only vocal part. In all these forms, *The Magic Flute* is enchanting.

Tamino and Pamina are thwarted by the machinations of the Queen of the Night, an evil spirit, and, as it first appears, by the high priest, Sarastro—who later divulges that he is, on the contrary, a benign not to say majestic being. His servant, the Moor Monostatos, has lascivious tendencies—there is an attempted rape *Act I, Scene II* which Mozart turns into a deliciously comic scene, making the amorous Moor mistake the little bird-catcher, Papageno, for the devil, while (as the audience knows) the bird-catcher is a craven little wretch, who is frightened out of his wits by Monostatos, whom Papageno believes *is* the devil!

Through two acts, and a total of thirteen scenes, the action piles one denouement on another, the music bears the sublime and the ridiculous on a great flood, and centuries before the development of cinema art Mozart and Schikaneder created what, in opera, cries out to be made into a moving picture since it is probably in this medium that the mysterious quality and the marvelous stage effects of *The Magic Flute* shall eventually be fully realized.

Thwarted love between a soprano and a tenor is the hinge on which great opera art swings, in the romantic pendulum animated by

Mozart, through his wondrously human characters, and into all the great operas of love, some comic in mood, others tragic.

In Verdi's *Rigoletto* the audience's sympathies are with an unprepossessing hero, the baritone (Rigoletto) for we know that the tenor means the soprano no earthly good. The tenor is the Duke of Mantua, full of charm, lacking scruples.

The soprano, Gilda, is Rigoletto's only child, whom he has reared in seclusion, far from the venal court where he serves the handsome, profligate Duke as jester. When Rigoletto finds out that the Duke has discovered this beauty and has designs on her (and that she has fallen madly in love with the wicked charmer, a veritable Mantuan Don Giovanni) he schemes to have a pair of assassins murder his master and undertakes to dispose of the corpse in a sack. By an error far from comic, Gilda is killed instead of the Duke and Rigoletto learns the horrible fact when he opens the bag to gloat over his enemy.

All this transpires not only because Gilda is beautiful and the Duke bad but because Rigoletto, a dreadfully flint-hearted cynic, had mocked a father tormented by the Duke's corruption of his daughter; an old man named Count Monterone. It is Monterone's fearsome curse on Rigoletto for making mock of him, and on the Duke of Mantua for laughing, which deprives these two of what they hold most dear—the Duke, his wayward but happy life, and Rigoletto, his daughter.

Verdi treats this lady exquisitely, giving her the celebrated air: *Caro nome*—Dearest name. The Duke and Rigoletto are equally well treated, and perhaps no other baritone in opera history has lovelier music to sing than proud, twisted Rigoletto.

If Verdi was a realist, so was his compatriot Rossini. Where some opera makers have experimented with works in the most gossamer and impressionistic styles, Rossini is the man who chose to take a fairy tale, *Cinderella*, and treat it realistically, throwing out fairy godmother, mice and pumpkin coach, *tout monde de fée* in which Weber and the others of the ilk revelled. Thus, Rossini's *La Cenerentola* is more *opera buffa* than anything else, complete with a prince in disguise as his own valet; the valet (Dandini) as his master, the character Don Magnifico, Baron of Mountflagon, who is an ass of the quality of Molière's *Le Bourgeois Gentilhomme;* and two sisters (Cinderella's) who are comic pieces by very reason of being who they are and what they are.

Once you know Rossini, you will readily understand Verdi and all that lies between these two, and all that follows after, in Italian opera. If you move backward from Rossini, you return to Scarlatti, and his compeers and predecessors—or you diverge and follow French opera from Lully, on into and out of Debussy.

Once you discover Mozart (and for many a theatre goer he is a key to opera, unlocking the secret wonders of music, the splendor of characterization and drama in music) you move easily forward to Wagner and all German opera, into Strauss; or backward and observe (with heightened awareness) the work of Gluck in France and of Handel in England, and, also, of all German opera in its *Singspiel* and other forms. For Mozart, who is not considered to have formally begun an era, nevertheless represents one. He stands alone but is not lonely or isolated because he is the key to a great deal in opera lore.

But these are not all, and are far from being the only opera makers you will discover, and want to know well, as opera makers and in their works.

If you are fond of Shakespearean plays or if, as a student, you are in a drama course, you might want to know the operatic versions— a whole world of opera in themselves. Verdi's three are *Macbeth*, *Otello* and *Falstaff* and the two latter operas are without peer. Verdi was particularly fond of Shakespeare, of whom he spoke familiarly and to whom he compared himself on occasion, speaking of their joint ability to "invent reality." He referred to Shakespeare as 'Papa,' saying that the playwright might have found a real-life Falstaff (as in the play, *The Merry Wives of Windsor*) but never a man as evil as Iago, or women as angelic as Desdemona, Cordelia and Imogen. These, Shakespeare had to create, as Verdi created or invented reality.

If you are fond of legends and fairy tales, opera libretti comprise a great store of the faërie and the supernatural, especially from German folklore. Wagner's operas are symbolical and mystical and based on myths, as is *Faust*, the subject of Goethe's celebrated drama, which inspired operas from Gounod, Berlioz, Boito (Verdi's librettist), Busoni and Spohr—Gounod's being the best known opera.

If you take your composers in anything like consecutive order, and in "national" opera traditions, you will come to Gounod after Daniel Auber, Meyerbeer, Berlioz and others, for Charles Gounod's most famed work, *Faust*, dates to 1859, mid-way in the 19th century. It was originally of *opéra comique* form (as was *Carmen*) but ten years after its Paris première Gounod altered it, adding recitative and the now-famed ballets in *Act V, Scene I* for the Walpurgis Night, a bacchanal which gives choreographers and dancers a chance at making their mark in opera.

If you study *Faust* before experiencing it as an opera in performance, note that it is a work which is produced in several different ways, some productions excising the Walpurgis Night ballets entirely, others also omitting *Scene I* of *Act IV*, and reversing the order of continuity for *Scenes II* and *III*.

This opera is frequently criticized (and this is understandable, since it is so subject to production changes) but its music preserves its popularity, and its theme (an old man bitterly resenting his aging body, longing for his lost youth, willing to commit suicide—or exchange his soul for a new life) has an eternal fascination. Faust deals with the Devil, who appears as a witty, worldly character in Gounod's opera. The role of Marguerite, the pure girl seduced by Faust, is one of the soprano's operatic prizes—although Faust has the title role, the focus of the opera is on Marguerite from about mid-way in the opera, which is in five acts in its uncut version. *Recitative* and *leitmotiv* patterns in this opera are influences of Wagner.

Operas out of the Bible include Verdi's *Nabucco*, which is seldom performed in the United States (it is still in Italy), Saint-Saëns' *Samson and Delilah* (1877), a fine example of French music and drama, and *Susannah*, by the American composer Carlisle Floyd, who transposed characters and events from a Biblical scene to the Tennessee mountains—here moving you into 20th century "American" opera.

By way of the French tradition you will discover Bizet's *Carmen*, and by way of the Italian not only Verdi but also Puccini and his compeers, and the *verismo* opera makers like Mascagni and Leoncavallo. Here you will have moved into the 20th century (which Puccini straddles) to find that Richard Strauss (as in *Der Rosenkavalier*) owes Mozart a great debt, but that Debussy, in French opera, refutes Wagner.

Claude Debussy (1862-1918) was the last of the individual

representatives of his era's Romantic period. *Pelléas and Mélisande*
marks the end of the great tradition of French romanticism. It is in the
artistic category of "impressionism" or antithesis of "naturalism"—
techniques and principles of which marked painting and poetry as
well as music.

Debussy's point of departure is Wagner's point of arrival and base
of operations in opera. Wagner's works were dramatic while Debussy's
ideals were to create an atmospheric or impressionistic opera whose
ideas are more tangible than the characters. Debussy, in a word common to colloquial use, was "cool" in his approach and in *Pelléas and
Mélisande* he succeeded in achieving (to quote Westerman's excellent
explanation) a unique masterpiece in an impressionistic opera—which
in itself is an absurdity.

You will find that the people in *Pelléas and Mélisande* are very
well bred—they seldom raise their voices but "speak" in soft, restrained
tones. The orchestral music "shimmers" in tiny graduations of harmonies and the music, as a whole, flows calmly, always with that sense
of restraint which even a child will perceive. The language of the
verse is appealing and the opera has a passionate passage in the finale,
like an all too human outburst from restraint. An example of its style
is in the passage, *modere*

> *Pelléas*
> *Je n'entends que ton coeur dans l'obscurité*
> I can just hear your heart beating in the night
> *Mélisande*
> *J'ai entendu craquer les feuilles mortes*
> I heard the crackling of dead leaves underfoot

When you know the story (that Pelléas has fallen in love with
Mélisande, his brother Golaud's wife) this musical passage in the opera
contains a breathless passion of its own, a terrible dramatic climax—the
lovers are suddenly aware that their forest rendezvous has compromised
them; Golaud is watching and listening.

Debussy's music for this, his only opera, is the masterwork of his
original techniques, experiments in coloring and patterning for the
orchestra. A respected opera authority has likened this music to an
incomprehensible murmuring interspersed with hiccoughs. A classicist

might dislike the scoring but an admirer of modernism or originality in the arts might rave over it.

Whichever type of music lover you might be I think it essential for you to know Maeterlinck's drama before you experience Debussy's opera. Maurice Maeterlinck's famous play is the basis of the composer's libretto, which Debussy set in entirety except for the omission of four out of eighteen scenes and some changes in a few lines of dialogue. Maeterlinck's play has been interpreted in several aspects, a poetic drama, an allegory, and a tour de force in mysticism. Debussy retained the poetic language of the original and to such extent that no extant opera better establishes the importance of the word—the absolute essence of what is said as it is sung.

The structure of this opera is nevertheless essentially a musical one; all the scenes are connected by orchestral interludes, and the five acts have a symmetry and musical continuity. The opera is a work of art that is both subtle and precise. Its haunting love-scene at the climax of *Act IV* is:

| *Pelléas* | *Mélisande* |
| --- | --- |
| *Tu ne sais pas que c'est parce que je t'aime . . .* | *Je t'aime, aussi* |
| You do not know it is because I love you . . . | I love you, too |

Here he has just told her that he is going away; the reason being that he cannot bear to stay near to her, married to Golaud—because he loves her. It is this love of Pelléas' for his brother's wife that poses the aesthetic riddle in Maeterlinck's play and Debussy's opera. Is it a sensual and earthly love, of a boy for a girl? Or is it a pure, ethereal love, of a poet for an ideal? As Golaud is fated never to know, the anguish is his at the end—the lovers who are suspect of gross sins are serene and aloof in their deaths. Golaud is a murderer.

Perhaps the most significant thing about *Pelléas and Mélisande*, from a dramatic point of view, is its expression of love. In one scene (*Act III, Scene I*) Mélisande at the window of her tower room lets down her long golden hair, which bathes the head and face of the ardent Pelléas who gazes up at her from below. They are too far apart for the tips of their fingers to touch and they exchange no words of love but their meeting here (and the harp music of the scene) conveys a quality of sublime rapture.

Mélisande sings: a song about the saints Daniel, Michael and Raphael, and about herself (she was born on a Sunday at noon):

*Mes longs cheveux descendent jusqu'au seuil de la tour!*
My long hair hangs down to the base of the tower!

The innocent lovers are interrupted by Golaud who, at this stage of the plot, believes (or pretends to believe) that his young wife's and young brother's love play is so much arrant nonsense. He persists in treating them as foolish children.

If, in one season, you experience Debussy's *Pelléas and Mélisande* and Wagner's *Tristan and Isolde* you will have the best idea of how these two composers thought of music (and of love) and the techniques and styles in which they expressed themselves in totally different ways or "languages," in an operatic theme of love and mysticism.

Pursuing the "modern" you may observe the works of Debussy's Spanish pupil, Manuel de Falla (who is classed with the 20th century French composers) and Maurice Ravel, also of the "impressionistic" school.

If, however, you incline to the preference of most *new* adult opera goers, you are likely to be more at ease with the traditional *dramatic* opera rather than the impressionistic or avant-garde, and with a dramatic opera of melodic score, instead of a score of atonal or other unconventional mode.

Any of the operas on the list of "best known, best loved" works in international repertory answers the description, and these are the operas you will generally attend in big opera company productions. Opera buffs who admire the new complain about the sameness of big opera company repertories but these are maintained because of their popularity with the largest audience strata—and because they are undisputable masterworks in which singers of succeeding generations strive to emulate and surpass the renown of older singers now legendary in some roles.

Romantic opera's most formal structure includes large choral scenes (which occur in *Aida,* and in *Otello* as well, as in the victory chorus when Otello safely disembarks from his wrecked ship) and some scene when a principal character commands the stage, drawing to herself or himself the focus of a dramatic and musical climax. This occurs in *Aida* when Aida on the brink of the Nile sings her *romanza,* the aria in which she mourns her homesickness. In *Otello, Act IV*, Desdemona has the Willow Song, a *scena* of heart-breaking melancholy:

> *Piangea cantando, nell'erma landa-*
> The poor soul sat pining, alone and lonely-

Both operas feature ballet, Verdi having inserted five dances as *ballabili* (short *divertissements* for *corps de ballet*) as the finale of *Act III* in *Otello* for its Paris première.

And both operas are tragedy, not comedy.

The overwhelmingly larger part of opera repertory is tragic, not comic. The tragic has always been taken by creative artists as the best means of depicting the noblest and ignoblest states of mankind. What is true of opera is also applicable to dance and drama, and to painting and poetry.

The best known and best loved operas include *Aida, La Bohème, Madama Butterfly, Carmen, Faust, La Traviata, Il Trovatore, Tosca* and *Rigoletto*, and Wagner's most generally admired works are *The Flying Dutchman* and *Tristan and Isolde*. These have at least one thing in common: sad endings. The principals of all these operas are dead by curtain fall and Faust, like the hero of Mozart's *Don Giovanni*, is dragged off to Hell by the Devil himself. If Rigoletto is alive at the close of his terrible drama then it is to eat his heart out in remorse for his crime: having, by error, murdered his beloved daughter Gilda instead of her hated seducer, the Duke of Mantua.

19th century opera habitually litters the stage with corpses and its characters usually come to their violent ends out of love. Love is the primary emotion and it is pre-Freudian in concepts because the best loved operas were composed at a time when art (like life) was a humanist passion and not a scientific curiosity. Audiences of certain styles of 20th century theatre, especially of ballet and music, are devoted to "cerebral" and abstract forms. In the dance, for example, movement is sufficient to itself and sometimes requires no music; drama and emotion are not within the content.

In Verdi's time, to the contrary, audiences had a totally human response to feeling, and the aesthetics of an art form incorporated expression as content as well as for style.

Life and death are the constants of the best loved operas, and the characterizations are painted in alabaster white and glossy black. There are no "grey" people in these dramas, and the events are colored, as it were, in brilliant scarlet, or in gold. Passion is the hall-mark of the great operas, and not only for those of tragic theme. The great *operas buffa* have an imperative and decisive quality, so that what might appear from the casual reading of a libretto to be a light, farcical play (Mozart's *Cosi Fan Tutte* and Strauss' *Der Rosenkavalier*, for example) are in themselves major works of provocative ideas, great characterizations and beautiful music.

These operas require time and care to know—but was there ever anything (or anyone) worth loving that did not extort from us understanding and patience? The slight work is stated glibly, it is designed to cause only a momentary diversion while it entertains us; opera makes a far more profound statement and thereby demands of us more profundity of response. The lightest satires, operas of the slightest plot, are aimed like arrows at the faults and foibles of human beings—when they strike their ludicrously painted marks and make us laugh they are also revealing to us manners and mores of societies within the eras and places where the operas are set.

The great operas are long and perhaps leisurely for contemporary theatrical fashion but they were created for people who regularly sat down to seven-course dinners and savored every course with discernment and abundant gusto. Those persons brought energy and individuality to the theatre, quarreling with passion and defending their opinions with the sword, the walking-stick, the pistol and the umbrella—fighting in theatre foyers to settle arguments that opera makers had raised as points of dispute on the stage.

And the greatest theatres in the Western world were built to house opera; opera itself is the greatest of theatre arts, the most sumptuous in its settings, the most eclectic in its command of musical, dramatic and scenic arts—the grandest in expression and therefore the most expensive to produce.

It is with the appreciation of what opera is and what opera is about that the opera goer enters the opera house to experience opera. Once you are there, enjoy it with your senses. At the opera, trust to your feelings for it is to the heart that opera speaks.

Science is a matter of fact but theatre is a matter of emotion.

## ❧ N I N E ❧

# An Approach to
# Opera Appreciation

Teacher-student use of this book is flexible. If opera is included in a music course it is feasible to use the material in the chapter *Opera: What It Is* . . . and extend from that chapter into other parts of the book, depending on class interest and time periods for the course. If, however, this book is used in the normal curriculum (within a general "Arts Appreciation" course, et cetera) then I suggest that the romance or story of opera precede the chapter *Opera: What It Is* . . . In my own experience, I find that a good working plan for teacher-student use is:

> *The Beginning*
> *Opera: What It Is* . . .
> *Opera After Gluck*

The social history of opera, and opera as entertainment, affords a lively introduction for the new opera goer. Above all, it relates the art to the artists, establishing for the reader the fact that opera is a human undertaking, a human commitment—*of* life rather than outside it and withdrawn from society. For the teacher, especially of the adolescent student, I feel I cannot emphasize enough the necessity of establishing theatre arts as valid *experiences*. The young person, particularly in contemporary society, is concerned with here and now. Theatre has the faculty of stopping time and holding up a mirror to real life, reflecting in realistic or fantastic images the place and time of which theatre is the product and the cultural extension. When the student is led to this discovery he ceases to distrust and dislike what is "classical" as being old, outworn and sentimental. It is of the utmost importance to convey to the student the fact that in *Cosi Fan Tutte* men and women move and behave in a *contemporary* manner—contemporary of their time and place. This is the sort of theatrical "reality" through which an 18th century artist communicates, on his own terms, in his own vocabulary, with audiences of the 20th century.

This fundamental validity is equally true with a work in fantasy rather than one of realism. Haydn's opera about people on the moon is essentially a divertissement of imagery, and as much so as though the American composers Samuel Barber and Menotti were to compose operas based on the first actual landing of men on the moon.

It is from *his* contemporary point of view that Haydn communicates a theory, quite fantastic to 18th century imagination but problematic and enchanting. Men were as much obsessed with human flight, human spanning of the universe then as they are now. The main difference between Haydn's time and Barber's or Menotti's is a scientific advance which makes the probable possible.

Quite young persons understand this point of view and apply it very practically and positively to the initial effort of understanding that *Cosi Fan Tutte* is valid in itself as an opera, regardless of the date of its first première. It retains its validity in their time and place because it is art, a magical dimension into which the audience enters and is made aware of aesthetic truths and values.

Also, the student likes and needs to know that opera was itself a revolution, that the Camerata's *Nuovo Musiche* was truly "new music," and that people continuously change in tastes while retaining a universal appreciation and emotional response to music—and that the makers of music are in themselves a rebellious, contentious lot. The nature of the art to great extent determines the creative artists.

These are some of the facts that emerge from the romance and story of opera and for this reason I advise a preliminary approach to opera through *The Beginning*. Depending on the class response, the teacher may then proceed directly into *Opera After Gluck*, which is basically a continuation of *The Beginning*. But my preferred arrangement is to diverge into *Opera: What It Is* . . . so as to have a working knowledge of the form, the better to perceive its contents and style. Form, content and style increase in scope and variety in the 19th century and the student is better prepared for *Opera After Gluck* for knowing something of opera's parts and sum, and having an understanding of the orchestra and the singers, as related in *Opera: What It Is . . .*

The chapter *Aida for Example* and its supplementary *Highlights from Aida* should serve you as the basis of formulating your own "how to look and listen" guide for opera. I think your essential approach should be the disclosure of *opera as drama in music*. I do not believe that the student is readily drawn to opera as "Art." Indeed, opera in the aspect of "Art" has assumed such solemnity that it terrifies the novice.

A technical knowledge of music will enrich the study but you do not need to be a professional musician to conduct a group investigation of what opera is and is about—sometimes, a non-musician has a wider concept of opera and is therefore able to relate it, for himself and a group, as art in life as well as art in theatre. A certain amount of preparation is necessary for your study course. You should have a point of commencement and one of "reach" if not termination in opera history and allow as great inquiry and investigation as possible within the margins, according to the time limit set on your course. I have in general set the margins within "romanticism" in opera but this book omits far more than it contains and only briefly describes examples of opera form and style. Yet my own study courses, in "Arts Appreciation," do not attempt to define an opera "study course" but to stimulate its beginning, in a group, and its individual members.

A cursory knowledge of the opera you set up as example is not sufficient; you must know the opera well and know, also, its identity as to form, style and influence in the historic operatic repertory. Pace your study course to the group progress, with predetermined bounds or margins for each series of talks or each "study course." This enables you to use a "block" method of inquiry and research throughout opera history. If I am limited in time or must work with a large group, I invariably choose *Aida* for example. Verdi is a remarkably versatile composer and his works provide the teacher with an ample opera repertory for reference.

Commencing with *Nabucco* (from the Bible), you will find examples in Verdi opera which you may use in actual historical perspectives. *Simon Boccanegra* (revised version, on the libretto by Boito) is factual, a Doge elected (their first) by the Genoese in 1339. This is an excellent opera for use within a historical perspective of the Guelph-Ghibelline family feud, responsible for the war that divided most of Italy in the 14th century. The operatic Boccanegra is so similar to the true life one that historians and history teachers who become opera buffs are astonished to find such veracity in melodrama.

*Un Ballo in Maschera* or *The Masked Ball*, has a libretto based on a play by the French dramatist August-Eugène Scribe, (a famous librettist who wrote 50 volumes of plays and 26 volumes of libretti, and became a member of the French Academy in 1836) on the assassination of Gustav III of Sweden. The king was an enthusiastic opera buff and was murdered by three peers, one the former Captain of the Royal Guards, in the Royal Opera House at Stockholm in 1792. Verdi's opera was written on this plot but before it could be premièred in Naples in 1859 the radical Orsini threw a bomb at Napoleon III of France. King Ferdinand of Naples thought it imprudent for the Italians to witness a king being assassinated in the theatre (Verdi's opera was due to be sung in Naples that season) and the royal censors altered the libretto so drastically that Verdi, the ardent old republican, withdrew the work altogether and offered it to the opera house in Rome, where it was premièred February 17, 1859—but with the locale ridiculously shifted to Boston, Massachusetts, U.S.A., where the Swedish monarch became an English governor. The opera has since been set in Naples as well as Boston, but is more understandable in a production which resets it in the original scene, Sweden—however, even so, "Gustav" is called "Riccardo." It does not matter, once he remains the king and is assassinated, giving credence to the opera's plot. The time is 1792.

*Don Carlo* is set in the Spanish court, circa 1560, and although the romance is imaginary the persons involved were real, these being Don Carlos, son of Philip II (1527-1598) by his first wife, and Elizabeth of Valois (called Elisabetta in the opera), the third of Philip's four wives. Elizabeth was 18 years younger than her husband and might, conceivably, have fallen in love with a younger prince—but the real Don Carlos was physically deformed and alleged to be insane. His father is believed to have had him poisoned; he certainly had him imprisoned, where Carlos (turned into Carlo in an Italian opera) succumbed mysteriously in 1568. Eboli (by this name in the opera) is also a historical character who was the mistress of Philip's chief aide, Perez. She was said to have been exceedingly beautiful although she had only one eye—"of surpassing brilliancy" an admirer reported; hence, the soprano in the role of Eboli in *Don Carlo* wears a black patch over one eye. Verdi and Scribe make Eboli the inamorata of Philip; history does not record this as fact but in her position as Perez' mistress she could have been Philip's as well, and in her society she probably had every encouragement to be.

What is important in the Verdi operas (*Nabucco, Simon Boccanegra, The Masked Ball, Don Carlo,* and, also, *Aida*) is that the teacher has a handle, so to speak, with which to approach opera *per se; a reality* for reference or base on which to approach opera as theatrical art. Any teacher will understand what I mean here, who knows that "art" has the connotation of "arty" for most students. In this connotation, opera is shoved outside reality, removed from "real" life, and grudgingly appended as a frill or superfluity which the student would as soon as not shear away from his general education or "culture." But if the student is shown the positive connotation in theatrical arts and life, between theatre and human "reality" in persons and events, then he is far more likely to become interested in the arts that, in the theatre, lie close to the inner or private, and outer or "real" aspects of life.

Verdi's operas will also serve as good examples of "periods" of creative work in opera, and as examples of creative empathy between the creator (the artist) and his created works. With this in mind I have included in this book a very brief summary of the composer's personality and his times, because his times, naturally, influenced him and his operas. *This is the aspect of reality which you must emphasize for the student in order to give him a genuine perspective in theatre arts.* Unless the teacher succeeds in this communication he will not communicate more than the bare statement that an opera is an opera. And that the student already knows, recognizably as to form—but probably does not know well enough to certify *what opera is* in its related factors in history as arts of man.

What the teacher must achieve in an "Arts Appreciation" course is an understanding, however elementary, of *the form of the art* which is the subject of the course, *the technique* or scientific method of training its artistes for expressing in that medium of art, and classical examples of the technique and art form *within styles.*

In short, the teacher must allow the student to know, and to provide opportunities for the student to have first-hand "experiences" of operas in production. Towards that knowledge, to qualify and inform the "experience," study your own capacity for communication, the tools or examples you employ, and the individual requirements (of a class, of a group) which you must satisfy . . . and also, stimulate to further, wider "experiences."

I conduct all my classes, whenever possible, towards culmination of the opera used "as example" in actual "experience." Happily, the present era allows the teacher almost anywhere in North America to provide opportunities for "experiences" of opera in theatrical productions—and happily, the chief means of providing this national opera experience, via the touring Metropolitan Opera National Company, allows the teacher an excellent sample "guide to the operas" in this company's primary repertory. Also, motion pictures of opera productions are becoming the vogue. Try, however, for "live" opera rather than the "canned" variety because the reality onstage is more immediately and urgently communicative than when it comes out of a motion picture reel stored in a can.

There are numerous schools where the teacher has no realistic method of introducing "live" opera to students. In such cases, a pragmatic use of the materials on hand must not only suffice but also inspire the student. The teacher can at least and almost always ensure an "approach" to opera, one free of artistic prejudice and the appalling sense of social and intellectual inferiority that so many persons, young and mature, confess to feeling about drama, dance, music and opera as "great" art.

A program for "Arts Appreciation" that includes opera may be adjusted to the Music course common to normal curricula or to a course in World History, and so on. Every group has special requirements and interests and only the teacher in the group can gauge the best approach, the most sensible pace of progress, and the terminal point at which to make evaluations of the project.

For the teacher hampered by a total lack of "live" opera I recommend the use of excerpts from vocal scores played on a piano for "illustration." The sound of "live" music is very important in the first phase of opera appreciation. From the piano score, the teacher may boldly extend the reality of the music into full-scale recordings and, also, into the opera in theatre.

While I prefer only to offer suggestions rather than advice for the teacher-student use of this book I strongly recommend that the teacher divide the "discovery" of opera (as through this book) from the "experience" of opera. The entire program or study course should explicitly establish the separate but correlated aspects of an approach to and an experience of opera. And in one form or another the students must extend the bare academic knowledge of the opera as form and content into the realization of the opera *per se*. Happily, such extension from the classroom into the theatre is becoming comparatively easy to achieve.

In very many instances, the arrangements have to be physically made—the students have to be transported to and from the opera house, and seating arrangements (like the purchasing of tickets for a performance) are often beyond the means of the students. Sometimes, but not always, school funds may be available for the theatre experience—but very often from a lack of understanding of theatre such funds cannot be expended for theatre arts' values in education. Some educators believe that theatre is a frivolity at least, and a wicked perversion at worst. We are not yet so emancipated that theatrical arts are universally recognized and accepted as part of the American cultural heritage.

The teacher must usually hope to obtain a theatrical experience of opera for the student by way of the opera house's or opera company's policies of encouraging student audiences to attend opera. This is most often in specially priced programs, at matinées, and the teacher can utilize such programs as an essential part of the study course—accompanying the class to the theatre and indicating the theatrical experience as a climactic point in the study course.

Opera has a seasonal character in the United States (as it does almost everywhere) and opera companies plan and usually publicize in local newspapers the dates of tour itineraries and the repertories on current tour. If you keep abreast of such news you will know, well in advance (sometimes, as far ahead as a calendar year, 12 months) what operas are likely to be within the physical area of your students. Towards the best use of the available current repertory, plan your "opera appreciation" course, integrating the opera or operas that are available for "experience" in the opera house into your plan.

Whenever possible, make the first opera experience for your students a romantic theme with strongly interpreted characterization in the libretto and a not too complicated plot—do not, for instance, fix on *Il Trovatore* if you can, instead, choose *Rigoletto*, because *Il Trovatore*, although one of Verdi's best-loved works, has an exceptionally confusing plot. Try for *Aida* and especially try for *La Bohème*, the opera with greatest empathy for adolescents.

The most extraordinary factor of the American opera renaissance (of which the establishment of the Metropolitan Opera National Company as a touring troupe is an important aspect) is the development of "regional" opera by way of permanent companies in communities with adequate theatre facilities. An excellent example is in San Diego, California, the nation's 10th largest city, where a 3,000 seat theatre, an opera house facility, was built expressly for opera—and three years before the city built a stadium, although it already supported a nationally ranked football team.

Observing San Diego (it is called the "most typical" city of its kind in the United States) as a community with a new opera tradition I note that the first opera produced was *La Bohème* (in English), under a resident director (W. J. Adams, Ph.D.) who is a professor of speech arts and drama at San Diego State College—typical conjunction of the "town and gown" or college and community interests in contemporary American theatre. For this opera production the local opera company imported its principals, and its Mimi was Maralin Niska of San Pedro, California—who went immediately into the Metropolitan Opera National Company to be starred in *Susannah*, in the company's première of Carlisle Floyd's opera.

The San Diego Opera next scheduled *Faust*, *The Barber of Seville* and *Aida* (in English), but sponsored the Metropolitan National Opera Company's *Madama Butterfly* in Italian for presentation in the 1965-1966 tour. And in San Diego, where there are two large universities and one of the major colleges in the California state college system (plus half a dozen other colleges) the local opera company has the policy which is more or less common to all such "regional" opera—pricing performances specially for "students" to encourage their attendance on "live" opera.

Combined with the prevailing "regional" opera company development and the annual tours of the professional Metropolitan Opera National Company is the current cinema opera theme, in which the La Scala production of *La Bohème*, under the Austrian conductor Herbert von Karajan (who comes closest to being the era's most dynamic opera conductor), is the chief example. In the summer of 1965, this film had national release in America, appearing in 1,050 cinemas to be viewed by more than five million persons, many of whom had never seen opera in any version ("live" or "canned") until that experience. At the same time the La Scala film was released its Mimi, the Italian soprano Mirella Freni, was featured in the Metropolitan Opera's production of *La Bohème*—singing, in the flesh, for houses of 3,600 persons.

*La Bohème* on film created a dimension of awareness in American audiences, particularly for the "student" audience which patronizes cinema almost exclusively, and "live" theatre only occasionally. This awareness, it must be noted, was to a *La Bohème* in Italian and the response was such as to support my belief that it matters, for the audience, more to have the opera audibly and visually exciting than for the audience, above all, to know what is *said* as it is sung.

The choice of *La Bohème* for a film to be released in commercial cinema (this *La Bohème* is released by Warner Bros.), and the frequent choice of *La Bohème* and *Aida* as première works in new repertories are knowledgeable choices by the impresarios or entrepreneurs who sell them to the American audience. In more than twenty years of observing audience responsiveness to opera in this country I have come to believe that *Aida* and *La Bohème* create instantaneous response, and especially in new opera goers of the "student" category.

My method of taking an opera apart and reconstructing it for its artistic sum has worked equally well with young and adult groups and I have found it especially useful for the teacher in the general educational curriculum because it permits expansion or diversion into other fields of study. A teacher working with *Aida* for example might consider the topic Music, but will also be working in such fields as ancient and modern philosophy and social manners and mores, in comparative religion and arts, and in history, past and present. *Aida* might open the topic of how the Egyptians built as architects or worshipped as a godly people, and what their ideas were about the emancipation of women and how their religious, matriarchal society functioned in that civilization. *Aida* might inaugurate a broad study of archaeology, as a study of people, customs and life in antiquity, a first class exercise in research in library materials, and in the art gallery and museum.

Once the teacher engages in the subject of art, and especially on the profoundly evocative art of music, there are no conceivable limits as to group discussion and interest and this is the essential structure (and the final merit) for a "discovery" of opera through teacher-student inquiry.

I am writing in this book about experiments which I formulated, conducted, supervised and helped to evaluate *within the broad educational curriculum* of what might be called the "normal" American public and private school system, ranging from high school through junior college. And a great deal of the material described here, especially the methodology, has been applied in practice by teachers to whom I lectured within my own ideas and principles of "the values and practical uses of theatre arts in education."

I stress the essential practicality of these methods of "Arts Appreciation" to reassure the teacher inexperienced in conducting group discussions on opera. Much of what I have written here especially for the teacher is readily applicable for groups outside educational fields who are interested in an approach to opera from the audience participation role. For such groups, almost everything described for teacher-student use may be adapted within the social-cum-cultural group, with a committee serving to compile materials such as phonograph recordings, books of reference and memorabilia, and to arrange the "experience" of opera in theatre by planned bookings, et cetera.

There is one other aspect of opera which I wish to relate here, because it is an obvious instrument of communication between teacher and student, and equally a force for social work emanating from just such social-cum-cultural groups as might employ this book as an approach to opera. I am especially concerned that groups of this sort, usually active in auxiliary guilds and associations working with "regional" opera troupes, recognize the enormous force as therapy which theatre exerts on the adolescent, the "exceptional," and the socially maladjusted child.

The students with whom I have worked include those who are considered "average" and those that are classified as "exceptional," and in this latter classification it is a generality of the U.S. educational system to designate children who are aurally deaf, children who are mentally retarded and children who according to intelligence quotient tests are called "above average" and "gifted." I have also worked with children of the so-called "minority" races in schools where an economic and residential segregation prevented them from acquiring "normal" knowledge of the "normal world" (in which theatre arts are a part).

To choose an incident for explaining the practical use of theatre arts in education, let me describe an "opera appreciation" program in which Negro high school students participated:

The class numbered thirty-three students, ages ranging from 14 to 19, all of female sex, all classified on school records as "socially delinquent" (meaning that they have acquired a reputation for showing little respect for their persons and properties, and for the persons and properties of others) and also as having, by intelligence quotient testing, more than average intelligence. The "course" was a requirement, not an elective, and three students attending the course had been formally ordered to do so by a juvenile court judge who had set the students on probation. Not one student had ever experienced "live" theatre, all were movie and television fans, few listened to radio and few were of families who owned radio or phonograph. All declared that they knew what opera was, none could articulate coherently what opera was about. 80% were vehement in stating they did not like opera (because opera was "not for them" either as a normal form of pleasure or from their sense of taste for pleasure through arts) and the remaining percentage were apathetic (they expressed themselves as not caring if they "liked" it or not). Less than 25% knew the name of an opera; the only opera named was *Carmen*, encountered on television by chance through a lecture-demonstration by the conductor Leonard Bernstein.

The précis of "discovering" opera was adapted to the group,

which spent a total of 28 hours with me, in classes of two hours each, these classes being supervised and monitored by the school's regular "English" and "World History" teacher in the normal curricula. At the end of the "study course" (which was so designated for the students and occurred in the daily calendar of their classes) the students were taken by chartered bus to a "live" opera performance in a neighboring city—a journey of about three hundred miles.

It was the longest distance they had traveled in their lives from their homes, except for two incorrigible runaways who had extensively traveled the southwestern states. It was their first experience of "live" theatrical presentation except listening to "pop" singers in concert halls, and this latter experience was by only two out of the thirty-three students.

On the basis of aural and written "reports" (on which the students were not graded and which they addressed to me, some of them as "private" letters) and the graded results of their school conduct in that semester, the students' school counselors and curricula teachers considered that a change had been experienced for the group collectively, and remarkable individual changes for more than 50%.

The collective change was not that thirty-three students became opera buffs after "discovering" through *Aida* what an opera is, and "experiencing" in theatre what opera is about. The change was not even in grades as much as it was, singularly, in attitudes about themselves (a 100% change noted) and certain attitudes about society, in general (a 50% change noted). These changes were attributed, by the students in their independent analysis of the "feeling" experienced, to knowing that an opera (*Aida* for example) can be and indeed has been made about a Negro, that a Negro girl can be and is the heroine of a tragic "serious" drama, that the drama is accepted as "Art" (an opera but not "soap opera") and finally, but not as inclusively of interest, that a Negro (Leontyne Price) can be and is a prima donna.

From this experiment with theatre arts in education I have these facts: thirty-three students of high school age, of above-average intelligence, of "underprivileged" class (their families were, without exception, on the county "relief" rolls, and the majority of the students had spent their lifetimes existing on this bounty, which in their district was called "aid to needy children"), learned from the experience of the opera *Aida* that opera art "tolerates" (the word is coined from the students' statements) the idea of a Negro in the "heroine image" in a romantic theatre piece (opera with a romantic theme), in which the Negress is a princess in her own country (a personage in her society), so desirable to a man of superior station and admirable presence (Radames) that she is more beloved than a woman of superior station and great beauty—that woman being of the man's "superior race," as was Amneris.

Ergo: the group said it learned that a Negress may be and is indeed depicted in "serious art" form (opera) as a person of quality and distinction. And as result it is possible for a Negro girl to "feel she can be as good as, better than, another girl" and, also, that the Negro has an ancient culture (as an Ethiopian), an "identity" which relates him to a civilization as old "and as famous" as that of the Egyptian—whose antique and modern civilization these thirty-three students were currently studying in the normal school curriculum.

This "experiment" was considered more therapeutic than artistic by its sponsor (the school) and was classed as an attempt to "rehabilitate" thirty-three high school students of above-average intelligence who were "delinquents." The rehabilitation was prescribed as an "enrichment" in introducing and exposing the students to a "culture" outside or beyond their social and educational bounds; meaning that they were considered (and considered themselves without great repugnance or concern) to be of a lower than average caste of American high school student. The prevalent mood of the group when we began the "experiment" was apathy. The school district psychologists determined that apathy as being a pernicious emotional anaemia, the chief reason for the students' disorientation in society—a disorientation which had so isolated them that they were, as had been proven, totally impervious to punishment and immune to "cures" through regulation school or court-appointed psychological counseling.

The requirement of me, in this instance, was to "break through" the apathy of the group. The true "break through" was achieved in the theatre, when the group experienced, in reality, the opera *Aida*. My part of the experiment was the studied methods I applied in the basic preparation, the attempt I made to reach them by "discovering" facts and some abstract ideas about the opera *Aida*. I worked on the theatrical concept of dramatic climax—suspense built on characters and plot and resolved as grand denouement, rising, scene on scene, to a series of climaxes with the end, or finale of the opera as the arc of emotion (the feeling and thought) circling into the spiral of inquiry as what *Aida* meant to every individual in the group, how each student responded.

In these terms, the experiment was considered successful, in that the group, collectively, was reached through *Aida*; all thirty-three students voiced (orally and/or in writing) what their opinions were about the opera of *Aida,* and about a great deal more that affected them because of the "break through" in *Aida*—and until *Aida* the group was unapproachable and unresponsive, either sullen or withdrawn.

The experiment might have been impractical without its realization of opera in the theatre. I believe that response to the "discovery" should have been negative or nowhere near the 100% response of the group to the "live" opera in the precincts of the opera house—which one student seriously described as being the largest building, save for a courthouse where she went to be tried for a felony, that she had ever seen and ever imagined. I am positive that all experiments with theatre arts in education should extend the "practical" use into professional theatre. This provision should be a matter of course aspect in educational "Arts Appreciation."

## TEN

# Contemporary Ideas About *La Bohème* and *Aida*

In many European societies, the Italian, for example, the music of theatre is the natural or normal music. In England, good little boys and girls are taught how to make music and, sometimes, how to listen appreciatively to music and look at opera and other of the "ocular" musical arts. But in America (as I have found after nearly a quarter of a century of working here) young persons are not content with looking and listening if they are touched or moved in any way. When they read a news account of a war far from home, they demonstrate; and if they take up a fashion it becomes a positive fad.

Americans are an emotional and demonstrative people, the ideal opera audience—which is why I feel certain of the 20th century opera renaissance which is already coming into being in the decade of the 1960's. Americans want to be more than opera audiences; they invariably want to "shape" opera. I frequently witness the act and fact of making opera, after I have conducted an experiment with theatre arts in education.

For my part, I eschew "Appreciation" and call all the preliminary investigation, the initial preparation for the new opera goer "discovery" because I invariably refer to looking and listening in the opera house as "experiencing opera." This "experience" in multi-faceted intellectual and emotional response becomes actual "experiments in art" for the group working in "Arts Appreciation." Where the teacher and his students are islanded (in an obscure community that may, indeed, be on an island, or in a desert oasis or a mountain area far removed from opera in theatre) free expressions of experimental opera are the only means by which the student may "experience" opera. I call these experiments or free expressions "ideas about" opera to separate the absolute and real theatre experience from the free-lance or improvised experiment in opera-making. Some of these are described here as contemporary ideas about *La Bohème* and *Aida,* noted for the teacher. These are physical exercises by young persons in high school and college but they have a certain value for the group working with a correlator—if only to illuminate, for the adult mind, the processes of communication and evoked responses in young adults in our society today.

The student responds as an individual to the experience of opera and if he is allowed to express response freely he will most often extemporize and improvise—because he expresses in his own language, on his own terms. A group will alter a masterwork, not to disqualify it but to possess it, so that it belongs to a new time and place—to students who at heart believe themselves to be the "new" people, and like no people who have existed before.

Such experiments with opera are like demonstrations and articulations and they prove that the students have been moved and touched. In my work, I am concerned primarily with communication, not with "art," and the reshaping of an opera does not appear as lese majesty but as part of the "experience."

For the teacher, it means that the students work—because revising an opera entails composition of new verse, rearrangement of the score, and resetting of the scenes. In the action or performance of these things a group is compelled to do or perform and sometimes it is stimulated to that type of thought and action that is termed "creative." If the results of the experiment with opera produce a work of validity, communicable to an audience, then the group has achieved a piece of theatrical craftsmanship.

Student groups appear to experiment more frequently with *La Bohème* than any other opera. *La Bohème* is the perfect "beatnik" opera, with its theme based on raffish romantics of the 1830's. It is not an opera of the form of *Aida*, which is a traditional form, but an opera rather in the style of impressionistic paintings—a series of vividly colored personalities which exist independent of place and time. The liaisons of Marcello and Musetta and Mimi and Rodolfo, and the bonhomie of the four young men (Marcello and Rodolfo and their friends Schaunard and Colline) were true to Puccini's time—he actually was one of such "four musketeers, all for one and one for all." The viable and valid elements combine as the one irresistible force in *La Bohème*.

*La Bohème* is episodic and is set on types rather than characters. It is thus easily adaptable as to scene and place and any young, eager and ardent amoralists can fit into the skins of the principals.

The poet Rodolfo, the painter Marcello, the philosopher Colline and the musician Schaunard live in a cheap, run-down rooming house owned by a landlord named Benoit, and patronize the Café Momus whenever they can afford it. The opera begins on Christmas Eve, in frenetic gaiety. Marcello has an off-again-on-again affair with a prostitute named Musetta. She lives by picking up foolish old men of substance (like one named Alcindoro, a city councilor) and because Marcello loves her he says she has eaten his heart away; he calls her a bird of prey. A new girl comes to lodge at the rooming house and meets Rodolfo; they fall in love at first sight and before the night is over they have formed a liaison. It is no happier than the tempestuous one between Musetta and Marcello because Rodolfo is insanely jealous of Mimi, whom he accuses of flirting.

She earns a precarious living by sewing and is quite ill, with a very bad cough—*una terribil tosse.* Her illness, and his inability to afford a doctor and medicine, drives Rodolfo wild. He rushes to Musetta and Marcello, who have set up light housekeeping at Café Momus (Marcello is paying for their board and lodging by painting a new signboard for the tavern); he and Mimi are finished—*è finito.* But when Marcello calms him down Rodolfo tells of his fears about Mimi, whom he feels to be dying. She overhears and decides to leave him for good (in an *addio* of her own), but they are reconciled—it is

Marcello and Musetta who have a row and part. All at end of *Act III* and in winter. (It is the bitter cold that emphasizes their acute pov- erty.)

Next spring, the four young men are again back together, Musetta having found another rich old gentleman to keep her and Mimi nothing less than a Vicomte. They are perfectly happy, these four young men, wrily condoling with one another—the women are not really important to them, until Musetta bursts in to say that Mimi has come back to die with Rodolfo near enough to hold her hand; the tiny frozen hand he warmed the first time they met. It is a touching ending, as Mimi succumbs in the garret despite being given Musetta's muff to warm her hands. She cannot wait for Marcello to get back with the doctor he has rushed to call, Musetta having torn the rings from her ears for him to pawn to pay the fee. Colline offers to sell his coat to have money to pay for the prescription. For Mimi it does not matter if she dies because she is dying near Rodolfo; his love has been her whole life. What joy to know, as she is leaving him, that he loves her still!

Groups of contemporary American students adopt this opera plot with marked empathy, changing the Parisian garret to its equiv- alent in our society today. When a literal transposition is made of the scene, the garret becomes, variously, a basement flat in the colder regions of the U.S.A.; a "shack" for itinerant farm laborers in the agricultural states; and "beach-house" of the kind put together with wooden crates and tarpaulin by the "beach bums" and "surfers" of the coasts. I have seen Café Momus reduced to a fruit-drink stand and also to a "dive" for supposed marijuana smokers.

But the contemporary Mimi does not die of consumption, which seems too archaic a disease to student groups; she expires of a mysteri- ous debilitation or anaemia like leukemia. Once, a group determined her as dying from pneumonia and was roundly abused by the student audience, because of the availability of penicillin and free clinical care for paupers. The student audience is, on the whole, inclined to be "precious" and sticklers for realism, identifying as closely with Puc- cini's types as do the amateur performers who undertake their char- acterization.

Now and then, hilarity begins where empathy achieves its most sympathetic perspective. A student group will see the irresistible advantage of turning pathos to bathos. *La Bohème* becomes *opera buffa*. One interesting "transubstantiation" (changing the opera's substance from Puccini's to the group's) condensed the *Acts I* through *IV* and set the scene entirely in and just outside Café Momus.

The college collaborated as a whole and Marcello was, in fact, a painter—on stage, he turned out a creditable new signboard for Café Momus. The set was cleverly designed, to allow its sidewalk to serve for all the action of Puccini's *Acts I & III* (these take place, respectively, in Rodolfo's garret and near the café). The façade was adjusted to provide this ample space and to put Marcello (*Act III*) on a step-ladder painting the sign. *Acts II & IV* were set inside the café, by the simple expediency of opening up the façade to reveal the inside room—where, in the last act, Mimi conveniently collapsed and "died" as well as she could have in the garret. The curtain fell on pathos and rose on a reprise of some of the music, notably Musetta's famous Waltz from *Act II*. It is 40 years later and Musetta is sixty instead of twenty, no one is keeping her in comfort and she works as a slatternly waitress at Café Momus—which the skinflint Benoit has acquired as well as all the business places on the street.

Rodolfo, forty years older, appears—he has been away all these years, from the moment he rushed out of the café, unable to bear the anguish of Mimi's funeral after her death. He inquires if she had a good turnout; if Marcello, his best friend, saw to her decent burial. Musetta tells him the unpalatable truth—Mimi collapsed but did not die; she revived, her care was so well undertaken by Marcello that she regained good health. These two got married and went off to live quite happily in a nice little place in the country where they are thriving as chicken farmers. Musetta sets one of these birds, roasted, before her old friend. Rodolfo throws the dish on the floor in a passion; he is outraged that Mimi did not die and so has destroyed love's idyll. For years he has cherished the grand amour of his life and now, disillusionment! But Schaunard and Colline turn up, also forty years older, and take their pal off to meet "another Mimi" a girl with tiny frozen fingers. Left alone, Musetta wipes the counter, thumps the coffee urn and sings the reprise of her song to the Madonna—this time for Musetta, not for lucky, lucky living Mimi!

These student excursions into opera production adapt the score of an opera to the action and alter opera to *opéra comique.*

Is the purpose worth the act in results? Are opera singers or composers "made" by these methods? I have no means of knowing and, to be truthful, I do not "research" to find out because I am of the belief that the artist is born, not made—that the singer (or dancer) may be ruined by bad teaching, but that no great singer (or dancer) has yet been manufactured or "made" by environment and influences "conducive" to making artistes. But I know what is obvious: that the opportunity must arise, the stage must be built, the opera must be composed, before the great diva can be heard singing her great role by the audience. And I have observed many instances of the opportunity occurring whereby the unconscious, unresolved young person became inspired or dedicated to an art.

One of opera's most dazzling new divas is Teresa Stratas, born in Canada of Greek parentage, who at fifteen was a successful "pop" singer on radio and television, planning a career as a movie and night-club chanteuse—and possessed of an exceptional soprano voice range. When she was sixteen she was given a ticket to her first opera performance, to which she went and sat "high in the rafters" in the cheapest section of the house. The company was the Metropolitan Opera on tour and Tebaldi was singing Mimi in *La Bohème,* and Teresa Stratas experienced an emotional earthquake—her life split into two. She says she thought, inarticulately: "Oh, my God, *this* . . ."—and *this* was the shattering experience (opera) which moved her as she had never been touched until then, because she suddenly conceived opera to be "the greatest art."*

The incident occurred in 1954 and as I write this in the early autumn of 1965 Stratas has just sung her first Mimi for the Metropolitan Opera, New York, where she is now a reigning diva. In an era when, as statisticians have compiled for us, there are more Americans alive under the age of twenty-five than within any other age strata, it is necessary as well as feasible to understand how Americans of the "student" category feel and think, how they respond and articulate, what their contemporary ideas are about art and nature or real

* The experience of Teresa Stratas' revelation about opera was recorded in *Life Magazine,* by Thomas Thompson, 1965.

life. And groups working in "opera appreciation" who exercise "experiments" in opera articulate very revealingly and eloquently, in *Aida* for example.

*La Bohème* and *Aida* are two works which have remarkable faculty in serving as catalyst between the new opera goer and opera art. Their universal appeal (plus the plain fact that their productions are fairly easy to arrange with minimal theatrical facilities) make them favorites with opera troupes, and is the primary reason why regional opera guilds, commencing new local opera traditions in their communities, often produce *La Bohème* or *Aida* as the première work. Some of the prejudices of the American audience divide opera buffs in debate about these operas; one half resisting the constancy with which Puccini's Bohemians and Verdi's *Aida* remain in repertory. For some opera buffs, these two operas fall in the categories of "chestnut" and "war horse," meaning that they are stale and static. In fact, they are ceaselessly new and animated for opera goers, and lend themselves to some of the most inventive and original ideas in transposition. Nothing that I have seen in amateur and educational theatre surpasses the agility with which *La Bohème* and *Aida* leap time and space to become topical of our age and place.

I have seen *Aida* literally transposed, geographically and historically, into Aztec time and place, Mexican Indians becoming Verdi's Ethiopians; Verdi's Egyptians turning into the Spanish conquistadores. In this transposition, the music and verse were left intact, but the plot suffered a change in administration, or executive power—the lovers died *à la Verdi* in a tomb but not in the Temple of Vulcan, which in Verdi belongs to the Egyptians, of which Radames is one. He was a Spanish captain, Amneris was a donna, and Aida, naturally, was an Aztec maiden. But the opera makers of this Aztec *Aida* put a twist in the old plot, turned the role of Ramfis, the high priest, upside down, and put him on the side of the Aztecs (according to Verdi, he should have been on the side of the Spaniards). But an Aztec temple and the Asiatic cruelty of the lovers' deaths fitted more neatly into this new concept than actual literal translation of the Ramfis role would have done—say: as a Spanish priest, even of the Inquisition. Whatever the aesthetic argument, the fact was that the new idea for *Aida* in this Aztec scene appeared perfectly valid.

Pictorially, the costumes of Spanish conquistadores and Aztecs aided the dramaturgical aspect of the Aztec *Aida*, and the contrast in weapons was such a novelty as to bring new excitement to the massed brigades with which *Aida* assails the opera stage. The Aztec scene was as somber as anything out of Egypt, from where possibly, the Aztecs may have come. The same peculiarly stony passion lay in landscape and priesthoods, in the Aztec *Aida*, as dwells in Verdi's Egyptian one. Altogether, this was the most apt and able transposition of Verdi's *Aida* into other times, other scenes, that I have observed and it grandly made use of Verdi's score and the libretto.

But I have seen other more inventive and topical versions of *Aida*, which rank higher in interest than the Aztec one. These were experiments in which music and drama departments collaborated and combined to produce opera of new ocular as well as new musical concepts, with the sangfroid of 19th century opera entrepreneurs.

In these instances, the libretto and score were bared to their bones, the opera makers choosing only what they required to effect contemporary versions of *Aida*, one established in Cuba, circa 1960's.

*Aida* in Cuba was scenically set against a great pair of gates, described for their purpose in the opera as "the gates of Guantanamo." They were Verdi's two "gates" superimposed as one; the Verdi "gates" appear at Memphis, *Act I, Scene I,* and as the triumphal entrance into Thebes for Radames, *Act II, Scene II.* For the other Verdi scenes, the opera makers of the Cuban *Aida* substituted a café and a prison instead of the palaces and pyramids in Verdi. On one side of the "gates of Guantanamo" were sketched military barracks, receding so starkly from the gates and the guard that the background stretched tautly behind him and away from him; he being the Cuban Radames.

He was an American Marine sergeant, the pivot in love between the same characters who plague Verdi's Radames. Here Amneris was an American nurse, very high-minded and altruistic as compared to Verdi's egotistical Princess, and Aida turned into more of a tiger cat than a kitten as a Cuban girl guerilla. But the triangle or love theme remained true. The issues at large were love of country versus love of self, because this operatic version defined Aida with greater passion and "human" aspect than Verdi's. She loved Cuba passionately, passionately believed in what she was fighting for (and Radames against) and happening to fall in love with Radames and he with her, she became dedicated to his "conversion" to her ideals.

Again here, the plot was given a twist, by which Ramfis came over to Aida's side, as a Cuban revolutionary, exercising the same powers of life and death on the Cuban lovers as Ramfis exercised over Verdi's.

The lovers die but instead of staging the finale in Verdi's "double chamber" this student group showed it in the "torture chamber" which was both a guardroom and a court of trial. An authentic Spanish Gothic architecture was contrived by copying the realistic "slave dungeon" style common to old Caribbean plantation houses, in which Spanish landlords made provisions for disciplining recalcitrant peons. The set had more verisimilitude, in the circumstances, than the conventional theatrical production of *Aida's* temple scene.

To allow for Radames dying on the other side (the wrong side) of the "gates at Guantanamo" the *Act III* was set in a garish cabaret, where the "ballet numbers" from Verdi's score were employed for music. Radames comes here, surreptitiously, to meet his Aida, who has undertaken (but not reluctantly) to turn him into a saboteur of his own military encampment. When Radames will not defect, Aida compromises him so that he hesitates to return through the "gates" and lingers long enough to be caught and tried and condemned by the Cuban Ramfis as an American spy and saboteur—thus, a death by firing squad which Aida elects to share with her lover. They die out of sight of the audience (a realistic sound effect notifying their demise) but the Cuban guerillas, made up to look like mesticos with beards, in rumpled khaki uniforms, remained in full view, in the guardroom.

The orchestra alone here played the music from Verdi's finale, Amneris' and the priests' parts were omitted, and instead of the great *Addio* being sung by the dying lovers (as in Verdi) it was rendered by a boys choir, taking on an unearthly quality like angels' voices. The lovers (and Amneris) were never seen again but as the *Addio* was being sung by the invisible choir the guardroom took on chilling realism.

Some of the soldiers squatted on the floor in a game with dice, one lay down on a wooden bench against a wall, an oil lamp was lowered from a ceiling hook and lighted, becoming the only light as the stage set gradually darkened. A woman came in with a tray and set dishes of food on the rough table where "Ramfis" sat writing. As she went out he looked up, cried out to her impatiently, and she hurried away, shutting a door with a great thud—which cut off the *O terra addio* as though the lid of a tomb had closed on the living singers.

The Cuban *Aida* was stark in scene and taut in dramatization, and was the product of a particularly idealistic group of students, which had been vehemently, if incoherently, voicing individual opinions about the Cuban internal conflict. In this instance, *Aida* was something like a safety valve, something like an experience (to quote the students) of "getting into the skin" of problematic but feasible characterizations. It was an uncompromising attempt to feel vicarious emotions; incidentally, it made an interesting theatre piece.

Another transposition of *Aida,* in more lavish scenic design but, again, with summary rearrangement of the score and some slight alterations in cast, set Verdi's principals in the South during the War Between The States, with Aida a slave girl and Amneris a Southern belle "from Memphis, Tennessee." Radames remained the romantic hero and whereas Amonasro had been deleted in the Cuban *Aida* he was retained in the Civil War version, but changed into a witch doctor or voodoo man, a slave like Aida but one of terrifying import to her, whom she obeys as Verdi's Aida obeyed her father. The Nile yielded to the Mississippi but Aida sang as poignantly here as she does for Verdi. This Amonasro required her to discover from her Radames much the same sort of strategic information as Verdi's did. And instead of urging this Radames to fly with her to Ethiopia this Aida wished him to go far enough North for them to be free of anti-African prejudices. In this production, Aida logically resents being enslaved, Radames is sympathetic but helpless to save her. Again here, the death by entombment was changed . . . these "Southern" lovers ran away together, knowing Aida would be hunted by dogs and men with guns; that they might die together, as they did. Again, the death was beyond the audience's range of view and the ending different from Verdi's *Aida.* Here the Southern Amneris sang the *Addio,* an elegy for the lost lovers and for *her* lost love.

The most effective of the "modernized" *Aidas,* including one set in Viet Nam where Aida became a Saigon night club singer who

doubled as a spy for the Viet Cong, was the Cuban *Aida.* The set was
of the simplest, the dramatic action the best resolved and the music
of an unusually high standard, in the singing and the orchestra. Also,
the dance scenes (which in Verdi's *Aida* are variously treated as
ballet) was more valid than many an "Egyptian" dance designed for
professionally produced versions of Verdi's opera. These were of two
kinds: ritual for voodoo, and the ritual Afro-Cuban adapted for
ballroom. Thus, the *naningo, santo bemba* and the drum dance called
*burandanga* in ⅜ compound meter were interpolated instead of Verdi's
"sacred" Egyptian music.

In the Cuban and Viet Nam *Aidas* café scenes (in place of the
*Act III* bank of the Nile) and change of music allowed the performance of contemporary dancing like frug, et cetera, and the gyrations
while remaining true to style were as orgiastic as is usual to see staged
in Verdi's *Aida.*

The experiments or "ideas" about *Aida* were by maximum student
effort with minimum supervision and the best presentations came
from collaboration between educational departments like music, art
(painting and design), architecture, dance and drama. Some but not
all the students had actual experience of professionally produced opera
but I must make it clear that these free adaptations were not wholly
in Verdi's form, since it was necessary for the students to improvise
and turn the form more towards that of *opéra comique,* interpolating
spoken dialogue in the singing.

This book allows me space only to offer examples and to make
broad generalities within these extensions of *Ideas About Aida,* which
contain some mention about another operatic catalyst: *La Bohème.*
I have shown the contemporary response for what it is worth to teacher-
student use beyond the basic information of "opera appreciation" into
"experiment" with opera. Response is always individual and therefore
always different for each opera goer.

The query has been made: is such tampering (as "experiment"
by students) with Verdi's *Aida* "good?" Is it "artistically permissible?"
Is it "aesthetically moral?"

I should think that Verdi himself replies to these queries when
he states "In the matter of musical opinions we must be broad-minded,
and for my part I am very tolerant indeed." (It is true that the com-

poser, in his lifetime, forbade theatres changing his musical works, on a threatened fine of 1000 francs for "the slightest change in instrumentation," but a good use of Verdi is not an abuse of his genius).

We know that Verdi in his life and music never hesitated to use what he wanted (as he used some Wagnerian ideas) for a purpose he believed good for him, and that he never ceased or hesitated (into his last works) to change, to be different, to experiment—and, sometimes, to borrow, as he is said to have borrowed from Wagner's dramatic tenets to consolidate his own dramaturgy.

The experiments here described in *Ideas About Aida* do not abuse *Aida,* because Verdi saw to it that the intrinsic values of *Aida* were incorruptible. And some vintners believe that new wines age better in old casks; so old casks are renovated by containing new wine.

# Index

# List of Sources

After more than forty years of study I find it impossible to compile bibliographies, especially when (as for *Enjoying Opera*) I have drawn on archaeology, comparative religions and philosophy as well as theatre and arts. I wish, however, to refer to the composer Cornelius Cardew as my authoritative source for contemporary music and its terminology, and to Dr. Gerhart von Westerman, former director of the Berlin Philharmonic Orchestra, as the authoritative source for German music, as they have written on these in *The Concert Guide*, published by the Oxford University Press, London, England, and by Arco Publishing Co. Inc. in the U.S.A. Sources for dates, spellings, et cetera are the *Concise Opera* and *Music* dictionaries (edited, respectively, by Harold Rosenthal and John Warrack, and Percy A. Scholes) published by Oxford University Press, whose *Universal Dictionary on Historical Principles*, 3rd ed., is my general source.

Throughout the text I have tried to identify sources for the reader, as for composers' letters contained in *Letters of Giacomo Puccini*, tr. Ena Makin, publ. J. B. Lippincott Co.; *Verdi: The Man in His Letters*, by Franz Werfel and Paul Stefan, tr. Edward Downes, publ. L. B. Fischer; et cetera. Unfortunately, almost all such sources are books now out of print. Particular to this book, in several instances, are translations from the Italian by Graciela Sanguinetti and from the German by Horst Spohr, and I am indebted to private collections of memorabilia and unpublished letters and journals for a great deal of description and anecdote.

Opera libretti excerpts are reproduced as described in *Musical quotations*, and photographs were selected for me by Anne Gordon, Jeanne Thomas and Dale Heapps of the Metropolitan Opera Association. The American composer Conrad Susa read my manuscript in early draft and made valuable suggestions; Elinor Parker, my editor, assisted me in final research. Numerous college and high school teachers compiled data under my supervision of pilot programs in Opera Appreciation, the sum of which considerably aided my research and evaluations.